My Union, My Life

Jean-Claude Parrot
and the Canadian Union of Postal Workers

Jean-Claude Parrot

Fernwood Publishing • Halifax

New

Editing: Scott Milsom
Cover image: courtesy of CUPW Communications Department
Printed and bound in Canada by: ~~University of Toronto Press~~ Thistle Printing Limited

A publication of:
Fernwood Publishing
Site 2A, Box 5, 32 Oceanvista Lane
Black Point, Nova Scotia, B0J 1B0
and 324 Clare Avenue
Winnipeg, Manitoba, R3L 1S3
www.fernwoodpublishing.ca

Fernwood Publishing Company Limited gratefully acknowledges
the financial support of the Department of Canadian Heritage,
the Nova Scotia Department of Tourism and Culture
and the Canada Council for the Arts for our publishing program.

Patrimoine canadien · The Canada Council for the Arts / Le Conseil des Arts du Canada · NOVA SCOTIA Tourism and Culture · CEP SCEP UNION LABEL GRAPHICAL 003G ®

Change to Our Union Bug – But Smaller

Library and Archives Canada Cataloguing in Publication

Parrot, Jean-Claude
My union, my life : Jean-Claude Parrot and the Canadian Union of Postal Workers / Jean-Claude Parrot.

Includes index.
ISBN 1-55266-164-4

1. Parrot, Jean-Claude. 2. Canadian Union of Postal Workers—Officials and employees—Biography. I. Title.

HD6525.P375A3 2005   331.88'113834971   C2005-900926-8

Contents

Dedication

I dedicate this book to the thousands of activists across the country who, after their hard day's work, give countless hours to fight in the interests of their fellow working people. I dedicate this book to all those activists who get involved in various struggles for justice and dignity for working people, both on the job and in their communities. I dedicate this book to all those women and men who take precious hours from their families because they care about the future we will leave our children and grandchildren.

I also dedicate this book to the families and friends of these thousands of activists. They accept and support their loved ones in their efforts to contribute to a better world for working people. My wife, Louisette, and my two daughters, Manon and Johanne, gave me profound support during all my years in the labour and social movements. I thank them for having always been there for me.

To all of you, I say thank you. I say thank you because without you there wouldn't be a labour movement, there wouldn't be a social movement, there wouldn't be hope that a better world for all can be more than a dream for working people. Thank you for caring for the most vulnerable people in our society. Thank you for believing that, together, we can build a better world.

The struggle continues.

Acknowledgements

Firstly, I wish to thank the members of the National Executive Board of the Canadian Union of Postal Workers (CUPW) for their moral and financial support. Through their generosity, I was provided with an office and equipment that facilitated both my research and the writing of this book. It was quite special for me to spend some time back in the CUPW offices. I wish to acknowledge all the people at the CUPW offices who made me feel welcome and assisted me as this book project proceeded. My particular thanks go to Evert Hoogers and Geoff Bickerton, who were assigned to follow up on this project.

Secondly, I wish to acknowledge the tireless efforts of Scott Milsom in the editing of my original manuscript. He was a great person to work with in this difficult task and made the long hours much more enjoyable.

Thirdly, I wish to recognize the assistance of John Willis and the Canadian Postal Museum. I am grateful that they agreed to keep the correspondence I received while in jail in their archives and make it available to those who wish to read any or all of it.

Fourthly, I want to thank all those, both inside and outside CUPW, who provided me with information and photos as I was writing this book. Space limitations don't allow me to mention all their names, but I wish to express my particular thanks to my late mother who, prior to passing away at the age of 91 while I was writing this book, provided me with many press clippings and photos that she had accumulated over the years.

Fifthly, I wish to acknowledge the interest shown in this project by Errol Sharpe of Fernwood Publishing and by Éditions du Boréal in the editing and publishing of both the English and French versions of this book. The assistance I received from their staffs was really special and pleasant. As I am writing these words, both publishers are working hard to ensure that both French and English editions will be delivered in time for our planned book launch at CUPW's 2005 National Convention in Québec City.

Finally, to my wife Louisette — who thought I had retired but who had to put up with my long hours of work during this process, especially during the last year — thank you for all your support. I assure you that I don't have any similar projects planned for the years to come.

Preface

When I decided to run for the position of Executive Vice-President of the Canadian Labour Congress (CLC), in 1992, I knew that, if elected, I was going to leave a union that had been my life. But, I felt that, after being the National President of the Canadian Union of Postal Workers (CUPW) for fifteen years and its Chief Negotiator for eighteen, it was time for me to leave my place to someone else. I sincerely believed that the union needed a new National President. I didn't like the idea that, more and more, the union was linked to my name. I was *not* the union, and it was important that the members recognized that there was a vast number of good leaders, and good activists, at all levels of CUPW's organization.

I believe when a leader is in office in any organization for too long, the internal desire for change lessens. This desire for change may not have seemed obvious in CUPW's case, due to the fact that the fifteen years I served as President were very active ones. But, I knew that staying on for a much longer period would be a mistake. With change, activists who had some ambitions to move up in the union would see opportunities open: the departure of a leader has a ripple effect on positions throughout the organization and leads to healthy debates that bring positive changes to the organization.

I had already decided I was not going to run again for President at the 1993 CUPW Convention. My decision to run for the CLC position was influenced by changes that were taking place in the direction of the CLC, with Brother Bob White, President of the Canadian Auto Workers (CAW), becoming the new CLC President. I respected him and wanted to be part of his team, along with Nancy Riche and Dick Martin.

In June 1992, I was elected Executive Vice-President of the CLC and resigned as CUPW's National President. I had been a national officer of CUPW for twenty-one years. And, prior to that, I had been an elected local officer in Montréal for seven years, the last three as full-time vice-president.

On June 14, 2002, the last day of the twenty-second CLC Convention, I officially retired from that organization after having been re-elected Executive Vice-President for a total of ten years. I was just two months away from my sixty-sixth birthday, and I felt I had a responsibility to leave CUPW with some history of the struggles we went through during my years of involvement in the organization. While this book is not a history of CUPW, it is an overview of its history, as I lived it, while I was involved in the union.

1

Writing about CUPW is a very challenging task, but one I felt needed to be done. No author could write about the history of the Canadian labour movement without talking about the important contributions CUPW has made to the movement. No writer could ignore what many people have come to recognize as the most militant of Canadian unions.

CUPW's achievements for its members, and for Canadian workers in general (especially employees of the federal government), are an important part of the history of the labour movement. Unfortunately, much of this has been ignored by many writers of the history of Canada's labour movement. This is probably due to the fact that CUPW has been seen by many writers as too young to have much of a history.

CUPW changed the way the federal government dealt with its own employees. In fact, CUPW and the Letter Carriers' Union of Canada (LCUC), now part of CUPW, were largely responsible for the inclusion of a provision in the Public Service Staff Relations Act that gave federal employees the right to strike. This entirely changed the way working conditions and compensation were negotiated.

CUPW has always chosen the approach of negotiating on the strength of its membership, with the understanding that it is not only because you have good arguments and a just cause that you win improvements for your members at the bargaining table. Only when the employer knows that you have the membership behind you and that you are willing, if necessary, to fight can meaningful gains be won. Thus has CUPW negotiated provisions that were previously nonexistent in the federal public sector, and in many instances, were nonexistent in the private sector as well. Many of these provisions have dealt with protections and benefits from new technology, benefits that were considered ahead of their time. CUPW has stood up for groups such as part-time workers, shift workers, women workers, workers with special needs, and others. CUPW has stood up for non-member postal workers such as cleaners, rural couriers, letter carriers, general labourers and trade groups, clerical staff, and others. CUPW has defended the public interest when it came to the closing of rural post offices and urban postal stations, and when it came to reductions in home delivery. CUPW has fought against a strictly business-oriented post office and for a post office for all Canadians. CUPW has adopted policies unique in the Canadian labour movement and often ahead of their time. CUPW has shown that "solidarity" is more than a word, making it something that postal workers are very proud of, which has earned the respect of others in the labour movement in Canada and even beyond. CUPW has been influential in changing the policies and orientation of the CLC.

CUPW has gained strong credibility among postal workers ready to fight for their rights, to obtain justice, to defend their brothers and sisters, and to move forward. Many CUPW members dedicate their time to fight for a better life for postal workers, and for workers in general. And CUPW has shown that there are times when you have to stand up to injustice, even when — and perhaps even especially when — an injustice is caused by an unjust law.

I served as Chief Negotiator of CUPW for eighteen years, beginning with a fourteen-day illegal strike in 1974 and ending in 1992, when I was elected Executive Vice-President of the CLC. I was also CUPW's National President for fifteen years, from 1977 to 1992. I played an important role in CUPW, a union that is clearly one of principles and determination. I hope that this book will make readers better understand how we were able to have such success, despite the odds. I hope that readers will learn something of the role played by CUPW, individual postal workers, and myself in those difficult but satisfying years. I hope readers will also find answers to many questions, such as:

- How did 23,000 postal workers spread out over 1,000 postal installations across the country defy the Trudeau government's back-to-work legislation in 1978?
- What was it like to spend two months of a three-month sentence in a dormitory cell with eighteen other inmates at the Ottawa Carleton Regional Detention Centre in Ottawa in 1980?
- Why did the media accuse the federal government of caving in to CUPW demands in a two-week illegal strike in 1974?
- What made postal workers, without the approval of their national union, walk off the job in 1965?
- Why did the general public support a boycott of the postal code in the 1970s?
- How did 23,000 postal workers go on strike for forty-two days to gain paid maternity leave in their collective agreement?
- Why has CUPW always been so principled and determined?
- How was it that a government that told postal workers in 1975 that they could stay on strike "until hell freezes over" then introduced back-to-work legislation on the first day of a 1978 strike?
- Did media coverage of labour disputes in the post office meet with the expectations of the general public? Did it treat postal workers fairly?
- Why did Prime Minister Trudeau decide overnight to turn the post office into a Crown Corporation?
- Why did CUPW, most other unions, and the CLC adopt resolutions supporting Québec's right to self-determination?
- Why do I hold Bob Rae responsible for the defeat of a New Democratic Party (NDP) government in Ontario in the 1990s?
- Does the labour movement have the strength we are led to believe it has?
- Can we do anything about the exploitation of children, women, and men around the world?

- Is it the proper role of the labour movement to be involved in politics?
- How did my family cope with my limited presence at home during these years? How did they manage while I was in jail?

No organization is perfect, and CUPW is no exception. In my years with the organization, I went through some difficult times. Throughout these years, we had to make some difficult decisions, and they were not always unanimous ones. We had our share of differences of opinion among ourselves. We had tough struggles during conventions. Still, we maintained our unity as postal workers when it came time to unite for progress.

I hope readers will enjoy learning more about postal workers, CUPW, and the role I played in it. I am proud to have been a postal worker and to have had the opportunity to play a major role in CUPW. I feel privileged to write this book, and I hope it will give readers a better understanding of the struggles of postal workers and the roles played by the media, governments, politicians, the labour movement, activists, and the public during those years.

In CUPW we have always believed we can change things. And we have done so, both inside and outside our union.

I trust that this book will help readers better understand why we believe that the fight of workers will never end, which is the reason for our slogan, "The struggle continues."

1 Early Years: From Association to Union

It all began in 1954. I was seventeen years old and worked as a clerk in a Montréal bank. I liked the work but, unfortunately, the pay wasn't great. I started there in 1952 at $900 a year and soon I would be getting $1,300 a year. I went to the bank because I like mathematics. While this was my first full-time job, I had worked with the public since I was ten years old. I delivered newspapers to people in my area six days a week, and on Saturday mornings I collected weekly subscriptions.

The summer I turned thirteen, I found a job as a bicycle delivery boy for a fruit store. I was paid six dollars a week during the school year and eight dollars a week during the summer. There was usually another dollar or two in tips each week. That summer, I worked Monday to Saturday from 8:00 am to 6:00 pm. On Fridays, I worked to 10:00 pm. I was fifteen when I began to work in the bank.

One day, my father, who worked in the post office, brought home an ad calling on people to apply for work there. They were hiring new people because they were implementing the five-day, forty-hour week, which happened following national consultations under the National Joint Council of the Public Service of Canada. In a brief presented by Brother Fred Whitehouse, National Secretary-Treasurer of the Canadian Postal Employees Association (CPEA), to the Council on January 17, 1952, it was estimated that the new measure would require a total of 1,875 new postal workers at an immediate cost of $3,768,000, and at an eventual cost of $5,114,250.

While I had not planned to work in the post office, I saw that my salary would almost double if I was to get a job there. In fact, the maximum salary for the job after six years was about the same as an accountant's in the bank who had been there for thirty-five years. So I applied, and a few weeks later I was called in to write an exam. I was then called for an interview before a three-man board. There had been several hundred applicants, but I soon learned I was number ninety-eight on the list.

On June 3, 1954, I was asked to begin work in the post office. Unfortunately, after I went through all the paper work, the personnel office discovered a message they had just received from Ottawa stating that they couldn't hire, as regular employees, people who were not at least eighteen years old. I was told they couldn't take me right away, but that they were going to hold a position for me because I was going to turn eighteen in less than two months.

I had already tendered my resignation to the bank, but they hadn't yet hired anyone to replace me, so they were pleased to take me back for a few more weeks. A week before my birthday, I went to the personnel office at the post office and was asked when I was going to turn eighteen. "Next Saturday," I said. I was asked to report on that day.

So on Saturday, July 24, 1954, on my eighteenth birthday, I became a postal clerk at a salary of $2,400 a year. When I showed up for work at 5:00 pm on the fourth floor of the post office at 715 Windsor Street (now Peel Street) in Montréal, I was told to go to an office and wait there for someone to take care of me. I waited twenty minutes before someone came and asked what I was doing there.

"This is my first day of work and I was told to come wait in this office," I replied. "Who the hell decided to have someone start on a Saturday?" he said, not expecting any answer.

He looked in some folders and then asked me to follow him. He showed me a big chart on the wall: it was the work schedule for everyone in that section.

"Your schedule will be number five and the chart indicates your days of work and your days off. So as you can see, you are off tomorrow, Sunday," he said. I remember thinking it strange to be off on my second day of work.

The man who seemed to be in charge then brought me to a row of racks and had me sit in front of one. "The mail on the ledge in front of you," he said, "comes from mailboxes on the street. The city mail has already been sent to the city section and this mail should be for anywhere else in Canada. To sort that mail in the rack you just have to put it in the corresponding case of the city to which the letters are addressed. Those that don't have a corresponding case go back on the ledge and someone else will sort them. We'll show you how to sort those next week."

That's how it started. Thanks to the five-day, forty-hour week, I was now a postal clerk. Neither the post office nor myself had any idea that I was going to become a national public figure, that I was going to become the Chief Negotiator and National President of what would become one of the most militant unions in the country.

My First Years in the Post Office

But things didn't happen overnight. Being rather shy, I did my work without getting very involved with other workers. I thought myself a good worker and conscientious in my work. I didn't know anything about unions and even less about collective bargaining. In those early days, the government unilaterally decided on our working conditions.

After a year at the post office, I asked for a transfer to the midnight shift in the registered mail section. I did so because, working the 5:00 pm to 1:40 am shift, I didn't have much of a social life.

My request was granted, and I found myself on the same shift with my father, though he worked on city mail while I dealt with forward mail. The registered mail section was in a secured area and someone had to open the door for us when we arrived for work. All the registered mail went through this section, including money packages and bags of currency for banks. I remember some of those bags were labelled with amounts of over $1,000,000 inside. One night, when we had finished our work early, we were waiting for workers who were going to pick up the mail from our section in the morning, and we were allowed to rest for an hour or two. I lay on the ledge using one of these bags as a pillow. For a young man like me, it was quite a feeling to know that I was sleeping with my head on more than $1,000,000.

My father died of cancer in July of 1957. About a year later I got a transfer to the postal stations, which was the only place where you could have a day-shift position if you didn't have much seniority. This is where I was going to discover the union.

When I was first hired, I was asked to sign a card authorizing the check-off for the CPEA. This check-off system had come into effect in July of 1953. Dues were twenty-five cents a month. I accepted the check-off because I felt it was "the thing to do," and I signed a CPEA membership card. There were then no full-time CPEA employees in our local. The Association's services were provided by the two full-time staff of our national magazine, *The Postal Tribune*, the official organ of both the CPEA and the Federated Association of Letter Carriers (FALC).

It was in the fall of 1961, seven years after I'd started in the post office, before I attended my first CPEA meeting. It was a special meeting called for postal clerks like me who worked in postal stations serving the public. Here, I learned that most of the complaints I had were the same as other workers had. At that meeting, I volunteered to sit on a committee that was going to report at the next CPEA meeting.

Over the next five years or so, I never missed a CPEA meeting. I became shop steward, a member of various committees, and an assistant secretary-treasurer. The situation in the post office was getting worse: our salaries were not keeping up with other workers' increases.

In 1959, the government cancelled postal workers' scheduled wage increases, but in 1960 it announced an increase, with a review to take place every two years. In 1962, the Pay Research Bureau of the federal civil service recommended pay increases, but its advice was rejected and a general wage freeze was imposed. It was only in 1963 that an increase of $360 a year was granted. We worked under a system where paternalism, favouritism, nepotism, discrimination, and a top-down military approach were the order of the day. Working conditions were deplorable.

At that time, 97 percent of full-time workers were men and 97 percent of part-time workers were women. That showed how little respect the employer had for women. At that time, women were just beginning to look for jobs and, in most cases, were seen by employers as good prospects for part-time work. Other than certain jobs traditionally viewed as "women's work," there were very few women in full-time jobs.

In the post office, part-time workers were under a "chips" system: each part-timer was given so many chips per tray of mail they sorted. The number of chips varied according to the type of mail in the tray. It was easier to sort letters when the address was typed than when the address was written by hand or when the letter came from a foreign country. A supervisor would often have a women "friend" or a very attractive woman sitting at the end of the row. The supervisor would spend a large part of his shift talking with that woman, so she obviously didn't do much sorting: still, at the end of the day, she would have more chips than the others. At the same time, a woman who might have sorted less than the criteria established by management would be disciplined, with no consideration of the reason for her low performance. Such practices amounted to discrimination or intimidation, or both.

Many of the part-timers weren't regular employees. A group called "casuals" was made up largely of friends or relatives of supervisors or people recommended by someone with local influence. After repeated representations by the CPEA, the Postmaster General abolished individual work measurement on November 20, 1963.

In the early 1960s, the militarist attitude of supervisors was never far from the workplace surface. One evening during the holiday season, I was asked to send a container of letters to Québec City. As I was about to transfer the mail in Québec City bags, I realized that most of the mail was addressed to different destinations all across the country. Obviously, this was mail picked up from a street box and it had not yet been sorted. I called the supervisor and told him about this. His answer was, "I told you to send that mail to Québec City." The tone of his voice was very clear: he didn't want me to argue with him — he was the boss. So I sent the mail to Québec City, knowing that most of it was going to come back to Montréal the next day. Although I didn't realize it at the time, I later came to understand that the whole purpose of this futile exercise was for the supervisor to show his superiors that he had been able to "clean up" all the mail with the staff he had on hand.

Another day, mail volume was getting abnormally low. Then, just thirty minutes before the end of the shift, a large load of mail arrived, and everyone was asked to stay to work overtime. Most of us didn't mind the overtime, as it was nice to get the extra money at the end of the month. But we discovered that the mail had been in the office for some time but had not been brought to us earlier because the supervisors wanted some overtime. This happened quite often.

Training was often lacking, so we had to learn on the job. When I transferred to the postal stations, I received minimal training from someone already too busy doing his regular work. I eventually took it on my own to train many new clerks.

Requests for transfers to other sections of the post office were dealt with in a very arbitrary manner. Seniority was rarely given much consideration. A joke made the rounds to the effect that a worker who wanted to be transferred to the postal stations serving the public had to do a bad job in hopes that the supervisor would recommend him for the transfer in order to get the employee out of his or her section. Though I didn't have to do this to get my transfer, the reality was that it was hard to understand why one request might be granted while another was denied.

Supervisors and inspectors used a series of observation galleries all over the post office from which they could see everything happening on the floor. They were, in effect, one-way mirrors, and they were used for security purposes as well as to check on workers' activities. There were even observation galleries in washrooms, and some inspectors exchanged jokes about the particular habits of some workers. Because there were some sections where no women normally worked, some areas lacked women's washrooms. There were problems with shift schedules, transfer requests, vacation schedules, discipline, health and safety, and other matters. Overall, morale was pretty low in the post office in the early 1960s.

At the time of the CPEA's National Convention in 1962 in Windsor, Ontario, we were under an "austerity program" of the Diefenbaker government. Wages were frozen and vacancies were not being filled. The wage freeze was finally lifted on December 10, 1962, but our working conditions were still determined solely by government rules and regulations

In early 1963 a general election was called and a minority Liberal government was elected. During the election campaign, all political parties pledged themselves to support some form of collective bargaining in the federal public service. In August of 1963 Prime Minister Lester B. Pearson followed up on this commitment and announced the establishment of the Heany Commission, which was to make recommendations for an appropriate form of collective bargaining and identify needed reforms in the system of classifications and pay structures in the federal public service.

The 1965 Strike

In the summer of 1965, the federal government again announced unilaterally that postal workers, along with others in the federal public service, were going to get a wage increase of $360 a year. The Heany Commission had issued its report, but it would not be dealt with by Parliament until it was due to convene in late September. But postal workers had had enough and were not going to wait any longer.

At the beginning of July, two weeks before the announcement of the

From left to right, three officers of the Montréal locals (in white shirts): CUPW President Willie Houle with Adrien Matte and Roger Décarie of LCUC. Standing to the left, a young Jean-Claude Parrot.

$360 increase, dissatisfaction was on the rise among inside postal workers. Management had issued an order stipulating that sorters would no longer have the right to sit at their seats during the first hour-and-a-half of their shifts and after meal breaks.

Every mail sorter has different habits, but it was rare to find anyone sitting all day while sorting. I was a sorter during my first years in the post office and I used my seat more to lean on than to sit in. The time spent by a mail sorter either sitting or standing varied from person to person, but a silly directive telling sorters when their legs needed a rest and when they didn't angered hundreds of workers. This national directive was seen by workers as yet another demonstration of how someone in an Ottawa office, with no understanding of how and why sorting is done a certain way, could be as stupid as the directive itself.

Because of this directive and the fact that no wage increase had yet been announced by Ottawa, there was pressure in Montréal on CPEA leaders to take some action. But it was the FALC local that first decided to hold an information meeting for the membership about the lack of any announcement of a wage increase. It was an explosive meeting, and it was agreed to hold a twenty-four-hour strike starting at midnight on July 19, with a call for a $660 increase retroactive to October 1, 1964.

On July 14 a delegation made up of officers of both CPEA and FALC locals went from Montréal to Ottawa to meet their respective national officers in an effort to get the support of the Postal Workers' Brotherhood for a national strike. The Brotherhood was composed of both Associations and the Canadian Railway Mail Clerks' Federation (CRMCF).

CUPW and LCUC members at a meeting in Montréal.

The delegation was told that the Brotherhood didn't have a mandate to strike and that it would be both premature and unconstitutional to do so without a referendum of the membership. A joint meeting then took place in Montréal and the strike deadline was extended to July 22. Other locals were contacted for support. I still remember that meeting: it was clear that postal workers were determined to strike.

On July 22, 1965, the members of both Associations in Vancouver, Hamilton, Montréal, and elsewhere in the province of Québec went out at the same time. The movement spread quickly across the country, and soon more than 80 percent of the national membership of both Associations was on strike.

Despite this, the national officers, who argued they didn't have a mandate to call a strike, never supported the strike. They were told very clearly to look outside, where 80 percent of their membership was on strike. They were asked, "Is that not a clear mandate?" Instead of answering, they tried to break the strike.

The Canadian Labour Congress didn't support the strike and asked its representatives to refrain from assisting striking locals. Maurice Hébert was one CLC representative who didn't listen: I remember him spending the full three weeks of the strike at our local headquarters.

Fortunately, Brother Louis Laberge, on behalf of the Québec Federation of Labour (FTQ), provided us with unconditional support and backed the decision of Brother Hébert to assist us. We really benefited from the experience of Brother Hébert and I personally never forgot his contribution. He was of great help to me in this first experience of being on strike.

We learned pretty fast and, despite our lack of experience, we put together a good strike organization in Montréal, with picket lines almost everywhere and good systems of communications. It was a great help that very many members stayed at our strike headquarters when they weren't on the picket lines.

At one point during the strike, a delegation went to Ottawa to meet with the Brotherhood's national officers and with government officials. There, the delegation learned that an *ad hoc* committee of the Brotherhood, on which our local president, Brother Houle, sat, had come to the conclusion that they would ask the striking members to go back to work. Their rationale was that the government had agreed that no disciplinary measures would be taken and a Special Commissioner would be appointed to make recommendations for changes in the post office. A resolution of the committee also provided that a national strike vote would take place within three days should the Commissioner's recommendations be unsatisfactory or too late in coming.

A Montréal delegation went to the train station to welcome Brother Houle back to strike headquarters. We arranged for him to meet with the officers and shop stewards of the two locals so he could see for himself the mood of the Montréal workers. There, he was told very clearly that, if he were to recommend to the workers that we should go back to work, he would be alone on the podium: none of us would support such a call.

We were not going to return to work on promises that things would improve after we went back. We wanted a real and immediate settlement of this dispute, and it was obvious to us that Brother Houle had been under a lot of pressure in Ottawa. The mood of the workers in that hall was incredible: people were raising their picket signs and singing, "We're not going back!" Brother Houle rose to speak and, if he had maintained any intention of trying to convince us to go back to work, by now he had certainly changed his mind. He gave what was probably the best speech he ever delivered. He talked about all the reasons why we should not go back to work and that it was time the government gave some respect to postal workers.

The CLC's Maurice Hébert was beside me at that moment, and he turned to me and said, "I never saw someone skate so fast! He just made a 90-degree turn!" Members, still chanting and raising their signs, voted unanimously to continue the strike.

That was Brother Houle's only moment of hesitation. I believe that, without him, we would not have been so successful in Montréal. He was a very good speaker and the members listened, ready to follow him in any actions required to win the struggle.

There were many more meetings before the 1965 strike was resolved.

CUPW and LCUC members in Toronto.

Many of them included speeches of support from Brother Louis Laberge, and his unconditional support gave us the courage to finish the struggle we had started. And, by now, the government realized that they needed to talk with the Montréal delegation. It was clear to them that they needed our participation if a solution was going to be found. Brother Laberge was part of the delegation that went from Montréal to meet the President of the Treasury Board, Edgar J. Benson. At one point in our negotiations, Mr. Benson indicated that the government might have no choice but to bring the army into the post office. (In fact, this idea had already been mentioned in the media.) Brother Laberge looked at him and said this: "Let me explain something to you. A good number of postal workers are veterans who have served our country in one of the two world wars. I'll make sure that they will wear their medals on picket lines that the army will be asked to cross. I'll also make sure that the media are there to see it all." The army was never called in.

The Montreal Gazette

CUPW and LCUC members voting by a show of hands to stay on strike. Though strike votes are always by secret ballot, in this case the mood of the meeting was such that a show of hands was all that was required.

Underhanded trickery was used to try to break the 1965 strike. Brother Joe Davidson, who preceded me as CUPW President, recalled a meeting in Toronto in his 1978 book, *Joe Davidson,* co-written by John Deverell:

> Les Hood, Arnold Gould and the Presidents of FALC and CRMCF then made a trek to Toronto, where the back-to-work appeal was ridiculed by our local strike committee during a late-night meeting at the Royal York. At a key point in the proceedings, however, someone produced a telegram bearing the names of Willie Houle and Roger Décarie declaring that Montréal was going back to work, and this took the heart out of the Toronto group. We concluded that the strike was finished and decided to recommend a return to work at a meeting the next day.

Both Willie Houle and Roger Décarie declared the telegram a forgery, but the repudiation came too late to influence the vote. A similar trick was played on the Vancouver local, which went back to work a couple of days before the Montréal local.

The spirit of the workers during the 1965 strike was very impressive. Montréal radio station CJMS stood against the strike, and the strikers, from the beginning: workers demonstrated outside its offices. Songs were written. Street demonstration followed meetings of workers. Officers from other Québec locals would come to our meetings in Montréal to support us. The atmosphere was electric. While most supervisors went to work during the strike, some, along with part-time workers, stayed out with us for the entire three-week duration of the strike.

After three weeks on the picket line, workers decided to go back to work after negotiations gained mail handlers an additional $510 per year, rather than the $300 that had originally been offered. As well, other workers earned a $550 annual salary increase, rather than the $360 that had initially been offered. And, a Royal Commission of Inquiry was appointed to investigate the working conditions of postal workers. (More on this Royal Commission in the following chapter.)

The 1965 CPEA Convention

The ninth triennial national convention of the Canadian Postal Employees' Association was held September 22–24, 1965 at the King Edward Hotel in Toronto. I still have a copy of the convention's program: on its cover is a photograph of what was then the new Toronto City Hall. Inside are greetings from both the Postmaster General and the Deputy Postmaster General. These are followed by greetings from both Toronto's Mayor and Postmaster, and messages from the CLC President, the Toronto and District Labour Council, and local CPEA leaders.

What hits me the most today, when looking at this publication, is the program itself, which provides a day-to-day outline of the three days of the convention, and at the end, a "Women's Program" for the three days. It outlines a tour of the city for the women on the first day, along with a visit to Casa Loma, and a dance and buffet in the evening. On the second day, there was to be a banquet and entertainment. On the final day, there was to be an excursion to a local shopping centre, followed by a farewell party in the evening.

Looking at this document early in the twenty-first century, it's hard to believe that women were treated this way. But, at the time, there were very few female delegates at our conventions. I have a photo of the Montréal delegation to that convention: it shows only one woman. I don't think there were more than five female delegates at that national convention, and all the men were dressed in two- or three-piece suits and ties.

Looking at this old convention document today makes me pause to reflect on how far women have come in our union over the years. At that time, women were seen far more as spouses of delegates, rather than as potential delegates themselves. Yet, by the end of this convention, we had become a union rather than an association.

On the convention floor, three outgoing CPEA officers ran for the position of National President. All were defeated: instead, Bill Kay, who had been one of the leaders of the Vancouver strikers, was elected to the position. When it came to the election of the Vice-President, the same three outgoing members ran for that post. But the incumbent Vice-President, Rick Otto, who had made clear in his written report to the convention that the CPEA's national leadership should have called a national strike when 12,000 of its members had already been on the picket line, was re-elected to the post. Finally, the incumbent General Secretary-Treasurer, Godfroy Côté, was re-elected to his post. That 1965 convention marked the end of the line for outgoing CPEA President Les Hood.

Also at the convention, full-time positions were established for field officers for the first time. Each of the eight regional caucuses nominated their preferred candidate, and each was then elected by all the delegates. A National Executive Board was formed, made up of the three national officers and the eight field officers. Salaries were set at $11,000 for the National President, $9,000 for the other two national officers and $7,000 for the eight field officers. (For the sake of comparison, the annual salary for a Member of Parliament at the time was $18,000.) Membership dues were set at four dollars per month, effective January 1, 1966.

In 1965, postal supervisors were members of the CPEA, but the issue of their ongoing inclusion in the organization was a matter of discussion among convention delegates. Willie Houle made a passionate appeal to the delegates on this issue:

> During the recent strike, the [supervisors] were the best-organized bunch of strike-breakers in Canada. During the first day of the strike in Montréal, these men were sent to different sections and they sorted a lot of mail. That mail was sent out to the smaller offices just to show the public that the [post office] was still operating.
>
> We have had these [supervisors] who were ready to break our strike....That is what happened in Montréal. I do not believe any good union would go along and try to get applications from those people. We do not need them. The sooner we get rid of them the sooner we will be a good union.

Delegates were determined to see change: they adopted a motion to get all supervisors and other management people out of the organization.

They also decided to exclude part-time workers. This was against the position of our Montréal local, where the regular part-time employees had all been on strike with us. Our position was supported by some other locals, such as Vancouver, where they had had similar experiences with part-timers during the strike. Another reason we opposed the exclusion of part-timers was that we knew another union, the Public Service Alliance of Canada (PSAC), would be happy to have them as members of its postal component and that this would complicate future negotiations. But most of the delegates had little or no experience in the real world of bargaining units, and the resolution to exclude part-timers was passed. (Fortunately, in 1966, the National Executive Board adopted a plan to recruit all part-time workers into the union.)

Another important resolution was adopted that called for the right to free collective bargaining with the right to strike. This was especially important in view of the fact that the Heany Commission, appointed by the Pearson government in 1963, had recommended only the right to negotiate and compulsory arbitration. Heany's recommendation would have meant that government would have continued to have the final say on our wages and working conditions. (As a result of our 1965 strike, of the position of the CLC, and of the position of the organizations of postal workers, Heany's recommendation was changed in the government's draft legislation to give federal public-sector employees the right to negotiate with a choice between conciliation with the right to strike or arbitration. The choice was to be made prior to the beginning of each round of negotiations.) Brother Andras from the CLC gave an excellent speech on collective bargaining and on Heany's report, along with upcoming tasks before postal workers.

Romo Maione from the International Department of the CLC also spoke at the convention. He had been appointed just three weeks before the convention to represent labour on the Royal Commission of Inquiry into the Working Conditions of Postal Employees, to be chaired by Mr. Justice Montpetit. He urged every local across the country and the national organization to prepare for the Royal Commission by presenting written briefs to the Commission along with oral submissions.

Finally, delegates voted to change the name of the organization from the Canadian Postal Employees' Association to the Canadian Union of Postal Workers. This was a clear indication of our determination to move from an association to a real union.

2 From Postal Clerk to National Union Officer

The Royal Commission of Inquiry

When the Royal Commission of Inquiry into the Working Conditions of Postal Employees, established as part of the resolution to the 1965 strike, came to Montréal, I was a member of the local's executive, and we decided to present a questionnaire to local members and ask them to identify important workplace issues. Fifteen percent of the membership replied to it. The respondents had an average of 10.8 years of service in the post office, and the biggest issue they raised — 82 percent of them — was health and safety. Salaries and other compensation issues were identified as important by 73 percent of respondents, while 70 percent said that scheduling and vacation leave were primary concerns.

Answers to the questionnaire helped a committee of five, of which I was a member, prepare a brief to the Royal Commission. It included more than sixty recommendations. Though we were a relatively inexperienced group, our local managed to put together a pretty good presentation to the Commission, largely because the results of our questionnaire gave us a working knowledge of the issues that most concerned our members. Though I played a relatively limited role in the presentation of our local's brief to the Royal Commission, I spent many hours preparing for it, and I gained experience in representing postal workers' interests. And, because our local had been on the front line of the 1965 strike, we knew the Commission would pay close attention to our brief.

The Royal Commission made 282 recommendations in the document it released at the conclusion of its proceedings. We were pleased with the recommendations in that document, known as the Montpetit Report. We also appreciated the first two recommendations addressed to the two parties. One of these called on government to study the possibility of turning the post office into a Crown Corporation, while the other urged the postal unions to be willing to take a positive attitude toward upcoming legislation in Parliament that would outline the process of negotiations among federal government employees.

But we knew our task was not over. Many of the Commission's recommendations dealt with consultations between the parties, while others were about negotiations that would take place once the legislation before Parliament was adopted and CUPW and LCUC were certified to represent postal workers. Change didn't happen overnight, and many of the problems detailed in the 1966 Montpetit Report still exist in the post office today. But the comments and tone of the Report reflected a real recognition of both the serious problems that existed in post offices across the country and the lack of understanding of labour-management relations on the part of senior management.

Though the issue of mechanization and automation in the post office was not seen as a major issue by either workers or management in 1966, the authors of the Montpetit Report wrote: "The issue of mechanization and automation is a problem of prime importance which should be looked into immediately by all interested parties since its effect will be very serious not only on job security, but also on job classification, seniority, etc." These words were to prove fateful.

The Report discussed staffing and working hours with this statement: "The fixing of working hours and the composition of shifts and their schedules create enormous problems for the Post Office Department. We feel, however, that the Department has, to some extent, lost sight of the human side of the problem and wonder if it has considered sufficiently the effects of constant evening or night work on the family and social life of an employee."

Comments such as these from the Montpetit Report give a sense of what working conditions and labour-management relations were like in the post office in 1966. We were determined to make improvements.

Negotiations of Wages, 1966

Though we had not yet formally earned the right to negotiate wages and working conditions by 1966, we nevertheless took part in negotiations with government about wages in the post office. At that time, a postal clerk earned $2 an hour when first hired and up to $2.51 after six-and-a half years of service. Mail handlers' wages ranged from $1.82 to $2.18. Letter carriers earned fourteen cents per hour less than a postal clerk, while mail dispatchers made a dime more. The Montréal local took the position that an increase of $1.25 an hour was appropriate, considering increases that were being negotiated by other unions on the eve of Expo '67.

One part of our research at the local level was to compare postal workers' salaries over time to those of other workers in a similar income bracket. We noted that, for a good part of the 1950s, postal workers were earning more than police officers, firefighters, and painters but, by the time of our 1965 strike, such workers were making between $800 and $1,200 more each year than postal workers. It was decided at the national level to demand an hourly wage increase of $1.00. (If not for our local's research, this figure would almost certainly have been lower.) In September, the national unions held a vote of their memberships to authorize a strike if we considered the government's offer unacceptable. All locals were to complete their votes by September 20. However, whatever the result of these votes, we knew that we had not yet been certified: Parliament had yet to pass the Public Service Staff Relations Act.

Around this time, the issue of wage increases and inflation was in the news. Prime Minister Pearson made a remark to the effect that the country was about to enter a period of inflation unless wages were kept down. The president of our Montréal local, Willie Houle, responded by saying, "Inflation began in 1534 with Jacques Cartier, when he asked for two or three furs from the Indians in exchange of his merchandise. When all goes well, workers are told: don't ask for big increases, or you'll create inflation. When all goes bad, the employers say: it's a depression, so we can't increase your salaries." (My own translation from the French original.)

Around the same time, there were satirical cartoons in the newspapers urging people to send their Christmas mail early. I remember one editorial cartoon that showed the Minister of Revenue holding a parcel from postal workers with the words "Don't Open Until Christmas" written on it. He was holding the parcel near his ear and could hear a "tick-tock" sound coming from it.

After negotiations with government, the postal unions settled for an hourly wage increase of $0.25 per hour. A central reason we got such a small settlement was a statement by Roger Décarie, the LCUC leader, that we wouldn't sit at the negotiating table unless an offer of at least $.0.50 was on the table. At the time, his remark prompted me to say, "We've just lost $0.50 cents on our demand for $1.00, and we haven't even started negotiating." Roger Décarie's statement had cost all postal workers dearly. We in the Montréal local were more than a little angry about the small increase that was finally agreed to. Meanwhile, we all waited for Parliament to pass legislation that would certify our union.

Certification of Part-Time Workers

Another project CUPW began in 1966 involved recruiting the part-time workers we had barred from the union at our 1965 convention. This plan to become certified to negotiate on behalf of part-timers was an audacious one, given that, as a result of the 1965 convention, we were widely seen as opposed to part-timers, and so it would not be appropriate for us to represent their interests in negotiations. It would take three years for us to succeed.

PSAC and CUPW were both engaged in efforts to organize part-time postal workers. The president of Montréal's CUPW local gave the task of organizing the part-timers to vice-president Marcel Perreault, who did a fantastic job in convincing them to come back to CUPW. He was helped by a number of female activists who were central to our success. (One of the key activists in that Montréal campaign was a woman named Madame Lebel, who I recently had the opportunity of meeting once again during the Montréal local's making of the film *Gains For Everyone*.)

I played only a limited role in this campaign because I worked at the time in the postal stations, where there were very few part-time workers. I did attend most of the meetings called for the part-timers and saw that some of the women were clearly working for the integration of the part-timers into PSAC.

When the vote was finally held and the results were announced on July 12, 1969, we prevailed. Almost 90 percent of the part-timers voted to be represented by the Council of Postal Unions (which included both CUPW and LCUC). In Montréal, we had feared that the national vote would be less clear than our local one, but these fears proved unfounded. Locals in Toronto, Vancouver, and elsewhere across the country did a great job in recruiting part-time workers to our side.

If the part-timers had voted to be represented by a different union, it would have presented great difficulties in our efforts to improve working conditions in the post office. But, once we were all in the same bargaining unit, we were better able to limit the number of casual and part-time workers by working to create more full-time positions, which part-timers were then able to fill. Our fight was not to divide one group of workers from another: rather, it was to stop the use of cheap labour by the employer. While we recognized that there was a legitimate need for part-time workers during peak periods, we fought to have them receive the same pay and benefits full-time workers received.

CUPW 1968 National Convention

By 1968, CUPW had the right to negotiate on behalf of inside postal workers. We had chosen to negotiate wages and working conditions through a process of conciliation backed up by the right to strike. CUPW's triennial National Convention was held in Montréal from May 27–29, 1968. We were approaching the conciliation process in our negotiations with management, and a strike loomed as a real possibility. A federal election had just been called on June 25, and Pierre Elliott Trudeau was the new Prime Minister and Leader of the Liberal Party.

Brother Roméo Mathieu, the chief negotiator for this round of negotiations, reported to the Convention. He remarked that, if we had chosen arbitration instead of conciliation with the right to strike, he would have refused to negotiate on our behalf. He then added: "I do not consider a strike as an end in itself. I consider a strike as a means to an end. I would prefer, needless to say, a settlement across the table, rather than a strike. But I will say to you also that you cannot have real collective bargaining at the table unless you have the big stick of the strike to hold above your head."

One of the resolutions adopted at the 1968 Convention raised union dues to five dollars per month, with two dollars of that to be sent to the locals. The increase in dues, however, would not take effect before postal workers received a substantial increase in wages through the current bargaining process.

A new, full-time, Ottawa-based position of National Director of Education and Organization was established, and the number of full-time field officers went from eight to ten. *The Postal Tribune*, which had served as CUPW's national magazine, became the magazine of our Montréal local. FTQ President Louis Laberge gave a rousing speech on the need for unity in view of the upcoming conciliation process and a possible strike. He underlined the fact that, had we not gone on strike in 1965, the labour movement would have taken many more years to organize within the federal civil service.

A new National Executive Board was elected on the Convention's last day. Brother Willie Houle was elected National President, Joe Davidson Vice-President, Paul Gruslin General Secretary-Treasurer, and Mel Wilde Director of Organization and Education. Rick Otto, the outgoing Executive Vice-President, was defeated in three efforts to be elected to the National Executive Board. Ten field officers, and their alternates, were also elected at the Convention. These field officers also served on the Board.

A Negotiating Committee was also elected, made up of Brothers Houle and Davidson, along with three field officers: R. Tremblay (Quebec North), Bill Kidd (Ontario North), and A.R. McLay (British Columbia).

The 1968 Convention was attended by 353 delegates, eleven national officers, thirty-one fraternal delegates, and 145 visitors.

First-Time Negotiations for Postal Workers

In 1968, CUPW and LCUC united in the Council of Postal Unions in order to become quickly certified to jointly represent postal workers, and we began our first round of negotiations with Treasury Board and the post office on a first collective agreement for our members. The Council's Negotiating Committee was made up of the five members recently elected at the CUPW Convention as well as five members from LCUC.

CRMCF, which represented mail sorters on trains, had also been a member of the Council of Postal Unions, but the employer had decided a few years previously to end the sorting of mail on trains, so CRMCF's role in the Council was very limited.

Expectations of these negotiations were high between both CUPW and LCUC members, given that the 282 recommendations of the Royal Commission on the Working Conditions of Postal Workers had outlined how bad working conditions and labour-management relations were in the post office. Many of these recommendations were to be the subject of our negotiations.

Negotiations were new to all of us. We had just completed our National Convention, and the president of our Montréal local, Willie Houle, had been elected CUPW's National President. Roger Décarie, the former president of the Montréal local of LCUC, was now serving as National President of that organization. Having these two strong people at the bargaining table, both of whom had been big backers of the 1965 strike, gave us hope that we'd be able to successfully negotiate better pay and working conditions. Union members were set to vote by mail in order to decide whether to give our negotiating team a strike mandate.

However, there was a lack of communication to the membership about what was going on at the bargaining table. In Montréal, I became involved in getting petitions signed by members of both unions calling for an information meeting with the Negotiating Committee and with the CLC's Chief Negotiator, Roméo Mathieu. More than 2,000 signatures were collected from members of both Montréal locals, and a joint meeting of the two unions was scheduled at Centre Paul Sauvé in early June. In fact, two meetings were held, in order to accommodate shift workers: one at 1:30 pm and a second at 7:30 pm.

I had been elected as an alternate to the field officer for Montréal, Brother Michel Lareau, who, in that capacity, sat on the National Executive Board. As an alternate, I received material from CUPW's national office that was meant for Board members. Among this material was information about the situation at the bargaining table.

At the 1:30 pm meeting, we were told that the Board wanted a strike mandate from members so they could achieve a set of demands that had been sent to us earlier by the Council of Postal Unions. Board members explained some of these demands, and, because I had access to more information than many members, I quickly realized that some of these demands had already been dropped at the bargaining table. I stepped up to the microphone and said that union members would have no problem authorizing a strike to achieve our demands, but that I had serious problems with the Board calling for a strike mandate based on issues that had already been dropped from the bargaining table.

At the evening meeting, the members of the Board said the same things they had at the earlier meeting, and I once again headed to the microphone to make the same point I had at the afternoon meeting. As I approached, I saw that there were people who wanted to stop me from getting to the microphone. I rushed there anyway and said that nobody was going to stop me from expressing my opinion and that the Board was misleading the members.

Both the meetings were very well attended. I think the Board members got the message that members were willing to give them a strike mandate, but also that the members demanded honesty from the Board about the issues actually in dispute. (This incident, along with a similar one in negotiations in 1970, gave rise to a policy being adopted at CUPW's 1971 National Convention that obliges union negotiators, when calling for a strike mandate, to inform members of what issues had been dropped before entering into conciliation.)

On June 10, 1968, the results of our national vote to give our National Executive Board the right to negotiate with the possibility of a strike, taken by referendum through the mail, were announced. Out of the 24,115 ballots mailed to our members, 21,144 returned their ballots, for a participation of 86.7 percent of the total membership. The result of the vote was 91.2 percent in favour of giving the Board a strike mandate.

A few weeks later, there was an election for first vice-president of the Montréal local. Marcel Perreault, who had previously held the position, had become the local's president after the election of Willie Houle as CUPW's Ottawa-based National President at our May convention. Several candidates indicated their interest in the vice-presidential position. Among the "progressive" activists in the local, two indicated their interest for the position: Brother Jacques Boismenu, who had been instrumental in getting me involved with the union, and myself.

Brother Boismenu and I both worked in the same section of the post office — the postal stations — and it was generally felt that candidates were most likely to have strong support from workers who worked in the same sections as they did. Local president Perreault, who was hoping one of us would get elected, called us to his office and encouraged us to reach an agreement about which of us would run so we wouldn't divide the votes from our section. I was convinced that Brother Boismenu couldn't win, so I maintained that I had a better chance, and so my candidacy should stand. Unfortunately, Brother Boismenu didn't agree with me: he would stay in the race as well.

In the end, there were seven candidates for this office, all men, from various sections of the local. I went to see local president Perreault and told him that I felt each candidate would get most of the votes in his section, but that I was also convinced I would pick up a lot of votes from other sections in addition to my own. There was a candidate from the city section, the biggest in the local, so I figured he had a pretty good chance as well. On one hand, with so many candidates in the race, there was a real chance of a split vote giving the election to the candidate from the city section. On the other hand, I was convinced I'd get most of the votes in the postal stations — despite Brother Boismenu's candidacy — and that I would also pick up a good number of votes in other sections.

The election was held through the mail, and the counting was done on July 14, 1968. I won election as first vice-president of the Montréal local. I received 727 votes, while the city section candidate got 493, and the other candidates received between 69 and 469 votes. Brother Boismenu received 367 votes. So, after fourteen years in the post office, I became a full-time officer for CUPW. (I was re-elected to this position in both 1969 and 1970, before being elected a national officer for CUPW in Ottawa in 1971.)

Meanwhile, negotiations for a new contract had been unsuccessful and a strike was imminent. So, I began my new duties just a few days before we would strike. Other than myself and local president Perreault, the only other full-time position with the Montréal local was a secretary-treasurer, Gerald Jenkins. I put together a schedule of how the members could cover the picket lines at the main post office throughout the strike. The three-week strike of 1968 unfolded with no major problems and was much better organized than our 1965 strike had been. And, this time, all locals across the country went out, unlike what had happened in 1965.

The atmosphere during the strike was incredible. Members took part enthusiastically in picket duties and many spent a lot of time at strike headquarters. In Montréal, CUPW and LCUC decided to have a joint strike headquarters and to hold joint meetings of members of both unions to strategize on a day-to-day basis, and this worked out well. (Across the country, some locals of CUPW and LCUC organized their strike activities separately, while other acted as we did in Montréal, by working in unison.) An incredible number of songs were composed during the strike. Almost every day, someone would adapt a then-popular song by embellishing it with new lyrics about our strike. And, we paraded on the streets of Montréal. One day we rallied in Laval, and then a procession of about 200 cars crossed the bridge and went through the streets of downtown Montréal and on to our strike headquarters. The police, though they initially wished to stop our rally through the streets, decided, when they saw our sheer strength of numbers, to simply block intersections and let us pass. People on the streets waved in support of us.

Our strike in the summer of 1968 ended when we signed a collective agreement that, for the first time, embodied, in a contract, rights and benefits that could no longer be taken away by the whim of management or the federal government. It provided better wages and some improved working conditions, and it obliged the employer to consult with the union on many issues that had previously been decided exclusively by management. And, a grievance procedure was put in place that allowed workers to deal with workplace issues.

Looking back on the 1968 strike and the meetings leading up to it, we proved that we could stage a strike on a national scale. It was an important moment in our history because it made postal workers across the country proud to act as trade unionists when the time came to take action against the employer. In a way, it was the end of postal workers thinking of themselves as "civil servants" and the beginning of thinking of themselves as "public sector workers."

The strike ended just weeks after the election of Pierre Elliott Trudeau's majority Liberal government. Soon after its conclusion, in view of the fact that I was now a full-time officer of the union, I resigned my position as alternate for the Montréal field officer. However, I asked the national office to continue to send me relevant materials. National President Houle approved my request.

Automation in the Post Office

Early in 1970, Postmaster General Eric Kierans announced the introduction of a six-digit postal code. This came about as a result of a study undertaken in July of 1969 at the request of the post office. This is the code still being used today.

During this period, CUPW's national office decided to study the automation situation in the American post office. A National Automation Committee (NAC), of the union was formed, made up of eleven leaders from the largest locals, and visits were organized to different American post offices. We broke up into teams, and I was on one that visited the post office in Philadelphia. Hearing about equipment recently introduced there, we weren't impressed with what we learned from the union local. There were lots of casual workers there, and it was difficult to determine how to classify them or to know what they were supposed to be doing. We got the impression that the union local there didn't know much about automation, and we couldn't tell whether the union had any objectives in that regard. On the floor, we noticed that most of those working on the coding desk had developed a work tempo based on some repetitive movement, such as tapping on the floor with a foot, moving the head or the top of the body, a certain rhythmic blinking of the eyes, or some such. We realized that these movements were based not on the pace of the worker, but on that of the coding machine, which was set at about sixty-two letters per minute. (Later on, management in the Canadian post office would fix the tempo of our machines at fifty-eight letters per minute — not to make things easier for workers, but because there were fewer breakdowns of machines at that rate than when it was increased to 60 letters a minute or more.) Montréal local president Marcel Perreault and myself were both at the Philadelphia facility, and we produced a report for the NAC, of which we were a part. The NAC then produced a report showing that management in the Canadian post office had planned its automation program in a cold, calculated manner focussed on both its own economic bottom line and eliminating the need to deal honestly with the workers' union.

High-level managers were hired from other industries and they formed a group that was given the power and resources to achieve the employer's objectives. Millions of dollars were being spent, but the NAC noted in its report that none of it was designated to provide postal workers a healthy and safe working environment. The objectives were to reduce the number of postal workers through lay-offs, to simplify the sorting process, to create new classifications of postal workers, to displace workers to other

Manual sortation of parcels by Montréal inside workers, prior to the introduction of automation.

distribution facilities, and to make unilateral changes in working conditions. The NAC report also recommended that CUPW undertake special organizing, mobilizing, and strategizing on the issue of automation in the post office. As well, it recommended that we approach negotiations with management with a special eye on reducing working hours, health and safety issues, and resolving problems such as seniority, classification, and wage issues.

The NAC's report on automation ended with the statement: "Our union does not exist to run an efficient postal service: that is the boss's job. Our union exists to look after the welfare of the membership."

This was but the first skirmish in the battle over automation and mechanization in the post office. Many more would follow, and I discuss many of these in later pages. But the history of that battle shows that CUPW fought for the interests of its members, and *also* for improved service to the public at large. Management's objective, on the other hand, was to provide better service to the business sector, especially large corporations.

The 1970 Negotiations and Rotating Strikes

In the summer of 1970, CUPW staged a series of rotating strikes across the country to back up our negotiating position at the bargaining table. All summer, the National Organization and Education Officer, Mel Wilde, went across the country to meet locals as their turn came to go out. He would explain to each local that they had to show that they could strike too: just as such-and-such a local had already shown. He might suggest that a local choose a Friday or Monday for its rotating strike, and so make a long weekend out of it.

This attitude seemed more than a bit cavalier to me. It appeared that the strikes themselves were becoming more important than the issues on the bargaining table. In Montréal, we accepted the concept of rotating strikes, knowing that the summer was not the most effective time for an all-out strike. It was our understanding that once fall arrived, we would go on a full-scale strike until we reached a settlement. That, however, never happened. The national office announced they had reached a tentative agreement with management and recommended that the membership accept the agreement. Our local was taken by surprise, because we knew that there were many issues that had not been resolved. I felt that many locals across the country had been more focused on the rotating strikes than on the issues themselves. We in the Montréal local were quite disappointed, but we were also aware that it was too late to turn things around.

The 1970 tentative agreement provided that letter carriers would receive overtime pay after eight hours of work, that there would be equal opportunity to members of both unions for overtime work, that there would be an increase in shift premiums, that there would be certain additional medical benefits and job protections, and that there would be a wage increase over several months adding up to $0.55 per hour. It also provided a commitment from management, outside the scope of the agreement itself, that casual workers would receive no less than the minimum pay for the classification in which they worked. There was also to be a cash settlement of $574 for all full-time employees and proportionately less for part-timers. Finally, the agreement included a letter from the Postmaster General guaranteeing job security for full-time workers.

In the vote of the membership, 88.2 percent of full-time employees approved the tentative agreement on October 16, 1970. More than 98 percent of part-time workers voted in favour of the agreement. It was signed on November 13, 1970.

The 1971 CUPW Convention — Calgary: Tough Battles, Tough Issues

During the period leading up to CUPW's 1971 National Convention, which was set to start in Calgary, Alberta, at the end of May, our Montréal local was very busy. We were determined to bring about some positive changes to our union's national policies and its constitution, and we were also concerned about some of the actions of the national union over the previous three years, particularly in matters of grievances and arbitration, communications, and several other areas. Our local decided to prepare for the convention with a series of meetings to propose and discuss convention resolutions, followed by two weekend seminars for our members who would go as delegates to Calgary. We divided into three groups: one dealt with non-financial resolutions regarding the union's constitution, the second solely with financial issues, and the third with other policy issues. During the first weekend, we went through all the resolutions our local had outlined for the convention and planned how we would intervene on the convention floor and put forward our arguments. By the end of the weekend, all delegates knew the roles they were expected to play at the convention, as well as the importance of being very disciplined.

We spent the second weekend reviewing resolutions that had come from other locals across the country. We looked for resolutions similar to ones we were proposing, at whether our not our local would support specific resolutions, and at how we would intervene in the discussions on the convention floor.

Both the president and the second vice-president of our local sat on a national committee dealing with resolutions coming from locals across the country, and they went off for meetings in Banff the weekend before the convention was due to begin. When our delegates arrived on Sunday, they were waiting for us, and we held a meeting of our delegation to discuss developments. There, the president and the second vice-president of our local, who had preceded us to Alberta, told us that resolutions dealing with constitutional matters that had been sent in by locals across the country would not be discussed on the convention floor, because an entirely new constitution, drafted by consultant Bill Walsh, was going to be discussed at the convention. We adopted a strategy for Monday morning, when the convention was due to begin, deciding to argue against any discussion of constitutional or financial issues until it was agreed that resolutions coming from the locals also be dealt with. We also had frustrations over some issues we felt the national union had not dealt with properly over the previous three years, such as automation, a dispute involving privately contracted drivers in Montréal, the way negotiations were going, a lack of communication, and the position of CUPW within the CPU.

In view of our opposition to having any discussions on constitutional and financial matters, the Executive decided to have the committee dealing with general resolutions report to delegates. These included policies on automation, negotiations, seniority, and much else. As we had agreed at our local's weekend seminars, I led our representations on the resolutions arising from this committee, and I found myself before the microphone far more often than I thought I ever would have.

On Tuesday, June 1, some delegates approached me and suggested that I run for the new position of National Chief Steward. Elections for this and other national union positions were scheduled for Friday, the last day of the convention, and I discussed this possibility with the other two full-time officers of the Montréal local on Wednesday. They had no objection to me running for the new position, and in fact, they said it would be good to have someone else from our local in the national office in Ottawa.

On Thursday, we had a presentation from Bill Walsh, the consultant hired to draft the new constitution. In putting his draft together, he had visited many of the locals across the country. We didn't know much about him in Montréal, but he was a nationally known progressive activist. He gave us worthwhile information on the mood within government during our rotating strikes the previous year and government's view of the settlement we'd reached. He then outlined the rationale behind the proposed constitution. It was to promote the militant unity of workers, help the union to operate democratically, and allow conventions to operate efficiently, with full opportunity for all the delegates to take part in the deliberations. It also outlined the rights and duties of union officers in implementing policies and tried to assure that lines of communications were opened — and were kept open — among the various levels of the union at all times (and especially during negotiations with management). It provided a structure to encourage mobilization of the membership in order that the union could bring its maximum strength to its struggles. It provided a means for the union to "police" the agreement through a new national officer to be called National Chief Steward. It outlined how officers would report to the membership and cooperate with other postal workers and the entire labour movement. Finally it provided for new, intermediate structures within the union, such as area councils and regional conferences.

Overall, we in the Montréal local thought that the proposed constitution was pretty good. But we didn't want to discuss it until we were assured that we would also have the opportunity at this convention to discuss resolutions coming from the locals. We especially felt that many of the issues we'd raised in our local's resolutions were not dealt with in the proposed new constitution.

The rest of Thursday was filled with points of order and considerable confusion about the various sections of the new constitution and the resolutions covered by it. At one point, the Montréal local walked off the convention floor. The end result was that most of the day was total chaos, and a decision was taken to extend the convention by another day.

Some national officers decided to call a meeting of the major leaders across the country to discuss how we were going to get out of this mess. At the meeting, held on Thursday night, the Montréal local along with others from the Québec region presented our priorities and concerns and indicated to all these leaders the issues we thought needed to be addressed to resolve our differences. They provided us with their own concerns, and we agreed to study one another's issues overnight. It was around 1:00 am when we went to our respective rooms. We met again at about 6:00 am.

I still remember how tired the national officers and the other leaders outside Québec looked when we gathered again in the morning. They had obviously worked all night studying our proposals. We, however, had decided to get a few hours rest so we'd be in decent shape when we resumed discussions. We finally reached an agreement on the sections of the new constitution that amendments would be proposed through.

At the opening of the Friday morning session, it was agreed that Dan Cross would chair the convention. Brother Cross was a former National President of the CPEA before it became a full-time position in Ottawa. He had played a major role in the organization and had devoted much of his time to the CPEA when it had no full-time officer. He was well respected and recognized as a good chairperson who knew the proper procedures for meetings such as this convention.

When the Constitution Committee began presenting the articles of the new constitution, they were adopted one after the other without any floor debate. Only a few sections were referred back to the Committee for amendment. Many of the delegates couldn't believe what was happening. Suddenly, things were moving at a speed no one would have expected the day before. (In the afternoon, all the referrals were reported back by the Constitution Committee and adopted without debate.) At the end of the morning session, André Marceau from Québec made the following statement: "I would like to thank the chairperson of the convention, and I would like to bring to the attention of the world... we're leaving this room this morning with the most united and the strongest union in the country."

The next debate was on a resolution to support the recommendations of the Royal Commission on the Status of Women, which recognized the basic rights of women and was supported by the CLC. The recommendation of the Resolutions Committee was one of non-concurrence. This came as a shock to the women delegates and to many other progressives. Sister Janet Renaud, who I believe was from the Toronto local, made this intervention: "I am really surprised that this resolution was rejected by the Committee. I really don't think there could have been any women on that committee. The recommendations of the Royal Commission are simply recognition of the basic rights of all women. It is not a bra-burning type of thing that people have associated with it. If we leave it up to each local, I don't think this will be very effective. I think we should stand united as a union and support this recommendation by the Royal Commission. So I disagree with the recommendation."

After this intervention, the recommendation of the Resolutions Committee was defeated. Then, a woman delegate I couldn't identify introduced an emergency resolution on the superannuation plan, which was adopted. This was the beginning of the participation of women and part-time workers at CUPW conventions.

The Constitution Committee then presented all the financial aspects of the new constitution. These included a new dues structure, the annual budget, new salaries and benefits for union officers, an education fund of $60,000 to be overseen by an education committee, and a provision that each member should contribute one dollar a month into a strike fund.

Several new union policies were also adopted, some of them dealing with automation, some with other matters. In view of these new policies, the union would not participate in the employer's publication, nor would the employer participate in the union's. Union members would not take part in employer's courses, other than those provided for in the collective agreement, such as job training and first-aid training. Both official languages would be used in negotiations. (I raised the fact that our demand to this effect had been dropped during the previous negotiations). All officers would be given the opportunity to become bilingual, with the union covering the costs involved. No person could be a delegate to convention if he or she accepted work in a management position. Nor could anyone be a delegate if he or she was on a waiting list to become a supervisor: any such people were obliged to leave any union positions they might hold. Union members were not to help management gather data related to employee files.

A resolution was adopted to implement universal seniority within the job classifications represented by CUPW, if approved by a referendum of the membership. (Changes that were to come with automation were a major element in taking this decision.) Another resolution called for a study of the consequences of the post office becoming a Crown Corporation.

Certain resolutions were also adopted relating to negotiations. A central information centre would be maintained by the union from the beginning of negotiations, in order to provide daily information to the field and to respond to requests. The union would reject any proposed "moratorium of silence" during the course of negotiations, and a public relations person would be retained during negotiations. Bargaining would be only at the national level, not the regional. Any memorandum of agreement signed during the life of a collective agreement would be submitted to the membership for ratification.

We agreed that a monthly, ad-free national newspaper in both languages would be mailed to each member. Each local would receive a monthly bulletin that included the minutes of the National Executive Board and any pertinent news that might be of interest to members. Another resolution was adopted that called on each local to send all minutes of their union-management meetings to their respective regional offices.

The fact that media representatives were present at the convention was discussed, and it was decided to maintain this practice rather than bar them. Another resolution directed that a national officer be present at the national headquarters at all times during regular hours of work. A "motion of blame" against the national officers was passed regarding a classification issue.

Two major debates took place at the convention regarding CUPW's future. The first was on a resolution to affiliate to the Canadian Union of Public Employees (CUPE). Delegates from Québec waged a strong campaign during, and outside, the convention on this issue. Our local had adopted a resolution to affiliate with CUPE during a meeting in July of 1969, and we had sent it to the national office for study and to have it sent to all locals across the country. A month later, the National Executive Board had adopted the resolution, along with an amendment that a study on this issue be submitted to the next Board meeting before being sent to the locals. In November of 1970, more than a year later, when a Board member had raised the matter, he had been told that one of the national officers would attempt to get more information from CUPE. By late 1970, any realistic idea of a real study being done was gone, despite the resolution the Board had adopted the year before.

Before the Calgary convention began, our local had asked that the national office provide all locals with the study that had been expected on the issue of affiliating with CUPE. It didn't happen, nor was any information on the matter provided to delegates — aside from resolutions from the Montréal local and others in Québec advocating affiliation. The resolution under discussion in Calgary called for the National Executive Board to negotiate affiliation with CUPE within four months. The Constitution Committee recommended that the resolution be rejected.

Our arguments in favour of affiliation were that CUPW needed certain technical services that CUPE might provide, such as legal advice, as well as help in such areas as communications, organization, job evaluation, and education. We also argued that affiliation would help us build a strike fund and also gain us easier access to translation services. As well, we pointed out that affiliation with CUPE could provide us with greater autonomy than what we then had under the CPU.

We didn't win this debate, and the resolution to affiliate with CUPE was defeated. But, our arguments for affiliation opened the eyes of many delegates, raising their expectations of what to expect from their own national union. It forced CUPW's leadership to be more attentive to the needs of the organization and to be more representative of the aspirations of the membership.

The second major debate on the union's future in Calgary dealt with our position in the CPU, established in 1966, pending a proposed merger of all post office unions — a merger that never took place. It was decided to debate this issue in a closed session on Wednesday evening. The full text of a legal opinion our local had obtained on the matter was read out. Basically, it explained the process by which we might disaffiliate from the CPU and

E. W. Cadman

National Executive Board members elected at the 1971 CUPW Convention. From left to right, back row: Alvin Clark (Atlantic Region), Michel Lareau (Québec Region), Bob Capstick (Western Region), and Arnold Gould (Ontario Region). Front row, from left: Secretary-Treasurer Paul Gruslin, Vice-President Joe Davidson, President Jim McCall, Chief Steward Jean-Claude Parrot, and Mel Wilde, Director of Organization and Education.

dealt with several complex legal and constitutional matters. The debate was quite interesting and, at the end of it, a motion was adopted calling for a meeting of the CPU to negotiate a new constitution. If that meeting failed to reach agreement on the issue at hand, a referendum would take place among our members on disaffiliating from the CPU. A deadline of December 2, 1971, was set for achieving a new CPU constitution

Because the convention had been extended by one day, the election of national officers was held Saturday morning. I had by now received the support of my local to run for the position of National Chief Steward. On Thursday I'd phoned my wife, Louisette, to tell her that we'd added a day to the convention, so I'd be back home Saturday night rather than Friday. I had also told her then that I was planning to run for a position that would mean we'd be moving to Ottawa if I were elected. She didn't show any opposition at the time. In fact, we hardly discussed the possibility at all in the course of that call.

There were three candidates for National President on Saturday, and Brother Jim McCall was elected on the first ballot. (This was the end of Willie Houle's presidency. He had sprung from our local in Montréal, but his defeat was not the result of our local's opposition to his re-election, though some at the time thought it was.) Brother Joe Davidson was elected National Vice-President by acclamation, and I was elected National Chief Steward in the same manner. Brother Paul Gruslin was re-elected National Secretary-Treasurer, and Brother Mel Wilde was acclaimed as National Director of Education and Organization.

After the election, I phoned Louisette and said, "Guess what? We're moving to Ottawa." She started to cry on the phone. It was the first time she really realized the impact my election as a national officer might have on our family. I knew that I'd have work to do on the domestic front when I got back home to Montréal.

Leaving the convention, I felt good about being the first person to fill the new position of National Chief Steward. I was determined to make shop stewards across the country recognize they could count on me to follow up their work in the locals. I knew I'd also be able to prepare recommendations for changes in the collective agreement based on our grievances at arbitration or simply based on difficulties faced by members over certain provisions of the agreement.

I was also pleased that we'd had some very serious, in-depth discussions at the Calgary convention. The debates on our relationship with both CUPE and the CPU had been, I thought, very educational for the delegates. Later, I would learn that they were a help to our union in what it went through in later years. I thought then that the adoption of policies on both negotiations and the integrity of the union were well-appreciated, and I believe that they still contribute today to the CUPW's credibility among the membership, especially among union activists.

On to Ottawa

When I came back to Montréal from the Calgary convention, I pretty quickly learned that neither my wife, nor my two daughters, nor my father-in-law — who was living with us at the time — were keen about moving to Ottawa. I argued that we'd find a better place to live in Ottawa, that my salary was better than before, that there were French schools available, and that it would be a great new experience for us. But I didn't really convince anyone.

We had arranged to rent a cottage that summer not far from Montréal. The rest of the family spent the summer there, while I took an apartment in Ottawa, attended to my new duties, and looked around for a place where the family might like to live. In September, Louisette came to Ottawa, and I showed her different places I'd found.

I wanted to stay on the Québec side of the Ottawa River, but I had only found one neighbourhood there that I thought would please her. One complication was that Louisette didn't drive — she still doesn't — and I knew that this neighbourhood wouldn't work out well because it was too far away from everything. Finally, we found a townhouse that was much

nicer than the place we were renting in Montréal, was close to two shopping malls and French schools, had good public transport — no more than
fifteen minutes to get downtown — and with other assets I felt would
make my family more comfortable with the move to Ottawa.

I knew that if I didn't want a divorce (which I certainly didn't) and if I
didn't want to move back to Montréal and give up my new position in the
national office, it was essential that my family feel good about our new
environment. Thankfully they did, and by the spring of 1972 they all told
me that they loved living in Ottawa and that they wouldn't want to move
back to Montréal. It really helped me in my new job to know that my two
daughters, Johanne and Manon, loved their new school and that Louisette
and her father were happy in this new period of their lives.

I worked really hard in my new position and was away from home a lot.
My work-week averaged over sixty hours a week — something I maintained most of my working life. This meant that I was not always there
when I was needed at home. One day, one of Johanne's school friends told
her that she had seen me on television the night before. "You're lucky,"
Johanne said, "I haven't see my father for a week." I felt bad about this, but
both Manon and Johanne told me they understood and that they supported me in my new work.

3 Through Adversity to Greater Strength

Getting On With the Job

I was determined to be a good national officer and to serve postal workers well. I quickly developed new methods for handling grievances and arbitrations. I also began to write a column in our national newspaper addressing specific cases and outlining the grievance and arbitration processes in an effort to increase workers' understanding of these matters.

A few months after I began my duties as National Chief Steward, I was invited to attend an important meeting of the Vancouver local's officers and shop stewards. The meeting was scheduled for 7:00 pm, and a seminar was set for the next day. Being new at the national office, I felt this meeting would be a test for me.

I was scheduled to take a morning plane from Ottawa, with a stop in Toronto on the way to Vancouver. But a big snowstorm descended on Ottawa, and no planes were leaving. In fact, it was announced that the airport was closed. I was really disappointed, but when the weather started to clear, I tried to reach Air Canada to see if I could get another flight. At first I couldn't get through on the phone, and when I was finally able to reach someone, the agent wasn't able to confirm anything about future flights.

At noon, I decided to go to the airport, still hoping to get a flight and make it to Vancouver in time for the meeting. With the three-hour time difference, I thought I might still make it. When I got to the ticket counter, there were a lot of people waiting, and I was told that there were no available seats on planes heading to Vancouver. "I can only give you a seat as far as Toronto," the representative told me, "but there are no available seats this afternoon to Vancouver."

I decided to at least take the seat to Toronto and hope for the best from there. From Toronto, the plane was scheduled to go on to Vancouver, arriving at about the time my meeting was set to begin, but my passage from Toronto wasn't confirmed. I was assigned a middle seat between two men, one of whom was flying on to Vancouver. A few minutes after take-off, the pilot announced we were returning to Ottawa because of a problem with the plane's flaps. A few minutes after that announcement, the pilot again came on the intercom, this time to tell us that were going on to Toronto because that airport was better equipped to deal with the plane's problem than was Ottawa. However, we would be cruising at low altitude and the flight, which normally took fifty-five minutes, would take an hour and twenty minutes.

The men on either side of me began to talk about our situation. One of them said he knew about planes, and if we had a problem with the flaps it meant we'd have problems landing. As long as we flew as we were, he said, there shouldn't be any problem. But the minute we try to land, the flaps would have to be working.

I could see that both these men were getting pretty worried, but somehow I was not. Finally, we approached the airport and the plane began to land. Looking out, we could see fire-fighters alongside the runway, but we landed safely. I rushed to pick up my bags, which had been dispatched only as far as Toronto, and then went quickly to the Air Canada counter.

I explained that I had originally had a flight confirmed to Vancouver, but find now that I'm not booked beyond Toronto. The agent took my ticket, looked in the computer, and told me to immediately go to the gate with my luggage. There would be no time to check my luggage, she told me, but they were expecting me at the boarding gate. I rushed to the gate and saw hundreds of people waiting to get on the flight. I ran to the counter with my luggage and the agent asked me whether I was Mr. Parrot. I said I was, and she took my boarding pass and told me to board the plane, which would be leaving very shortly. I was the last passenger to get on.

In a way, I had been lucky that the plane had had problems with the flaps, because it caused a half-hour delay in leaving Toronto, and I never would have made it on board because of the time it took to retrieve my luggage. But it was now quite late and there was no way I was going make it to Vancouver in time for the meeting. The flight was now scheduled to arrive around 8:30 pm Vancouver time.

I didn't know whether anyone would be there to meet me, but I knew where the meeting was and the hotel where I was staying that night. As it turned out, there was someone waiting for me at the airport, and he gave me a lift to the meeting. To my surprise, all the stewards and officers were waiting for me. I was quite impressed that they had waited and I told them of my travel adventures of the day. They laughed, especially when I spoke about the discussions between the two men when we learned about the problem with the flaps. "But," I added, "I learned something today. If you really want something, it's amazing how you can manage it. I wanted to be with you tonight, and here I am. I was even able to fight my shyness when I got to Toronto. But there was no way I could have fought the weather if it had stopped any plane leaving Ottawa today." I believe this was my first time in Vancouver, and I was quite impressed by the nice weather there in the middle of February.

My First Confrontation with a National Officer

I really enjoyed my new work in Ottawa, but it wasn't always easy. I had my first major confrontation with other officers of the union about a year and a half after my election. It might have led to my resignation and my return to Montréal.

When I first arrived in Ottawa to take up my new position, I spoke very little English, and I soon learned what it was like to have to often work in a language I wasn't comfortable with. It was difficult for me as a French-speaking person from Québec to find myself on the National Executive Board with English-speakers whose origins were in England, Scotland, Ireland, and different parts of Canada (including Newfoundland). Though they all spoke English, with their different accents and ways of pronouncing words, it seemed to me that they were all speaking different languages. In those first meetings, I don't think I understood more than about twenty percent of what was said. I was in my second year, working on grievance and arbitration issues, when something happened at a meeting of the five national officers in Ottawa. As was the general practice, I was making recommendations on grievances that were going to arbitration. One grievance filed by an aboriginal woman in Calgary claimed that racial discrimination was behind management's denial of her request for a position in a postal station. A hearing before an arbitrator was scheduled where both sides would argue their cases, and I recommended that another of the national officers accompany me to Calgary to argue on the woman's behalf. I knew the case well and wanted to assist the other officer in making our argument.

The Secretary-Treasurer, a French-speaking person of Belgian origin, objected to the cost of having two officers go to Calgary and said that the only reason I wanted someone to come with me was because my English was very poor. Instead, he said, we should hire a lawyer to argue our case and added that we were going to lose it anyway.

I confess that I felt insulted, especially by the tone of his argument. I felt betrayed by a fellow francophone who surely knew how difficult it can be to work in a language you don't know very well. The National President supported his argument that we should use a lawyer and that we were bound to lose the case. Hiring a lawyer would cost much more than sending two officers to Calgary, so it was obvious that cost was not the main thing at play here.

I was shocked. It had never occurred to me that we should retain a lawyer for the simple reason that we thought we would lose the case anyway. We did use lawyers in some very complicated legalistic cases, but in this instance I felt that a union representative who knew the case well would do as well as a lawyer. I knew it was certainly possible that we would lose the case, but I thought it well worth fighting on the worker's behalf because, as I saw it, it clearly was a matter of discrimination.

I have always had a bit of a temper, and much more so in those earlier years than today. I stood up and said, "If that's the way you feel about this case, I'll take it by myself," and I left the meeting without waiting for any reaction. I studied the file, and then spoke with Eric Robichaud, the Calgary local's chief steward, who was responsible for local grievances. I told him that I'd decided to argue the case myself, and he then told me that he had already hired a lawyer on instructions from the National Secretary-Treasurer. My temper flared at hearing this and I said, "Listen to me carefully, Eric. I am leaving you the choice — you can let me take the case, or have the lawyer do it. But if you choose the lawyer, I'm going back to the Montréal local." He responded that he didn't want to get caught up in arguments among the national officers, but that if I wanted to take the case, it was fine with the Calgary local.

I wondered whether I would be able to do justice by this aboriginal woman. I knew it would be a difficult case. I had learned from the leaders of the Calgary local that they thought this woman was a victim of discrimination and that management, realizing the importance of the arbitrator's decision, had hired a very experienced lawyer to handle the case on their behalf.

I told the national officers I was going to leave two days before the hearing was scheduled so I could meet with all possible witnesses in this case. I didn't give the officers a chance to react, saying only, "This will cost you less than a lawyer." I then left the office and had no contact with them before I left for Calgary the next day.

I had asked Eric in Calgary to arrange a schedule for me to meet all possible witnesses, including the woman who had filed the grievance in the first place. That day full of meetings was a difficult one for me, and that evening Eric and I reviewed all the notes we had taken. (It helped me that Eric was bilingual.) I was convinced we had a case of discrimination before us, but I knew that we didn't have everything necessary to prove it. I also knew that the text of the collective agreement stipulated that positions in the postal stations were to be given, in order of seniority, to those competent to do the job. I told Eric I was going to build the case on discrimination and would also argue that the woman was competent, and therefore entitled to the post because she had more seniority than the person who was given the position. My task wasn't going to be easy, especially in light of the fact that the three men on the job selection committee — there were no women in such positions at the time — had interviewed our aboriginal sister along with all the other candidates and had unanimously decided that she wasn't competent for the position, even though she had the necessary seniority.

Against this, my witnesses were all going to say that the woman was very good at her work. By itself, I knew that this wasn't going to be enough to convince the arbitrator. However, I had a sort of ace in the hole: the president of the job selection committee that had deemed her incompetent was known among the staff to be a racist. He openly used derogatory terms to address different ethnic groups: words like "frog" in reference to French-speaking people, for example.

The day before the case was to be heard, I spoke again with some of my witnesses and asked them whether they thought the immediate supervisors of the aboriginal woman considered her incompetent in her work. Their answers were unanimous: none believed that her supervisors found her incompetent. After further discussion with Eric, I chose eight witnesses to appear before the arbitrator. Eric wrote out in English all the questions I planned to ask these witnesses, which was a great help to me.

The arbitration hearing was set for 9:00 am in the morning, but I was there at least a half-hour before to meet with all the witnesses and have a further talk with Eric. All went well with our witnesses except for one who was nervous, but he didn't cause any damage to our case. Without a doubt the most interesting part of the hearing, headed by arbitrator Ted Joliffe, was the testimony of our sister's two immediate supervisors, who were called by the employer.

When the first supervisor answered questions from the employer's lawyer, it seemed to me that he wasn't showing any antipathy toward our sister. In the cross examination, I had a gut feeling that made me break one of the basic rules of examining of a witness, which is that you don't ask a witness a question if you don't know what the answer will be. I asked the supervisor if he thought the report he had prepared for the job selection committee was favourable or unfavourable to our sister. My gut feeling turned out to be right: the supervisor claimed that the report he had written had been favourable, and I asked no further questions. The employer's lawyer then called the second supervisor. When I got the chance to cross-examine him, I asked him the same question, and got the same answer.

The main witness for the employer was the president of the job selection committee. I asked him about his use of racial epitaphs when referring to members of different ethnic groups. He replied that he had always done so, and thus the use of such words didn't constitute discrimination because he used the same words with everyone, regardless of their personal ethnic origin.

We finished our two contending presentations around 8:50 pm. Mr. Joliffe offered us a twenty-minute break to prepare our final arguments. I said that twenty minutes wouldn't be enough time for me to prepare. (I hoped to gain more time so Eric could help me prepare my arguments in English.) "Mr. Parrot," Mr. Joliffe said, "you have demonstrated that you know your case very well, and I think twenty minutes will be enough time for you to prepare your final arguments. We have to finish tonight, because I can't come back tomorrow."

So, we were soon back making our final arguments. I listened carefully to the employer's lawyer and heard nothing I thought would affect my own argument. It was then my turn, and I argued that it was clear the decision taken by the job selection committee that our sister was incompetent was flawed, because it was based on the reports of the two immediate supervisors, both of whom had thought their reports were favourable to our sister. And, because she had the required seniority, she should have been given the position in the postal stations she had asked for. The only reason she hadn't, I concluded, was that she had been discriminated against.

It was past midnight by the time the hearing ended, and we would have to wait about three months to hear of Mr. Joliffe's final decision. But, I was somewhat encouraged by his parting remarks to me: "Mr. Parrot, your English was much better this morning that it was this evening, but I want to say that if your union continues to act as you did in this case, your members will always be well represented."

When I returned to Ottawa, I didn't speak to the President or the Secretary-Treasurer about the Calgary case. When Mr. Joliffe's written decision finally arrived, I flipped immediately to the last paragraph and read: "For all these reasons, the grievance is granted." We had won.

Mr. Joliffe sustained the grievance on the basis of the collective agreement, stating that our sister should have been given the position because she was the qualified employee with the most seniority. As I expected, he rejected my argument of discrimination, but he asked that the employer give courses to its representatives to increase their understanding of personnel relations.

I immediately made two copies of the decision and asked the Secretary-Treasurer to join me in the President's office. I gave them each a copy, saying, "This is a copy of the arbitration decision of the case in Calgary you told me I shouldn't have taken because my English wasn't good enough. You wanted us to hire a lawyer because we weren't going to win it anyway. Read the last paragraph before reading the rest."

The President congratulated me on Mr. Joliffe's decision to order the employer to give our sister the position, but the Secretary-Treasurer didn't say a word. (The officer who was originally to accompany me to the Calgary hearing was very pleased with the decision, because he had not been happy with the way I'd been treated in the matter by some of the other officers.) From that day onward, I never hesitated to take arbitration cases in English. I even began to give trade-union education courses in English, and I'm sure I made quite a few people laugh because of my accent and the mistakes I made using the wrong words, but I knew I had gained their respect. Looking back at this experience, I think the Secretary-Treasurer's attitude had compelled me to jump into doing something that I otherwise might have taken a few more years to do, though I knew him well enough to know that this hadn't been his intention.

Saul Alinsky

In July 1971, CUPW invited a populist leader of American social movements to Canada. As we wrote in November 1971 in our national newspaper, Saul Alinsky was "a man who for many years has been dedicated to the fight of minority groups against persecution of any kind. He has been in the forefront of the fight by black and Mexican poor people's groups, organizing them and encouraging them in their fight for social justice. He is the author of a book on John L. Lewis that should be read by every trade unionist. He is also the author of *Rules for Radicals*, a book which should be on the bookshelves of every trade union."

Saul Alinsky's strong personality impressed us all in his talks with CUPW's national officers and with members of our Wage and Contract Committee. The theme of his message was that no employer, private or public, is concerned with the justice of any particular issue: their concerns only arise when the people suffering from injustice decide together to fight to resolve their problems. We were then in our third round of negotiations with a new National Executive Board. We heard from some staff at post office headquarters that management was worried about the impact Saul Alinsky might have on CUPW leaders.

Personally, I was very impressed with Saul Alinsky and also pleased that someone of his stature was helping us organize to fight for justice. I will always remember him. During the several days he was with us, I had the good fortune to lunch with him and a couple other officers at a restaurant in Hull, on the Québec side of the Ottawa River.

After the meal, which included great stories about intriguing aspects of his life, I offered him a ride back to the hotel in Ottawa where we were meeting. As he was about to get into my car, he told me that he had to make a phone call in the next few minutes, and perhaps he should make it before we left the restaurant. I told him not to worry and that we'd be back at the hotel in time for him to make the call from his room.

So, I wasted little time in getting back to the hotel. Back in 1971, it wasn't common practice to use a seat belt, but I noticed as we drove along that Saul had put his on. When we got to the hotel, he told other union members that it had been a pretty fast trip back from Hull and that he had resorted to using his seat belt. "But you arrived back in time to make your phone call," I said to him. "I sure did!" he replied.

Saul Alinsky was such an inspiration to us that we eventually had *Rules for Radicals* reproduced and distributed to all our shop stewards and other officers across the country. We even had it translated for our French-speaking stewards and officers. Sadly, a year after his visit with us, Saul Alinsky passed away. Those who had the opportunity to meet him will always remember him, as will all those on whose behalf he fought against injustice of all kind. The world today would be a far better place if there were more like Saul Alinsky to stand up and fight for social justice.

In February of 1972, students in Québec City developed a strategy reminiscent of what we had learned from Saul Alinsky. The Urban Community Transportation Commission implemented new rules that effectively amounted to a rate hike for public transit. Students organized what became known as "The Penny War." For two weeks, they paid their fares in pennies, depositing them into the fare box one at a time. Of course, this caused delays in bus schedules and required a lot of time at the end of routes to count all the pennies. The students' strategy was such a success that the Commission cancelled the rate hike.

Negotiations 1972–73

The negotiations with management that we began in 1972 were the first since our 1971 National Convention, where I had been elected a national officer and Brother Jim McCall from Vancouver had been elected National President. Post office management may have wondered what this would mean to the negotiations, as we were both seen as coming from militant locals and leaders of the 1965 strike.

One of the features of the new constitution adopted at the 1971 National Convention was the establishment of a Wage and Contract Committee, made up of three members from each of the four regions. Looking at the list of its original members, it's almost impossible to believe that not one of its twelve members was a woman. Nor were there any members of visible minorities or any representatives of part-time workers. As well, there were no representatives of such groups on the union's National Executive Board. Today we have a woman as CUPW's National President, Deborah Bourque, while another woman, Lynn Bue, serves as First Vice-President and Chief Negotiator. Much has changed over the past thirty years, and these changes within CUPW are reflective of similar transformations throughout the entire Canadian labour movement.

In the early spring of 1972, the Council of Postal Unions published a paper outlining the demands we would present to the employer at the outset of negotiations. These demands had been agreed to by members of the Council's Negotiating Committee, which was made up of one member of CUPW's Wage and Contract Committee from each of the four regions along with our National President and five representatives from LCUC.

In June of 1972, the Council's Negotiating Committee issued a letter for distribution to members of both unions. It read, in part: "One of the main differences in 1972 as against previous years is the application of psychological tactics by the employer in dealing with the memberships of the public unions and the ultimate effects with the general public and the Parliament." It then went on to explain the employer's negotiating tactics and how they might play in the media and among the general public. It detailed how the employer might try to split the membership with proposals such as regional pay differentials. It then called on the members to stay united, to not act on their own, and to be prepared.

This letter ran in our national newspaper. In the same issue, I wrote a column in which I advised members not to fall into the trap of discussing the employer's proposals for rollbacks, because that would take the focus off our own demands for improvements. Instead, I wrote, members should talk about the demands we had on the table, and I then touched on a number of them.

This was going to be a very important round of negotiations, because the employer had developed a $70-million program to bring new equipment into the post office. The new coding machines had already been brought into the Ottawa post office and were due to enter into production in August of 1972. Management claimed that the equipment would pay for itself in a relatively short time, in view of the savings that would be made through a reduction in the number of postal clerks. Further savings would be realized by operating the machines around the clock, seven days a week. Management also boasted that these machines wouldn't need lunch, work breaks, or annual and other leaves. Nor would they be late for work, have their schedule affected by weather conditions, traffic jams, or any of the other things that affect human beings. Finally, management unilaterally decided that those working on these new machines, the coders themselves, would receive seventy-five cents per hour less than manual mail sorters were getting at the time. So, all the benefits of automation would go to the employer, with not even a thought of sharing any of them with postal workers. Management was unwilling to wait to have the issue of the new technology worked out at the bargaining table. Nor would it wait for a hearing on the issue before the Public Service Staff Relations Board, scheduled for September.

The post office had contracted with the firm KPMG to study the issue of automation, and it had produced a report entitled *Blueprint For Change*. That report served as the basis of its automation plan, yet management decided to ignore many of its recommendations. A few quotes from the report, taken from our national newspaper in August of 1972, are in order:

> The change to automation should be undertaken with the objective in mind of equipping the Canada Post Office to fulfill its responsibilities to the country while at the same time upgrading the work content, morale, and job satisfaction of postal employees....
>
> For the Post Office, dollar savings, while significant, must be secondary to its wishing to take its position alongside the other major postal systems in the world....
>
> The introduction of automation on a large scale in the Canada Post Office has to be evaluated critically and the ramifications of such a change should be accommodated so as to provide service and maximum benefit in the long term to employees.

I have always been a strong believer in the idea that the benefits of technological change should be shared with workers. The fact that this rarely happens today in our society will not make me change my views on this issue, because workers in particular, and Canadians in general, are not responsible for these changes. They shouldn't have to pay for them while the corporate sector, which introduces the technological changes in the first place, gets *all* the benefits.

On July 25, 1972, the National Executive met with representatives of the fifteen locals that would be first affected by automation. As a result of this meeting, protests were organized across the country focusing on the fact that the newly hired coders who would work the machines would be paid only $2.94 per hour, instead of the $3.69 manual sorters were receiving. (Because of this wage differential, manual sorters wouldn't apply for the new jobs on the machines.) We set up information pickets to bring public attention to our situation. The major message on our picket signs was, "Sorting mail is our job." In one of many efforts to make members and the general public aware of the problems and dangers that could arise from these new machines, the Québec City local sent two or three busses of postal workers to visit the Ottawa post office to see how the new machines, and those who worked them, were operating.

What Brother Joe Davidson called management's "arrogant take it or leave it attitude" prompted the Council of Postal Unions to call for the establishment of a Conciliation Board. Owen Shime, Vice-Chair of the Ontario Labour Relations Board was appointed as its chairperson, Bruce H. Steward, a lawyer from Toronto, would represent the employer, and Bill Walsh, the Hamilton labour consultant who had been instrumental in drafting the new constitution CUPW had adopted at its 1971 National Convention, would represent the union.

Along with management's imposition of the new "coder" classification of worker, to be paid at a lower rate, to work the new machines, Treasury Board offered postal workers a 13-percent wage increase over a three-year period. This was at a time of significant inflation, and wage settlements in Canada were averaging 9.6 percent per year. Having already fallen behind in wage rates in recent years compared to the private sector, there was more than a little incentive for postal workers to prepare for a strike to press their demands.

Just before the start of conciliation in October, I wrote about another threat to postal workers. A management representative had said at a labour-management meeting that it wasn't fair that an employee requiring less knowledge to sort mail than another worker should be paid the same salary. Even the other employees, he said, wouldn't think this was fair. We replied that postal clerks were still available to sort mail in other areas requiring more knowledge and that, although automation might mean that postal clerks needn't be as knowledgeable as before, other factors would come into play with the new machines, such as productivity, dexterity, and flexibility. Our bottom line was that, however the mail would be sorted in future, it should remain the work of those classified as postal clerks.

On October 30, 1972, a minority Liberal government was elected with thirty-one New Democrat Members of Parliament holding the balance of power.

A Major Internal Problem About Negotiations

In December 1972, it was time to make a recommendation to the membership, and a split occurred on the Council of Postal Unions' Negotiating Committee, on CUPW's National Executive Board, and among the leadership of LCUC. A majority recommendation of the Negotiating Committee was to reject the Conciliation Board's report and authorize strike action to achieve our aims. Six members of the Negotiating Committee supported this recommendation to the membership, while four opposed it.

An air of secrecy surrounded negotiations. Members of the Negotiating Committee weren't allowed to discuss progress, or the lack of progress, with anyone other than fellow members of the Committee. So, unless CUPW's National President, who sat on the Committee, brought us up to date other CUPW officers were in the dark about most of what was going on at the bargaining table. So, the Conciliation Board's report gave rise to serious concerns for me and many other CUPW members. One cause for these concerns was the Board's recommendation for a Manpower Committee, which would transfer negotiations on the impact of new technology to a "consultative committee" during the life of the agreement. We figured that if we had been unable to reach agreement with the employer during negotiations in which we had the power to call a strike if necessary, that we'd carry even less weight in any "consultation" process.

I sent out a bulletin to all officers and shop stewards to explain my position. We don't know, I wrote, the employer's position on the issues in dispute, and we don't know what demands we are being asked to fight for by the Negotiating Committee. I knew that some demands had been dropped, but not which ones, and that others had been amended, but, again, I lacked any detail.

What the situation boiled down to was that we were being asked to strike to achieve a situation we might not agree with, such as the Manpower Committee, as well as the introduction of a provision stipulating that there would be no strike during the life of the agreement. The minority recommendation to accept the Conciliation Board's report made no sense, because it was incomplete. There were no recommendations on many issues affecting members in different classifications or on issues affecting all members. What was perhaps most incredible was that there was no recommendation at all on part-time workers. It was as if they didn't exist, or didn't have a right to a collective agreement. Nothing at all was recommended for them, not even wages. How could anyone recommend that members accept the recommendation of the Conciliation Board? Yet, somehow, this was what four members of the Council's Negotiating Committee were recommending. I ended my bulletin to officers and shop stewards as follows:

> Under the present circumstances, I urge you to recommend to the members to vote no and, in doing so, reject the recommendation of the Negotiating Committee. By such a vote, the members will express their will to know what they are getting involved in before giving the Negotiating Committee such a mandate. A no vote doesn't bind the members to the minority recommendation of the Negotiating Committee. How could part-time members be bound by a Conciliation Board report that makes no recommendation for them?

The result of the vote, tabulated by a coordinating committee of which I was a member, was 10,128 full-timers opposed to the Negotiating Committee's majority recommendation, 9,047 in favour of it, with 197 spoiled ballots. Among the part-time workers, 1,089 were opposed, 432 in favour, and there were 21 spoiled ballots. So, the recommendation of the Negotiating Committee to reject the Conciliation Board's report was itself rejected. However, it was also clear that this result did *not* mean acceptance of the report by the membership. Then, to further cloud this murky situation, a majority on the Council of Postal Unions chose to interpret the result of the vote as acceptance of the Conciliation Board's report by the members. They rejected the claims of some on the Council who argued that the members had been confused about what they were voting for. On that basis, the Negotiating Committee went back to the bargaining table, but gained nothing more than had been in the Conciliation Board's report. An agreement was reached between the Council of Postal Unions and management on February 2, 1973, pending acceptance by a vote of union members.

I received many requests to make my views on this tentative agreement known, so I issued a bulletin saying that we must vote against it. I then outlined the clauses or articles we objected to as well as the many issues that had not been addressed. I found myself in the position of opposing the recommendation to accept the tentative agreement made by a majority of the Council's officers and its Negotiating Committee. There was, though, unity among the officers on one issue: that the unions reserved the right to strike regardless of which side won the vote.

In a limited number of local meetings I attended in the field around this time, I expressed my view that we shouldn't accept the tentative agreement simply because negotiations had lasted "long enough," or because the "best" time to strike had passed. I argued that we could do better by rejecting the tentative agreement and continuing negotiations. And, if we had to strike to earn more in a future agreement, so be it.

Unfortunately, when the members voted the results among the full-timers were 16,070 in favour, 6,154 opposed, and 118 spoiled ballots. Among the part-timers, it was 1,053 in favour, 567 opposed, and 13 spoiled ballots. The members had accepted two collective agreements, one for full-time workers and the other for part-timers, and this was the end of this round of negotiations.

Aftermath of Agreements

It came as no surprise to me that the new agreements didn't work. It led to our 1974 strike and to the resignation of Jim McCall as CUPW's National President. At our 1974 National Convention in Québec City, it led to a series of amendments to our constitution and policies. And, it led to the end of the Council of Postal Unions.

The signing of these two agreements brought about serious change in CUPW's orientation and organization. We now had five official consultative committees and many other areas where consultations could or would take place. In the year that followed the signing of the collective agreements, the employer continued to introduce new equipment and other technological changes and the issue of pay scale for the coders remained unresolved. The lack of information from the employer continued, and frustration rose among the activists across the country.

At our 1974 National Convention, we voted to make changes to our constitution, bringing the Negotiating Committee under the responsibility of CUPW's National Executive Board and giving the Board responsibility to make recommendations to the members, taking that power away from the Negotiating Committee. Elected officers were made more responsible for their actions, or inactions, and would have to defend their actions before delegates at future conventions. These changes led to a transparency during negotiations, so our members would know details of ongoing negotiations. There would be no more moratoriums of silence. Members would no longer vote on reports of a Conciliation Board. Rather, they would vote on future tentative agreements and on whether to strike to achieve clearly identified goals. In fact, our transparent and open policies only added to our strength.

4 A Stronger Union for Harder Struggles

The 1974 Two-Week Strike

As the new technology was introduced, management brought in the new "coder" classification and began hiring people off the street to fill these positions. CUPW resisted management as it implemented this agenda, and we responded with a "Boycott the Postal Code" campaign, because we knew that if the public and business sector didn't use the new postal code, the new equipment would be useless.

As a result of the frustrating 1972–73 negotiations, we had to deal with the issue of new technology through a new "Manpower Committee." Clearly, the issues would be discussed through this mechanism in a framework where postal workers had no power and no real say in the making of decisions. This was part of the employer's strategy to keep as many issues as possible away from the bargaining table.

After I had been a national officer in CUPW for some time, it became clear to me that management habitually divided our demands into five categories: those that were not negotiable under law, those that were not negotiable because they were covered by government policies for the whole federal public service, those that were considered to be management rights, those that should be dealt with by a "consultative committee" after negotiations, and finally, the few they considered were truly negotiable. This was no joke: it really was their approach. In effect, the employer was saying, "We don't believe in collective bargaining, but in consultations. We will decide issues, and then consult with you." This is exactly how they introduced their new classification of coders, where they unilaterally reduced pay from the $3.69 per hour manual sorters were making to the $2.94 per hour they decided coders would receive. At the same time, there was a lot of provocation by supervisors in the field, who came to see themselves as part of a management team permanently at war with workers and their union.

Eric Taylor, a well-known Ontario consultant, was appointed to facilitate discussion on the Manpower Committee, but the talks were going poorly. We were pushing to have the coders working the machines paid the same wages as manual sorters, for a reduction in the use of casual labour, and for a reduction in working hours (with no decrease in pay), for our members as a means to protect jobs and as a benefit from the new technology, but were getting nowhere. It was plain to us that, for management, the "consultation process" with the union was a mere formality. So, locals across the country found creative ways — using pamphlets, buttons, tee-shirts, advertisements, and other tools — to promote our boycott of the postal code, and these efforts had an impact on management's timetable for implementing its automation program.

The Montréal local conducted a months-long, aggressive campaign against the abuse of part-time and casual workers, protested the way automation was being introduced, and promoted the postal-code boycott. When workers began to wear "Boycott the Postal Code" tee-shirts to work, local management suspended a number of workers indefinitely, just a step short of outright dismissal. The Montréal local then walked off the job and asked me to represent them in talks with management over the issues in dispute, threatening to walk away from the discussions if I didn't participate. National President Jim McCall saw this as a vote of non-confidence in his leadership, and he wrote a letter of resignation to the National Executive Board, which accepted his resignation with little real discussion. As provided by CUPW's constitution, National Vice-President Joe Davidson then became National President.

After talking with Brother Marcel Perreault, president of the Montréal local, and seeing that the situation was deteriorating, Brother Davidson called a meeting of myself and the two other national officers. Brother Davidson had originally come from the Toronto local, and he decided to contact his old local to get their support behind the Montréal local's strike. Without hesitation, Brother Lou Murphy, head of the Toronto local, who had much respect for Joe Davidson, told him he would get his members out on strike in support of the Montréal local. The Toronto workers then walked off the job, and Joe Davidson called a national strike, which was supported by LCUC. We were suddenly in what was considered an illegal national strike. The central issue for us was the discriminatory pay scales of the coders (many of whom were women), as well as the disciplinary measures taken against our Montréal members.

Given that the minority Liberal government of the time needed the support of New Democrat Members of Parliament, we had some clout. It was arranged for top-level management, along with someone from Treasury Board, to enter into negotiations with us. Joe Davidson asked me to be CUPW's spokesperson in the talks. The National Executive Board decided that both of us would be on the Negotiating Committee, along with Roger Décarie and Jim Mayes, respectively President and Vice-President of LCUC. Eric Taylor was appointed conciliator to help resolve the dispute. We demanded that coders working the new machines be re-classified as postal clerks and so be paid $3.69, rather than the $2.94 management had decreed. The employer argued that while the coders required a certain dexterity, they needed little knowledge and so weren't worth what manual sorters were receiving. They also argued that CUPW members had job security, and so nobody would lose his or her job because of automation. We argued that such job security didn't apply to part-time workers, but only to full-time workers employed at the time of the signing of our previous collective agreement in March of 1973. Management remained unwilling to act on our demand for the withdrawal of all disciplinary measures taken against our Montréal members.

In the middle of the strike, I accepted an invitation from a French-language television station in Montréal to debate the dispute and strike with Postmaster General André Ouellet. We both had the opportunity to outline and debate our positions in the course of an hour-long presentation. Other than comments made to the media before or after meetings, this was my first experience on television. I heard later that the government had agreed to this debate only because they thought I was going to lose. I was up against a Cabinet minister well experienced in dealing with the media. But I knew my subject matter, and the next morning I read a newspaper editorial that judged the debate a tie.

The Night of the Settlement

The national strike dragged on for two weeks, and it gradually became clear that the government was willing to address our issues. Eric Taylor called the two parties together on the evening of Thursday, April 25, 1974. We had two press releases ready, one announcing a settlement and the other underlining that the strike was still on.

We had heard concerns from field representatives that we wouldn't be able to maintain the strike much longer. This was especially true of LCUC members, many of whom felt that this wasn't their strike. Earlier that day, LCUC's Roger Décarie had spoken to Joe Davidson and me, saying that we needed to reach an agreement because it would be difficult for him to keep his members out another day.

That evening, serious discussions took place on our proposals for a settlement of the dispute. The employer brought up the issue of our boycott of the postal code, but we made it clear that this issue was not going to be settled. But it was understandable why they raised the issue: since we began the boycott in 1972 it had been fairly effective. Both the general public and many businesses were still taking a "wait-and-see" attitude toward using the postal code, and this had hampered management's automation plans. (There may also have been a fear among some customers that if they used the postal code, workers might be less than anxious to move their mail efficiently through the system.)

At about 10:00 pm, the management side decided to meet in caucus. We then issued our press release saying that the strike was still on. We did this to let our members across the country know not to show up for work the next day. At about 2:00 am, management came back with a document that seemed to us to contain the elements needed for a settlement. Both sides had their lawyers present, and we confirmed that the wording in the document, entitled "Terms of Settlement," was acceptable. It recommended the lifting of all disciplinary measures, including cases then before the courts, and extended the job security enjoyed by full-time CUPW members to part-time workers as well as all members of LCUC. It referred the issue of coders' wages to a third-party committee. I knew that, at this stage, we were not going to get management to give away its right to classify workers, since that would set a major precedent for the entire federal public sector. I saw the employer's move to allow a third party to decide on the issue of coders' wages as a face-saving mechanism for the government and as a major step in achieving our objective. Management had dropped its demand that we abandon our boycott of the postal code. They knew that postal workers were not willing to give away our most effective way of exerting pressure to ensure that the employer would share the benefits of automation with workers.

Before signing the agreement, we held a short caucus meeting. I asked our lawyer, Morris Wright, if I was right in thinking that the only person who had the authority to withdraw cases currently before the courts was the Minister of Justice. He agreed, so at about 2:30 am, we went back and said we were ready to sign the agreement as long as the Minister of Justice also signed it. They argued that this was unnecessary, that it was enough that those present signed it. I still remember that moment: I asked Morris Wright again whether I was right on this point, and he said I was. Management's lawyer, Walter L. Nisbet, who I respected, replied, "We are not going to wake the Minister of Justice up in the middle of the night for this." Morris Wright then offered to wake the Minister himself. At this juncture, the management team asked for a caucus, and said they would get back to us. (We knew they were using their caucuses to meet with members of the Cabinet, who were the ones making the critical decisions.)

After they left, I noticed that Brother Décarie of LCUC looked very worried. Joe Davidson came to me and asked, "Are you sure you know what you are doing?" "Yes Joe," I replied. But, deep inside, I wondered whether I had pushed my luck too much. On one hand, I was concerned that management might have got wind of the idea that we might be in trouble with our membership in the morning. On the other hand, I knew they were in too deep to break off talks at this point. There was only the Minister of Justice's signature between us and an agreement.

It was almost 6:00 am on Friday, April 26, 1974, when they came back with a letter signed by the Minister of Justice authorizing their lawyer to sign the agreement on his behalf. Both Brothers Décarie and Davidson looked at me. I was not going to push this further, and I said, "I think we have an agreement."

Before 7:00 am, we had our copy of the signed agreement, and we went out to face the reporters who were still waiting to learn the outcome of the talks. I had already ensured they knew we were coming out so they would have time to set up their cameras and reach reporters who were in a special room. I had promised them I would notify them in advance when we'd be coming out so they wouldn't have to stay up all night in the corridor. (I think members of the media appreciated the way I treated them: my good relations with them surely didn't hurt in 1975 when I became CUPW's Chief Negotiator.)

We issued the second press release we had prepared the day before announcing a settlement. When reporters saw what was in the agreement they were shocked at the terms we had got the employer to agree to. I remember the headline of an editorial in one of the newspapers that morning: "Postal workers bring the government to its knees." Thus ended the two-week strike of 1974.

(Needless to say, with such headlines in the newspapers, the Liberals weren't too happy about the embarrassment they were subjected to by postal workers across the country. But, by the time we had entered into our next round of negotiations in January of 1975, the Liberals would have been re-elected, this time with a strong majority.)

We immediately informed postal workers across the country of the settlement. We got almost everyone back to work that day, though some got the news too late and went in the next day. In any event, workers had up to twenty-four hours to report back to work.

Looking back on the 1974 strike, one thing that impresses me is the number of new activists that got involved in CUPW's work. Many of these new activists would eventually take on different positions at all levels of the union's work.

In the aftermath of the strike, we paid close attention to the proceedings of the third-party committee charged with dealing with the issue of coders' wages. It made a decision on a new wage rate for coders, and the impact of that decision meant that coders' wages were now higher than those of some workers in a higher classification. This left the employer no choice but to review the classification of coders, and by the end of the year we got management to agree that coders would have manual sortation added to their job descriptions, and so would receive the same pay as manual sorters. It had taken two-and-a-half years, but we had finally won this battle. Those hired after the introduction of the new technology were finally being classified at the same level as sorters hired before its introduction. For the coders, this meant a wage increase of $0.75 an hour on top of other wage increases negotiated during that period.

While pleased with the final result, it had taken a long time to win this victory. I have always argued that by not getting this issue settled in our 1972–73 negotiations, we had shown management a sign of weakness. But it

From left to right: Gilles Payette, Richard Forget, Guy Senecal, Jean-Claude Parrot, Marcel Perreault, and Clément Morel celebrating victory at the end of the two-week strike in April 1974.

also shows what can be accomplished when union negotiators have the strength of the membership behind them to back up the strength of their good arguments.

The 1974 CUPW Convention

The 1974 CUPW Convention was held from June 3–8 in Québec City. It saw a real debate in the union between those seen as on the "left" and those seen as on the "right." Personally, I think it was a debate between the more progressive forces and those who were more moderate in their aspirations for the future of postal workers, between those who believed in negotiating on the strength of the membership and those who thought dialogue and good arguments were the best ways to make progress.

There was one important matter decided at the Convention that didn't spark much controversy or debate. On Friday, June 7, 1974, delegates adopted a resolution calling for CUPW to disaffiliate from the Council of Postal Unions and for the filing of CUPW's application for certification before the Public Service Staff Relations Board. This reflected the recognition among all delegates that, between 1971 and 1974, the Council of Postal Unions had not been democratic and did not serve the interests of CUPW members.

This Convention saw some very tough debates over the orientation the union would take in the years to come. Delegates were passionate in their interventions and were divided into two contending forces. The situation got so bad that, at one point, Brother Joe Davidson announced that he would not run for President. At that stage, we clearly looked like a union completely divided, with neither side prepared to compromise.

Fortunately, with the help of delegates from the Western region who moved on their position, a positive orientation and great policies were adopted. CUPW was ready to face the upcoming struggles for a better future for postal workers. Delegates opted for a union based on the strength of the membership, one where our negotiations were based on that strength, rather than one where our negotiations were based on consultation and cooperation with the employer in the hope of achieving success.

Before the election, a Credentials Committee announced that there were 220 registered delegates, including the four trustees and the eight national officers. After chairing a difficult convention, Brother Joe Davidson, nominated by Marcel Perreault from Montréal, was acclaimed as National President, and delegates gave him a standing ovation. I believed he had shown great leadership since the resignation of former President Jim McCall. He had also demonstrated that leadership in the way he tenaciously chaired what must have been one of the toughest CUPW conventions in our history.

I was nominated by Lou Murphy of the Toronto local and acclaimed as National Vice-President. In my short acceptance speech, I thanked delegates for their support and Brother Davidson for having reconsidered his earlier decision not to run. I also thanked my wife Louisette, who was in the observers' area, for her constant support.

Brother Paul Gruslin was re-elected National Secretary-Treasurer, Brother André Marceau as National Chief Steward and Sid Baxter as National Grievance Officer. Brothers Darrell Tingley, Clément Morel, Arnold Gould, and Frank Walden were elected National Directors for the Atlantic, Québec, Ontario, and Western regions respectively.

At the 1974 Convention, those who wanted a more conservative union were defeated. Instead, we came out of it with a progressive orientation and good policies adopted by the delegates. This progressive orientation would be confirmed and underlined yet again by the incredible and united 1977 Convention in Halifax.

1975 — First Negotiations as CUPW

When we began negotiations in the first months of 1975, the context was quite different than it had been in the previous round. We now had a majority Liberal government that was really angry with CUPW in particular and with postal workers in general. The progressive forces in the union had prevailed over conservative forces at our recent convention. We had held a referendum authorizing our departure from the Council of Postal Unions. CUPW was now certified to directly represent its members. Joe Davidson was now our newly elected National President, and I had been elected National Vice-President. The National Executive Board had also appointed me Chief Negotiator.

Our withdrawal from the Council of Postal Unions in October 1974 led to its decertification. CUPW members had voted 86.2 percent in a national referendum to withdraw from the Council. They had also voted 86.8 percent in favour of CUPW becoming their official bargaining agent in the Council's place. (LCUC had won certification to represent letter carriers and would later also be certified to represent mail service couriers.)

In January 1975 we began our first negotiation as CUPW. For the first time, all full-time and part-time workers would be covered by the same collective agreement. (While we technically didn't have an agreement — the previous one had been with the Council of Postal Unions — management had indicated at hearings before the Public Service Staff Relations Board that it would maintain existing working conditions for union members pending the negotiation of new collective agreements with both CUPW and LCUC.)

I was really excited that I would finally have the chance to live through a round of negotiations where CUPW had the sort of democratic structures, procedures, and policies in place that I had always promoted in our union. While I knew that being the Chief Negotiator was going to be a lot of hard work, I was confident we were going to do well. I had a good understanding of the membership across the country and of their differences. I had a good team with me on the Negotiating Committee. We had a very good understanding of what our membership wanted in a new collective agreement. I had the confidence of my friend, National President Joe Davidson, and of the rest of the National Executive Board.

We were a completely new team of negotiators with no experience at all in negotiations. I was sure that, if we were to succeed, we needed the strength of the members behind us. The National Executive Board took the steps necessary to ensure that strength was there.

We adopted a theme — "This is the Year" — that we felt was going to do three things for us. First, it would be a clear message to the employer that we were serious. Second, it would be a call on activists to mobilize. And third, it would be a clear appeal to members to be ready to fight for our rights. "This is the Year" was printed on all our communications during negotiations.

After gaining a majority government in the election of July 1974, Prime Minister Pierre Trudeau appointed Bryce Stuart MacKasey as Postmaster General. He was very experienced in the field of labour relations and had been a major player in the adoption of the Canada Labour Code. On October 22, 1974, he spoke at the opening of a new mail processing plant in Calgary:

I would expect in the next collective agreement to put an end to the men's concern about automation being a threat against job security. This is consistent with my philosophy that men should not be displaced by machinery, that they should have some input into the effects of automation on their lives. This is a philosophy that I have been synonymous with in the private sector when I was a Minister of Labour and expect to see it carried on in the Post Office.

Hearing this, we might have thought we were entering a new era. Here was a minister who had forced private enterprises to negotiate technological changes with their employees through their unions, a minister who had been considered a friend of labour, and a minister who had vast experience in the field of labour-management relations. He had been appointed Postmaster General because of these qualifications, but we would soon come to know that his government's aim was "to put postal workers in their place." He would spearhead one of the most vicious attacks any Canadian union has ever faced. He quickly went from being "a friend of labour" to simply being "BS" MacKasey.

When we began negotiations, we didn't know we would face such an attack. But we knew that without the support of our membership, management wouldn't budge at the bargaining table. Under CUPW's constitution, our program of demands needed to be ratified by the membership. While we were preparing material and briefing leaders in the field prior to this ratification, the National Executive Board decided to authorize the Negotiating Committee to begin talks on four issues: we demanded an immediate adjustment of salary to regain the bargaining power we had lost during 1973–74, immediate legislative amendments to permit free collective bargaining by turning the post office into a Crown Corporation, a deferral in the introduction of technology and relocation of workers until a collective agreement had been signed, and simultaneous translation in negotiations, to be paid for by the employer.

In presenting these demands at the outset of negotiations, we knew that the employer was not simply going to agree to them, but by putting them forward it would allow for open — and perhaps, constructive — discussions while we waited for the ratification of our broader demands by the members. While we were doing this, CUPW held a meeting in Ottawa of all the regional staff representatives, followed by a meeting of the presidents of the thirty largest locals across the country. (Smaller locals would be kept informed by the union's regional representatives.) The purpose of these meetings was to demonstrate to all that these negotiations were going to be transparent, as far as our side was concerned. We were determined to keep all our members informed of where we stood with management as negotiations proceeded.

At the meeting of local presidents, I explained our program of negotiations, spoke of our latest efforts in our campaign to boycott the postal code, and talked about how the union and its members might benefit if the post office were to become a Crown Corporation. Brother Davidson began the meeting by welcoming the participants and wrapped it up by explaining the role of leaders at all levels of the organization. This was a successful meeting, and I think that the most important aspect of it was that it was apparent to all that we really *did* know what we were doing and that we were well prepared. It was clear to all that negotiations were not going to be a private affair for just a few leaders: rather, we were going to be open and transparent throughout the course of negotiations. I made it clear that the CUPW policy of "no moratorium of silence during negotiations" was going to be respected. Participants in the meeting understood that "the team" was not just the Executive or the Negotiating Committee, but all of us in our different functions in the union. I knew that they were pleased with this approach.

Our program of demands was ratified by 87.4 percent of the membership. Our objective in this round of negotiations was to ensure that there would be no rollbacks or loss of existing provisions, but real progress for all 23,000 postal workers. "This is the Year," we said, that postal workers have the right to a better standard of living, real benefits from automation, and full job protection. Each of our specific demands was to serve one of these three purposes.

Among our specific demands were: a substantial wage increase and a cost-of-living allowance, an increase in the overtime rate, shift and weekend premiums, recognition of the rights of shop stewards during hours of work, proper notification of technological changes along with the elimination of their adverse effects, a clear process to ensure proper negotiation of these technological changes during the life of a collective agreement, health and safety protections (including fully paid injury-on-duty leave), proper staffing, a salary adjustment for the 2,200 mail handlers, and that, on a *pro rata* basis, part-time workers receive the same benefits as full-timers. It was an ambitious program, but many of these demands were not new, and we felt it was time to win them. They were geared to achieving bigger objectives, such as more day-shift positions, more full-time workers, and less use of casual labour.

One big problem for us was that many issues were considered "non-negotiable" under the law, so we had to address these issues through a series of demands to circumvent the law.

We had to negotiate several demands to achieve an objective that we could not address directly because of the law. Prior to conciliation, we had had to appear before the Public Service Staff Relations Board to determine whether our demands were "negotiable" or not. Jacob Finkleman, the Chairperson of the Board, gave what was, in our view, very broad interpretations of what constituted a "non-negotiable" demand.

Postal management was hiding behind these interpretations and would regularly argue that such-and-such a demand was not negotiable. We were trying to remedy the fact that there had been major wage increases in recent years in other sectors that increased the gap between postal workers and those other workers. As well, we needed to renew all the other provisions that had existed in the previous collective agreements covering both full-time and part-time workers.

LCUC also began negotiations in January, and we knew that the employer would try to play CUPW members off against LCUC members. But, wages aside, we weren't worried about any precedents being set in LCUC's negotiations. Other than wages, LCUC's main interest was the working conditions of letter carriers and mail service couriers, which we saw as quite different from the working conditions our members faced.

When we attended our first negotiating meeting at the end of January 1975, we were prepared, but we didn't know that we were entering into what was going to be a very vicious round of negotiations, thanks to the so called "friend of labour," Postmaster General Bryce Stuart MacKasey.

A First Obstacle

At that first meeting, the employer's representatives began the meeting by explaining that, "as was the normal practice," they were ready to make the efforts necessary to reach a negotiated settlement with us. They also told us that it was normal practice for the talks were to be in English, that we would negotiate all the wording of the new agreement in an English text and, after ratification, the entire collective agreement would be translated into French by "professionals." A clause in each agreement would stipulate that both texts would be considered official. It didn't even occur to any of the representatives of Treasury Board or the employer that this was an unacceptable way to proceed in a country where French and English were both official languages.

We knew that this practice of negotiating only an English text had caused problems in the past. Often, especially in Québec, workers had filed grievances, convinced they had a right or a benefit, but had lost at arbitration because the translated French text didn't reflect the English text. At other times, workers might not even have filed grievances because thought that they didn't have a case, even though a reading of the English text clearly showed that they did.

Our negotiating team was composed of one member from each of the four CUPW regions, Brothers Leroy Hiltz (Atlantic), Marcel Perreault (Québec), Carman Robinson (Ontario), Eric Robichaud (West), as well as myself as Chief Negotiator. On the employer side were national representatives of both Treasury Board and the post office. Everyone on their team was a native English speaker, while our team was made up of a mix of unilingual French and English speakers, as well as people who understood both languages to varying degrees.

By 1975, the issue of respect for both languages had become a delicate national issue. So, speaking in English at that meeting, I presented them with our four demands, listing as the first of the four that the employer, at its own expense, provide simultaneous translation at the bargaining table. Their reaction was immediate: this was "not the practice," and they were unwilling to accept this "costly" demand. They were obviously concerned with the precedent this could have for the whole federal public service.

I immediately called a caucus of our representatives and we quickly agreed to a strategy. We went back to the meeting and I began to explain, in French, the entire rationale behind our demand for simultaneous translation. After a couple of minutes, I was interrupted and asked a question in English. I replied in French, and the other side immediately called for an adjournment until the next day.

When we came back the next morning, we had simultaneous translation equipment and translators in the room. Obviously, management realized that, with two official languages clearly being the policy of the federal government, they had no choice but to comply with our demand here. If they had not, this issue might have become a damaging national issue for the Trudeau government. This was a very good start for us. Not only had they changed a longstanding practice in negotiations in the federal public sector, but it also helped set the tone for the rest of negotiations. They now knew that we were serious and not ready to accept a "no" to our demands based on simple arguments such as "this is not the practice." They would have to argue on the merit of the issues in front of them.

I then suggested that any agreement on the wording of a clause in one language would only be initialed by the two parties once the text in the other official language had been agreed to. This was agreed, and we then outlined our other three preliminary demands. (At this juncture, our membership had not yet voted to ratify our entire program of demands.)

The Montréal Strike and Firings

Ratification of our program of demands by CUPW's membership followed soon after these initial January meetings, and we entered into full negotiations. But after a few unproductive meetings, we began to see that this wasn't going to be an easy round of negotiations. The employer knew that the use of casual labour was an important issue for us and that if our demands in this area were implemented, it would lead to the eventual elimination of casual labour. This is when we began to see the strategy of the new Postmaster General really take shape.

The use of casual labour had been a source of frustration for years, particularly among postal workers in Montréal. As we began negotiations, the employer increased its use of them, especially in Montréal. Even though they had agreed to carry on with existing working conditions at the time of the dissolution of the Council of Postal Unions, they now argued that, because there was no legal collective agreement in effect, they were free to increase the use of casuals. They also argued that it was already their right to use casual labour, and they would continue to do so. They refused to even recognize that the issue of the use of casual labour was a subject for negotiations. They simply argued that it was a management right, and they proceeded to call in more casual workers than ever. So, workers on the floors in Montréal responded by escorting casuals who arrived for work to the doors.

One might have thought that the employer would have called a meeting with the union about this, but they did not. So, for three months, workers in Montréal continued to show casual workers the door, and there were no reprisals from management for this action. Then, on March 7, the employer sent a letter to the Montréal local saying there was a problem with weekend work and inviting the union to meet about the issue. Meetings took place and two alternatives were discussed: a change in the rotation system for regular workers and the use of part-time workers on weekends. The meetings continued, and on Thursday, April 10, 1975, the union local presented statistics that we claimed showed that the use of weekend part-time workers was not the solution. The employer argued that the local's statistics were faulty and asked for another meeting the following week. Then, the very next day, management issued a bulletin outlining that the consultations were progressing well and, as a result of these discussions to date, it had decided to call in casual labour for weekend shifts.

On the morning of Saturday, April 12, hundreds of casuals showed up to work. So the regular workers, as they had been doing since January, escorted them to the door. More than 300 workers were then immediately given letters by their supervisors telling them they were suspended for the rest of their Saturday shifts. These letters had obviously been printed and signed before the shift had started: all supervisors had to do was to write the name of the individuals being suspended. Clearly, the employer had planned these suspensions beforehand.

CUPW National President Joe Davidson immediately contacted the Deputy Postmaster General, John H. Mackay, in an attempt to arrange a meeting that evening in Montréal. He also informed him that I would be available for that meeting. Management's District Director for Montréal-Metro told me three times on that Saturday that there were no management officials available to meet that evening. I told him, in view of the urgency of the situation, that I was willing to meet at any time through the night to discuss the urgent issue at hand with the employer. Later that evening, I went to the main post office with some of the local's officers to see whether there were any problems. While there, we saw many management officials, including the District Director and the local Staff Relations Officer, coming out of the building. These were the very officials I had been told would not be available to meet on this night.

Around 3:00 am on Sunday, two postal officials banged on the doors of fifteen of the suspended workers and handed each of them a letter of dismissal. These workers had their spouses and children awoken in the middle of the night by management representatives there to tell them they were fired. It was obvious to us that this was not "normal practice," and we were certain that the delivery of the dismissal letters in the wee hours had been undertaken as a follow-up to a decision taken by management on Saturday evening, in order to ensure that the this would be a *fait accompli* before any meeting with the union took place.

At about 10:30 on Sunday morning the District Director contacted me and invited us to meet with him at 2:00 pm that afternoon in the regional office. Of course, this meeting was completely unsuccessful: if they had wanted the problem to be resolved, they would have called a meeting on Saturday night before the dismissals were delivered.

Things were made much worse in Montréal on Monday, April 14, a day when there were no casuals foreseen on the schedule, but hundreds appeared on the floors. Of course, they were escorted to the door, and this led to 250 more suspensions. The following day, hundreds of casuals showed up again, and union members again escorted them to the door. Another 300 workers were suspended. More letters of dismissal were delivered to suspended workers.

During these three days of suspensions and dismissals, supervisors had been telling CUPW shop stewards that they were going to "get them." Of the first twenty-four workers who received letters of dismissal, ten were shop stewards, six were former shop stewards, and one was a member of the local executive. In all, thirty-nine workers had received letters of dismissal, and 700 had received suspensions.

This is how Postmaster General MacKasey began his attack. Having felt humiliation in the settlement of 1974, the government had given "BS" MacKasey a mandate to extract revenge in 1975. In his turn, he gave management in Montréal a blank cheque to set up our members there. MacKasey hoped to isolate the Montréal local from others across the country. To a certain extent he was successful, because in the spring of 1975 we felt our membership across the country didn't want a national strike over a situation in Montréal that many saw as a local issue. In his crusade to get rid of militants in the Montréal local, he also arranged for local management to prosecute in the courts the workers that had been fired. So, these workers were to be doubly punished by management: once through their firing and a second time through the courts. This led Jacob Finkleman, Chairperson of the Public Service Staff Relations Board, in a

June 25, 1975, appearance before the joint House-Senate Committee on Employee-Employer Relations in the Public Service, to say:

> I do not know whether what has been happening in the Post Office in Montréal in the last while reflects a policy that disciplinary action should be substituted for prosecution or whether the disciplinary action that has been imposed is a prelude to further recourse by way of prosecution. If it is the intention of the employer to proceed by way of prosecution in addition to the disciplinary action that has been taken, I am impelled to say, even at the risk of prejudging the case, that the employee would be placed in double jeopardy, something that I regard as being highly undesirable and that other labour relations boards have held to be undesirable, except in very special or extraordinary circumstances.

Some CUPW members were prepared to take action at the time of these suspensions and firings to support their Brothers and Sisters in Montréal, but we heard a clear message from our members across the country that this wasn't so for the vast majority. They *were* ready to fight for their collective agreement, but they believed a strike, at this stage, wouldn't help them achieve it. I believed, though, that most of those who didn't then support the idea of a strike would support dealing with the situation in Montréal once a collective agreement had been agreed to, but before it was signed.

Management, under the leadership of Postmaster General MacKasey, had begun to play a dirty form of hardball. Unfortunately, we were about to learn that it was about to get a lot dirtier.

5 Descent into Strike, Rise to Resolution

Negotiating Troubles

On April 14, 1975, the same Tuesday Montréal postal workers were receiving notices of suspension and dismissal, Postmaster General MacKasey rose in the House of Commons to speak about an "offer" of overtime work to 2,000 postal workers in Montréal and elsewhere. As the *Montreal Gazette* quoted him three days later, the gist of what he told Parliament was, "We can't get the sons of bitches to work."

Of course, this was a lie. Postal workers across the country had worked more than 600 person-years of overtime in the previous year alone. During the previous days of suspensions and dismissals, postal workers in Québec had accused MacKasey of trying to use anti-French bias to split anglophone from francophone CUPW members and had pointed to management's dishonesty in its dealings with postal workers.

After MacKasey's statement to Parliament, CUPW President Joe Davidson called on the Prime Minister to start talking some sense into his Postmaster General and said to the media, "Mr. MacKasey is playing a divisive and dangerous game by singling out and vilifying the Montréal postal workers. The Postmaster may believe he can take advantage of anti-Québec sentiment in the rest of the country to misrepresent and destroy our union in Montréal, but it won't work." He added, "The post office is pretending that the firing of thirty-nine workers and the suspension of over 700 others in Montréal is just a local issue, but the issue of casuals is nationwide, and the action undertaken by the Montréal workers [escorting casual workers to the door] has been repeated elsewhere without reprisals."

On May 29, 1975, CUPW's National Executive Board unanimously adopted the following motion:

> Be it resolved to support the strategy recommended by Brother Davidson. To the utmost of our abilities we will lead this struggle for the collective agreement and for the protection of all CUPW members engaged in union activity and do everything in our power to counteract and overcome the divisive strategies and

tactics of post office management.

We will be carrying out further plans of action within the next few days that will show our displeasure over the employer, who has deliberately stopped negotiations, stalled the grievance procedure, acted in an authoritarian manner, created a police state in the Montréal post office, and flouted the collective agreement.

Our members are only decent working Canadians who can only stand so much intimidation before they lash back. And when they lash, their sting will be felt in every part of the country.

The statement also mentioned that the employer was breaking terms of the collective agreement in the area of sick leave. The statement ended with a warning that, if the Postmaster General wanted a fight, then a fight he would get.

During this period, we held a meeting in Ottawa of the presidents of the thirty largest locals in an effort to raise morale and solidarity, and to further explain our negotiation strategy. But the meeting took a wrong turn when some locals, led by Mel Wilde, a representative from the Western region and a former national officer, demanded that we speed negotiations by making a whole series of concessions. They also expressed the concerned that I would put the Montréal firings and suspensions ahead of my overall responsibility as Chief Negotiator for the national union. Joe Davidson recalled this meeting in his 1978 book:

> After several hours of their sniping, I concluded that shock treatment was needed to bring that fractious and quarrelsome lot back into line. Banging the gavel on the table, I said, "If this is the best you can do as the top leaders of this union, then get yourself another President," and with that I walked out, followed closely by Brother Parrot.
>
> I had once more been forced to play my trump card, which often seemed my only card in a union where the President's powers are quite limited. The critics could complain all they wanted, but they could mount no credible alternative to our leadership. The thirty presidents went home, and we vowed it would be a long time before they saw each other again at union expense.

The only offer we obtained from the employer that spring was on wages, which matched that in a recent settlement reached with LCUC. It provided for a $1.70 per hour increase. I was surprised that LCUC had agreed to this, because that union was in a good position to insist on more. Our own demand was for a raise of $3.25 per hour, and we produced evidence that such an increase was in tune with the reality of the day. In presenting the $1.70 offer to us, the employer knew we would reject it, and we knew the employer and the government were going to try to play the two unions against each other, as they had in the past. But now that we were negotiating as separate entities, we felt able to come to the negotiations to fight for the interests of our own members, whether or not these were the same as the interests of LCUC members.

Around this time, the government was talking about introducing "wage and price" controls in an effort to tackle inflation, and most in the trade union movement feared that wages would be controlled far more closely in any such scheme than would prices. (In fact, the Liberal government did implement such controls in October of 1975, and the one-sidedness that trade unionists had feared was to prove all too correct.) Such talk may have been a factor in LCUC's acceptance of the $1.70 per hour offer.

As noted earlier, we had had our differences with LCUC in the past, while we had been together under the umbrella of the Council of Postal Unions. Nevertheless, I always had respect for that union. They were there with us in the 1965 strike, they stuck with us in 1968 and 1970, and they joined us in our 1974 strike. And so I was very disappointed in February of 1975 when LCUC National President Roger Décarie announced that his union would no longer support our boycott of the postal code. It was quite a shock for us to see LCUC, a sister union in the post office, drop its support for CUPW. Other unions were more supportive. A few weeks after Décarie's announcement, CUPW organized a National Boycott Day, and we received support from the Canadian Labour Congress, provincial Federations of Labour, district labour councils, and other central labour bodies in Québec, including the Fédération des Tvavailleurs du Québec (FTQ), the Confédération des Syndicats Nationaux (CSN), the Centrale de L'enseignement du Québec (CEQ). And, despite the position of its leadership, many LCUC members joined in our information pickets that day.

As noted earlier, our boycott of the postal code was designed as a weapon to prevent the employer from introducing technological change at the expense of our members. At a press conference held jointly with CSN and CEQ in March of 1975, FTQ President Louis Laberge made the following statement: "At this time, [the employer] denies postal workers the right to negotiate the effects of technological changes. Why does the government force private enterprise to negotiate technological changes, but not act in the same fashion itself?" The three central labour bodies then confirmed their full support of our boycott of the postal code. Roger Décarie was now the only national trade union leader not supporting our boycott. Despite this, the Postmaster General persisted with statements that only "a handful" of workers supported the boycott.

Given the marked lack of progress at the bargaining table, on May 22, 1975, we decided to apply for a conciliator and, a few days later, the employer agreed to this in principle. On June 2, we applied to have a special mediator appointed to deal exclusively with the more than 1,000 disciplinary cases that had arisen from union-management conflict since April 12. On June 5, locals across the country organized information pickets to urge the government to act on both of these requests. On June 16, 1975, Judge René Lippé was appointed as conciliator to assist the parties in negotiations. Mediation lasted three weeks, but went nowhere. Unfortunately, management continued to oppose the appointment of a special mediator to deal with the disciplinary issues that had arisen since April 12.

Also in June of 1975, post office management placed a very disturbing ad promoting the postal code in *Byliner*, the magazine of the Toronto Men's Press Club. In response, Joe Davidson issued a statement describing it as the "most sexist advertising" he had ever seen in a Toronto publication, adding, "The ad depicts a man painting the postal code on the posterior of a woman wearing only a string bikini. There is also a degrading poem with the ad.... This is an absolute disgrace. I wonder, is this how the post office views its women employees?"

A few days after this, Postmaster General MacKasey was asked in the House of Commons about the cost of management's automation program in the post office. He replied with a figure of $96,000,000. We knew, however, that the employer's own figures added up to $683,534,000 for major postal facilities, as well as an additional $181,000,000 for smaller facilities. This was certainly far from the only time that the employer tried to use fuzzy arithmetic to mislead the public about goings-on in the post office, but when Byrce Stuart MacKasey lied to Parliament by hiding almost 90 percent of the real cost of automation, he revealed the real quality of his character.

The summer of 1975 saw many inflammatory statements by the Postmaster General, as well as intimidation by management all across the country. With the blessing of the Postmaster General, the employer now felt free to do whatever it wanted. Rather than working to resolve outstanding issues in labour-management relations in the post office, the Trudeau government chose instead to encourage the employer, at all levels, to take on the union, union officials, and postal workers themselves. This only served to increase solidarity at all levels of the union.

It was around this time that postal workers fell victim to a new virus, and huge numbers of postal workers were waylaid by it, as the malady spread quickly across the country. After certain investigations about the cause of this phenomenon, we received reports that this new virus was called the "MacKasey flu" and that it was easily transmissible to co-workers.

After the weeks of unsuccessful mediation efforts of Judge René Lippé, the Public Service Staff Relations Board agreed to the appointment of a Conciliation Board chaired by Judge Jean Moisan, with labour lawyer

Irving Gaul sitting as our nominee, and Guy Dancosse as management's. We spent much of the summer of 1975 before this Board. However, the Board was limited by its terms of reference, and many issues, including the whole issue of technological change, were referred to it with the caveat that its recommendations couldn't override the employer's rights under the law. Management negotiators saw the Conciliation Board's proceedings as just another process to go through, so, in fact, there were no real negotiations at all. We spent our efforts trying to convince the Board that our demands were fair and could be supported, and we received some real sympathy from Board members.

Seeing that our position was strengthening, Postmaster General MacKasey tried an old trick: get the union's leader to break ranks with his team or, failing that, raise suspicions among the union's other officers by getting their leader to meet privately and secretly with the other side. MacKasey invited President Joe Davidson to meet with him to discuss the present situation. This was his style: invite you to his apartment to resolve problems over "a few drinks." A few days before, he had told the media that he was prepared to solve the problem of technological change, so this was his lure. He indicated to President Davidson that he wanted to meet alone with him.

I remember Joe coming to me and telling me of this invitation. He said he shouldn't accept the invitation because we had all agreed from the beginning that myself and the members of the Negotiating Committee would be open and keep one another up to date on what was happening at the bargaining table. He also told me that he thought there might be something MacKasey wanted to offer but he wanted to check it with me before accepting MacKasey's invitation.

I told him that he had the full confidence of the Negotiating Committee and that we had no objection to him finding out what the Postmaster General had in mind. I knew Joe enough to know that he would never agree to anything at that private meeting without coming back to us, even if he himself felt the offer was acceptable.

But, he didn't go alone: John Rodriguez, the New Democrat Member of Parliament who was also his party's postal critic, went with him. At the meeting, MacKasey produced a certain document and said it might be incorporated into the collective agreement. Joe brought that document back to us and told us that it had been both the first and the last time he would meet privately with Bryce Stuart MacKasey. We couldn't agree with what was in the document, so the matter died there. It had never been an official offer in the first place.

After this, the Postmaster General made statements in the media, often outlandish ones, more and more often. So, Joe Davidson countered with more appearances of his own in the media, in which he responded to MacKasey's statements and put the union's case forward. One day, at a press conference during the Conciliation Board's meetings, reporters asked him questions about what our position was in regard to the effect of any possible strike on the general public. Brother Davidson explained that it was out of concern for the public that he was attempting to explain through the media where negotiations presently stood. I was there at this press conference to field questions from French reporters. The question of any strike's impact on the public was asked again, and Joe indicated that CUPW members were going to be the first affected by not being paid and added that a strike was a legal right that could be used in negotiations.

"What if the public do not understand?" asked a radio reporter. "I believe they will," said Joe. "But what if they don't?" said the same reporter again. Joe came back with a similar answer, but the reporter kept coming back with the same question. After five or six answers in the same vein, the reporter again asked, "What if the public still don't understand?" Joe, angered at the reporter's unwillingness to accept all his previous answers to the same question said, "Well, then, to hell with them." At that moment, I don't believe he realized what he had just said.

Of course, this was front-page news in most newspapers across the country and the lead story on radio and television newscasts. It was a shock for everyone in the union, understanding the impact such a statement might have on postal workers and their union. Naturally the employer, along with right-wing politicians and columnists, used this statement to attack CUPW as a union that doesn't give a damn about the public.

Although there was a feeling of regret in the union that Joe had made such a statement — one that would be used so savagely against us — there was also a sense that perhaps Joe had said something that does express the feeling of many: we *do* have the right to strike and we shouldn't have to forever defend this right against attacks on the pretext that it would affect the public. We would only use our right to strike to defend the issues we are fighting for. Unfortunately, some representatives of the media weren't interested in learning about those issues. For them the issue was the strike, and the issues underlying any strike were of no interest to them. In any event, we couldn't turn back the clock, and we'd have to live with this statement from our President. I know with certainty that postal workers across the country continued to have great respect for Brother Joe Davidson, their leader.

After the hearings, the Conciliation Board members were given time to write their report. One day, while waiting for the report to be completed, I received a phone call from our representative on the Board, Irving Gaul, who had discussed with us earlier the possibility of his writing a minority report. He told me he was at the Chateau Frontenac in Québec City and both Mr. Finkleman, the Chair of the Public Service Staff Relations Board, and Conciliation Board Chair Judge Moisan were pressuring him to change his position about writing a dissenting, minority report. I suggested that he leave the hotel and not allow himself to be pressured any longer. I immediately phoned the Québec local and, within a few minutes, a group of postal workers were protesting in front of the hotel.

The days dragged on, and still there was no Conciliation Board report. We held a press conference to protest the delay, and we speculated that it was caused by government efforts to see that the report would contain so little that we would have no choice but to call a strike vote.

In the final days of conciliation meetings, a certain document came into our hands. It clearly outlined management's contempt for our demands. The document listed ninety-eight demands, with handwritten indications of management's attitude toward each of them. Beside seventy of those demands were written the words "not negotiable," while three more were marked "limited negotiability."

How had we obtained this document? Someone on the employer's negotiating team carelessly left it at the bargaining table. One of our negotiators felt that it was intended that we have it, so he took it. In light of the deceptive shenanigans of "BS" MacKasey in his public pronouncements, we had no hesitation reproducing this document for the media.

I wrote of this document at the time, saying that it:

> shows beyond doubt that the post office negotiators had absolutely no mandate to deal seriously with our demands. This document should be evaluated carefully and the truth of Mr. MacKasey's many declarations judged accordingly. I think you will have to conclude that the Minister has been misleading Parliament and the public about what is happening in this complex dispute.

Two days after our press conference protesting the delay in issuing the report, Jacob Finkleman called and told us we could go to his office and pick it up. Joe Davidson and I were soon there, and we were invited to wait in a boardroom. A few minutes later, Mr. Finkleman came in, threw two copies of the report on the table, said, "Here it is," and left. He seemed very angry, and when he closed the door, I thought it was going to open on the other side.

The Conciliation Board report was reasonable in the issues it dealt with, but many issues were set aside, and this prompted our representative, Irving Gaul, to issue a minority report. We never found out with certainty why the Conciliation Board's report was delayed, but I believe that, given that the government was upset about the settlement of the 1974 strike and wasn't ready to give us any more than what had been agreed to by LCUC on monetary issues in the spring of 1975, it badly wanted a unanimous report in order to put us under heavy pressure to accept it. That's why there was pressure on Irving Gaul, and almost certainly on other Board members behind the scenes, as the report was being prepared.

Aftermath of the Report

When we finally received the Conciliation Board's report, we saw that in many areas, it made good, solid and progressive recommendations. However, it failed to make any recommendations on some very important issues for postal workers. On wages, Judge Moisan offered us exactly the same $1.70 that had been agreed with LCUC earlier in the year. But, I must say that Judge Moisan made some very significant comments on the process of negotiations under the Public Service Staff Relations Board. Basically, he agreed with our argument that, given the blue-collar type of work our members did, it would make more sense for our negotiations to fall under the Canada Labour Code than under the Public Service Staff Relations Board, which was designed for negotiations with federal civil servants.

Our representative, Irving Gaul, refused to sign the report because of its lack of recommendations on some very important issues, and instead issued his own minority report. The employer's representative, Guy Dancosse, did sign the report, although he disagreed with some of its recommendations, objections that he outlined in his own addendum to the report. However, according to Judge Moisan, Mr. Dancosse did support an article on technological changes, as well as a rationale elaborated by Mr. Moisan in the report on the issue. (More details on this matter later, but this fact is quite important, because the terms of this article would form part of the agreement signed with the employer after the strike we would soon wage. In every round of negotiations since then, up to and including negotiations in 2002, the employer has sought to have these terms changed in its favour. Management has also through the years continually challenged the provisions of this article, forcing union members to grieve countless individuals' arguments before an arbitrator.)

Another important point made in the report by Judge Moisan dealt with the attitude of the employer. He wrote:

> The Employer appears to have experienced difficulty accepting the idea that an individual can be both an employee and a member of a union, clearly preferring the employer-employee relationship to the employer-union relationship. It has undoubtedly developed a more modern concept of this relationship since 1969, when the Chief Adjudicator of the Public Service Staff Relations Board severely criticized its attitude, but it should be noted that this paternalistic attitude and this preference for the employer-employee relationship still persists to some degree.

Soon after the release of the report, "BS" MacKasey publicly stated that Judge Moisan's report constituted an offer to CUPW members. However, we knew he was opposed to both shift and weekend premiums, and to the technological change article recommended by Judge Moisan, so we made it clear that any offer from management would have to be presented from them to us in writing, if we were to believe that any such offer was legitimate.

Primarily because of the failure of MacKasey and his negotiating team to deal adequately, or at all, with many issues and recognizing our need for a clear mandate and the strength of the membership behind us, we prepared for a strike vote among our membership. Furthermore, Moisan's report referred some issues back to the parties, and management was unwilling to move on them. What was the employer's offer on these issues that were referred back to the two parties? Simply to write in a collective agreement that they were "referred back" to the parties? Perhaps the Postmaster General was told that CUPW negotiators had no experience in negotiations, but it was long past time for his team to recognize that we were neither stupid nor naïve. Rather, we understood very well what was necessary to protect our members.

In order to ensure there wouldn't be any confusion among our members about what they were being asked to vote for, as had happened in 1973, we worded the ballots with one simple question: "Do you support the recommendation of the National Executive Board?" There were two boxes, labelled "Yes" and "No." All members attending their local's meeting to cast their votes were also given a copy of the unanimous recommendation of the National Executive Board, which read, "Your National Executive Board unanimously recommends that you give your Negotiating Committee a mandate to negotiate a collective agreement based on the minority report submitted by Irving Gaul, which contains your main demands, and that you authorize the National Executive Board to call a strike in order to achieve this objective." Everyone who cast a ballot was also given written information on why the National Executive thought they should vote "Yes" as well as on exactly what a "Yes" vote meant in the context of negotiations and any possible strike. National and regional CUPW representatives attended local meetings to provide information to members on the content of the Conciliation Board report, the minority report, and Mr. Dancosse's dissenting addendum to the report before they cast their votes.

We were determined in these 1975 negotiations to show our members that they were entitled to the respect of their union by keeping them informed about where negotiations stood and what precisely their decision in the voting booth meant. During the entire course of negotiations, we issued at least one bulletin a week for posting on bulletins boards, and we also produced notes for local officers and shop stewards so they could clearly communicate to our members what they were being asked to vote for.

The deadline for locals to send in the results of the their votes was 11:00 am on October 15, 1975. When we tallied the national result, it was 68.3 percent in favour of supporting the recommendation of the National

Executive Board. This was a smaller majority than we might have hoped for, even though it was a clear one. It showed that "BS" MacKasey had met with some success in his efforts to divide the membership and convince some of them that the real issue was the firings and suspensions in Montréal rather than the situation at the bargaining table. The offer of a $1.70 wage increase may also have swayed some members to vote "No."

It would be seven days after this vote of the membership before we could legally strike, and both parties agreed to enter into intensive negotiations during this period. We put the Moisan report forward as the foundation for arriving at a written agreement with the employer, but we underlined that there were at least five major non-monetary issues left unresolved in the report that needed to be dealt with. We were asked if we would accept the offer of a $1.70 per hour wage increase, as recommended in the report: my response was that we would agree to discussions on wages once all the non-monetary issues had been resolved.

During these few days of negotiations in a highly pressurized environment, we actually made some real progress. In fact, we managed to come to agreement on every non-monetary issue outlined in Moisan's report, but this is where real negotiations ended. As well as the monetary issues, there were at least another five issues not touched on by Moisan that we felt needed to be resolved, but, at this point, management refused to discuss these with us.

On the evening of October 20, we received a phone call from the employer's spokesperson, Ed Waddington, telling us that there was no hope of further progress and therefore no need for further meetings. My reaction was to ask, "So, you're breaking off negotiations?" Mr. Waddington replied that, no, his side was not breaking off talks, but unless we agreed to the monetary package, the central feature of which was the $1.70 per hour wage increase, there was no point in further negotiations.

I then spoke with other members of our Negotiating Committee and we came to the realization that management was trying to make it seem that our side was responsible for the breaking off of negotiations. We were in a desperate situation, so I did something desperate that, up to that point in my life, I never thought I'd do. I phoned Mr. Waddington, and said, "I just want to be clear: we have a negotiating meeting scheduled for tomorrow, but you say there is no need to meet now. So, you're breaking off negotiations?" He replied, "Yes, you can take it this way, unless you agree to the monetary offer." After a few more minutes of discussion, we ended our phone conversation.

What I hadn't told him is that I had taped the entire conversation. As I had expected, the employer, and especially "BS" MacKasey, accused us the next day of having broken off negotiations through our intransigence at the bargaining table. I then called a press conference and told media representatives in a packed room that the Chief Negotiator for the em-

During the 1975 strike at the Vancouver post office, from left to right: CUPW President Joe Davidson, Frank Walden, National Director for the Western Region, and Peter Whitaker, President of the Vancouver local. Behind them is Larry Honeybourne, Staff Representative for the Western Region.

ployer had phoned us the previous day to tell us that there was no reason to continue to meet and that this left us with no choice but to call a strike as of midnight tonight. As I expected, media representatives reacted to this by saying that that the post office claimed it was we who had broken off negotiations. I responded: "I know that the employer is feeding you with all kinds of questionable information, so I want you to listen to a tape I made yesterday of my conversation with Mr. Waddington." I explained that it had been very difficult ethically for me to do such a thing as tape a conversation without the other party's knowledge, but that the vast disinformation campaign of the Postmaster General had left me with no alternative action that would make clear just who had cancelled the meeting set for the next day and so had broken off negotiations. I then played the tape and let them listen to it from beginning to end. The conversation was in French, but with simultaneous translation at the press conference, everyone present heard how the conversation unfolded.

This tape was helpful to us and extracts were played on radio and television stations and appeared in newspapers. The decision to break off negotiations was obviously part of MacKasey's efforts to divide the members and turn them against their union. CUPW members across the country walked off the job just after midnight on October 22.

On October 23, I wrote Postmaster General MacKasey the following letter, which was delivered at 6:02 pm that evening and released to the media the following day:

> As we have stated publicly, the Canadian Union of Postal Workers is prepared to resume negotiations with representatives of the employer on two hours' notice. The sole condition the union attaches to the resumption of bargaining is that all outstanding issues be negotiated without any rigid limitations on the order.

The next day, I received this reply from the Postmaster General:

> In reviewing your letter of October 23, 1975, I have noted that you wish to resume negotiations without any limitation on the items still outstanding.
>
> You may recall that the position of the Post Office, revealed to you after the issue of automation had been resolved, was that we were then prepared to move to our ultimate position of a wage increase of $1.70 spread over an agreement of 30 months, a cost of living allowance, [and] improvements to vacation entitlement, consistent with the recommendations of Judge Moisan, Chairman of the Conciliation Board....
>
> We are not concerned with the order in which the outstanding items are discussed. When negotiations are resumed, we intend to present a package proposal with respect to those items still outstanding and including the wage position described above.
>
> We note that you are prepared to resume negotiations on two hours' notice and we will inform you when we are ready after we have finalized the package proposal. In other words, we are asking you to acquiesce tacitly with respect to our position on wages, recognizing that this acquiescence can be revoked by you if the outstanding items are not settled to your satisfaction.

On October 25, I replied to him as follows:

> Your letter of October 24, 1975, indicates clearly that your attitude remains unchanged with respect to your ultimatum on the wage issue.
>
> There can be no question of the Union "acquiescing tacitly" to the wage offer that you still consider as final, that is $1.70 over 30 months, including a [cost-of-living] clause and the annual leave provisions contained in the Letter Carriers' collective agreement.
>
> Since the order of items to be discussed is of little concern to

you, we think it normal and desirable that the wage offer be the last item to be discussed.

While our attitude is not inflexible with respect to possible solutions, we trust we are not being presumptuous by expecting the same attitude should prevail on your part.

This being understood, our Negotiating Committee is prepared to meet with your representatives.

Any counter-proposals will be carefully considered and we expect that they will reflect concessions, such as was the case with our counter-proposals submitted to your Negotiating Committee.

Our attitude is not inflexible and we sincerely hope that you will return to the principle of collective bargaining rather than that of ultimatum. It is possible to find a compromise if a comprehensive attitude is shown on both sides.

Finally, on October 26, I received this from Bryce Stuart MacKasey:

I have your letter of October 25. It seems to me that by continuing an exchange of letters we shall not bring about any early resumption of the postal service of Canada so very much desired by your members and the people of Canada.

For the record, it is necessary to deny strongly that any ultimatum was given or intended or that we departed from the principles of collective bargaining in any way.

As indicated in my letter of October 24 to you, we have completed the preparation of a package of outstanding items, one of which is the wage item I spoke of in my previous letter. Items of the package can be discussed in any order desired.

I have instructed my negotiating team to be available to meet with you at 2:00 pm, October 27, 1975, at Place Bell Canada, 21st floor in the Board Room.

We resumed negotiations as suggested on the 27th, and management finally agreed to discuss the five non-monetary issues that Judge Moisan had failed to make any recommendations on. However, they were still not ready to move on monetary issues. We resolved at least one non-monetary issue every day, until we were left with only the monetary issues. After each meeting in which a non-monetary issue was resolved, I was asked by the media whether we were now ready to accept management's offer on monetary issues. Each day, my answer was the same: we would deal with the monetary issues when the time came.

One of the contentious issues we resolved dealt with management's earlier reluctance to create more full-time positions, with the work increasingly being done by part-timers and casuals. We agreed that part-timers were needed during peak periods on evening shifts in major offices, but we wanted casual labour kept to a minimum. During a "Hire Permanent" campaign we had waged in 1973, we conducted a survey that indicated, on average, about 10.5 percent of postal workers were part-timers and 15.2 percent were casuals. The use of such workers had been on the rise, especially in some centres, such as Winnipeg. The agreement we came to would reduce the use of part-timers and, particularly, the use of casuals.

After two weeks of strike and negotiations, we were left with only monetary issues to deal with at the bargaining table. I indicated that we weren't in a position to accept the employer's proposal because there were some specific monetary issues we felt needed to be addressed. Among them was our demand for a ten-cent adjustment in salary for mail handlers, who had seen their wages lag behind those of workers in other classifications in recent years, that the benefits enjoyed by full-timers be given to part-timers on a prorated basis, and fully paid injury-on-duty leave. I also indicated that the $1.70 wage offer was insufficient. In response to arguments that we should accept an offer that had been good enough for members of LCUC, I countered that the very reason we were no longer united with LCUC in the Council of Postal Unions was that the needs and priorities of our members were different from the needs of theirs. So we would not feel bound by what had been negotiated with any other union. Talks broke down, and Byrce Stuart MacKasey was quoted as saying that CUPW members could strike "until hell freezes over."

"Hang a Parrot"

At this point, the Postmaster General — that so-called "friend of labour" — came up with yet another anti-union strategy. He publicly challenged us to put management's last offer to a vote of the membership and implied that the union leadership was hiding things from its members. My response was that it was not up to "BS" MacKasey to decide for the union when we would submit the employer's offer to our membership. We had obtained a clear strike mandate and we were not going to run to the membership each time the employer put an additional cent on the bargaining table. MacKasey also said that what CUPW leaders really wanted out of this strike was a resolution of the suspensions and dismissals in Montréal. This only confirmed what we had said all along: that the dispute in Montréal was a set-up by management to divide the membership. There were no negotiations going on at all, and there was lots of pressure on union leaders at both the national and local levels. A very few small locals had even returned to work.

In some locals, there was a lot of pressure for local leaders to hold a vote on returning to work. Striking is never an easy thing to do, and the government's campaign against CUPW was getting steadily more vicious. Post offices that had been closed due to the strike were reopened. Street mailboxes were unlocked and the public was encouraged to start using the mail again. In response to the government assault, some locals began to hold votes to show MacKasey that we remained united. I argued strongly against such votes, because a poor result in a weak local could give the other side exactly the ammunition it needed. I also argued again that it was not up to the Postmaster General to tell us when to vote.

Despite my arguments, many locals held such votes and, thankfully, the results were always to continue the strike. The Toronto local was under particular pressure to hold a vote. Pressure had come from a group of members who wanted to go back to work. They went to a local meeting and demanded that their local recommend to the national leadership a nation-wide vote on whether or not to return to work. The local's executive informed me of the situation and urged me to go to Toronto and explain to local members why they should opt to stay out. I had faith in the good judgement of the membership when they well understood what was at stake in any vote, so I went to Toronto on the weekend of November 8–9, 1975.

On Saturday, I arrived to a hall packed with postal workers. The local executive had decided not to make any recommendation on whether to hold a vote recommending a return to work, but indicated it would abide by the decision of its membership. Some people were clearly demonstrating their desire to go back to work. One worker held a long stick, at the end of which was a stuffed parrot with a rope around its neck. This teasing with my name made the front page of many newspapers the next morning.

It seemed clear to me that the local executive was right in its assessment that most of these workers were ready to vote to go back to work. I explained the points still in dispute and the importance of resolving them. The vote was determined only by a show of hands, because this was not a vote authorized by our constitution.

It was a close vote, but after the show of hands, local president Lou Murphy ruled that a majority was in favour of continuing the strike. From my view on the podium, I thought he was right, but if he had decided otherwise it would have been very difficult to argue with him. A good number of members then walked angrily from the hall. A challenge to the president's ruling then took place, but given the large number who had left, this effort was unsuccessful.

I think Brother Murphy showed courage at that meeting, because it would have been easier for him to determine that the show of hands was in favour of a vote to go back to work. But I also think he knew that it would have isolated the Toronto local from others, that it would have divided the national union, and that it would probably have divided the local even more deeply than it was then.

Perhaps this, written in the December 2, 1975, issue of the *Globe and Mail* by reporter Wilfred List, best describes the position Brother Murphy found himself in:

As the strike progressed, Mr. Murphy was at loss to understand the quixotic positions adopted by the national Negotiating Committee and the National Executive Board in the face of the realities of the government's position. If he had his way, the previous membership meeting would have adopted a motion calling on the National Executive Board to hold a referendum on the government's position.

But when someone missed a signal and offered a motion that combined a demand for a referendum with a proposal to return to work in Toronto, he could not support it because of its implications for the unity of the union as a whole — disenchanted as he appeared to be with the position taken by the bargainers in Ottawa. At the same time, he was equally tough in his view that Postmaster General Bryce MacKasey was not offering enough.

After that Toronto meeting, I knew, as I'm sure Brother Murphy did also, that there were going to be strong picket lines in Toronto over the following hours and days made up of those who wanted to continue the strike. In fact, the next day, nobody went back to work and the strike continued all across the country, with the exception of a few small locals, mostly of less than ten members, that had never gone out in the first place or that had gone back after a day or two.

On the same weekend of that Toronto meeting, many other locals across the country decided to take votes to demonstrate to Bryce Stuart MacKasey, despite all his efforts to divide us, the solidarity of members with one another and their support for CUPW's National Executive Board. I'm convinced that the Toronto vote and the others held during that weekend were an important turning point in our strike. Around the same time, all the major locals in the four western provinces met in Vancouver to express their complete support. The thirty-nine locals in southwestern Ontario passed a unanimous motion to continue the strike until asked by the National Executive Board to return to work. The sixteen locals in northern Ontario unanimously passed a similar motion. On Sunday, November 9, close to 600 members of the Ottawa local voted 99 percent in favour of a motion expressing their solidarity and complete support of our National Executive Board. The Québec region informed the Board that none of its members intended to return to work before being asked by the Board. Locals in both Saint John, New Brunswick, and St. John's, Newfoundland, passed unanimous resolutions in support of the Negotiating Committee and the National Executive Board. Over the course of the following week, many other locals passed similar resolutions.

A New Difficulty — No More Strike Pay

As the weeks passed, another difficulty faced us. In late November, we had to announce to our members that starting with the fifth week of strike, there would be no more strike pay because our strike fund was now depleted. Under the terms of our national constitution, there is no strike pay for the first two weeks of a strike, so this meant that, during the entire six-week strike, our members received only two weeks of strike pay.

Despite this, after more than five weeks on strike, the Postmaster General had to come to the conclusion that postal workers were not about to go back to work on the basis of his campaign to divide them from their union. Despite some significant differences among our members, and especially sharp differences between the national officers and some local officers in the Western region, no locals took a stand to take a vote on management's latest offer. Despite the end of strike pay and the announcement of the federal government's impending adoption of wage-and-price controls, picket lines were solid all across the country and there was no sign that the strike would collapse anytime soon.

During the course of the strike, the Montréal local developed an interesting strategy by starting a "worker-controlled messenger service" within the Montréal metropolitan area. On November 19, it issued a special $1.25 stamp for businesses and another, valued at $1.00, just over a week later, for the general public. The stamps were limited to 35,000 in sheets of 20 stamps. The idea quickly became very popular and postal workers took part in the service enthusiastically. It helped keep morale high among Montréal workers, despite the situation they found themselves in. (This strategy would be the subject of much discussion at CUPW's National Convention in Halifax in 1977. More on this in the following chapter.)

In late November, negotiations resumed after an intervention by the federal Department of Labour. It suggested that both sides needed help to move things forward at the bargaining table, and each side was asked to appoint an additional person to their team. The idea was that these two appointees would meet separately and try to make some progress regarding the outstanding monetary issues.

Bryce Stuart MacKasey appointed his good friend Bernie Wilson to join his team and we called on Shirley Carr, Vice-President of the Canadian Labour Congress, to join ours. By this time, we had reached a point where, in addition to the $1.70 wage offer, there were three other monetary issues we wanted to work out. The first was our demand for a ten-cent-per-hour salary adjustment for mail handlers, whose wages relative to other workers had fallen in recent years. The second was our demand that the salaries and benefits of part-time workers be the same, on a prorated basis, as full-time workers. The third was our demand that any injury leave approved by provincial workers' compensation boards be fully paid.

On November 29, 1975, after their respective sides had briefed the two new representatives, Shirley Carr and Bernie Wilson met privately. At the end of that meeting, Shirley came back and told us that Wilson had agreed to our three monetary demands. Shirley explained to me what Wilson had said, and I suspected, because of previous experiences in negotiating with management, that there might have been a misunderstanding between the two. (I was quite certain that MacKasey would insist that the cost of these three demands be deducted from the overall cost of the $1.70 wage offer.) I told her simply, "Shirley, you did a great job, but I won't be surprised if they renege on the agreement you just made with Mr. Wilson."

We then met again with the management group and, as I had expected, it presented us with a proposed agreement different from what Shirley had told us had been agreed between her and Mr. Wilson. I turned to Shirley and said, "You see how they are? You reach agreement, and then they turn around and deny it." Shirley was angry, and she turned to Mr. Wilson and said: "Have we not reached agreement on these issues?" He responded positively. Postmaster General MacKasey then asked him to confirm that he had agreed with Shirley that each of our three monetary demands would be met. Wilson looked at her and said, "I guess I did." MacKasey then said, "We have an agreement then. I'll live with what my representative committed to."

It was a great moment for us, and I immediately indicated that we would submit the overall package — which included the $1.70-per-hour wage increase — to the National Executive Board with the Negotiating Committee's recommendation to submit it to a vote of the membership. However, I added that I couldn't guarantee whether the Board would recommend that the membership accept it, especially given that management had refused to deal with the issue of the firings in Montréal and other disciplinary measures taken during the negotiations and strike.

As it happened, the Board agreed to put the proposed settlement to a vote of the members, but with its unanimous recommendation that they reject it because of its failure to deal with disciplinary measures taken against Montréal workers. In the end, despite all the difficulties we were faced with before and during the strike, the membership almost turned down the agreement. Although some locals voted to reject the offer — incredibly, some locals that had originally voted against striking now voted to reject the agreement — nationally it was accepted by 51.8 percent of the members. The forty-two-day strike of 1975 was over.

This result of the vote was a shock for many in the union who had been convinced that the members were determined to go back to work, particularly among some local and regional leaders in the Western region who had challenged the national leadership in the latter days of the strike, during a very delicate phase of negotiations. (These Western leaders were among few across the country who recommended acceptance of the agreement despite its lack of resolution to the Montréal situation.) It must also have been a shock to the Liberal government to see that, even after MacKasey's campaign to divide and discredit our union, postal workers, voting by secret ballot, almost turned down the agreement.

Two Final Hurdles

One of our demands in the 1975 negotiations was to delete a clause stipulating that workers would not strike, and the employer would not lock workers out, during the life of the collective agreement. This clause had been introduced during the 1972–73 negotiations under the Council of Postal Unions.

I've always had a problem with the idea that workers' right to strike is the "equivalent" flip side of the employer's right to lock them out. If they are judged to be equal and they are then both disallowed, then workers have no means by which to force the employer to move in negotiations. Clearly, the only one to benefit will be the employer.

I never understood our side's attitude on this issue in the 1972–73 negotiations. It had been the subject of a real battle within CUPW. Some, such as Jim McCall, then the National President, had argued that it was no big deal because labour law that governed postal workers beyond the scope of the collective agreement — law administered by the Public Service Staff Relations Board — already prevented both a strike and a lockout during the life of an agreement. Others, like myself, had opposed this clause, arguing that management had introduced it as a means of not having to justify before the Public Service Staff Relations Board any disciplinary actions it might take against striking workers. Furthermore, we had argued, if the law already covers it, why then do we have to put it in our collective agreement?

So, in the 1975 negotiations, management was determined to keep this clause in the collective agreement, while we wanted it deleted. All through negotiations and the strike, management insisted that the clause remain in the agreement. On the last day of the strike, after we had reached agreement in the presence of the Postmaster General, a final meeting was scheduled for both sides to initial every clause of the new collective agreement. Quite a ceremony had been prepared: this was, after all, the first time we were signing a collective agreement as CUPW.

We were presented with the customary three full sets of clauses to be initialed, one for each side and one for the records. On our side, we were carefully checking the wording of each clause to be sure it was what we had agreed to. All was in order until we came to this clause that stipulated that there be no strike and no lockout during the life of the collective agreement. I said that we had never agreed to this.

Bryce Stuart MacKasey then read the clause and, without talking to his team said, "You don't want it, you won't have it. This is a provision that already exist in the law anyway." Saying this, he took the sheet of paper with the clause written on it and tore it apart in a way that meant, "I don't mind, I've got it in the law anyway."

I remember the looks on the faces of the management team that had been so determined to keep this clause in the agreement. The way they looked at MacKasey, I thought they were going to kill him! For our team, it was one of these moments of satisfaction, a moment where we felt like saying to the management team, "It's about time someone put you in your place." For us it was a personal victory over an employer team that had made everything personal in these negotiations.

There was yet one final hurdle to get past. In the weeks before and during the course of our strike, Ottawa had implemented a policy of wage-and-price controls, and a new federal Anti-Inflation Board (AIB), was just finding its feet. One of its first judgements was that the monetary aspects agreed to in the collective agreement went beyond its guidelines and so should not stand. But the government knew I was serious when I said to "BS" MacKasey that if this AIB ruling was a new trick on government's part, he could be assured that the strike would continue and he would face a guerrilla war with postal workers for months to come.

The case was referred to the Governor in Council. (Essentially, this is the federal Cabinet.) The final judgement was that the proposed agreement should stand despite the AIB's ruling, because further attempts at negotiation to modify its terms would not serve the national interest.

One regret I had about the agreement was that we were unable to resolve the issue of the Montréal workers who had been so unfairly fired. These cases went through arbitration and, in the end, only about half were eventually reinstated.

Important Progress

The new collective agreement included many important advances. On the non-monetary side, an entire article dealt with technological changes. It included a clear definition of "technological change" itself, outlined a clear consultation and arbitration process, identified specific types of information the employer was required to provide to the union ninety days prior to the introduction of any technological changes, obliged the employer to eliminate any adverse changes that arose from such changes, and guaranteed that all workers would keep their jobs in the same classification level and at the same wage rates after technological changes that they had enjoyed before. Other non-monetary gains were that management was now obliged to use full-time workers over casual labour, transfers within a region would now be by seniority, there would be fewer "consultations" and more negotiations and arbitration during the life of the agreement, there would be no individual work measurement, one level of the grievance procedure was eliminated, there were now more protection and more rights for shop stewards, as well as many other improvements.

On monetary issues, although the wage increase of $1.70 per hour was less than we had hoped for, we made progress in many other areas. For the first time, there would be a cost-of-living allowance, and there were increases in the number of days allotted for vacations and special leaves. We made important improvements for minority groups among postal workers, an increase in shift premiums, and new weekend premiums. We won our battles for part-timers to get the same benefits as full-time workers on a prorated basis, for the ten-cent adjustment of mail handlers' wages, and for fully paid injury-on-duty leave. We won double time for work on a day of rest and other improvements.

Looking back, I think we achieved more in the 1975 negotiations than we had expected when we began them but less than we had expected by the end of the process. But, we had raised the morale and the expectations of postal workers across the country. And, it was clear that the Trudeau government's strategy for "dealing with postal workers" had failed.

6 Employer Attacks, Government Assault

Aftermath of the 1975 Strike

The Liberal government's failed 1975 strategy for dealing with postal workers had four main aspects. The first was to get a quick settlement with LCUC in order to show that CUPW was being unreasonable in not agreeing to a similar settlement. The second was to sow division among CUPW members through a set-up of workers in Montréal that it hoped would turn some members against them. (Later, during the 1975 strike, this move also helped sow seeds of doubt about the motives of the national leadership among some members.) The third strategy was to give negotiators no mandate to negotiate most issues on the bargaining table, while making repeated statements in the media to discourage workers and divide them from their leaders. The fourth was to provoke a strike, create confusion around the Conciliation Board's report, and then accuse the union's leadership of being afraid to submit the employer's last offer to a membership vote.

All through this period, we faced a campaign of attacks, both public and behind the scenes, against the union and its leadership by "BS" MacKasey. Before the strike, we saw constant attacks at the workplace, where the rights of shop stewards and other union officers were denied, in the hope that workers would see this as a demonstration of management's strong determination to settle the dispute on its own terms. Still, despite these and many other obstacles placed in our way, the government's strategy didn't bring the results it wanted. Indeed, it failed almost completely.

Technological Change:
Management's Battering Ram Against the 1975 Agreement

On February 5, 1976, CUPW officially called an end to our "Boycott the Postal Code" campaign. We had begun this boycott in late 1972, and it had been quite successful. That success had created problems for management, and it was probably one of the reasons management had taken such a tough approach at the bargaining table in 1975.

But the boycott had also allowed us to gain protections while technological changes were being introduced and to win a small share of the benefits arising from the new technology.

So, while we hadn't got all the benefits we were looking for, we nevertheless felt that it was time to end the boycott. We felt that, having reached an agreement with management after a long struggle, this would send management and the government a message that perhaps we could develop a more decent way of dealing with one another. Unfortunately, we were wrong. Many managers never accepted the 1975 collective agreement, feeling that it had been imposed on them and, therefore, they had a right to ignore it.

We thanked the backers of our boycott, and the general public, for their understanding and support. Boycotts are very difficult tools for workers, or any other group fighting for justice and dignity, to use effectively, and I felt we had been privileged to receive the support we did.

Soon after we dropped the boycott, the employer began to challenge us, again and again, over what had been agreed to in 1975. This was a period when the post office, government officials, and many other employers across the country were trying to sell new technologies by saying we were entering a new era in which there would be much more leisure time for people. We were told there would be more time off for workers to spend with their families, that working hours would be fewer and leisure hours greater. Some went so far as to tell us that new technologies would mean early retirement and that, in the years leading up to retirement, workers would only have to be on the job for a few weeks each year. What they were not telling us back in the 1970s is that any reduction in time worked would see an equal reduction in pay. Today we see that technology has meant that many workers now have to cobble together a number of part-time jobs to make ends meet, and most workers now labour through far more hours than in years past. Meanwhile, others can find work only part of the time, at best.

Given the attitude of management in the preceding years, we were very sceptical about the sincerity of these people who were telling us how much better technology was going to make our lives. In fighting to assure that the new technology would not have a negative effect on jobs in the post office, we were fighting against both layoffs and to maintain jobs for the next generation of workers. When we had drafted our program of demands prior to negotiations in 1975, we were guided, at least in part, by the rosy future we were being told technology would bring us. At the negotiating table, we won a guarantee that we would be given accurate information about technological changes, that we would be consulted prior to the implementation of such changes, and that the employer would eliminate any adverse effects arising from them.

Management wasn't pleased by the fact that Bryce Stuart MacKasey had compromised in order to resolve the last three issues on the bargaining table, which led to the end of our 1975 strike and the signing of the collective agreement. They decided to challenge almost all the improve-

ments we won through the negotiations and strike of 1975. And, technological change seemed to them a good place to start.

Despite the agreement we had signed on technological change, in 1976
the employer provided us with incomplete information — when they
provided any at all — about the implementation of new technologies.
Proper notice of the implementation of changes wasn't provided, the
pledge to eliminate any adverse effects was totally ignored, and the process
of consultations was nothing more than farce.

We fought to have the terms of the collective agreement observed, but
it took months before we finally obtained a ruling from an arbitrator that
the employer was violating the provisions of the collective agreement.
That arbitrator, Ted Joliffe, ruled in two cases that "the employer was in
violation of the collective agreement in several respects," that it was taking
"a 'specious' and 'nonsensical' approach to the definition of technological
change," and that it was guilty of "failure to give proper notice, failure to
provide required information, and failure to engage in constructive and
meaningful consultation."

Unfortunately, the arbitrator felt he didn't have the power to force the
employer to stop implementing these technological changes. So, management simply continued with impunity to introduce changes that were in
violation of the collective agreement. However, we won some cases where
arbitrators forced the employer to eliminate the adverse effects of technological changes as provided for in the collective agreement, and compensation was granted in other cases where the elimination of the adverse
effects wasn't possible.

As well as disregarding our rights in the area of technological change,
management ignored many of the other provisions in the collective agreement. By the time we entered into negotiations again in 1977, our members
had filed 42,000 grievances.

I remember one case where the employer argued that the arbitrator
could not rule a violation of the collective agreement because the provisions of the collective agreement themselves were in violation of management rights as outlined in the Public Service Staff Relations Act. Fortunately, this was an arbitrator with some backbone: he asked the employer's
lawyer, "Are you telling me that you negotiated these provisions with the
union in bad faith and now you are counting on me to tell them that what
you both signed and agreed to is not valid?" The lawyer responded to the
effect that the employer's representatives didn't have the authority to sign
such provisions. The arbitrator then said, "Don't count on me to rule in
that direction. I will only determine whether or not you are in violation of
the provisions of the collective agreement that you signed and agreed to."

This is the level of arrogance we faced: management taking the position that their representatives at the bargaining table — those from
Treasury Board and from the post office, including the Postmaster General

himself — had signed provisions that are management rights under the law and, therefore, management has no obligation to respect these provisions. Their strategy was clearly to make CUPW members feel they had fought for nothing in 1975 and so to turn them against their union.

In 1976 alone, we received twenty-one notices of technological changes to be introduced in the post office, and each of these prompted negotiations on their implementation at each particular location. In some cases, we managed to reach agreements with management, though in others we failed to do so. But even when we managed to reach agreement on technological changes in particular locations, the employer refused, in violation of the provision signed by them in the 1975 negotiations, to incorporate such agreements into the collective agreement. Had the employer done so, it would have provided affected workers with the right to grieve any violations of those agreements.

The situation became impossible. Despite winning case after case at arbitration, management simply continued to ignore the collective agreement. Our demand that management postpone further introduction of technological changes until the problems arising from it were resolved was flatly rejected. So, workers in different offices across the country began to walk off the job in an effort to resolve their problems locally. We decided to support these strike activities with rotating, one-day local walkouts. The Vancouver local went out on October 4, 1976, Ottawa on October 5, St. John's and London on October 6, and Edmonton on October 7. They all called for the postponement of technological changes.

On October 5, the employer applied to the Federal Court for an injunction to stop the rotating strikes. We counteracted on October 12 with an application before the same court for an injunction to stop the introduction of technological changes in the post office. Both parties then agreed to a mediation of the dispute by Dr. Noel Hall, who was appointed by the Public Service Staff Relations Board. With his appointment, we put any plans for further walkouts on hold.

Near the end of mediation, in an effort to reach an agreement, we proposed a three-point offer: the immediate settlement of issues related to seniority, staffing, and closed-circuit television, that the next round of contract negotiations would begin as early as January 1977, and that all outstanding problems arising from the introduction of technological changes be tackled in the upcoming negotiations.

The response from the employer was a partial solution on the issue of seniority — a proposal on staffing for Toronto only, without the right to grieve — and a six-month postponement of the introduction of closed-circuit television for the surveillance of employees. Management refused to begin negotiations in January, under the pretext it would be illegal, and suggested that all other appropriate points be referred to the next round of negotiations, set to start in May of 1977.

It was as clear as ever to us that the employer saw the mediation process as another means of delay as it continued to press on with the introduction of technological changes, in contravention of our signed collective agreement. The mediation talks ended on December 15.

In the last weeks of 1976, it became clear that management was conducting a major campaign against CUPW across the country. It seized upon different local issues and resorted to tricks at the local level, but it was obvious that the thrust of management strategy was coming from the very top. One of management's main arguments at this time was that, in its dealings with postal workers, it was following guidelines set down in a document written by former mediator Eric Taylor, who had participated in union-management meetings — under the Manpower Committee — following the 1974 strike. This argument took no account of the fact that we had never agreed to most of the points in that document, nor that we had since gone through a full round of negotiations that had resulted in a new collective agreement.

Another of management's arguments was that thirteen issues had been resolved during the recent mediation efforts of Dr. Noel Hall. I was the CUPW spokesperson during that mediation, and what management was saying to our members in the field was, simply, a lie. I challenged the employer to specify the issues that had been resolved and the nature of their settlement. Of course, management could not respond to this challenge.

On December 10, 1976, I wrote to members across the country that we have a collective agreement, and *it* is the bible, not some report from mediation efforts that had taken place more than a year before both sides had signed a collective agreement, and certainly not vague management promises. "Your legal rights are in your contract and the union is determined to defend your contract," I concluded.

The double-dealings of management during this period were very frustrating to us. "Say one thing one minute, another the next," seemed to be their guiding principle. The Trudeau government had shuffled its Cabinet, and on December 16, 1976, the new Postmaster General, Jean-Jacques Blais, told the House of Commons of his decision not to proceed with early negotiations. (He pretended, falsely, that he was restricted by the Public Service Staff Relations Act.) But he told a group of postal workers who "greeted him" in Burlington, Ontario, on February 19, 1977, "We are willing to negotiate at any time."

When the employer announced in early 1976 that new technology was going to be introduced in Windsor, Ontario, one of the issues we asked to be included in consultations was the impact that the sorting of more mail in Windsor would have on other post offices in the region. In March, workers in Amerstburg, Kingsville, Leamington, and Essex, Ontario, were told that all mail bearing the postal code must be forwarded to Windsor. In

May, Mr. Fultz, the post office's National Director of Mechanization Program, guaranteed us that no mail from other post offices would be sorted in the newly mechanized offices. On July 14, Mr. Lockman, the Manager of the Consultation Division of the National Mechanization Program, told us that Fultz had never given us such a guarantee, that he had only been speaking of management's "intention," rather than its obligation under the terms of the collective agreement. On November 8, the employer, through mediator Dr. Noel Hall, stated that only if mail were to be processed on an ongoing basis at another post office would the article dealing with technological changes apply.

During this time our members saw that the quality of postal service to the public was deteriorating, with heavy backlogs of mail in many major sorting centres. We knew that management would use this to try to turn public dissatisfaction with mail service against postal workers themselves. Given this and the many other problems in the post office, CUPW announced a new public campaign to demand that the government establish a Royal Commission of Inquiry to investigate the causes of poor postal service to the public, financial mismanagement, management's refusal to implement the recommendations of various reports, and the cause of poor labour-management relations. This campaign lasted six months, but the government refused to establish any such Royal Commission. Needless to say, the corporate sector, which was quick to blame postal workers for the deteriorating service, didn't support our call for an impartial investigation.

We used the first months of 1977 to communicate with our local officers and shop stewards about the introduction of technological changes and other violations of the collective agreement on management's part. A series of one-day meetings was organized across the country, both to inform union activists and to counteract the repeated attacks of the employer against the union and its members.

The next round of negotiations with the employer, which had been set for May of 1977, actually began on April 20. However, little progress had been made before our triennial National Convention in Halifax, held July 25–29.

1977 CUPW National Convention in Halifax

Everyone who attended that National Convention in Halifax would agree that we made great strides forward in our organization, primarily because of resolutions sent to the convention by locals all across the country. In fact, this was the only convention in CUPW's history where all local resolutions were dealt with on the floor.

It was at this convention that we had our first all-night session, simply because delegates wanted to see all the work we needed to deal with be completed. Far more than in any previous convention, delegates seemed to work in harmony, with a determination to come out of the convention with

From left to right: Jean-Claude Parrot, Joe Davidson, and Darrell Tingley demonstrate in support of striking Ottawa postal workers during the 1977 CUPW National Convention in Halifax.

strong policies that would serve us well as we faced the employer in the upcoming years.

On the Thursday night, the Halifax local had organized a banquet, dinner, and dance, so delegates could take a break from our heavy schedule. Given the agenda before us, it seemed that we wouldn't have time to cope with all the issues we had to deal with, and so a suggestion was made that we cancel the banquet and dance to consider the business at hand. After a short discussion and after offering our apologies to the Halifax local and banquet organizers, we cancelled the dance but not the dinner, because we all had to eat in any event. After dinner, we went back into session, and something incredible happened: we pursued our work non-stop through to the next morning, taking just the time necessary to refresh ourselves, have a good breakfast, and return to the convention floor at 9:00 am.

One of the things discussed in depth at the Halifax convention was the worker-controlled messenger service that the Montréal local had organized during the 1975 strike.

On one hand, many activists suggested that this strategy had amounted to scabbing against our own strike. Most Québec delegates, on the other hand, argued that it had hurt management in the area of revenues and that it had helped us gain public sympathy, as we also had when we had organized special shifts during the strike to sort pension and other benefit cheques.

As it turned out, a majority of the delegates voted in favour of a resolution calling on the union to oppose such strategies in the future. It was never tried again, but I am not convinced that the debate on this issue covered all its aspects. When the Montréal local started this strategy, they were inspired, I think, by examples of workers in other industries who had taken over the employer's business after it had been closed because of a strike. To me, what is most important in today's context of more back-to-work legislation and greater flexibility of employers do their business in different places is for workers to be more and more imaginative in our strategies, while maintaining the right to strike as our central strategy in negotiating collective agreements.

In response to the attacks of the government and the employer, we adopted an emergency resolution that recognized our legal rights as bargaining agent, as well as our contractual rights as union representatives, including our right to distribute information to our members at their place of work. A second emergency resolution called for a Royal Commission to inquire into the administration of the post office.

I remember Frank Hilliard, a CBC Television reporter who covered the Halifax Convention. He was known for not being very supportive of CUPW, but he still gave us fair coverage. By the time the convention ended, his opinion of CUPW had changed drastically. He said he had discovered a union that was an example of dedication to its members. He was impressed with the quality of the delegates' interventions in the debates and with the democratic way the convention had been conducted.

The election of national officers took place on the last day of the convention. Joe Davidson, I believe, would easily have won re-election if he had wished to run, but he had decided to step down as National President, and he nominated me to succeed him. I was elected by acclamation, little knowing I would remain in that position for fifteen years. (This would be a surprise, both to me and everyone else involved in the union, given that no National President had ever before been re-elected for a second three-year term.) Brother André Beauchamp — who had missed the beginning of the Convention because he had been leading a strike in the Ottawa post office — was elected First National Vice-President, David Jones as Second National Vice-President, Leroy Hiltz as National Secretary-Treasurer, and Sid Baxter as National Chief Steward. The regional directors were Brothers Darrell Tingley (Atlantic), Clément Morel (Québec), William Dalgleish (Ontario), and Frank Walden (Western). Together, we made up the new National Executive Board.

Delegates adopted new policies and mandates that gave me, in my first term as National President, a clear direction on how to move forward in the future. I knew that this clear direction, along with a good team of national officers and union representatives across the country, would make CUPW stronger than ever in the upcoming round of negotiations. I left the convention confident we could face up to management's challenges in the coming years.

Eighteen Months of Meetings and Conciliation

In early 1977, discussions had been taking place across the country about the development of our program of demands for the next round of negotiations. We took into consideration the overriding attitude of the employer on the existing collective agreement. A final program of eighty-three demands was ratified by 87.8 percent of the membership.

For the first time we had a woman on the Negotiating Committee, which was composed of four local presidents, Sister Martha Stockwell of St. Catherines, Ontario, Brothers Ted Penney of St. John's, Marcel Perreault of Montréal, Stan Darlington of Victoria, and myself as Chief Negotiator.

When we began negotiations on April 20, 1977, we tabled our program of demands and demanded a full list of all the technological changes that were either underway or were to be introduced over the next three years. We also made proposals to reinforce the guarantees we had negotiated in 1975 to eliminate the adverse effects of such changes and, where this was impossible, that proper compensation be provided. Because we foresaw that the new technology would mean fewer jobs, we also demanded reinforcements to the 1975 provisions dealing with the conversion of part-time, casual, and overtime hours into full-time positions. We also sought a wage increase, together with a shorter work week without loss in pay after that increase took effect, pre-retirement and paid maternity leave, and more vacation leave, and other improvements. All these demands were in line with the prevailing philosophy of the 1970s that technological change would result in more leisure time for all workers.

Our collective agreement was set to expire on June 30, 1977, and we informed the employer that any agreement made after that date would be retroactive to the expiration of the previous contract. So, we urged management to keep careful track of hours worked, including overtime hours. (In past negotiations, management had always fought to have workers receive a lump-sum payment, rather than consent to have a new agreement provide for retroactive wages. Such lump-sum payments, in the case of the vast majority of workers, were less than what they would have received had the agreement been retroactive.)

But, our difficulties were only just beginning. From September of 1976 to the start of our strike on October 16, 1978, we faced problem after problem put before us by management. The number of grievances we filed in this period had no precedent anywhere. With almost no exceptions, local grievances were not settled at the local or regional level, so almost all reached the national level. Even then, they weren't settled until referred to arbitration, a hearing date scheduled, and a decision subsequently rendered. (In a large number of cases, management knew it would be the loser in arbitration, but nonetheless, they would still wait until a hearing date was scheduled before settling the grievance.) The arrogance of managers in the field, who repeatedly violated the signed agreement, prompted many spontaneous local walkouts.

Interventions by Cabinet Ministers seemed to only invite more confrontation. An announcement by Postmaster General Jean-Jacques Blais that there could be a strike in the post office as early as May 24, 1977, was far from helpful. There had only been three negotiating meetings by that point. Perhaps Blais knew, given the mandate he was going to give his negotiators, that we wouldn't have any choice but to strike.

Even before the beginning of negotiations, the employer established a direct communication link to our membership. It went by the name of "Comteam" and it was used to bypass the union, interfere with our internal communications, and denigrate union negotiators in the eyes of postal workers. It would fill too much space to detail all the misinformation management was spreading by this means, but suffice it to say that it was saying different things in different part of the country, and it spread blatant lies about what was happening in our negotiations.

In August of 1977, we came into possession of a number of internal management documents that proved the employer was using a vast amount of public funds in these efforts to weaken the position of our Negotiating Committee and undermine our union. One of these documents was a letter signed by the Assistant Deputy Postmaster General, John Paré, whose job was to try to introduce "industrial democracy" to the post office. One of his key tasks was to get the unions in the post office to deal with issues away from the bargaining table. In this letter, he described some of the tactics used by the employer to support its negotiating team. They included "effective external communications" (a $350,000 advertising campaign), stepped-up internal communications (Comteam), and a proposed multi-union conference." He continued: "We need to come up with a great variety of other ways to support our negotiating team." The Postmaster General said that the $350,000 advertising campaign was to inform the public, hiding its real purpose: to support management negotiators.

Mr. Paré continually invited us to attend sessions away from the bargaining table — which management called "Intergroup" sessions — where we could have "open discussions." It was our position that the bargaining table itself was the appropriate place for such discussions. In the fall of 1977, Mr. Paré said the following about management-union meetings:

If the managers and the business representatives and union stewards work from the assumption that they share common objectives, it's likely they can do a lot jointly and effectively. However, this is giving up management's decision-making rights. I am not advocating sharing decision-making. It's not in the interest of either party. Where they can get together, however, is in problem solving, with management reserving the right to make decisions, taking into consideration the union's perception of problems and their recommendations. In this way, management has the right to decide on the most appropriate solution to an issue, and the union retains the right to protest and appeal management's action.

On another occasion, Mr. Paré gave the following view of contracts between management and labour: "The contract is nothing more than a set of rules to which the parties agree in order to aid in creating and maintaining the kind of relationship they want. If the contract is a barrier to achieving this relationship, then a change would be beneficial to both parties."

In CUPW, we prefer that management take decisions that live up to the provisions of the contract it has negotiated rather it making decisions following union-management meetings. The contract between the two sides was legally binding. While it recognized that union-management meetings might be called for to deal with issues not covered by the terms of the contract or to deal with specific issues such as health and safety, the outcome of such meetings cannot be in violation of the provisions of the collective agreement.

After launching its Comteam plan for communicating directly to our members, the employer took an additional step: it declared an end to our right to distribute literature on the employer's premises outside working hours, such as during breaks and lunch periods. It also declared an end to the right of shop stewards and officers to call meetings of CUPW members in the workplace during breaks and lunch periods. Such rights had been common practice for many years. This was a clear attack on the democratic right of workers to be informed by their union.

We filed an immediate complaint and stopped all negotiations until this issue was settled. We involved our locals in hearings on our complaint and so created greater solidarity among our members. On August 30, 1977, an arbitrator recognized the "right" and "duty" of the union to communicate with its members. Three weeks later, we agreed to resume negotiations after the employer reinstated the rights of shop stewards and officers to communicate with our members on the employer's premises. We then provided shop stewards and other activists with reams of information for our members, and it was all read avidly. Management's strategy had backfired: more members were now reading union material than before our right to distribute it had been taken away.

In October of 1977, just a few weeks after the arbitrator's decision to reinstate our right to communicate with our members, our National Office issued two bulletins reproducing articles from the *Globe and Mail* and the *Toronto Star*. On October 14, the *Globe and Mail* ran an interview by Marina Strauss with Tony Hornick, management's Director for Staff Relations in Toronto. He said that transforming the post office into a Crown Corporation would be the best remedy for its current troubles, but that it would never happen. He mentioned that management "can't make any decision without going from one person to another person to another person... and they haven't a clue how the post office should be run or staffed.... It's a horror story."

The next day, the *Toronto Star* reported that Hornick had been given sick leave and that he would be off work for three or four weeks. On October 18, Marina Strauss wrote another article in the *Globe and Mail,* which included a statement from Assistant Deputy Postmaster John Paré, who said that Hornick "went too far" in his statements to the press.

Not surprisingly, the Postmaster General couldn't resist getting in on the act. When asked whether the many different government agencies responsible for running the post office were hampering management, Mr. Blais said, "That's a bunch of baloney." However, he acknowledged that, "Because of the heavy benefits paid out in the past years, the Treasury Board has put a freeze on hiring and kept a watchful eye on staff changes."

Despite the arbitrator's earlier decision to restore our right to communicate with our members, management in some post offices denied our right to post the two bulletins relating these stories on union bulletin boards in the workplace. Having successfully defended our right to communicate with our members, we had to defend that right again and again against management attack. Other demands for bulletins to be posted on union bulletin boards in the workplace were denied under all sorts of pretexts. Sure, we won such cases at arbitration, but only long after the situation and the reasons for posting the bulletins in the first place had changed. How could postal workers develop any respect for management when it was so obvious that it had no respect for workers? The simple answer was that they couldn't.

Attacks against union activists continued. A broad array of arbitrary measures was used against workers, and especially against union activists. The principle of "innocent until proven guilty" became a farce. In the previous three years, management had been obliged to pay close to $1,000,000 to CUPW members who had been unjustly suspended or dismissed. But this figure is nothing compared to what it would have to pay in the following years for its arbitrary actions during this period.

In keeping with management's vicious campaign, there were several cases of retaliation against postal workers for filing grievances. I remember Brother Darrell Tingley, National Director in the Atlantic region at the time, denouncing the Postmaster of Port Hawkesbury, Nova Scotia, for having transferred a part-time worker to the night shift when he continued to file grievances. He filed his grievances because the Postmaster was using casuals and part-timers in a manner that was clearly in violation of the collective agreement. His twenty-four hours of weekly work were changed from day-shift hours spread over five days to night-shift hours (2:00 am to 6:00 am), six days a week. And Port Hawkesbury was far from an isolated example: when it came to using casual labour, many managers in the field did exactly the opposite of what had been agreed in the collective agreement. This provoked both discontent and spontaneous walkouts among our members.

Brother Tingley denounced another situation in which employees were disciplined, or were threatened with discipline, if they continued to "abuse" the grievance procedure in response to local management's clear violations of the 1975 collective agreement. It seemed that local management was taking its cue from the Postmaster General.

On October 11, 1977, I announced at a press conference that CUPW would launch an intensive information campaign on October 13 by placing ads in major newspapers across the country to explain to Canadians the true problems in the post office and to identify issues that were obstructing negotiations. The ad underlined the fact that there had been seventeen studies in the previous eight years that had all blamed problems in the post office on poor management and recommended its conversion into a Crown Corporation. The ad was entitled "Return to Sender" and it read in part, "Make the mail system work better... we're all for that!... Eight years, seventeen studies, and five Ministers later... Without exception, these many studies agree on the need for a Crown Corporation. Why? One Employer Will Deliver."

The employer continued to make a mockery of the collective agreement signed at the end of our forty-two-day strike in 1975. An increase in our cost-of-living allowance was provided for in the agreement, but this was denied until we had expended much time and energy to get it paid to our members.

By now, it was crystal clear that management was going to use every trick in the book, and even tricks from outside the book, against CUPW and its members. Their purpose was to make it clear that they were not about to give anything away in this round of negotiations and that they were going to take back some of the gains we had achieved in 1975.

Despite these assaults, strategically, we decided to stay at the bargaining table. We filed complaints against the employer regarding the cost-of-living allowance, its denial of our right to post bulletins, and its vast disinformation campaign against our members. We also filed a complaint regarding stories in the media about the Royal Canadian Mounted Police reading citizens' mail. On November 30, 1977, the employer decided to apply for conciliation.

Members of CUPW's 1977–78 Negotiating Committee, from left to right: John Fehr, Martha Stockwell (the first woman to serve as a CUPW Negotiator), Jean-Claude Parrot, and Marcel Perreault join a demonstration on Parliament Hill in 1978.

It was unusual for an employer to apply for conciliation. Normally it is the union that, facing stalling strategies on the part of the employer, decides to move to this next step. It was clear to us that the other side knew it had the full support of the government and was anxious for these face-to-face negotiations to end.

I believed that the management team realized we knew that they were ready to go for the kill. Officially however, the employer argued that the two sides were diametrically opposed in their points of view and it felt the parties would be unable to come to agreement without the aid of a third party. At the same time, however, it publicly invited us to take part in "intensive negotiations" pending an upcoming conciliation process. We knew we had to be well prepared for the conciliation process and that management's public invitation was simply a tactic to keep us busy while its staff prepared for conciliation. We didn't have anything near the resources of the other side, so we put our energies into getting ready for conciliation.

We confirmed our acceptance of the establishment of a Conciliation Board on December 7, citing the obvious lack of authority of the employer's team to negotiate seriously with us. But the employer's game was far from over: on December 19, it asked for a delay on the pretext that it had to study our demands to assess their admissibility before the Conciliation Board, despite the fact that they had had these demands in their hands since April.

We suspected that the government really wanted the extra time to find someone to chair the Conciliation Board who would be to its liking.

In December, the two sides nominated their respective representatives to the Conciliation Board. Roy Heenan, the employer's nominee, was a lawyer who worked for a law firm well known for representing employers. Ours was labour lawyer Irving Gaul, who had represented us on the 1975 Conciliation Board and had filed a minority report at the conclusion of that Board's hearings, despite immense pressure from government not to do so. But it wasn't until February 3, 1978, that the Public Service Staff Relations Board appointed Louis Courtemanche, a lawyer who acted as an arbitrator in Québec, to chair the Conciliation Board.

Before beginning the conciliation process, we had to appear before the chair of the Public Service Staff Relations Board, J.H. Brown, in order to get a determination on whether any of our demands weren't negotiable under the law. The employer took the position that the Conciliation Board should not be permitted to make recommendations on seventy-one of our eighty-three demands. On March 29, 1978, Mr. Brown handed down his decision. It stipulated that twenty-five of our demands couldn't be addressed by the Conciliation Board and that thirty-two others were referred to it with caveats, conditions, or deletions, for a total of fifty-seven of the eighty-three items in dispute. Of the twenty-six he agreed could be dealt with by the Conciliation Board, Mr. Brown said that seventeen were referred because the employer had withdrawn its objections.

This was an incredible decision. Some of the items Mr. Brown had not referred to the Conciliation Board had already been the subjects of provisions in the collective agreement signed by both parties in the previous round of negotiations. It was clear to us that this decision was part of the government's overall strategy to weaken CUPW, if not to break the union entirely. We knew that Louis Courtemanche wouldn't deal with items outside the mandate given him by Mr. Brown, and so the conciliation process would be quite limited. (We appealed Mr. Brown's decision in Federal Court on May 26, 1978, but the conciliation process was completed by the time a decision was made, rendering our appeal irrelevant.)

Gilles Lamontagne had replaced Jean-Jacques Blais as Postmaster General on February 2, 1978, and during the entire conciliation process he made many statements attacking the integrity of postal workers. In these attacks, Lamontagne was continuing in the tradition of his predecessors as Postmaster General, but he raised his attacks to a new level of viciousness. The outright lies and threats he made in this period made it once again clear to us what the government's objective really was.

On March 31, 1978, Mr. Lamontagne, speaking in Edmonton, said that CUPW had not presented its demands until January of 1978. This was quite surprising, considering that the employer had summarized our demands in a Comteam release dated April 19, 1977.

On the first day of the Conciliation Board's hearings in mid-April, the employer submitted a document claiming that our demands would cost $1.9 billion and would required the hiring of 44,888 new employees. This was almost twice the number of postal workers CUPW represented. The employer's calculations were based on double- and triple-counting procedures, as we would soon demonstrate publicly. Nevertheless, Mr. Lamontagne used these figures in public statements in an effort to discredit our position.

Given such statements, it wasn't long before the Postmaster General lost his credibility with the media. We, in contrast, were able to provide the real facts and figures. On July 11, 1978, we made a four-hour presentation to the Conciliation Board in which we exposed management's double- and triple-counting practices. We refuted virtually every one of their calculations, including one on a "travel time" demand, which they estimated would cost, by itself, more than $900,000. (Travel time was almost non-existent in the CUPW bargaining unit.)

On April 28, Mr. Lamontagne, speaking in Vancouver, said CUPW was not cooperating with the Conciliation Board. This statement was incredible, given that none of the senior management team attended the sessions of the Conciliation Board, while CUPW's National President actively participated in all of them. On May 2, having been heavily criticized for this accusation, he denied ever having made it.

On May 29, Mr. Lamontagne said this in the House of Commons:

> There are four principles, for example, on which we are not prepared to negotiate. We intend to proceed with technological change. We want to have freedom to contract out some of our work. We want our casual and temporary employees to meet peak demands, and we want to be able to measure quantity and quality of employee output, which we do not have at the moment. The workers previously acquired certain rights and we would like to negotiate in that area.

Basically, the Postmaster General had no intention of negotiating seriously.

Mr. Lamontagne often contradicted his own statements. One day, he denied there were any plans for staff cutbacks. Not more than a few minutes later, he said that cutbacks forecast in eastern Ontario and outlined in a management study would "be made with the collaboration of the union and will come mainly with attrition."

In the first week of June 1978, Lamontagne gave an interview to Kit Collins, a reporter for the *Ottawa Citizen*. Speaking on the issue of the constant hiring of casuals, he said, "If every worker in CUPW did a good day's work, there wouldn't be so much need for casuals. It's our responsibility to see that the mail goes out." Even some on the management team would have gagged at the idea of blaming CUPW members for the increasing use of casuals. In fact, management was arguing before the Conciliation Board that casuals were necessary because of the fluctuating mail volumes, not because of any laziness on the part of CUPW workers.

After having repeatedly denied in the House of Commons that the government intended, or was even considering, cutbacks in mail delivery, he said in that same *Ottawa Citizen* interview: "Expectations have to change. Canadian taxpayers are dreaming if they expect the same postal service as fifty years ago. In the old days, milk and bread and groceries were delivered to your door — now there's no milk at the door. We are living in 1978." I responded at the time that the only ones getting "milked" in 1978 were taxpayers, who couldn't even get the same statement twice from the Postmaster General.

Lamontagne tried to personalize the dispute by saying, "Jean-Claude Parrot is too much of a politician. He seems to want to attract attention, to make the headlines, instead of communicating. The Conciliation Board — that's the place for negotiations." This was exactly what we'd been trying to tell him for months while he and his team were arguing that some issues, such as those arising from technological change, should be resolved in informal chats, rather than at the bargaining table.

On June 12, 1978, Mr. Lamontagne, speaking before the House of Commons Committee on Transport and Communications, again attacked the integrity of postal workers:

> In other areas again, with the inside workers, the CUPW members, you have to admit that everybody is not doing their job. I mention a visit I made to Alta Vista [the Ottawa mail processing centre], with the Deputy Minister at one o'clock in the morning, and we found the guards sleeping and things like that. Somebody, it is plain to see, was sleeping at the switch somewhere.

I had two points to make in response to this statement. First, CUPW did not represent the security guards in the post office. Second, I had worked night shifts myself, and I knew that a night worker might sometimes choose to take a nap during lunch break, but that this was in no way a sign of a lazy worker.

Before the same Committee on that same day, the Postmaster General showed complete ignorance of the grievance procedure when he said:

> Mr. Chairman... I think you do not take that seriously when the union gives you 42,000 grievances in the short time that they have done it. Obviously, they are promoting grievances in one way or the other. I mean, if you have one grievance on one worker, well,

you try to make the others sign the same grievance — instead of having one, which you can discuss and settle for all the others, you have maybe 150 others sign the same thing. You can go up to 75,000 grievances that way very easily.

This was in contradiction to a written affidavit before the Supreme Court in which Deputy Postmaster General Jim Corkery estimated that for every grievance on a particular article in the collective agreement there were ten grievors and, consequently, the 2,700 grievances filed under that article actually represented the grievances of 27,000 employees.

On June 22, Mr. Lamontagne denied that management negotiators were trying to eliminate contractual rights of postal workers outlined in the collective agreement. Rather, he said, they were trying to "clarify the existing language." I reacted strongly, calling on him to read the employer's brief before the Conciliation Board. I read its proposal for a rollback of our contractual rights to the media, and then added:

> All of his actions and statements since his appointment on Febru-
> ary 2 are proof that Mr. Lamontagne was appointed solely to be
> the Liberal Party's "hatchet man" to provoke a postal strike as part
> of its election strategy. Unfortunately for the Liberals, the Cana-
> dian public may not buy this strategy, where they are used as
> pawns and postal workers are used as scapegoats, while the postal
> service continues to deteriorate.

On July 7, speaking in Halifax, Lamontagne blamed the extensive overtime and casual hours worked in Halifax on CUPW members, who, he claimed, were unproductive and deliberately slow. When questioned on this attack on the integrity of Halifax postal workers, he had to admit, "The production figures for the Halifax plant are the highest in the country."

Needless to say, by this time, I considered the Postmaster General to be nothing less than incompetent. It must have been hard for Pierre Elliott Trudeau to hear, day after day, just how badly his Minister was performing.

Because of its narrow mandate, the conciliation process was, just as we had expected, less than fruitful. On August 16, 1978, we gave the required seven days notice for the Conciliation Board to adjourn and begin to write its report.

During this period, we conducted a campaign to have the post office become a Crown Corporation. The campaign was going well, and many workers were wearing buttons in support of it. The employer took discipli-nary measures against some of the workers who wore these buttons, but many others insisted on their right to wear them. To counter these but-tons, managers designed a button similar to ours, but which read, "I'm proud to work for the Post Office."

Finally, a week before the union acquired the right to strike in October of 1978, Mr. Lamontagne threatened to legislate postal workers back to work if we struck. He repeated the statements a few days later and added that the employer wouldn't negotiate until we put aside our strike threat.

By 1978, the Trudeau majority government had been in power for four years and there were election rumours in the air. Early in the year, the government passed legislation, titled the Postal Services Operations Act, 1978, that denied CUPW the right to strike at any time between the dissolution of the House of Commons — the announcement of an election — and twenty-eight days after the anticipated 1978 election. Not only did this repressive legislation make a mockery of workers' rights recognized by law, but it also discriminated against CUPW specifically. CUPW was singled out: no other unions representing workers in the post office had their right to strike taken away during the anticipated election campaign. (As things turned out, the Trudeau government did not call an election until the spring of 1979. So, although this legislation was never actually used, the fact remains that it was directed specifically at CUPW.)

Our collective agreement had expired on June 30, 1977, but it contained a clause that stipulated its provisions would remain in effect until either a new contract was signed or we acquired the legal right to strike. Before the passing of the Postal Services Operations Act, 1978, Brother Joe Morris, President of the Canadian Labour Congress, issued a press release inviting individual Members of Parliament to break party ranks and vote to reject the special bill. He argued that voting against it would be in the interest of justice, that the union had been without a contract since June of 1977, and that the legislation was nothing more than an act of government provocation.

So, the long and frustrating process of negotiations and conciliation lasted from April of 1977 to October of the following year. This was a much longer period than was provided by law, but we had agreed to the extension of time because we wanted to make the process work. Unfortunately, the Chair of the conciliation board, Louis Courtemanche didn't have the courage to strike compromises.

The Conciliation Report was released on October 6, 1978. (We had acquired a copy previously through our representative on the Board, Irving Gaul, who needed a copy of it in order to write a dissenting minority report.) Reading it, one could see that Louis Courtemanche certainly didn't have the backbone that Judge Moisan had shown during the 1975 conciliation process. Judge Moisan had not hesitated to break new ground and propose real solutions to the problems between the parties. But, Louis Courtemanche's 1978 Conciliation Report was nothing less than a copy of the employer's proposal, which contained rollbacks instead of progress and completely ignored our demands. In my eyes, and in those of the other union negotiators, officers, and activists, Louis Courtemanche was either anxious to get more of this sort of well-paid government work, or he was simply unable to summon the courage to stand up to the government and its sweeping plans to roll back our hard-won rights.

A Conciliation Board's report is not binding on the parties. Its purpose is to make recommendations to assist the parties in arriving at an agreement. Courtemanche's report did the exact opposite: it ensured that the parties would remain far from any agreement, and it forced postal workers to resort to their right to strike.

On October 1, 1978, CUPW's National Executive Board decided to proceed with a strike vote. All locals were provided with the necessary materials for the vote, including the recommendation of the Board, for distribution to our members. Even as we prepared to vote, the government announced it would step in with legislation to end any strike that might occur.

The National Executive Board's recommendation to the members read as follows:

> In accordance with the objectives of the Canadian Union of Postal Workers to negotiate improvements in the collective agreement while maintaining all acquired rights of the membership, and:
>
> In accordance with the Program of Demands ratified by 87.8 percent of the membership in March, 1977, and the Wage Demand ratified by 91.4 percent of the membership on July 11, 1978, which:
>
> Authorized the Negotiating Committee to effect improvements in 362 clauses of the collective agreement, of which 264 remain in dispute:
>
> Due to the intransigence of the employer, both at the bargaining table and during the conciliation process, combined with the employer's strategy of demanding rollbacks in the acquired rights of postal workers, and:
>
> Recognizing that the Chairman's Conciliation Board report, which is not binding on the parties, is an abdication of the responsibilities delegated to him, but in any event, does not contain recommendations which could be the basis of a settlement; and
>
> In the understanding that it is imperative that we achieve solutions to the problems which have led to numerous work stoppages and over 56,000 grievances by improving our collective agreement and including clauses that will force the employer to honour what he signs, and:
>
> Realizing that it is a fact in the coming year the employer's program of automation will continue to adversely affect ever-increasing numbers of postal workers, both directly and indirectly, and:
>
> In the knowledge that it is absolutely essential that we achieve

the necessary improvements, protections, and guarantees now in order to maintain and protect those rights until the signing of a first collective agreement under the Crown Corporation:

The National Executive Board unanimously recommends that the membership vote "Yes" to authorize the Board to call a strike in order to achieve a collective agreement based on the principles and objectives contained in the Program of Demands.

All nine members of the National Executive Board signed this recommendation, which was distributed to members attending meetings in every local across the country. Votes were to take place in the various locals across the country no later than Sunday, October 15, and an agenda for local membership meetings was prepared and sent to all locals. All full-time representatives of the union were called upon to participate in the meetings in the field.

We were well prepared for this vote and on Monday, October 16, the compilation of votes from every local across the country showed that 78.5 percent of our members were in favour of a strike. We had been in a legal strike position since October 13, and the National Executive Board decided to call a strike in line with the mandate we had received from our membership. Last-minute meetings between Shirley Carr of the Canadian Labour Congress and the acting Minister of Labour, André Ouellet, failed to find a solution. The strike was set to begin at 12:01 am the next morning

In fact, several locals across the country were already out. Given that the government had already announced it would introduce back-to-work legislation in case of a strike, the result of the membership vote constituted a strong mandate for the National Executive Board.

The Strike

It was just a few minutes after 10:30 pm in Ottawa on October 16 when we received word that locals in Newfoundland were out. It was midnight there, and the first day of the 1978 CUPW national strike had just began. Half an hour later, postal workers in Nova Scotia, Prince Edward Island, and New Brunswick walked out. As the hour of midnight marched westward across the country, postal workers walked off the job and picket lines were organized.

After eighteen frustrating months of negotiations with management, we had finally acquired our legal right to strike, the only tool at our disposal to try to persuade the employer to give a mandate to its negotiators to enter into serious negotiations. Despite the threat of the Trudeau government that back-to-work legislation would be put before Parliament, postal workers in every local across the country were now on strike.

At 2:00 pm on Tuesday, October 17, the first day of our legal strike, the government introduced Bill C-8 in the House of Commons, the "Postal Services Continuation Act." It stipulated that postal workers return to work and required me to inform our members that the strike has become invalid and they must return to work. The Bill had obviously been prepared long before the strike.

Bill C-8 also stipulated that a mediator-arbitrator would be appointed to, first, mediate the dispute between the parties and, failing any agreement, then determine a new collective agreement for postal workers. The law was not passed in the Senate until Wednesday, October 18, thanks to John Rodriguez, the New Democrat Member of Parliament for Nickel Belt, who made a strong and lengthy intervention on this unjust law in the House of Commons, preventing its adoption by the Senate on Tuesday night.

Before the passing of Bill C-8, I made it very clear through the media that if back-to-work legislation was adopted, postal workers would then face a dilemma. On one hand, we were on strike under legislation that gave us the legal right to strike after we had gone through the process of negotiation and conciliation provided by law. On the other hand, here was other legislation that told us our strike was now terminated and replaced by a process of arbitration.

In order to acquire a legal right to strike, the union had had to indicate to the federal Department of Labour, before the beginning of negotiations, which of two routes to follow in an effort to reach a new collective agreement. One was compulsory arbitration, in which an arbitrator would decide how points in dispute between the parties would be dealt with in the collective agreement. The other option was conciliation with the right to strike, which dictated that if, after a process of mediation and conciliation, there is still no agreement between the two parties, that the union and its members would then have the right to strike in an effort to reach an agreement with the employer. Before negotiations began in April of 1977, CUPW had chosen the second option, because the right to negotiate without the right to strike guarantees little beyond "consultations" with the employer. Now, more than eighteen months after making that choice, we were faced with legislation that imposed compulsory arbitration. In essence, Bill C-8 both took away our right to strike and made the law retroactive to the very day we had filed our notice to bargain with the employer.

In the face of such disregard of the legal process we had followed, I made it very clear before the passing of Bill C-8 that after its passage we would face a situation of having two laws telling us two contradictory things. Therefore, we were going to respect the law we felt would be most appropriate under the circumstances. Bill C-8 was unfair, unjust, and — especially — dishonest on the part of a government that gave us a legal right to strike only to take it away on the first day we decided to exercise that legal right.

On the morning of Wednesday, October 18, 1978, the Senate passed
Bill C-8, which, following swift Royal Assent by the Governor-General,
would enter into effect on Thursday, October 19. This meant that it would
be workers on the coming midnight shift who would be the first to face
this legal dilemma.

That day, the National Executive Board reviewed each of Bill C-8's
articles and listened to reports by each of the National Directors about the
situation in their respective regions. There followed a full discussion,
during which every officer expressed his — there were still no women on
the National Executive Board at this time — view on the position we
should adopt. The National Executive Board then voted unanimously to
continue the strike.

Around 2:00 pm, while we were having these discussions, we issued a
statement that we would make our decision known to our workers in the
field through a press conference at 7:00 pm that night. We reserved the
National Press Gallery on Wellington Street in Ottawa, which was a large
room with facilities for simultaneous translation. We sent this 2:00 pm
statement out to local and regional offices across the country by fax. They,
in turn, found ways to bring this information to workers on the picket lines.

Around 4:00 pm that Wednesday afternoon, the president of one local
phoned me and said, "Jean-Claude, I want you to know that, should the
National Executive Board decide to stay on strike despite the law, I will be
with you. But I will be alone. My members are going to go back to work."
This was a local of close to one hundred members, and I replied, "Thank
you for your support, but I'd appreciate if you would phone me back
tomorrow at the same time."

We came to our decision around 5:00 pm, and, for whatever reason, I
wasn't nervous about what we had decided or the upcoming press conference. But I knew that I had to make it clear to our members — the vast
majority of whom were going to learn of our decision through the media —
exactly where we stood.

Defying Back-To-Work Legislation

I will never forget the moment: the room was packed with print reporters,
photographers, and television workers wielding cameras and other gear.
There were also CUPW members from the Ottawa local and members of
the Executive Board and Negotiating Committee present. I said the following to those gathered in the National Press Gallery:

> In the last few days, I have told you all the reasons why I felt
> postal workers were being denied their right to negotiate and now
> their right to strike. So I will not wait to tell you that I have
> received the unanimous support of my Executive Board to inform
> our members across the country that, in line with the mandate we

received from them, the strike continues, and picket lines will be maintained in every workplace across the country. I am asking all postal workers across the country to continue the strike and maintain our picket lines at all postal installations.

Members of the Ottawa local immediately reacted with cheers of approval. After making it clear that the strike was still on, I explained that this was the second time in six months the Trudeau government had adopted legislation to deprive postal workers of their right to strike. This, I said, had encouraged management and Treasury Board negotiators in their refusal to negotiate in any serious way. I then added:

> It was scandalously obvious last night during the debate in the House of Commons, with the employer's chief negotiator, Mr Paul Pageau, sitting in the House giving directives to the Minister of Labour on behalf of the employer during the adoption of various clauses of Bill C-8, and with regards to amendments proposed by Members of Parliament. All amendments which did not reflect the employer's position at the bargaining table have been rejected.

This was, I believe, the largest press conference I ever gave. I spent more than an hour answering questions from reporters and giving one-on-one interviews. Many reporters asked me how I thought the membership would react to my announcement. My answer was that CUPW members know this is an unjust law from a dishonest government.

After the press conference, I went back to the office to hear reports from the field.

The first came from Newfoundland just after 10:30 pm Ottawa time, and it confirmed that nobody had gone back to work in St. John's. Similar reports came in as the night went on: local after local reported that the strike was still on. Though many of our leaders were worried about the day shift, staffed by our more senior members, on Thursday we received word that our locals were still out. By the end of that day, it was clear to everyone in the country that our strike was still on, and still strong.

I spent much of that Thursday doing interviews on different radio and television public-affairs programs and to newspaper reporters. In every interview, I underlined that the strike was not over and that picket lines would be maintained.

This strength of our membership in the face of adversity must have come as a shock to a government that had been led to believe that the strike would collapse. It also must have been a shock for an employer that never believed postal workers would stand up for their rights. As the days went by, very few postal workers went back to work. I will always remember the encouragement I felt when I learned that in Inuvik, Northwest Territories, not only were the three regular postal workers on strike, but they were joined on the picket line by that office's three casual employees.

Also that Thursday, I got a call back from the local president who had phoned me the day before the strike to tell me that he would support us if we decided to stay out, but that he thought he would be alone among his members in that support. "Jean-Claude," he said, "you wouldn't believe it! I am flying high here! Not only haven't the members gone back to work, but the vast majority are also on the picket lines with me, and they are proud of it. All the people who were telling me yesterday that they were not going to disobey the law are with me."

I must say that I was flying high too. For me, our members' defiance was a great way to let Prime Minister Trudeau know that, in future, he shouldn't trust the information he receives from those guys in Treasury Board and post office management.

In the days immediately following our defiance of Bill C-8, the media reported that, if anything, the net effect of the legislation was to strengthen our picket lines. One evening, while we were still in defiance of the law, Patrick Watson interviewed me on CBC Television, and many postal workers across the country tuned in. In answer to a question about how I felt about engaging in illegal activity by defying the back-to-work legislation, I answered, "My conscience is clear." Later, someone from the Vancouver local told me how tremendously inspiring this was for fellow members who had gathered in a hall to listen to the program. Their cheers and clapping could be heard by those on the picket line.

I suddenly felt relieved of all the fatigue and stress of the previous months. I knew that we had gained the respect of our enemies, as much as that of our friends, whether in government, postal management, the labour movement, the general public, and — especially — among ourselves. Postal workers all across the country were standing proud in defence of their rights. For a whole week, postal workers showed no weakness, and, though I knew that our defiance didn't necessarily mean we were going to win a good collective agreement, I was really proud of the message postal workers were sending to both the government and the employer.

On the Friday after the adoption of the law, a reporter asked me during a press conference whether our strike was collapsing. He pointed to the fact that the post office in Orangeville, Ontario, was open and postal workers there were at work. I reacted by saying: "Orangeville! Where is Orangeville?" I wasn't at all impressed that some reporters would bring up that fact that workers in a small town had returned to work in an effort to question the solidity of our strike. Like me, they knew that these few workers couldn't get the mail moving across the country.

In the following days, the government applied to the courts for injunctions in different cities across the country to deprive workers of their right to picket. I found it quite strange that the government would ask judges to tell us to stop picketing when special back-to-work legislation had failed to do the job. Nevertheless, several hearings were held across the country. In both Halifax and Montréal, the courts refused to hear any arguments from our lawyers, and I immediately held a press conference and asked members in both cities to maintain their right to picket in the face of another unjust legal attack on them.

In the few days after Bill C-8 was adopted, management officials said they were unwilling to negotiate while we maintained what they called an illegal strike. But, on the weekend, we did meet with Labour Minister André Ouellet in an effort to reach a settlement. We provided a list of seven points that would serve as a basis for settlement of the strike.

On the political front, New Democratic Party Leader Ed Broadbent was enthusiastic about giving us his party's support. However, the CLC Executive decided not to support what they viewed as an illegal strike, and this caused Mr. Broadbent to reluctantly withhold his party's support of postal workers. CLC President Dennis McDermott said that CUPW was giving the labour movement a bad public image, something I strongly disagreed with. This lack of support from the CLC was upsetting to our members, and I believe that the CLC's decision not to support us came as a surprise to Mr. Broadbent.

On October 19, we met with the CLC Executive Committee and Ed Broadbent. Realizing that the members of the CLC Executive were not going to change their minds, we asked that they at least refrain from making public statements about the situation. We were told that, while they would not speak out in support of us, neither would they speak out publicly against postal workers. On October 20, McDermott sent this message to CLC offices across the country: "Suggest you refrain from commenting on rights of current postal strike until such time as the CLC has had an opportunity to clarify its position." Fortunately, members of many CLC-affiliated locals and unions across the country continued to support us, and many of them showed up on our picket lines.

On the morning of Wednesday, October 25, we met with John Monroe, a former Minister of Labour, and some others from that department. We were told we would soon receive copies of documents related to the seven proposals we had made on the weekend. Might these documents show that the government was willing to make some move to end the strike? No: fifteen minutes after we left that meeting, John Monroe contacted me and told me that no such documents would be forthcoming. I wasn't surprised: the Liberal government hadn't acted the way it had toward postal workers for the previous two years only to suddenly compromise with us.

When we returned from that meeting, we learned that the Royal Canadian Mounted Police were searching our offices. It became clear to us that, while we were meeting with the Department of Labour, a decision had been taken by the government to throw the whole weight of the judicial system at us.

Workers were now threatened with fines and jail sentences. Our members received letters from management telling them that, if they remained absent from their job for seven days following the adoption of Bill C-8 on October 19, then, under the terms of the Public Service Employment Act, they would be considered to have abandoned their jobs.

This threat was a real one. After denying postal workers their rights to negotiate, to strike, and to picket, the employer was now going to deny them their right to defend themselves by firing them for "abandonment of position" when it was clear that this was strike action, not abandonment. A worker has neither the right to grieve, nor the right to appeal a dismissal, for abandonment of position. Even if it might have been possible to appeal on the grounds that it wasn't an abandonment of position, but rather a case of discipline, I knew that, in the meantime, many of our members would go through a long period without a job, pending decisions on their cases. I also knew the employer would use this process as an opportunity to reinstate many postal workers, while denying the same treatment to those they saw as union leaders and activists.

October 25, 1978, was a day of decision. At this stage, the government had gone too far to relent at the last moment. With workers now threatened with dismissal for "abandonment of position," what had up to this point been a great show of unity within the union could turn suddenly into a real nightmare for our members. We had only a few hours in which to act, so we asked every local to call a meeting of its members before the end of the day, and to remain on strike until they received a recommendation to the contrary from the National Executive Board.

In view of the situation, I told our Executive Board that we had no choice but to inform our members that the strike was over. They all looked at me with pained expressions on their faces, but they knew, deep in their hearts, that I was right and that this was a very difficult position for me to take. It certainly was not an easy decision for me, nor was it an easy decision for any of the others on the National Executive, given the great strength that CUPW members were showing all across the country. But they agreed with me, and we hastily scheduled an early-evening press conference.

As had been the case a week before, the National Press Gallery was packed with reporters. I made a very clear statement, informing them all of our decision to call on our members to go back to work for their next shift. (This would prevent them from being deemed to have abandoned their positions.) I urged our members to go back with their heads held high and that nobody could take away from them the courage they had demonstrated. Negotiations, I added, were not over, and would not be over, until we signed a collective agreement that was then duly ratified by postal workers.

I later had the opportunity to speak to many local presidents who had also found it very hard to ask their members to return to work, but they too knew we had no other choice. Many of them told me that, never in their whole lives had they seen so many people with tears in their eyes on hearing we were going back to work. I myself saw men and women crying when they heard the news.

As hard it was, they all knew it was the right decision. They knew that this was not a sell-out, but a very tough decision for their leaders to make. They knew that staying out any longer would have had serious consequences. But they also knew that we had shown the Canadian public how a government can abuse its power by attacking its own employees.

And, most importantly, they knew we were not asking them to go back because we feared for the strength of their resolve.

I understood the members' sadness, but I knew that neither the National Executive Board nor myself had the right to bring these workers to the point of no return, to that point where many of them stood to lose their jobs. And, it was clear that staying out any longer would have destroyed CUPW, the only organization these workers had to defend their rights and protect them against dictatorial decisions by post office management. Now, postal workers needed their union more than ever. We had made our point loud and clear, and I knew that no management representative would dare laugh at these workers for coming back to work at this stage.

In fact, we recommended that our members go back together arm-in-arm, with heads held high. They did so, with many also chanting, "It's only a beginning! The struggle continues!" The message we sent to our members and to the employer was that this round of negotiations was not over: it would only end when we signed a negotiated collective agreement that was ratified by postal workers.

On Tuesday, October 24, 1978, the police officer in charge of the Commercial Crime Section of "A" Division in Ottawa obtained warrants that allowed police to search several CUPW premises, and this is what led us, on returning to our offices after a meeting on the following day, to find the police scouring our national offices. Of the warrants granted, one was for our national headquarters in Ottawa, one for our Western regional office in New Westminster B.C., two each for the Montréal and Halifax locals — both the office and the strike centre were to be searched in these two cities — and one for the Toronto office.

The raids took place at 2:00 pm on October 25, the same day we decided to ask our members to return to work. The search warrant presented to me allowed police to seize "notes, memoranda, minutes of meetings, telexes, telegrams, reports, releases, resolutions, or other records or copies thereof, relating to the decision of the union to continue the strike despite the coming into force of the Postal Service Continuation Act." All such items were taken, along with "lists of the union's officers and representatives, its constitution, strike declarations, authorizations or directions, or copies of them, pursuant to the offence under Section 115 of the Criminal Code.

Within two days of our return to work, charges were laid against all members of the National Executive Board, and we were all arrested. We pleaded not guilty and were sent to trial.

7 Judicial Process, Penal Experience

Of the four trials that took place as a result of our defiance of Bill C-8, mine was the only one that resulted in a jail sentence. In the spring of 1979, I was sentenced to three months in jail, with eighteen months probation. (More on my trial and time in prison later.) Brothers Clément Morel, National Director for the Québec region, and Darrell Tingley, National Director for the Atlantic region, both pleaded "not guilty" and were given suspended sentences. Brother Frank Walden, National Director for the Western region, also pleaded "not guilty," and was found to be so on the basis that he was in Ottawa, not British Columbia, when the offence he was accused of occurred, and so British Columbia's Supreme Court had no jurisdiction to hear this case.

The charges against the officers were not made under Bill C-8 or the Public Service Staff Relations Act, but under the Criminal Code, which is very rarely invoked during a labour dispute.

Charges against Leroy Hiltz, National Secretary-Treasurer, were dropped. The other members of the National Executive Board, Brothers André Beauchamp, First National Vice-President, David Jones, Second National Vice-President, National Chief Steward Sid Baxter, and William Dalgleish, National Director for the Ontario region, all eventually pleaded "guilty" and received suspended sentences. I know that some of our members were upset at them, but I was not. These officers had stood shoulder to shoulder with other officers and members when we took the decision to defy the law. Their pleas saved us time, energy, and money. I didn't see how "not guilty" pleas would have added anything to our cause at that stage.

During the negotiations between the Crown and these four officers, it was agreed that charges against CUPW itself would be dropped in exchange for their guilty pleas. This was important, in view of the time, effort, and money our defence would have taken and because of the possibility of a heavy fine if we had been found guilty.

An Abuse of Judicial Power

After my arrest and my appearance before a judge in late October of 1978, I was released on bail until my trial, which began on April 2, 1979. However, the conditions of my bail presented me with a dilemma: along with the usual conditions of bail for someone charged under the Criminal Code, such "keeping the peace," the judge demanded that I tell our members again that the strike was over, using the same methods I had used to tell them to stay on strike. I had, in fact, already done so, and everyone knew that postal workers were all back at work. Perhaps the judge simply meant to humiliate me, but I thought it was an abuse of power on his part and that he had already decided I was guilty, in spite of the principle of "innocent until proven guilty."

Postal workers had just returned to their jobs, and, although circumstances had changed, the struggle was still as important as ever. We needed to maintain our solidarity and at the same time send a clear message to government and the employer that, as far as we were concerned, negotiations were not over. (In fact, we also had to send that message to the CLC.) But first, I had to make this very difficult decision about whether or not to accept my bail conditions.

Although I was inclined to refuse to sign the terms of my bail, after further consultations with some other members of the National Executive Board and my lawyer, I decided to do so. The coming weeks were going to be very difficult for CUPW members, and I was told I needed to be on the job. So, I told myself that we had already made our point and that I wouldn't add anything to our cause by not signing the bail conditions. We needed to develop a program of action to deal with the impending mediation-arbitration process, and I wanted to take part in that process, so I signed the paper outlining the conditions of my bail and was then released, pending trial.

Late that very night, in order to meet the terms of my release on bail, I held a press conference, in which I had to make a very silly statement urging workers who had already returned to work to go back to work. I hoped that the late hour would discourage many from attending, and I was pleased that, other than CBC or Radio-Canada (I forget which), there were no other television journalists present. I made my statement briefly and, on being asked further questions, responded only that I could add no further comments.

The next day, we began to put in place our plan of action. Our objective was to acquire all possible support for the next round of negotiations. Our basis was the conviction that, no matter what might be imposed on us through arbitration, this round of negotiations would not end until we had signed a negotiated collective agreement and our members had approved it.

As we expected, the government appointed as mediator-arbitrator someone who wasn't going to be friendly to our side. Judge Lucien Tremblay had no experience in the field of labour relations. A rumour even circulated that someone in government had contacted the wrong Mr. Tremblay and, because he accepted immediately, it was then too late to correct the mistake.

Despite his appointment, we did our homework and were ready to undertake as much damage control as possible during mediation. On its first day, November 7, 1978, Treasury Board officials refused to discuss the issues and displayed such an arrogant and high-handed attitude that Judge Tremblay was forced to agree to our request for separate meetings.

During the week preceding this meeting, thousands of our members received letters from the employer telling them that their actions during the strike were being investigated, despite the fact that the Attorney General had already stated publicly that he had no plans to indict individual CUPW members.

The mediation hearings didn't last long, and early in the New Year we moved to the arbitration phase. These lasted several weeks, during which we submitted more than 150 exhibits to Judge Tremblay to bolster our arguments. This was part of our damage-control strategy, as we knew that, being a judge, he would make his decisions on the basis of the evidence before him. We wanted to make sure he was made clearly aware of the impact of any decisions he would render. At the end of this process, both sides summed up their arguments, and Judge Tremblay then retired to write the report that would outline the terms of a new collective agreement.

This report was issued on March 31, 1979. On a reading of it, it seemed to me that some of our arguments had held some weight for Judge Tremblay, because he didn't give the employer everything it wanted in the new agreement. However, he did take away many of the rights and benefits we had acquired for our members through past negotiations. Judge Tremblay allowed wording in the collective agreement that permitted the employer to implement both individual work measurement and electronic surveillance of postal workers. On wages, he decided on a package that was less than what the employer had accepted in Louis Courtemanche's Conciliation Report the previous October. He also ruled that wage increases would be expressed in percentage terms, rather than in the absolute figures we had successfully bargained for in the past, and this meant that wage gaps among the various classifications would increase. This would eventually eliminate the adjustment we had won for mail handlers at the end of the 1975 strike. On retroactive pay, he decided in favour of a lump-sum payment rather than by calculating actual hours worked, which would have brought more to most workers. He decided that the final payment of our cost-of-living allowance would be paid on December 31, 1979, rather than continuing until the signing of a new collective agreement, as had been the case with the 1975 agreement. And, he changed, to the employer's advantage, the way of calculating severance pay in cases where a full-time employee had also worked part-time for a period of time. Along with all these rollbacks, the employer's position was also imposed on us on many other issues. Judge Tremblay simply ignored most of our arguments.

When we read Judge Tremblay's arguments for his decisions, we realized that on the issue of wages he felt constrained on what he could offer by the terms of the Trudeau government's Anti-Inflation Act. We appealed his decision before the Federal Court of Appeal, which, on Tuesday, December 18, 1979, declared Judge Tremblay's decision null and void and sent it back to him for review on the basis of the court's decision. On April 1, 1980, he rendered a new decision that provided for an additional increase that made the wage package similar to the position the employer had agreed to in the Conciliation Board.

This imposed, thirty-month collective agreement didn't affect our determination or the implementation of our plan of action. The agreement was retroactive to June of 1977, so we were only few months away from a new round of negotiations. We were determined to negotiate hard to reach an agreement we could put to a vote of our members.

One of my successors as CUPW President, Brother Dale Clark, once recalled to me that he was hired not long after the 1978 strike. "It was incredible," he said, "the strength of the union in the post office in Winnipeg. There was such a sense of strength that I very soon knew that I wanted to get involved with the union."

Trial, Verdict, and Sentence

My trial began on April 2, 1979, and I was charged that morning at 11:20 am as follows:

> Jean-Claude Parrot stands charged: that he, being an officer or representative of the Canadian Union of Postal Workers, the employee organization described in the Postal Services Continuation Act, on and after the 19th day of October, 1978, at the City of Ottawa and elsewhere in Canada, without lawful excuse contravened subsection 3(1) of the said Act by wilfully omitting to do a thing required to be done by the said Act, in that he did fail forthwith on the coming into force of the said Act on the 19th day of October, 1978, to give notice to the employees described in the said Act that any declaration, authorization or direction to go on strike, declared, authorized or given to them before the coming into force of the said Act, had become invalid by reason of the coming into force of the said Act, thereby committing an indictable offence contrary to subsection 115 (1) of the Criminal Code of Canada.

In other words, I was charged with not having ended the strike since I had not told postal workers "forthwith," or immediately, that the legal strike had become invalid.

After a trial of several days, on April 10, the Honourable Mr. Justice

From left to right: Daughter Manon, wife Louisette, Jean-Claude Parrot, and daughter Johanne entering court on May 8, 1978.

Evans, asked, "Members of the jury, have you agreed upon your verdict? Do you find the prisoner at the bar guilty or not guilty of the charge?" He received this reply: "My Lord, we, the jury, find the accused guilty."

Ironically, this was precisely two years to the day since we began negotiations.

My sentence was to be rendered on May 10. At 2:30 pm that afternoon, Justice Evans spoke to me: "Jean-Claude Parrot, stand up. Do you wish to say anything before the sentence of the court is passed upon you?" I replied:

> Not really, my lord. I think you are well aware of this problem, and there is not too much — well there's maybe one point, if you don't mind, I might add. There was a lot said this morning about those 23,000,000 Canadians that I didn't seem to be caring about. I would just like to say in what happened last year, our union has asked, on behalf of the 23,000 postal workers, that there be a Royal Commission of Inquiry into the situation in the post office, and I hope, not only for you and me, but for the 23,000,000 Canadians, which includes the 23,000 postal workers, that this inquiry will take place. That's all, sir.

I had not prepared a statement, but I reacted to something that had been said in court that morning — that postal workers didn't care about the public. I think my lawyer was afraid of what I was going to say, because it could have had an influence as to the sentence the judge decided on. After a long preamble, Justice Evans then rendered the following sentence:

> Will you please stand, Mr. Parrot? A jury of your peers has found you guilty. On the evidence before them I do not believe they could have arrived at any other verdict. They did their duty and I now must discharge my responsibility. In my view the imposition of a fine in your case would not satisfy, would not meet the seriousness, with which this offence must be regarded.
>
> It would make a sham and a mockery of justice, and it would appear to almost condone illegality and render ineffective the element of deterrence. There are many Canadian cases involving contempt of court in which substantial jail terms have been imposed. I do not consider a challenge to Parliament less important.
>
> However it is not my intention to punish you as an example to others by imposing a severe sentence. In passing sentence, a judge does not give a personal judgment but a judicial judgment. He is governed by those principles which courts have declared applicable in the determination of the appropriate sentences for particular offences.
>
> One cannot help but feel a certain sadness for you and for your family because I consider you to be an honest and dedicated man whose loss of objectivity has warped his judgment and launched him on an ego-satisfying, but disruptive, course of action, which one labour leader is quoted as having described as one "that would take us down the road of anarchy, leave the labour movement in total disrepute and possible destruction." I agree with those comments.
>
> Rationalization is an exercise in which many misdirected zealots engage. There is no evidence to indicate that you feel any remorse for your action. You have convinced yourself that in defying the law you were motivated by an honest belief in the righteousness of your cause. I do not anticipate that any sentence that I impose will convince you that you acted unlawfully. I can only suggest that you might reflect on the possibility that you, like the rest of us, may err, particularly when frustration arouses anger. Hopefully you will come to recognize that a biased individual opinion is no substitute for the objectivity of the law.
>
> You have in effect set yourself up above the law and have used your position to influence others to ignore the law. Such action involves a highly dangerous philosophy, which our society views with condemnation.
>
> I sentence you to be imprisoned for a term of three months,

and in addition you will be placed on probation for a period of eighteen months on the usual statutory conditions. The person having custody of you shall, prior to your release, comply with the provisions of s.663 (4) of the Criminal Code of Canada. You may sit down.

The labour leader the judge had quoted was CLC President Dennis McDermott. A few minutes after the passing of my sentence, I was taken in a police car to the Ottawa Carleton Regional Detention Centre. We left the courthouse through a secondary entrance in order to avoid numerous workers who had gathered at the front door in support of my cause.

Prison

During the drive in the police car, I thought to myself how fast things were happening. I was then put in a cell in a waiting area. At one point, they brought me some food, but I didn't eat much of it.

Indeed, food would be an ongoing problem for me during my time in prison. I had a history of odd eating habits. Until the age of twenty-six, three years after I got married, I never ate meat, fish, pasta, eggs, cheese, or many other foods. I ate little other than white and brown bread (sometimes toasted), peanut butter, potatoes — especially french fries — potato chips, fruit, and various sweet desserts. The only vegetable I'd eat was raw carrots. During my early years in the post office, my favourite meal was six slices of toast with french fries. When I switched to day shifts, lunch would often be a bag of potato chips and a Pepsi. If I brought a lunch to work, it would be something like eight buttered crackers, four slices of buttered white bread, a piece of cake, and a small milk. Years before, when I was still in school, I remember one of my teachers offering a week free of homework if I would only eat some meat. I never met this challenge.

By the time I was twenty-six, my first daughter was two, and my wife Louisette was finding it difficult to prepare meals for the family because of my very limited diet. Louisette and I had a conversation about my eating habits, and she noted that I wasn't providing a good example to my daughter. So, I made special efforts to change my eating habits, but it was not working very well: every time I ate meat I was unable to keep my food down.

So I went to the doctor, and he told me about a new medication that he said would help me. It was delivered by injection, and I had six shots of the medication in the course of just a few weeks. I thought at the time that I might be being used as a guinea pig, as this medication was pretty new on the market. It increased my appetite, but I found I was just eating more of the same old things I was comfortable with, and I had little stomach for anything else. In order to make the medication more effective, I stopped smoking. Within six months I went from 115 to 140 pounds, and I was still not eating properly.

One day before I reached the age of twenty-seven, I went to a park at lunchtime, sat down, and thought to myself, "Jean-Claude, it's obvious that your problem is in your head and in the way you try new foods." From that day on, I began to really try new things and slowly I began to eat them. As the years went by, I added things to my menu. I learned that part of my problem was a difficulty I had in swallowing, so I would chew my food far more than was necessary, and I had trouble with some of the tastes that were new to me. But I worked at it, and my eating habits improved somewhat, though I was still a fussy eater.

So, here I was in jail at the age of forty-two, still fussy about food. This caused me problems while in prison, but I became very popular with other inmates who where happy to get a second helping at mealtime. And, by eating bread, fruits, and other things I had by now taught myself to eat, I managed to get through my sentence without losing weight.

After this short meal on my first night in jail, I was asked if I wanted to have a cell to myself. "I haven't asked to be here and I don't want to be treated differently than others," I said. "Fine," came the response, "we prefer it this way." I was taken to another area and asked to remove my clothes and shower. I was then given what would become my prison clothes: underwear, jogging pants, tee-shirt, socks, and felt shoes. I was then taken to a large dormitory cell with nineteen beds, but there were no other inmates there. I saw other dormitory cells housing many inmates but, for whatever reason, I was alone in this one.

I fell asleep quite early that night. The next day, a photograph of me asleep in my cell appeared in the newspaper. It seems a newspaper photographer had been allowed in to take my picture. Perhaps this was why I was put in the cell alone that night. Nobody had told me that any such a thing had been arranged before I went to sleep.

I didn't give this incident much thought at the time, but when I though about it later, I wondered who had the power to arrange something like this. I never again saw that cell I had slept in that night empty, and I never saw anyone inside the detention centre who wasn't either an inmate or someone employed in its operation. I certainly never saw a newspaper photographer during my time in prison. I guess I'll never know now whether someone at a low level was paid to arrange this, or whether someone in high authority might have had some other motive.

I was released the next day, pending my appeal to the Ontario Superior Court, but I returned to the Ottawa Carleton Regional Detention Centre in mid-October of 1979, when my appeal was heard before that body. I was put in the same cell I had occupied that first night, but this time there were other inmates there. The following day I was transferred to another dormitory cell for inmates who worked in the laundry, where I put clothes and linens in the washing and drying machines and separated them afterwards. The following day I was released again, pending my appeal before the Supreme Court of Canada.

That appeal hearing took place in mid-December, and the judge reserved his judgement for later, which prompted some in the media to say that I had received a nice Christmas gift, which was true: I spent the Christmas season with my family.

On January 29, 1980, the Supreme Court denied my appeal and told me to present myself to the detention centre that afternoon to serve my full sentence. They didn't direct the Royal Canadian Mounted Police to escort me to jail immediately, but agreed to my lawyer's request that I be given a few hours to prepare for my incarceration. So I reported to the Ottawa Carleton Regional Detention Centre under my own steam, accompanied by Louisette, our two daughters, and a number of union activists. But, before doing so, I issued the following statement to CUPW members:

> One thing is sure, putting me in jail won't change my attitude towards our struggle to have our right to negotiate recognized. I'm asking the membership not to overreact to this decision of the Supreme Court, but to keep our energies for the real struggle that is coming, the struggle for our legal right to negotiate, the struggle for which I'm in jail. You don't have to walk out on the street to prove to me, to the union, or to yourselves that you are there, united and determined. What you've done in the past speaks for you.

I was put in the same cell as the two previous times I had come. I knew by now that this cell was only for new inmates on their first night in prison, while they waited to be assigned to a particular task, which then determined the cell they would be assigned to for the longer term.

On facing this cell from the corridor, there was a long row of beds along the two walls on each side — eight on the left side and eleven on the right. Before the rows of beds, on the left-hand corner were a small table and four chairs, some games, cards, a radio, and a small television on the wall. On the right were two toilets and two showers with partial doors that provided a minimum of privacy. The front of the cell, including the door, was made of steel bars. There were some windows high up on the left-side wall; though they were too high to allow inmates to look out them, they at least provided some natural daylight.

That night, the cell was pretty full, and most of the other inmates were young men. It was pretty quiet, but the television was showing the latest news. Suddenly, one of the young guys, who was on a bed on the other side of the cell facing the television, looked at me and said, "That's you on television!" I turned around to look and saw footage taken earlier that day of myself being shown arriving at the detention centre with my family and a group of supporters.

"Yes," I said, "that's me coming here today." This inmate then got up, shook my hand, and said, "It's very nice to meet you." He then went around the cell and told everyone that I had just been on television, and many of the inmates then came over to talk to me. Eventually, some began to ask me about their rights, and I had to explain that, in here, there were really no rights other than the right to have visitors. Everything else was a privilege granted or denied, such as the possibility of getting out on weekends or evenings. When asked about rights to appeal convictions or other legal matters, I could only say that such issues needed to be addressed by their lawyers.

On my second day in prison, I was assigned to what they called the "outside gang," which was given such tasks as snow-shovelling, feeding small animals at a prison farm attached to the facility, and washing the entrance, both outside and inside the facility, where visitors came in. I moved to a cell similar to the one I had occupied the night before, and I remained there for the duration of my time in this facility. After a couple of weeks, I was relieved of almost any task for about a month. I think this relief was prompted by a couple of things that set me apart from most of the other inmates. Firstly, I received far more mail than any of the other inmates, and I was allowed to spend my days replying to it. Secondly, I received visits almost every other day from my lawyer, who also worked with CUPW's Negotiating Committee. He was often accompanied by one or two of the union's national officers.

I soon noticed that, after prisoners had been in the facility for several weeks, the daily chores were curtailed for most of them. I concluded that there were more inmates than there was routine work to be done, and so the inmates who had been in for a longer time were given more free time. (Those whose sentences were longer than three months stayed at this facility only for a day or two before being shipped elsewhere to serve the balance of their terms.)

This free time gave me a chance to visit the prison library for reading materials and to look at other union material relating to ongoing negotiations, some of which needed my signature. About once a week, we had an opportunity to go to a games room, where we played ping-pong and engaged in similar pastimes. I enjoyed ping-pong, and in one tournament I survived to the semi-final. But, most of my free time in jail was spent responding to letters I received.

While in jail, I received more than a thousand pieces of correspondence. It was quite an inspiration to see the kind of support I got from so many people, most of them postal workers. I received more than a hundred letters, several hundred cards, magazines, books, and other forms of correspondence.

I tried to reply to every one, but it wasn't easy. I had only a limited time in which to make my replies, mail piled up every day, and I had to use paper and pencil (no pens allowed) provided by the institution. I think I did pretty well in replying to most of them.

The letters and other materials I received from individual postal workers, or groups of workers, were particularly encouraging. Some of the cards I received were huge, signed by all the workers at a plant. I enjoyed writing directly to CUPW members at home and, in some cases, at work. I later heard that, on some shifts, the fact that I had answered a particular piece of correspondence was the subject of discussion among workers. Some wrote again to thank me for replying, or simply to provide me with further thoughts or information. Many people used cards CUPW had produced to raise awareness about the history of postal workers to send me messages of support.

But not all the letters were from CUPW workers. Many came from trade unions across the country and from workers around the world. The Postal, Telephone, and Telegraph International, to which CUPW was affiliated, provided its affiliates with a history of our struggle, along with my address in jail, and I received many messages of support in this way. I also had many other letters from Canadian activists both within and outside the labour movement. Finally, some of the letters were from members of the public who wanted to express their gratitude and support. One letter came from an elderly man in British Columbia who wrote about how proud he was to see that there were still leaders today who were willing to stand up for their rights. I was in prison on Valentine's Day, and I may have received more Valentine's Day cards than anyone else in the country. They contained words of encouragement, jokes, and messages of support.

I will always remember one letter from Julia Vanessa Spencley, a ten-year-old girl from London, Ontario, who I had met while at an event there. She wrote:

> I do not hope that you're having and will have a terrible time in your lovely cell. On December 14 I turned ten. At Christmas I got everything that I needed or wanted. Right now my school is being renovated and we are being bussed out to Stinson. Yesterday and today my class got a substitute teacher by the name of Mrs. Button, and I hate her guts. Well I've gotta go now.

Julia also wrote me a second letter in which she said she was sad because her parents were divorcing, but that she was still going to be my friend. I replied to her letters, but we never did have the opportunity to meet one another after my release from prison. I hope things went well for her in school and that she's now happy in her adult life.

Another letter came from United Church Minister Reverend Bruce Wallace, who wrote:

Recently I saw your address in one of the current left periodicals. So I thought I would drop a note of cheer and let you know that you are not forgotten. I respect your stand tremendously. As a clergyman, I try to keep alive the vision of social justice that I remember from university in the late 1960s. An example of courage such as yours helps to shape my concept of ministry.

You stood by your workers and didn't let them down. You could have held out but risk destroying the union — or you could have given up without a fight. But you did neither. Your course of action was entirely appropriate, and has the dignity of the late Dr. Martin Luther King in my estimation.

I look forward to your release. Keep up your spirits, for you are remembered among the population.

This letter from Lois Hutchinson touched me:

I am the wife and mother of postal workers, and I wanted to write to you at this time. I personally do not think you should be in jail — it is truly a miscarriage of justice! I do appreciate the steps you took in the fall of 1978, and I remember back to the days of the [Canadian Postal Employees] Association. This letter doesn't make much sense, but I wanted you and your wife to know that others care about you and your present situation.

I received a number of letters from fellow trade unionists who had been in jail before me. Some had spent only a few hours in jail, some a few days, and some longer periods. Among these correspondents were Louis Laberge, President of the FTQ, Sean O'Flynn, President of the Ontario Public Service Employees' Union, Jess Succamore, Secretary-Treasurer of the Canadian Association of Industrial, Mechanical, and Allied Workers, and Bill Walsh, a long-time union activist. Every one of their letters has a special place in my heart. I think that this, from the late Louis Laberge, written on February 14, 1980, expresses the feelings of all of them:

These are just a few words from an ex-detainee to a current resident of the Ottawa Carleton Regional Detention Centre.

Know that I greatly sympathize with your current situation, and I apologize for not writing to you sooner.

Thousands of people who abuse the system, and crooks of all kinds, not to mention the police who illegally steal, set fires, and blow up buildings, are still running free, while you, who only carried out your duty with honesty, have been put away.

I am confident that this temporary detention will have no impact whatsoever on your determination to continue representing your

A newspaper cartoon that appeared on February 4, 1980. The three caricatures are, left to right, of Marcel Pépin, Louis Laberge, and Yvon Charbonneau, leaders of the Québec labour movement who were jailed in the 1970s for defying provincial legislation. Jean-Claude Parrot is saying, "It really feels good… to finally be admitted to the trade union movement's hall of fame."

members and workers in general as best you can.

At least we have the consolation of knowing that our cause is just and that together, we will continue the struggle.

In the process of writing this book, I received a copy of a letter I sent from prison to a young woman, Diane Castonguay, a CUPW member who had written me while I was in jail. During the strike, she had made the front page of the *Montreal Gazette* with an article in which she explained why she had taken her nine-month-old daughter with her to the picket line, in defiance of the law, and why she was ready to go to jail. Here's my own translation of what she wrote to me on February 7, 1980.

How are you? Are you getting used to the atmosphere of a world without sun? It must remind you of the good old days at 715 Peel Street. This is just another small letter to say hello. You probably don't miss the office: I understand you had much work to do there. I too would like to get a few months vacation paid for by Her Majesty.

Outside your jail, and inside ours, it's always the same. Each day we have to face a working atmosphere where the word "humanity" doesn't exist. If your guards get a little bit crazy sometimes, remember that they cannot be as bad as the supervisors in the post office.

I have some trade union documentation. If interested, let me know and I will send it to you. It deals... with pension funds, shift work, piecework, health and safety issues, grievances, and other matters. These are well done and easy-to-read documents. I also have a book entitled *The Damage of Progress* that might interest you. This is only if you have time to spare. I will write you again soon.

On February 22, I replied to her with this:

I received your letter dated February 7, 1980. It is very nice of you to take the time to write me. Since I've been here, the nicest moment of each day comes around 4:30 pm, when I receive my mail. It's heart-warming to read comments from members of our union.

Thank you for your offer to send me certain documents.... However, I don't think I will have the time to read them during my stay here....

In a few minutes I am going to attend a meeting to finalize preparations and the approach we will take during conciliation. The meeting will take place here at the detention centre. We met all day yesterday, and will continue today.

My morale is still very good and I do not intend to give up. Quite the contrary, in fact.

In view of the large number of letters I received, I tried to be brief in my replies. Perhaps I sometimes didn't manage to write the best letters in the world, and I'm sure that sometimes there was little continuity from one paragraph to the next, but I really enjoyed writing back to all these people. I would have liked to keep copies of some of my replies, but this wasn't possible under the circumstances.

All the letters I received were special to me, but the ones I received from family members were perhaps most special of all. In addition to their regular visits, sending me written assurances of support was another way for Louisette, my two daughters, Manon and Johanne, and my father-in-law to show their love. I had not been home a lot in the months prior to serving my prison term, and that made their letters all the more touching to me.

I also greatly appreciated the letters of support I received from my mother, who passed away at the age of ninety-one while I was writing this book, from my two sisters, and from my brother, all from the Montréal area.

When I was deciding whether or not to accept my bail conditions after charges were first laid against me, my father-in-law, who lived with us, gave me a letter in which he wrote that I shouldn't think about the family when making my decision and that they were all fully with me in whatever decision I might make. I was very touched by this letter.

All the mail I received while in prison was opened before it came to me, and the stamps, as well as the gummed flaps used to seal the envelopes, were removed. This was because the glue might have been used as a means of getting drugs into the prison. Brother Michael Duquette was a local officer of the Scarborough local, who was always constant in his devotion to our struggle for justice and dignity. He was also a talented artist, and he sent me some of his work while I was in prison. This artwork would normally have been considered unacceptable for the same reason stamps and envelope flaps were and would have been destroyed by prison authorities. Instead, they very thoughtfully offered to keep it for me until my release. I was grateful, because it was a real piece of art. (As of this writing, Michael's artwork can be found on the internet at <http://www.civilization.ca/cpm/chrono/chs1951e.html#1977>. Then click on 1977, click my name, scroll down to the third image, and click the red button to enlarge it.) They were also kind enough to keep some other pieces of mail until my departure, including large cards of support from the Edmonton and Calgary locals signed by postal workers.

On opening my mail one day, I smiled when I saw that a postal worker had sent me some magazines, among them a copy of *Playboy*, along with a letter saying he would send me any other magazine I wished to read. I wrote back thanking him, but didn't ask for any more magazines. I also received a number of books from activists in the labour and social movements.

I was an unusual inmate in the amount of contact I had with the outside world. I noticed that some inmates never received a single letter, and many others received mail rarely. But I was asked almost every day, "How many letters today, Jean-Claude?"

All the correspondence I received while in jail is now in the hands of the Canadian Postal Museum, part of the Canadian Museum of Civilization in Ottawa. All these letters are available for anyone who wishes to read them.

My correspondence in prison was fun, but not everything there was. Perhaps my worst prison experiences were those occasional searches for drugs that staff made of all prisoners. There was, of course, never any notice of these searches. Two guards would come into a cell and ask all prisoners to strip naked. We were then asked to stand about a foot away from the wall, spread our legs, and put our hands against the wall. They then checked every orifice of every inmate. Next they would search each inmate's clothes and, returning them, ask us to move to another cell to put them back on. Finally, they would search every bed and table, as well as the rest of the cell. Only when they had finished their search were we able to return to our own cells. In the two months I was there, this happened three or four times.

One day, when I had been there for less than two weeks, the person in charge told me I was entitled to apply for a weekend pass. It was a common thing to see an inmate returning from his weekend leave on a Sunday night. So, because I was entitled to it, I applied. A few days later, I was called to the office of the committee that decided on such matters.

"Mr. Parrot," I was told, "we would like to grant your request for a weekend pass, but it is a bit too early, especially given that your case was very public. But you can apply again two weeks from now." I asked: "Will that request be granted?" I was told that it would not be decided until the time came. "Well," I said, "I'm not going to apply again. I'll just do my time."

They tried to convince me to apply again but I wouldn't, for two reasons. First, I didn't like the fact that they had asked me to apply, yet they had then turned me down. It was just another way in which they seemed to make inmates beg for any privilege that might be granted. Second, on thinking it over, I realized I had made a mistake in applying for the pass in the first place. At this time, I was a very public figure, and, if I had been granted the pass, people would see me on the streets and perhaps conclude that I hadn't even served my sentence. I imagined the sort of editorials that might appear in the right-wing media if they got wind of the fact that I was walking the streets of Ottawa. We might have lost the sympathy and understanding of some of our supporters across the country.

Most inmates were allowed two visits per week from family or friends. As well, inmates might, or might not, be granted the privilege of a third weekly visit. Making a phone call was also a privilege that could be granted or denied. I never had a problem getting that extra weekly visit, and this was great, because I was able to see my wife and family on a regular basis.

When it came to phone calls, our only right was to speak to our lawyers, and even then it was at the discretion of the person in charge. Any other calls had to be explicitly approved.

One day, I wanted to speak to Louisette, so I went to the office of the person in charge and asked for permission to make the call. Before giving any answer, he reminded me, in more ways than one, that I had no right to make such a call. He finally granted me the privilege, and told me to use the phone in the office. He was still behind his desk as I dialled the number.

At just that moment, someone else came into the office, and the person in charge began to explain to the newcomer that he had granted me the great privilege of calling my wife. He did this in a very paternalistic manner that I thought very inappropriate, and I got angry. I banged down the receiver, told him I was not a child, suggested where I thought he should "put" his privilege, and left the office.

He tried to stop me, but I was already walking down the corridor, passing other cells as I made my way to my own. There, I waited for a guard to come unlock the door so I could get inside. Seeing that I wasn't going to come back to his office, the person in charge returned to his desk because, I think, he didn't want others to see that someone was standing up to his bullying, paternalistic manner.

Several days after this incident, I had to wash some floors, including this man's office. He sat at his desk looking at me, and it seemed to me that he was enjoying the spectacle, though we never exchanged a word. I suspect he was responsible for me being assigned this chore, perhaps in an effort to embarrass me or make me feel stupid, but, I'm not sure it was me who looked stupid as a result of this incident.

On another occasion, another inmate and I were asked to take the garbage out. When we went to the garbage room, I saw that there was food and other slop on the floor and, to say the least, the smell of the place was hardly delightful. The other inmate immediately began to pick up some of the slop off the floor, but I said to the guard, "I'm not going to do this work without a pair of gloves." He said that they didn't have gloves for this sort of work and that it was my turn to do this chore today. I told him that, although I wasn't refusing to do the work, I was insisting on gloves for health reasons.

The guard left, but came back a few minutes later with a pair of gloves. There were some holes in them, but I felt I could use them to pick up the garbage. As I was about to do so, the other inmate told me not to bother, that he would do it all. He insisted, and he even got in my way so I couldn't pick any of the garbage off the floor. I realized then that he had been pleased with the stand I had taken and that this was his way to show his respect for me. Nevertheless, I managed to make him realize that my objection was not against the idea of doing this kind of work at all, but rather was based on the principle that we shouldn't have do the work in a way that risked our health. The guard was silent, but I had a feeling he knew I was right.

One tragic incident occurred while I was serving my sentence. A young inmate — I think he was seventeen years old — had managed to get his hands on a bottle of white-out, the fluid used to make corrections on a typewriter. In bed at night, he and a friend sniffed this stuff under their bedclothes. Suddenly, this young fellow stood up, with a look on his face that gave the impression he was somewhere very far away. His friend asked him what the matter was, but no answer was forthcoming. He then fell on the floor unconscious, and in a few minutes it was confirmed he was dead. The other inmate was brought to the prison's small medical clinic where, I think, he had his stomach pumped. (This didn't happen in my cell, so I heard of this only the next day.) For several days after this incident, security was reinforced, and we were not allowed to leave our cells to go to the games room or for a walk in the yard outside.

As I mentioned before, the cells each had two showers and two toilets. I joked that the doors of these facilities had been designed to hide only the most intimate parts of one's anatomy. In fact, if an inmate were particularly tall or short, the doors failed even in this limited purpose. I may be exaggerating a bit here, but it gives an idea of how small these doors were. However, I never saw or heard of any incidents in the showers and toilets while I was there. On the contrary, there was a clear rule of discretion observed by the inmates when it came to the use of the showers and toilets.

Another inconvenience was that we had only one razor for the whole cell. It would appear near the door of the cell very early in the morning, and, being an early-morning person, I was usually the first to use it. I knew if I weren't among the first to use the razor, the quality of my shave would suffer.

Once a week, a canteen truck came to the detention centre and we had the opportunity to buy magazines and snacks. I usually bought a couple of bags of potato chips and some chocolate bars, because on some days I didn't eat very much of the prison food. I kept these treats in the drawer of my bed-table, and I never had anything stolen.

I had good relationships with other inmates, but I never imposed myself on them or asked why they were there. I knew they were in for many different reasons: for unpaid fines or parking tickets, for being drunk and disorderly, for using or selling drugs, for break-and-enters, for theft, and for many other offences. And some were there waiting for trials, or for transfers elsewhere.

There was one particular inmate who was already there when I arrived. Soon after, he was released, came back again, was re-released, and then came back yet again before I was released. He drank a lot and lived on the streets, and the police would pick him up regularly. I think it was beneficial for him to be there, because this was in the winter.

Once, I was walking back and forth in the cell with another inmate, something many of us did quite a lot, both for the exercise and just to pass the time. At one end of the cell, my companion would stop and do some push-ups before resuming his walk. So, I began to stop and do push-ups with him. I remember that this fellow loved to tease me about being in jail: "This is what happens to criminals like you," he would say, laughing.

Another inmate talked to me about some of his problems and asked me to help him write a letter. Sometimes I played cards with some of the inmates. Most of them knew why I was there, but, though I was able to take a pretty good guess sometimes, I had no direct knowledge of why they were there. In all my time in prison, I never had a problem with even a single inmate.

The guards were very decent and I had great respect for the work they do. Their jobs are not easy.

During the period I was in jail, CUPW was involved in important negotiations with the employer, and I was regularly permitted to review documents in my cell. I was once allowed to meet for a day and a half with my Negotiating Committee in a room near the prison entrance. Committee members ordered out for lunch, and so I had meal from a St. Hubert restaurant that I very greatly appreciated.

I think my time in prison might have been harder for my family than it was for me. I saw visitors through a window, which meant it was impossible to have even a short hug with my wife Louisette, or with my daughters, Manon, who was nineteen at the time, and sixteen-year-old Johanne. Because I was allowed only a limited number of visits, I sent word to my friends not to visit me so I could have more visits with my family.

It was hard for Louisette to know that my lawyer and some union officers were sometimes able to meet in the same room with me, but that she only ever saw me through a glass window. (Visits between inmates and their lawyers were private, and were in a room set aside for that purpose.) She told me later on that the toughest part of her visits was while sitting in the waiting room. One time, she saw two women who had come to see the same inmate fighting in the waiting room: one was his wife and the other his girlfriend. When she would be called from the waiting room, she would always sit on a chair in front of the window where I would appear. After a while, she got to know when I was coming by counting the number of doors she heard opening and closing.

Louisette gave me amazing support, and she never argued that I shouldn't have done what I had. On the contrary, I think she was proud I did what she knew needed to be done. For my two daughters, I think the visits to see me must have been hard: it must have been difficult for them to know their father was in such a place. But I knew that my family understood my situation and my commitment to obtain justice and dignity for workers in general, and for postal workers in particular. So I can only thank them from the bottom of my heart for having been there for me, for their unwavering support. After forty-five years of marriage, two daughters, and now two granddaughters, I confess that I am one very lucky man to have these five women in my life.

During my last two weeks in jail, I was given more chores to do than I had been given during most of the previous weeks. I think the authorities didn't want me to say that I hadn't been given my fair share of chores to do while in prison. When I left the Ottawa Carleton Regional Detention Centre for the last time, I had spent slightly less than two months there since last entering it. (The days I had spent the two previous times I'd been there were counted as part of my overall sentence.) Unless they lose the privilege through the attitude they display while in custody, prisoners are routinely released when they have served two-thirds of their sentences. And, so it was in my case.

8 1978–1983
Years of Struggle, Years of Change

Arrested in October of 1978, I was convicted on April 10, 1979, and that night was my first at the Ottawa Carleton Regional Detention Centre. Following my unsuccessful appeals to the Ontario Supreme Court and then the Supreme Court of Canada, I completed my two months in prison in March of 1980. Meanwhile, CUPW was very active in defence of postal workers across the country.

Program of Action Following the 1978 Return to Work

After the strike ended, we established a program of action designed to ensure that our members, the trade union movement, social organizations, politicians, the media, the public, and the government would all know how determined we were to obtain justice in the next round of negotiations, which were due to begin in the fall of 1979.

We immediately put in place a system that assured every grievance filed by our members would have as a preamble, "I grieve against a violation by [management] of the collective agreement imposed by the Trudeau Liberal government through Bill C-8." This was a way both to remind our own members that the struggle was not over and to let the employer know that we were already working towards the next round of negotiations. Given management's ongoing attitude of contempt for both our members and the very concept of a negotiated collective agreement, the employer was not happy to see this preamble to the hundreds of grievances filed by CUPW members every week. As we had designed, it reminded them that our struggle was not yet over.

National and regional representatives of our union attended local meetings all across the country. I myself managed to speak at meetings of all the major locals, at gatherings of many of the smaller locals, as well as at area and regional meetings attended by activists at those levels. We stressed that Bill C-8 had not ended the negotiating process, only delayed it. At the beginning of negotiations in 1977, post office managers had sent a message up the chain of command that postal workers had no stomach for a strike and that, even if there were one, the spirit of postal workers wasn't strong enough to sustain it for long. Our task now was to ensure that the correct message was sent up management's chain of command, from the shop floor all the way up to the federal Cabinet: that postal workers across the country are willing, if necessary, to strike, and to stay on strike whatever the legal ramifications, if their demands are not met.

In January of 1979, we produced a small, sixteen-page booklet, titled *Postal Workers' Struggle Continues*, for broad distribution to the entire Canadian labour movement. On its cover was the following:

> Confronted with an employer who wants to mechanize the post office at their expense, who refuses to honour their collective agreement, who refuses to acknowledge their right to negotiate, and who resorts to any number of repressive measures to impose his will upon them, the 23,000 postal workers in Canada are in the midst of a long struggle to win the right to negotiate the effects of technological change, defend their job security, improve their working conditions, ensure compliance with their collective agreement, and win back the freedom to bargain. The consequences of their success or failure will be felt throughout the whole labour movement.
>
> To win, they need the solidarity and concrete support of all workers.

CUPW activists attended meetings of every District Labour Council and every provincial Federation of Labour across the country to explain our determination in upcoming negotiations. I spoke at many of these meetings and also at most of the major union conventions held across the country in this period, and many resolutions were passed supporting postal workers in our negotiations. Many of these were sent to the CLC for its upcoming convention in May of 1980. We knew that it was essential to have the support of the entire labour movement during our next round of negotiations.

Our members wore buttons that read "The Struggle Continues" and we displayed labels and bumper stickers with the same slogan. On specific days of nationally organized actions, we distributed pamphlets to the public in every community across the country. We wanted to both reach out to the public and again let the government know we would be determined in the next round of negotiations.

I remember walking the streets of Ottawa around this time and seeing that most mailboxes were decorated with our "The Struggle Continues" stickers. Management tried to remove them, but the glue on them was of high quality: weeks later, they were still there.

In February of 1979, we launched a publicity campaign with ads on radio stations and messages in major newspapers. We then declared Valentine's Day as "National Federal Member of Parliament Day" and, to celebrate the occasion, produced a special four-page tabloid that sported an "I Love You" message to Pierre Elliott Trudeau on the front page. Inside, we detailed his government's track record against Canadian workers: fewer jobs, lower wages, higher prices, fewer services, and more profits and subsidies for employers. On the back page, we detailed his government's track record against postal workers: 65,000 grievances, rollbacks, the suspension of our right to strike, and an imposed collective agreement.

When the Trudeau government called an election for late May of 1979, we produced another four-page tabloid, titled *Which Side Are You On?*, which was addressed to our elected representatives in the House of Commons and to Canadian voters. On the front page, we reminded Canadians that Parliament had been called upon to vote on regressive pieces of legislation that had given us wage controls, reduced funding for education and medical services, greater police powers, the denial of Unemployment Insurance benefits to 250,000 Canadians, the denial of air-traffic controllers' right to strike and the imposition on them of a collective agreement, the denial of our right to strike should a federal election be called, and, finally, the back-to-work legislation we had defied. On the inside pages, we listed the name and party affiliation of each Member of Parliament and how they had voted on these various pieces of regressive legislation. When the votes were counted, Joe Clark's Tories won election in a minority government that would prove to be short-lived.

We spoke at public forums and made presentations before municipal councils. We prepared background documents, both for our own activists and for those in other unions across the country, on the issues we insisted be addressed in the next round of negotiations. We worked to assure that members of other unions across the country understood our determination to make gains in the upcoming negotiations. We wrote to every Member of Parliament and met with the caucuses of each of the parties in Parliament to underline our determination.

We contacted non-governmental organizations in the women's, peace, environmental, anti-poverty, students', seniors', religious, unemployed, aboriginal, and other organizations across the country asking that they offer us their support, or at least explain our case to their own members.

We used the media intensively to outline our position through press conferences, letters to the editor, op-ed articles, press releases, and briefings of journalists and editorial boards. I did several media interviews and appeared on phone-in and public affairs programs.

After the imposition of Judge Tremblay's new collective agreement in March of 1979, CUPW was often in the public eye, and this helped keep our campaign alive. My trial attracted a lot of media coverage, as did my appeals, my comings and going at the Ottawa Carleton Regional Detention Centre, the court cases of CUPW's other national officers, and the start of the new round of negotiations.

In summary, after our return to work in October of 1978, we focussed our efforts on ensuring that *everyone* knew our struggle wasn't over and that we were *determined* to make up lost ground in the 1980 negotiations.

1980 CLC Convention

As noted earlier, the national labour body, the CLC, had not supported CUPW during our defiance of back-to-work legislation in 1978, and, as the date of its May 1980 National Convention neared, many of our locals elected delegates who were determined to express our dissatisfaction over this matter. As well, since being released from prison in late March, I had spoken at many labour council meetings, conventions, and conferences, and many resolutions critical of the CLC and its leader, Dennis McDermott, were sent to its National Convention for debate. Many of these resolutions called on the CLC to support CUPW should we once again be forced to take strike action. As well, more than a hundred CUPW delegates were determined to make their unhappiness with the CLC and Dennis McDermott known far and wide. Clearly, there was great potential for serious conflict within the national labour movement at this CLC Convention.

As much as I felt it necessary to denounce the CLC's lack of support for us, I never lost sight of our ultimate aim: a negotiated collective agreement ratified by postal workers. I knew that if we were to achieve this, we would need the CLC's support. Just prior to the Convention, I called a meeting of all CUPW delegates and explained to them that the most important thing for our membership was not how successful we would be in condemning McDermott but how successful we would be in winning the CLC's support in our current negotiations.

I suggested that I meet with McDermott and tell him that we were faced with a clear choice. We could have a huge fight on the convention floor that would result, regardless of who carried the day in the debate, in a weakened national labour movement. Or, we could agree to have all the resolutions dealing with our past differences replaced by one resolution of CLC support for CUPW in our current negotiations. Despite the strong personal distaste for McDermott among many CUPW delegates, they agreed that gaining the CLC's support was most important.

I met with McDermott and he agreed, so he asked the members of the committee dealing with these resolutions to convert them to a single resolution expressing the CLC's support for us both in our current negotiations and in the event of a possible strike. When this new resolution came to the convention floor, all major leaders spoke in support of it. The CUPW delegation had agreed that I would be the only delegate from our union to speak on this resolution. The last speaker before me was CLC Executive Vice-President Shirley Carr, who made a strong intervention in support of us. When I came to the microphone, I received a long standing ovation from the whole Convention. This was a moment that neither I nor any of

National Executive Board members elected at the 1980 CUPW Convention. From left to right, back row: Darrel Tingley (Atlantic Region), First Vice-President André Beauchamp, Frank Walden (Western Region), Chief Steward Sid Baxter, Joe Alviano (Ontario Region). Front row, from left: Clément Morel (Québec Region), Secretary-Treasurer Leroy Hiltz, President Jean-Claude Parrot, and Second Vice-President Mason Duffy.

the other CUPW delegates present will ever forget. When the applause subsided, I said: "Before you vote, I want to make it clear that you may be voting to support an illegal strike, because we will not go back to work until we have an agreed collective agreement."

McDermott, who was chairing the Convention, then said: "There are no strings attached to our support." This statement was followed by another outburst of applause from delegates, many of whom had long wanted to openly show their support for CUPW. It was an incredible feeling for me to hear that applause, and when it finally died down, Dennis McDermott announced that the resolution was adopted by the unanimous consent of the delegates.

The unanimous passage of this resolution was a powerful message to government, to post office management, to the media, to the public, and obviously to the whole labour movement. And, it was a huge encouragement to CUPW members, and it strengthened our resolve in the current round of negotiations.

The 1980 Negotiations

Approaching the 1980 negotiations with the employer, our goals were clear. While we certainly wanted to win back the gains that had been taken away from us by Judge Tremblay in 1978, we were also ready to fight hard to assure that our members would share the benefits of new technology, particularly in the area of job security. And, we saw a shorter workweek for our members — without a drop in pay — as one of the means to achieving that job security. We also sought to safeguard and extend protections acquired in the past, to improve our working conditions, and to ensure respect for the collective agreement with an efficient and expedient grievance procedure.

Our comprehensive program of demands for the 1980 negotiations was approved by a referendum in all locals across the country during the summer of 1979. While ambitious, I believe it was a fair program. We made it clear to all from the beginning of negotiations that, if necessary, we would strike and that, if forced into a strike, we would not go back to work under any circumstances until we had obtained a fair collective agreement that had been approved by postal workers all across the country.

After negotiations began in the autumn of 1979, we went through the processes provided for by the Public Services Staff Relations Act, and a Conciliation Board was appointed, as in previous negotiations. On January 22, 1980, CUPW's National Executive Board approved Jacques Desmarais, a man of long experience and strong reputation who had helped bring all of Québec's major labour bodies together in a "Common Front" in the 1970s, as our nominee on the Conciliation Board. Germain Jutras was named to chair the Board, and he took a much more constructive approach than had Louis Courtemanche, who had held the same position in 1978. After the release of the Conciliation Board's report it became clear to me that management negotiators had been given a real mandate to settle this round without a strike, and we were able to make a lot of progress at the bargaining table.

There was no mention of rollbacks in Mr. Jutras' Conciliation Board report. Instead, there were recommendations for important improvements in monetary benefits — including a sixty-six cent wage increase — a shorter workweek, an increase in shift and weekend premiums, important improvements in non-monetary articles, and a mechanism to deal with 30,000 accumulated grievances.

Mr. Jutras' approach was to consider our demands and our arguments on their merits, and his attitude was very helpful in resolving problems. I was encouraged to see a Conciliation Board chair not abdicating his responsibilities, as Louis Courtemanche had done in 1978, thus making a strike inevitable. It seemed that the 1980 Conciliation Board report was going to help the parties resolve this round of negotiations without a strike. Jacques Desmarais supported the report's recommendations, with the exception of five he thought should have gone further towards meeting our demands. We soon reached the stage where the only major outstanding issue was our demand for a shorter workweek without loss of pay.

For us, the shorter workweek was a strike issue, because it was the only way to win a share of the benefits of automation and to at least protect existing jobs, if not gain additional ones. Well remembering the lack of support we had received from the CLC during our 1978 strike (more on

CLC President Dennis McDermott, left, with CUPW negotiators Jean-Claude Parrot, Marcel Perreault, and Jim Hall, preparing a counter proposal for Postmaster General André Ouellet in May 1980.

relations between CUPW and the CLC in Chapter Eleven), I suggested to CLC President Dennis McDermott that someone from his office attend that part of negotiations so he would be aware of the issues and attitudes of the two parties at the table. This also seemed a good way to convince the employer, and the government, that, without doubt, the CLC stood with CUPW this time around.

Mr. McDermott sent two representatives to observe negotiations, and they kept him informed of developments at the bargaining table. After the release of the Conciliation Board report, the parties resumed negotiations. We managed to resolve many issues, but we were approaching an impasse on the issue of a shorter workweek. In an effort to resolve the issue, Postmaster General Ouellet joined the management team, although he did not himself appear at the bargaining table. Knowing the importance of his presence with the management team, I called Dennis McDermott and asked him to accompany us at the bargaining table. While he had a very busy schedule, I managed to convince him that he could have an important impact on these last-minute negotiations. After making it clear that he would come to the table not as a mediator but as part of our team, he agreed to attend the negotiations.

I felt that the Postmaster General wanted to resolve the issue of the shorter workweek, but that something was preventing him from putting an offer on the table. He asked for a private meeting with Dennis McDermott, and I urged him to meet with the Minister. Dennis then asked me, "Don't you have a policy in your constitution that no CUPW representative will meet the employer alone?"

He was, of course, correct in this. It wasn't that we thought one of our representatives might sell-out the union in a private meeting: it was meant to assure, firstly, that the employer could not claim that we had agreed to something when we had not and, secondly, that CUPW members could trust the integrity of their negotiating team.

When Dennis asked me this question, I responded, "Are you a member of CUPW?" Of course, he responded negatively. "Then," I told him, "the policy doesn't apply to you. I believe the Minister has something for us that he doesn't want to put on the table without being sure that we will agree to it." Dennis went to the private meeting with the Minister, and when he came back I learned I had been right. Dennis then told us that Mr. Ouellet was willing to shorten the workweek from 40 to 37.5 hours.

However, a problem remained. The Postmaster General was concerned that paying the same weekly salary over 37.5 hours rather than 40 would increase the hourly wage rate, and so the hourly rate for overtime would be higher than he could agree to.

We understood his problem, and our team realized that the solution was to find a way to maintain the hourly wage rate based on a 40-hour week while in fact reducing the workweek by 2.5 hours. We proposed that thirty minutes of each worker's daily meal period be paid, and therefore be included in the 40-hour workweek. This would have the effect of actually reducing the workweek by 2.5 hours while not increasing the overtime rate.

Dennis McDermott again went to meet privately with the Minister and made this counter-offer, and a few minutes later he was back saying that the Postmaster General was going to come to the bargaining table himself and make this an official offer from the employer.

The Postmaster General did just that, and, despite the opposition of his negotiators, we had him agree that the shorter workweek would take effect immediately. Like us, he knew that this would mean that, until new schedules were put into effect, the employer would have to pay workers overtime for an additional 2.5 hours per week. But he also knew that this would pressure management to move quickly to put new schedules together, something we wanted as well. After these last-minute negotiations, we finally reached a tentative agreement.

This agreement reversed the rollbacks we had suffered through the imposed 1978 settlement, won us some very important gains in the area of benefits from automation, and included important improvements in non-monetary areas. The members of the National Executive Board were very pleased with the results our Negotiating Committee had achieved, and they recommended to our 23,000 members across the country that they approve the tentative agreement in referendum.

Meetings of our members were held across the country to explain the terms of the tentative agreement, and myself and other national officers attended many of them. We all had the same message for our members, I recall giving that message to our members at a number of meetings in this manner:

This is the result of the unity you showed in the 1978 negotiations, your participation in implementing our program of action, and the determination you showed in the preparation of this round of negotiations. As we told you before, we are not going to consider negotiations over until you approve a collective agreement. We now have in front of us the result of both the strong solidarity postal workers have shown and the clear message you gave to the employer that you were ready to fight for your rights. It is without any hesitation that your National Executive Board recommends that you vote in favour of this tentative agreement.

This message was well received, as were the gains laid out in the tentative agreement, and 89.8 percent of postal workers voted to accept the new collective agreement. We were proud to announce the result to all our friends, those both inside and outside the labour movement. "We began negotiations in the spring of 1977," I wrote at the time, "and we signed a collective agreement in the summer of 1980. What happened in between is part of the history of courage, determination, and unity displayed by the 23,000 postal workers all across the country."

Today, I am still proud of those 23,000 postal workers, and I consider myself privileged to have led them, as National President and Chief Negotiator, in our long struggle together.

1981: A Strike Caused by the President of Treasury Board

Some in the government weren't happy with the collective agreement won by postal workers in 1980. We were soon to discover that one of the unhappiest of all was Don Johnston, President of Treasury Board.

The 1980 contract remained in force until the end of June 1981, and when we began negotiations in the spring of that year, we were determined to continue our struggle for our share of benefits from automation and for further improvements in working conditions. We knew it wasn't going to be easy, but having found a better atmosphere at the bargaining table in 1980, we were hopeful of further progress. We were ready to present our case and to listen carefully to the employer's arguments.

We prepared seven background papers, each about twelve pages long, which outlined the rationale for our demands in each of seven areas: health and safety, reduced work time (outside the parameters of the shorter work week), parental rights, accidents and injuries, noise, night work, and justice, equality, and dignity. Each paper included statistics and information about other existing collective agreements that already provided the benefits we were demanding for postal workers. These background papers were distributed to union activists, especially shop stewards, so they would be able to answer members' questions about our demands during the course of negotiations.

Health and safety issues were very important to us in this round of negotiations, and we adopted a holistic approach in this area. Workplace accidents and injuries were on the rise, and noise — certainly a related issue — had become a serious problem in mechanized plants. Our demands were designed to prevent accidents and injuries, to promote the general health and well being of our members, to encourage preventive health care, to reduce night work, and to provide adequate rest periods. In all, we put forward eighteen demands to achieve these objectives. Other demands were designed to protect jobs through longer vacations, pre-retirement leave, and more paid holidays.

Our central demand in the area of parental rights was for seventeen weeks of paid maternity leave. In 1980, translators working for the federal government put this issue on the bargaining table and eventually went on strike. However, they dropped this demand in the course of negotiations that led to a new contract. Despite their lack of success, I thought they did a fantastic job in putting this issue on the public agenda and, speaking at one of their rallies, I congratulated them on this.

The Trudeau government had clearly indicated that the issue of maternity leave was on its legislative agenda, so we knew it was a very topical issue and decided to make it a priority in negotiations. Québec public sector workers had earned the right to paid maternity leave several years previously, but no other government workers in the country were so fortunate.

We stressed the issue of paid maternity leave throughout the labour movement, in the media, to Members of Parliament, to the various social movements, and everywhere else we thought our demand would resonate. We contacted more than 500 women's organizations across the country, and we received widespread support for our demand for paid maternity leave. We felt that all women had an interest in this, and we were determined to win this right for our members at the bargaining table. Granting postal workers paid maternity leave would not involve a huge expense for government, and so we had little cause to think it would be a major sticking point in our negotiations.

However, it seemed that Treasury Board President Don Johnston had not been pleased with the settlement we had won in 1980 through the intervention of Postmaster General Ouellet. We heard rumours that Johnston was critical of Ouellet and that he felt the shorter workweek was too costly. So, in the 1981 negotiations it seemed that he wanted to give the Postmaster General a lesson in how to bargain with postal workers.

But Don Johnston obviously forgot the mistakes then-Postmaster General Gilles Lamontagne had made in the 1977–78 negotiations. That approach helped bring about the unity of postal workers in defying back-to-work legislation and brought the full weight of the labour movement onto our side in the 1980 negotiations.

From the very beginning of negotiations, Don Johnston followed the same pattern that Lamontagne had in 1978. He attacked CUPW in the employer's communications to postal workers and in the media. He said our demands were too costly and that the government couldn't accept them. He then tried to say the real issue was not paid maternity leave and that this was just a union strategy to make everyone forget what our real demands were. However, he found himself unable to explain his refusal to accept our demand for paid maternity leave, which was going to cost the employer the equivalent of about a two-cent-per-hour wage hike, while the employer had already offered a fifty-cent wage hike at the bargaining table. It didn't take Don Johnson long to destroy his own credibility in the media.

He then argued that, because the issue of maternity leave was soon going to be dealt with by legislation in the House of Commons, we should set aside our demand for *paid* maternity leave until Parliament had taken action on it. My answer to this was: "We have the right to negotiate parental rights under the law — this is not one of the demands identified as non-negotiable by the Chairperson of the Public Service Staff Relations Board — and therefore, this being a priority for our members, and the cost being very minimal for the employer, we have no intention of waiting for the government to decide on this issue. We have the right to negotiate *paid* maternity leave and we will not wait to be told later on that such leave will be unpaid. We have no trust that such legislation will allow for paid leave."

Mr. Johnston continued his campaign of disinformation, attacking the union's leaders and accusing our negotiators of intransigence at the bargaining table. We applied for conciliation, and Pierre Jasmin, the Chairperson of the Conciliation Board, recommended paid maternity leave in his report, along with other improvements to the collective agreement. Still, the President of Treasury Board maintained his refusal to grant us paid maternity leave. We called a strike vote and received a strong mandate from the membership for strike action. In June, picket lines went up across the country.

It would take a forty-two-day strike before the government agreed to our demand for paid maternity leave. But those forty-two days were incredible: for the first time in my life, I saw an issue being negotiated between an employer and a union become the subject of widespread public debate. While a strike can sometimes overshadow the issue (or issues), surrounding it, now the issue of paid maternity leave was overshadowing our strike.

Newspapers across the country ran editorials about paid maternity leave, and there was a constant flow of letters to the editors on the issue. Columnists felt obliged to add their two cents worth on the matter. Phone-in shows across the country were abuzz with talk of paid maternity leave. Guests, especially women, on public affairs programs weighed in on the issue. I was asked on many occasions to explain our position and, in some cases, to confirm that we were really serious about getting paid maternity leave in our collective agreement. I received phone calls from members who asked me whether we really were on strike for paid maternity leave. My answer was always, "There are some other issues, but we aren't going back without paid maternity leave." To which, the caller would respond: "Okay, Jean-Claude, I understand."

The summer of 1981 was generally a very nice one, and many of our members who never had the opportunity to take summer vacations took the opportunity of enjoying the season with their families. Our picket lines were very limited, but there was no talk of any of our members going back to work before the issue was resolved in our favour. Our members knew that one of our objectives was always to make gains for those relatively disempowered, in this case women. They also knew that I, as Chief Negotiator, felt it was an achievable demand.

As the strike wore on, it became clear that the government was losing both the public debate and credibility on that issue of paid maternity leave. The employer's own monetary offer on the bargaining table amounted to more than seventy cents an hour, yet it remained stubborn on this two-cent issue. After having settled a collective agreement without a strike the year before, it was sad to see the Trudeau government yet again take on postal workers and provoke a strike on such an issue.

I didn't understand why Prime Minister Trudeau allowed the President of Treasury Board to act in such a manner as to have his government lose so much credibility over this issue. Whenever postal workers struck or threatened to strike, government always argued that it was essential to the lifeblood of the country that the mail keep moving. But by allowing a strike over an issue of human rights such as paid maternity leave — an issue it would have cost relatively little to concede — the Trudeau government revealed how little it really cared about keeping the mail moving. It showed that it was still out to get postal workers and it showed how out-of-touch the Trudeau government was with the needs of workers, especially women.

The government finally accepted our demand, and we negotiated the inclusion of seventeen weeks of paid maternity leave into the collective agreement. We had not achieved all of our major demands, but we won new health and safety provisions, a ban on the further introduction of closed-circuit television in the workplace, improved rights for part-time employees, increased protections regarding disciplinary actions, and protections during the transition of the post office into to a Crown Corporation. (More on this matter below.)

Postal workers were proud of having been the central part of this successful struggle for paid maternity leave, and I was very proud of both our members and the patience shown by those in other postal unions affected by our strike. For postal workers, a forty-two-day strike was a high price to pay for achieving the right of paid maternity leave. But postal workers know that because of their stand in 1981, today all federal employees have this leave in their collective agreements. And, for showing such courage in such a cause, postal workers earned tremendous respect among the general population.

Not long after the 1981 strike, the post office became a Crown Corporation, something CUPW had been advocating for years. Looking back on the struggles we waged before it became a Crown Corporation, we're proud of what we accomplished. We're proud of the outcome of the 1975 negotiations and strike, of the outcome of the 1978 strike and negotiations — which really only ended in the summer of 1980 — and of the outcome of the 1981 negotiations and strike. These were difficult times for postal workers across the country, but we all had reason to be proud of what we had done and what we had achieved. We showed remarkable unity and determination. We made real progress. And we proved we could change things for the better. (For a visual illustration of progress we made in negotiations through the years, see the appendix.)

Canada Post: Becoming a Crown Corporation

On October 16, 1981, the post office became a Crown Corporation with the proclamation of Bill C-42, the Canada Post Corporation Act. It was well known that CUPW had long called for turning the post office into a Crown Corporation and that we had launched a series of campaigns over the years toward this end. In fact, without our input the post office may not have become a Crown Corporation until many years later.

But, considering all the studies and recommendations that had been made by third parties and internal government studies over the years, dating all the way back to 1965, it's hard to understand why the Trudeau government waited so long to make that decision. It was on August 1, 1978, that Prime Minister Trudeau first announced the post office would become a Crown Corporation, but it was more than three years later before it became a reality.

Trudeau's announcement seemed to have come out of the blue. Even the then-Postmaster General, Gilles Lamontagne, who had argued against such a move just six weeks earlier, was taken by surprise. Why such an announcement at that time? I believe that this was because the Prime Minister had had enough. Management-labour relations in the post office were a constant headache for the Trudeau government. Negotiations at that point had dragged on for almost fifteen months, with constant public declarations from both sides, and these often didn't reflect favourably on the government.

The Prime Minister must have realized that post office management was hiding behind the federal government in its approach to labour relations with the postal unions. From his own experience as a labour lawyer, he must have realized that, by transforming the post office into a Crown Corporation, negotiations between the employer and postal workers would fall under the Canada Labour Code. This would remove the need for his government to continuously have to intervene in postal negotiations while still allowing it to exercise control through the Cabinet Minister responsible for the new Crown Corporation.

I believe that the Prime Minister's reasons for making the announcement were strictly political. It was certainly not because he suddenly believed that postal workers should get a fair share of the benefits of automation, which was our main issue in negotiations at that time. I think it was his way of letting the parties know that they should take into account in their negotiations the fact that they would soon be operating in a new context.

We had argued long and hard for a Crown Corporation because it would mean that our relationship with management would then fall under terms of the Canada Labour Code, rather than the Public Service Staff Relations Act. This latter legislation had been designed years before to govern the manner in which mostly white-collar civil servants bargained with the employer, and we believed it wasn't appropriate that its terms dictate the manner we bargained for our members. Under its terms we were required to go through the following series of complex steps in every round of negotiations:

1. Before the beginning of negotiations, inform the Public Service Staff Relations Board of our choice between two options: to negotiate through conciliation with the right to strike or to negotiate through a process of binding arbitration that precluded the right to strike. (CUPW had always, without exception, chosen the former option.);
2. Without any time limit, to negotiate in "good faith";
3. When areas of disagreement are identified by the negotiating parties, to have a Conciliation Board (or Conciliation Officer), appointed;
4. To appear before the Public Service Staff Relations Board, which would rule on the Conciliation Board's (or Officer's) terms of reference;
5. To proceed with conciliation, a fourteen-day process unless extended at the request of the negotiating parties or the conciliator;
6. After the release of the Conciliation Board's (or Officer's) report, which is not binding on the parties, allow seven days to pass before the union acquires the right to strike.

This process restricted us in several ways. In negotiations before becoming a Crown Corporation, the employer would argue that it had to get the approval of Treasury Board, the Public Works or Finance ministries, the Public Service Employment Board, or other government agencies or departments before they could agree to a particular point. Under a Crown Corporation, we would deal directly with one employer.

The process of appearing before the Public Service Staff Relations Board to determine the terms of reference for the Conciliation Board and identify demands judged to be non-negotiable was a particularly awkward one. The interpretation of law in these hearings was narrow, and often left little room for the parties to work out agreements. Some decisions in the terms of reference were ridiculous.

For example, the Board determined that appointment to positions was a management right and therefore non-negotiable. Management was guided by the merit principle and so, only when two candidates were judged to be equal would seniority then apply. We demanded that seniority apply to workers in the same classification, but this was not negotiable according to the Board. However, it was okay to for us to demand that seniority apply to workers in the same classification who wish to move from one shift to another, but not to demand that seniority apply to those wishing to move from one section of the post office to another. The whole system was so impracticable that most Conciliation Boards ignored the terms of reference identified by the Public Service Staff Relations Board and simply made recommendations they felt would help the parties reach agreement.

This process also led to unnecessarily complex collective agreements. Because of restrictions on what demands were negotiable or non-negotiable, we often had to make a roundabout series of demands in order to achieve a relatively simple end. For example, before the post office became a Crown Corporation, there were twenty-one clauses in the collective agreement related to the protection of work performed by our members. Under the Canada Labour Code, only two to five clauses would have been necessary to achieve the same result. And, it would have meant far less time in front of courts and arbitrators that had to rule on interpretations of the collective agreement.

The complexities of what was negotiable and what was non-negotiable also led to problems in resolving grievances. Because conciliation efforts often sidestepped the rulings of the Public Service Staff Relations Board in this regard, after a few rounds of negotiations, one could argue that a large part of our collective agreement was illegal because it contained provisions that were determined to be non-negotiable under the law in the Board's terms of reference. When a grievance was arbitrated, the employer's lawyer often argued that the arbitrator couldn't sustain a grievance even when the wording of the collective agreement was clearly in favour of the grievor. This was a real nightmare for arbitrators. On one hand, by sustaining the grievance the arbitrator knew he was agreeing to provisions that were normally not negotiable under the law. On the other hand, he knew that denying the grievance would confirm that the employer had negotiated in bad faith, because that judgment would imply that the employer had agreed to the contract without the intention of abiding by it, and this was clearly illegal. So the best an arbitrator could do was to look at what was negotiated between the parties, assume it was what they both wanted, and simply avoid making any ruling on the agreement's legality.

Negotiating under these conditions was a nightmare for the union. The advantage of the Canada Labour Code is that there are no restrictions to negotiations. The employer can't hide behind the law or force the union to go through a process of determining whether a demand was negotiable or not. Under the Code, the employer has to deal with real issues, rather than convoluted processes.

We never assumed that, on coming under the Canada Labour Code, the employer would suddenly become a model of good, cooperative management. As I've always said, "An employer is an employer, and will always be an employer." By this I meant that employers will always try to get as much as they can out of workers and give them as little as possible in return. However, coming under the Code would force the employer to stop playing games with processes.

Despite Prime Minister Trudeau's 1978 announcement that the post office would become a Crown Corporation, it wasn't until the spring of 1981 that legislation was drafted to this end. At the time, we were in the midst of conciliation, but we understood the necessity of having input into this legislation, and we dealt with it as an issue separate from the conciliation process. Postmaster General André Ouellet and other high government officials sat down with representatives of all the unions in the post office (under the umbrella of the CLC). We discussed, article by article, the legislation that would be introduced in the House of Commons.

I must say that the Crown Corporation was set up in a way that recognized the contribution of the postal unions in raising the matter in the first place. With Postmaster General André Ouellet in charge of the consultations, we had real discussions and real input into the legislation that would create the Crown Corporation. We reached agreement on most of the wording of the legislation before it went to Parliament.

We won the protections we needed regarding acquired rights and the protection of bargaining units. On the financial side, although Canada Post was expected to break even, we won assurances that profits would not take priority over service to the public and human resources within the post office. We accepted the legislation as something we could live with. The legislation was adopted on April 14, 1981, although the Crown Corporation did not come into being until that autumn.

Section 5 (2) of the law creating the Crown Corporation, which provides clear instructions on the mandate of Canada Post Corporation, reads as follows:

While maintaining basic, customary postal service, the Corporation, in carrying out its objectives, shall have regard to:

- The desirability of improving and extending its products and services in the light of developments in the field of communications;
- The need to conduct its operations on a self-sustaining financial basis while providing a standard of service that will meet the needs of the people of Canada and that is similar with respect to communities of the same size;
- The need to conduct its operations in such manner as will best provide for the security of mail;
- The desirability of utilizing the human resources of the Corporation in a manner that will both attain the objectives of the Corporation and ensure the commitment and dedication of its employees to the attainment of those objects; and
- The need to maintain a corporate identity program approved by the Governor in Council that reflects the role of the Corporation as an institution of the Government of Canada.

Note that this section begins with the phrase, "While maintaining basic, customary postal service…" We stated at the time our support for this mandate as follows:

- We believe it reflects the importance of the postal service in promoting the cultural, educational, and commercial objectives of Canadian society, in all communities, regardless of their geographic location;
- Financial self-sufficiency is described only as a goal to be pursued, but not at the price of reduced services;
- In addition to requiring Canada Post Corporation to maintain basic, customary service, the legislation instructs the Post Office to have regard to "the desirability of improving and extending its products and services…" For CUPW, this is clearly the direction the Corporation must follow if it is to reconcile the three objectives of improved service, deficit reduction, and improved labour-management relations.

On November 27, 1980, the Postmaster General, André Ouellet, appearing before Parliament's Miscellaneous Estimates Committee to discuss the legislation that would create the Crown Corporation, made a strong commitment to preserve postal workers' right to strike:

The reality, Mr. Chairman, is that, while [some might wish] to make a system by which it will be impossible for our employees to strike, you might take away the legal right to strike, but you will never take away the illegal right to strike. And the fact of the matter is that we are living in an environment where there have been discussions, difficulties, and no one will solve the problem by putting their heads in the sand. We felt that it was unrealistic to put in our legislation provisions that will forbid our employees to legally strike.

With the proclamation of the Canada Post Corporation Act, the post office became a Crown Corporation, and our rights to negotiate under the Canada Labour Code and to strike were recognized by that legislation.

1981–1983

Nineteen-eighty-one was not only the year we became a Crown Corporation and won a forty-two day strike for paid maternity leave: across Canada, there was much ferment in the labour movement. Many workers were just ending important strikes and many others either remained on, or would soon set up, picket lines. And many other developments were having an effect on workers across the country. A brief excursion into a number of these struggles and developments will provide some context for our own work during this period.

The year 1981 began just after the conclusion of a sixteen-month strike by Local 2693 of the Lumber and Sawmill Workers' Union at Boise Cascade plants in Fort Frances and Kenora, Ontario. Despite the full support of the entire labour movement, this multinational successfully isolated this local from four other unions representing Boise Cascade workers, all of which signed contracts, leaving this group on its own. With workers divided into several bargaining units, the company was able to import scabs. In spite of the strike, large numbers of Ontario Provincial Police officers helped the company maintain production levels.

CUPW adopted, as did many other unions, families of these striking workers for the duration of their strike. These workers struck with tremendous courage, as our National Vice-President, André Beauchamp wrote: "For sixteen months, the members and their families had to withstand incredible police harassment and enormous financial hardship. Still they fought on, until victory was impossible."

Another strike that lasted for several months in 1981 was that of workers at Stelco in Hamilton, under the leadership of Cec Taylor, president of Local 1005 of the United Steelworkers of America. During this strike, Dave Paterson, who had led an eight-and-a-half-month strike at Inco in Sudbury just two years earlier, was elected Director of the United Steelworkers of America District 6 (Ontario), bringing a more militant spirit to that organization.

The same year also saw a strike by CUPE hospital workers in Ontario. I had the good fortune of addressing a rally in Ottawa just before they held a province-wide strike vote. The union conducted the vote, and they struck, in defiance of provincial legislation that denied them that right.

In October, I had the honour of addressing a rally in support of 4,000 striking Cape Breton miners, members of the United Mine Workers of America. For me, it was an emotional event. Their strike was settled after eleven weeks on the picket lines.

There were many other strikes across the country in 1981, as workers in both the private and public sectors fought for their rights under difficult conditions, but with determination and courage. This labour unrest in Canada paralleled American President Ronald Reagan's firing of thousands of air-traffic controllers, who had dared to go on strike in 1981. While the American labour movement organized a large demonstration in New York, the first such rally in thirteen years, and another large one in Washington on September 20, 1981, it was unable to stop Reagan's attacks on the controllers. Reagan's success sent a false message to governments and employers on both sides of the border that they could "put unions in their places" without fear of a massive fightback from the labour movement.

Less than two months after we became a Crown Corporation, on November 21, 1981, the CLC organized the largest demonstration in modern Canadian history to protest the economic policies of the Liberal government. More than 100,000 workers protested on Parliament Hill in Ottawa against a government whose policies permitted interest rates of more than twenty percent, which had a devastating effect on workers and their families. It was a day I will never forget, and all who took part in it were very proud to have done so.

Before we began our first round of negotiations with Canada Post, we had good reason to believe we were entering into a new era where labour-management relations would be largely improved. The appointment of Michael Warren as the first President of Canada Post Corporation was, in our opinion, a good sign, in light of the three central objectives that had been established for Canada Post by the legislation that had created it: improved service to the public, financial self-sufficiency, and improved labour-management relations. Mr. Warren immediately took an interest in working with the postal unions, and all went well at the beginning. Management indicated it was going to pursue the three mandated objectives with equal vigour.

In the fall of 1981, however, we expressed strong reservations about the possibility that management would set too rigid a deadline for achieving financial self-sufficiency. We argued that, if such a deadline were adopted, the likelihood of achieving the other two objectives would diminish. Governments being what they are, our fears were confirmed on November 12, 1981, when Finance Minister Allan MacEachen established 1986 as the deadline for Canada Post to break even.

We considered this a unilateral decision without public justification and that management had offered no explanation of how the setting of this deadline would affect Canada Post's ability to achieve its other two objectives. No rationale was offered for Canada Post to be singled out as the only major federal service to be denied federal funding. There were no efforts to reconcile instructions from Parliament — to see all three objectives pursued equally — with instructions from the Finance Department. It was simply a deadline, with no thought of its consequences.

The years since the post office became a Crown Corporation have demonstrated that our understanding of the legislation that created it was less than perfect. So far as the protection of acquired rights and of the rights of the bargaining units went, things unfolded as we had anticipated. But, on the financial side, one thing we did not foresee was that government would, over the years, come to interpret "breaking even" as equivalent to making a fifteen percent profit every year. (More on this later.)

I believe that in the setting of this deadline for breaking even, the government was probably in violation of the legislation that had created Canada Post. Certainly, it was not respecting the intent of the law. But we all know that if the government were told by the courts that it was in violation of the law, it would simply change the law to its liking. At least under the existing law, it had to demonstrate it was making the goal of better service and improved labour relations a priority.

Unfortunately, soon after we became a Crown Corporation, we were deprived of our right to negotiate. In June of 1982, the federal government introduced legislation imposing wage controls on 500,000 federal workers. Our collective agreement, which was set to expire on September 30, 1982, was extended for two years, with a provisions for a 6-percent wage increase in October of 1982, and another of 5 percent the following year. In the same month the 6-percent increase took effect, the employer proposed either reopening our collective agreement to reduce labour costs by $18,000,000 or the elimination of 600 jobs. We refused this blackmail, opposing any measures to reduce services or cutbacks to staffing. Instead, we initiated a campaign designed to improve and extend services.

In 1983, teachers in Québec's English-language public education system went out on legal strike. In response, the Québec government passed two very repressive pieces of legislation. Bill 105 provided for wage cuts of 19.45 percent and massive layoffs. Bill 111 suspended the Charter of Rights for strikers, demanded they go back to work, legalized arbitrary firings, and made the legal assumption of guilt a priority over the assumption of innocence. Together, these two bills represented the most repressive legislative assault on workers in the history of the country.

As someone who had faced back-to-work legislation before, these pieces of legislation struck me as particularly unfair and created a dangerous precedent. While the government gave workers the right to strike with one hand, they took it away with the other when workers used that right effectively. In fact, this package of legislation was going to do far more than take away the right to strike: it would impose a collective agreement with wage cuts, layoffs, arbitrary firings, and the denial of basic rights. I brought the issue to CUPW's National Executive Board, asking that we provide substantial assistance to these workers. I said that if such back-to-work legislation was what other public sector workers had to look forward to, then we were in for a period of very difficult struggles all across the country. I proposed that we ask the CLC to call on each its affiliates to collect five dollars from each of their members' bi-weekly paycheques to help the teachers' union for the duration of their strike and that CUPW conduct a referendum among our members on making a similar donation. The National Executive Board agreed unanimously to these actions.

This was an ambitious plan on my part, and though it may have also been somewhat naïve, I thought that by calling on the support of every CLC affiliate and organizing a referendum in my own union on the issue, I was encouraging the entire Canadian labour movement to action in support of the striking teachers. However, the CLC soon reacted to our call, not by saying that supporting the striking teachers wasn't very important, but by criticizing CUPW and myself for not first presenting the proposal to the CLC's Executive before writing to its affiliates directly.

I wasn't happy with this reaction from the CLC but was even more distressed by the reaction of some of CUPW's local leaders to our call for a referendum. When I found out that Marcel Perreault, president of my own local in Montréal, objected to it, I asked that I be allowed to present the views of myself and the National Executive Board before a meeting of the local's members. (Though I was now National President of the union, I still served in that position as a member of the Montréal local where I came from, so it was only right that I be able to speak at a meeting of my own local.)

I was given five minutes to present my case. This wasn't much time, but I knew the procedure for deciding on referendums in Montréal was always short, so I didn't complain. Before giving me the floor, Brother Perreault spent a lot of time arguing that the proposed five-dollar assessment went against both CUPW's spirit and its constitution. I then used my five minutes to argue that holding a referendum of the membership was a purely democratic process and then explained the seriousness of the issue and why we needed to support the teachers.

Realizing that I may have had some impact on the members, Brother Perreault then took the floor and denounced the National Executive Board and myself in a manner I felt was totally inappropriate. The tone he used was vindictive, and it made it look as if we were thieves who wanted to steal money from members' pockets. He repeated his points that this was against both the spirit and the constitution of the union. This was followed by a strong attack on the National Executive Board. He then proceeded with the vote, giving me no chance to answer his attacks.

Unlike other locals across the country, in Montréal there were no question periods or debates at referendum meetings. In Montréal, referendum meetings normally lasted about forty minutes, including the time for voting. Local members liked this process, and it ensured a greater participation in the vote. The process was based on the concept that the members had faith in the local executive they had elected, and so they were only interested in its recommendation, along with a few explanations, before they voted.

Members supported their local executive and voted against the five-dollar-per-pay assessment for the striking teachers, but many workers came to me after the meeting and told me they thought I was right on the issue, but they had to go along with their local president. Some also thanked me for having had the courage to stand before the local membership and put forward my views and expressed their disagreement with Marcel Perreault's attack on the National Executive Board.

I confess I was hurt by this rejection of our recommendation by my own local: not because we lost the Montréal local's referendum, but because Marcel Perreault never showed any sensitivity to the issues underlying our call to support the teachers. For him, CUPW's National Executive Board was the villain, and it was the sole target of his criticism. Not a word against the Québec government that had introduced the legislation in the first place. No recognition that we were trying to help the teachers win their strike and prevent the future adoption of similar legislation elsewhere across the public sector

There were two reasons why I couldn't understand the argument that supporting the teachers in the way we proposed went against the spirit of CUPW. First, we were asking the members directly, in a democratic manner, whether they supported our proposal, rather than doing it by executive order, or even through a convention. Second, we were trying to show tangible solidarity with a group of workers who at that moment faced an even worse form of back-to-work legislation than we had defied in 1978.

I was also hurt because I was aware that Brother Perreault knew I had convinced the Executive Board to take this action. He knew that I believed in surprising others with strategies unexpected by the other side. He knew that this legislation was a very dangerous precedent. He knew that I was only trying to do a decent job in representing our members. And he knew he was hurting a friend, one who dared to ask to speak at the local's referendum meeting. I have no problem when there are disagreements within any organization. But, I do have a problem when debates around these disagreements take a demagogic tone.

After the Montréal meeting, I went back to Ottawa to find that, across the country, support for our proposal was less than solid. It was becoming a divisive issue within CUPW, so I recommended we cancel the referendum. I also felt that losing it could hurt the teachers.

After the announcement that the referendum had been cancelled, many locals took up voluntary collections for the teachers among their members, and we turned this into a national campaign. We collected around $50,000, which we knew wouldn't be enough for them to win their struggle. I accepted responsibility for the failure of an action that might have changed the way governments treat the right to strike in our country. I also recognized that I hadn't followed the accepted procedure in asking for the cooperation of the CLC's Executive. I had seen an urgency in moving forward within CUPW to support the teachers, but in the end, the decision-making processes within the union had proven too slow to adapt to my sense of urgency.

Throughout my life in the trade union movement, I took part in many different struggles. I always did my best to assure that my own ego never clouded my judgment on an issue I felt strongly about. But, in this instance, I was hurt by the arguments used against my solidarity plan, because I saw my plan as a way of building support for a group of workers in great need of support, while at the same time raising awareness among other workers across the country about the issues the strikers faced.

On reflection, what I learned from this is that I, as National President, was responsible to ensure that our actions bring about the solidarity we are looking for. In this case, I had not taken the steps within CUPW, or within the broader labour movement, to ensure that we had the best chance of gaining that solidarity.

1983 National Convention

By 1983, CUPW's triennial National Conventions had become increasingly busy affairs, most notably because they represented the highest level of our democratic structure and it was through these gatherings that the representations of the grassroots could most formally be put forward to those at higher levels of leadership. There was so much to deal with at our 1983 National Convention, in fact, that there was still unfinished business at the end, and it was agreed to hold a second session in the fall.

The first days of the May session were devoted to reports from the National Executive Board, from the individual national officers, and from the National Board of Trustees. Debates surrounding these reports indicated that, among some CUPW members, there was opposition to the way union leaders were conducting themselves.

Ever since our 1971 National Convention, the view that CUPW's constitution should provide guidance for every contingency had been growing, and the 1983 gathering dealt with proposed constitutional amendments that would define specific responsibilities and direction for individual officers and executive bodies. While many of the problems raised by these proposals were real, it was obvious that solutions to them required something more than alteration to constitutional wording.

One of the major issues discussed at the May session arose from some resolutions put forward that suggested our priority should be restricted to matters that directly affected the well being of our members and the day-to-day workings of the union: negotiations, grievances, arbitrations, conciliation, mediation, health and safety issues, and other related matters. While these are obviously central and legitimate concerns of any union, these resolutions reflected a narrow view of the role of unions in the broader society. There were negative references in these resolutions to the involvement of the union and its officers in the wider labour and social movements. The debate revealed two views of what CUPW's orientation should be: one side argued that the union should limits its activities to the direct defence and representation of its members' interests; the other that, in order to best represent its membership, the union must also involve itself with broader issues in our society that affect our members.

The debates and resolutions put forward by the Montréal local made it clear that there was strong opposition from that source to any absence of officers from national headquarters in order to attend gatherings about issues that were beyond the scope of a narrow understanding of what was in the best interests of the membership. While I recognized that this Convention was the proper place for such debate, I was in total disagreement with the concept behind such arguments and, if the narrow view had prevailed, I would have withdrawn my nomination to continue serving as National President, because I could never lead an organization if I was in disagreement with its basic orientation.

At the time of the 1983 Convention, we were under wage-control legislation that denied all public sector workers the right to negotiate, and the CLC had organized a fightback campaign on this issue. There were important issues such as unemployment, widespread layoffs across the country, the denial of women's rights, and many other aspects of what was an overall attack on working Canadians by employers and their friends in government. The adoption of these proposed amendments to our national constitution would have limited the ability of the National Executive Board, of myself, and of other officers to identify and deal with issues that would have a major impact on the membership. It would have also limited my relationship with members and with activists outside the union. I often accepted invitations to speak at conventions of other unions, at May Day rallies, to workers of other unions on their picket lines, to conferences dealing with issues such as peace, poverty, unemployment, technological change, the right to strike, negotiation, privatization, "free trade," and other important social issues. I also participated in panel discussions and debates on such issues.

I used these opportunities to share CUPW's position on the different issues, but I also used them to meet with CUPW's local officers, shop stewards, and activists, to attend meetings of members, and to tour post offices. I often joined locals that were making presentations to city hall or to public meetings. I met with the media and participated in call-in shows to talk about the purpose of my visit to a certain area, to discuss the situation in the post office, and to defend the interests of postal workers.

Certainly, there has to be balance between "direct" (strictly membership affairs) and "indirect" (actions in the broader social and political fields) activities in any union. However, this isn't something that can be written into a constitution, because it involves assessments that can only be made as circumstances evolve. (I think our program of action after the 1978 strike was a successful example of a case where we unanimously decided we needed to reach out to the wider labour and social movements in order to be better positioned for the next round of negotiations.)

One of the arguments used through the years to criticize certain of our activities was that we were not the CLC, and so we shouldn't try to act like a central labour body. This argument implied that it was the CLC's responsibility to deal with broader issues and that CUPW should tend to the far narrower interests of its members. I disagreed with this argument. Were these people suggesting that the CLC is not the sum of its affiliates? It seemed strange to me that the same people who had long been saying that CUPW was made up of its members and not the National Executive Board were now telling us that the CLC was made up of its Executive rather than its affiliate members. In my view, there would be no CLC without its affiliates, just as there would be no CUPW without its members.

The right of workers to freedom of association, to negotiate, and to strike are fundamental rights that I will always defend and promote. So, I often had to fight beyond the bargaining table when governments tried to take away these rights. And, I often had to fight against employers who tried to blackmail workers into accepting concessions.

I feel strongly that CUPW has to be there to support other workers fighting for dignity and justice. We have to be there for the unemployed and the underemployed, who are so often abandoned by our society. We have to be there to fight neo-liberal concepts of privatization, deregulation, contracting out, and the so-called free trade agreements (I call them "free investment" agreements), which in fact only free investment capital from any social restrictions, including our rights to freedom of association, to negotiate, and to strike.

I feel strongly that CUPW has to be there to denounce the fact that a million Canadian children are living in poverty. We have to be there to speak out on environmental issues, such as pollution of our forests, rivers, and cities. We have to be there to promote peace. We have to be there to ensure a better future for our children and grandchildren. We have to be there to oppose racism, homophobia, sexism, and all other evils that serve only to exclude and divide.

The bottom line is that as unionized workers, we will not safeguard the gains we have made or make further progress if we are not concerned about the exploitation of others and the denial to others of the fundamental rights we enjoy. CUPW should always be there to represent the concerns of its members, both in appropriate forums and in our broader society as a whole. This is what solidarity is all about.

These were the arguments that others and I made against the proposed constitutional amendments from the Montréal local. Thankfully, our arguments carried the day by approximately a two-thirds majority, and, interestingly enough, Brother Clément Morel, who had argued in favour of the resolutions, nominated me for another term as National President.

Some delegates to the May 1983 session also criticized national officers for our travel expenses, suggesting that we pocketed money by abusing them. In fact, most of the time our *per diem* was less than the cost of hotel and meals, and we had to supplement it from our own pockets.

As CUPW's National President, I was sometimes called upon to attend international gatherings, but it was often difficult for me to get authorization from the union to attend them. One of these meetings I managed to get authorization to attend in the autumn of 1981 was the international convention of the Postal, Telephone, and Telegraph International, to which CUPW was affiliated. It was a five-day gathering in Tokyo, and some remarked that it was nice for me to be able to take such a trip. I arrived in Japan after a sixteen-hour trip, and I went to a small hotel away from the convention site because it was the cheapest one on the list provided by the organizers. I received the same *per diem* that I would have if the convention had taken place in Toronto, and you can imagine, if it wasn't usually enough to cover my hotel and meal costs in Canada, how far it went in Japan. That trip cost me more than $300 from my own pocket, and I returned to Ottawa and my office at the end of the five days.

Louisette didn't come with me to Tokyo because we couldn't afford it. While there, I met three LCUC officers: they were all staying at the hotel nearest the convention site, which was paid for by the union, and they had $1,000 in expense money for the five days. LCUC also paid for their wives to accompany them and provided them with expense money.

I never asked or expected that CUPW officers receive such generous travel benefits. I agreed with the principle that a *per diem* should provide enough so that officers are not left out of pocket. But, in most of our travels, our *per diems* weren't sufficient to accomplish this.

A CUPW Christmas Gift

As the 1983 Christmas began, we had many reasons to be displeased with Canada Post, which had used the period we had been deprived of our right to negotiate to pursue its business plan, ignoring our representations about the future of the Crown Corporation.

After the second session of our National Convention in the autumn, the National Executive Board adopted a plan to reduce postal rates for the general public's Christmas cards. We felt that the Canada Post was more and more becoming a service to the business sector and less and less a service to the general public. We argued that the public should be entitled to a special gift during the 1983 Christmas season.

We announced publicly at a press conference that, during this Christmas season, the general public could mail their Christmas cards at a rate of ten cents and postal workers would sort and deliver them, just like any other mail. The standard letter rate at the time was thirty-two cents, and Canada Post was so taken by surprise by our announcement that, before they could react, many postal stations ran out of ten-cent stamps.

In the following days and weeks, the media covered this matter with a sense of incredulity. Editorials spoke of anarchy in the post office, comparing our position with workers in a store who simply decide to sell merchandise at a lower price than that decreed by the owner. Cartoons of me in a Santa Claus suit appeared in some newspapers, and some columnists condemned our union.

For management, this created a real problem, because ten-cent mail was going through and there wasn't much it could do about it. The sorting machines did their work regardless of how much postage was on the mail.

Reporters tested the system and found out that, as long as there was a stamp on the envelope — the amount of the stamp didn't matter — the machines would sort the mail and it would reach its destination. With that kind of reporting in the media, regardless of what the post office said to the public, mail continued to pour into the post office with ten-cent (and even cheaper) stamps.

Canada Post then threatened to discipline postal workers if they processed this mail. But if, during the busy Christmas season, workers had had to examine each piece of mail to determine how much postage was on it, the entire system would have come to a shuddering halt. The entire automation system would be rendered useless, and management's production standards would be nothing more than a joke.

Not being able to control the situation in the plants, management asked LCUC members to intercept mail without proper postage. LCUC replied that checking for proper postage was not in letter carriers' job descriptions and that forcing them to check for proper postage would make them miss delivery deadlines, even for mail with proper postage.

Next, Canada Post complained to the Canadian Labour Relations Board, arguing that, in fact, this action constituted a strike on the part of CUPW. We appeared before the Board to argue against management's position.

Meanwhile, millions of Canadians continued mailing letters, as well as cards, without proper postage. We said this was proper compensation to the general public, which had seen services being cut to them, while the opposite was happening in the business sector, which saw improved services and reduced rates.

The Canadian Labour Relations Board moved quickly to render a decision in mid-December. It ruled with the employer, judging our action to be an illegal strike. When the media contacted me for my reaction, I said, "Does this mean that when we win back our legal right to strike, it will be legal for us to reduce mail rates for the general public?" Another reporter looked at me, and said, "You know, I didn't think about that angle, but you're right. It opens the door to another way for postal workers to strike in future."

We suspended our ten-cent campaign, but the public continued to respond to it through the rest of the Christmas period, and things returned to normal after the Christmas season. Interestingly, the employer soon issued new stamps that allowed sorting machines to detect whether or not letters had proper postage.

9
Turmoil 1984–87

1984–85 Negotiations

Before we entered into the next round of negotiations in the summer of 1984, we developed a program of demands that reflected the many problems we had faced since the post office became a Crown Corporation in October of 1981. Our hopes that management would act differently as a Crown Corporation, which had been based on the legislative mandate that had been agreed to between the parties prior to October 1981, had been dashed over the course of the ensuing three years.

The employer had introduced a variety of measures that were contrary to the interests of both postal workers and the general public. These included the unilateral extension of our contract through anti-inflation legislation, cutbacks in services, massive new technological and organizational changes, inadequate staffing, the stockpiling of mail, increased postal rates, and greater intimidation and harassment in an effort to achieve greater productivity.

So, despite the Crown Corporation, we still had the same old employer. We would have to bring to the bargaining table all those issues that had been deemed non-negotiable before the creation of Canada Post. Through the years, we had made some progress on some of these, but now we would be able to confront these issues without having to find ways to circumvent the law. We wanted to be ready to use our collective strength to achieve real long-term security. Our overall theme for the 1984 negotiations was "To Secure Our Future," which, as I wrote in the first paragraph of the national program of demands submitted to a vote of the membership, would win for postal workers a workplace "free of uncertainty, doubt, and hassles."

Our demands were organized into sub-themes for these first negotiations under the Canada Labour Code. These were "Total Job Security," "Reduced Working Time," "Job Creation," "Equality," "Preserving our Income," "Health and Safety," "Adequate Staffing," "Protection from Arbitrary Measures," and "General Demands." It was an ambitious program but one that addressed real issues, many of which had previously been considered non-negotiable under the Public Service Staff Relations Act.

The program of demands was built on the basis of proposals that came from regional pre-negotiation meetings, and they took into consideration the situation as we regained our right to negotiate.

The issues of job security and job creation were central to our program. More than 2,000 CUPW jobs had been eliminated in the two previous years, and Canada Post had plans to eliminate 3,000 more, which would mean a 20-percent decrease in the size of our bargaining unit. Canada Post proposed incentives to these 3,000 workers now considered "surplus" to either take early retirement or resign their positions. These job reductions came at a time when mail volumes were up 19 percent, to new record levels. Canada Post was busy replacing full-time workers with part-timers, who already represented 16 percent of our members.

Our program of demands was presented to the membership in the spring of 1984 with the unanimous recommendation of the National Executive Board that it be presented to the employer for negotiations along with our notice to bargain on July 2, 1984. It was distributed to all members attending meetings across the country. In brief, the program took into consideration demands and considerations from the field: the fact that the collective agreement had been in effect for more than three years because of the two-year extension due to federal anti-inflation legislation; that this was our first round of negotiations with a Crown Corporation under the Canada Labour Code; our responses to the numerous management attacks to prevent workers from exercising their rights; the many arbitration decisions that had been rendered since the last round of negotiations; management's many efforts to achieve rollbacks and to implement changes that negatively affected our members' jobs; and existing political and economic conditions.

Included with the National Executive Board's recommendation of acceptance was a detailed sixteen-page program that set out our demands, dividing into the nine sub-themes. It was designed to secure the future of postal workers across the country. It was ratified in June of 1984 by 91.4 percent of members who exercised their right to vote. (Later in the course of negotiations, our National Executive Board submitted a separate wage demand to our members, and it, too, received the endorsement of the vast majority of the membership.)

Our Negotiating Committee was made up of Gordon Ash from the Atlantic region, Marcel Perreault from Québec, Bob Borch from Ontario, Peter Whitaker from the Western region, and myself as Chief Negotiator. Brother John Fehr, National Chief Steward, acted as Technical Assistant to the Committee.

On the occasion of New Year's Day, 1983, the Episcopal Commission for Social Affairs of the Canadian Conference of Catholic Bishops had issued a statement titled "Ethical Reflections on the Economic Crisis." This had received a lot of attention in the media at the time, largely because of its moral arguments against the increasingly unfettered power of capital in our society at the expense of working people. Before we began our 1984 negotiations, we received a request from the Commission's Chair, Bishop Remi De Roo, that we meet with him at our Ottawa office on May 1, 1984, the same day the Commission was due to hold a press conference to release a paper titled "Ethical Choice and Political Challenge," a follow-up to its 1983 New Year's statement. Bishop De Roo and his colleagues were most interested in our efforts to create new jobs at a time of high unemployment.

After our meeting, Bishop De Roo and his Commission members visited three workplaces to meet with workers who were facing the impacts of technological change. After visits with Mitel workers and women operators at Bell Canada, he went to Canada Post's Alta Vista Plant in Ottawa, where we encountered some difficulties in securing the cooperation of plant management.

Then, in September, Bishop De Roo met with our Negotiating Committee. We were very encouraged that the Catholic Bishops felt that our negotiating approach to creating jobs seemed so important to them.

Negotiations with Canada Post began on July 2, 1984. In my opening remarks in presenting our program of demands, I made it clear that we were prepared to make all reasonable efforts to reach a negotiated collective agreement, but that we were not prepared to accept rollbacks.

Jean-François Boyer, Chief Negotiator for Canada Post, indicated that he understood the problems we had encountered in past collective bargaining efforts. However he said, Canada Post needed "more flexibility to meet new realities" and that the employer was undertaking these negotiations to secure its own future, that of the Crown Corporation. He added that his team had received a mandate to settle an agreement.

When management tabled its series of demands, we saw that theirs were far more numerous than ours and that most of them involved rollbacks. In sum, insecurity, harassment, discrimination, and a further deterioration of working conditions were what Canada Post was offering postal workers. After a series of July meetings, we wrote to Labour Minister Labour André Ouellet, informing him that we were convinced that no settlement would be possible before we had gained the right to strike. We therefore asked him to appoint a Conciliation Commissioner, as this would be the fastest route to put us in a legal strike position under the terms of the Canada Labour Code. We believed that, once we had attained such a position, Canada Post would be much more likely to engage in serious, substantive negotiations.

Instead, the Canada Labour Relations Board decided to appoint Roland Doucet as Conciliation *Officer*. (The legal distinction between a Conciliation Commissioner and a Conciliation Officer meant that, after Mr. Doucet had finished his conciliation efforts, we would still not be in a position to legally strike.) After just a few meetings, it was clear we were getting

Meeting with the chairperson of the Episcopal Commission for Social Affairs of the Canadian Conference of Catholic Bishops on May 1 1984. From left to right: John Fehr, Bill Chedore, and Jean-Claude Parrot of CUPW with Bishop Remi De Roo and Tony Clarke from the Commission.

nowhere. Still, Mr. Doucet insisted that his conciliation efforts continue.

Meanwhile, throughout the summer, Canada Post had sent letters to several employees informing them that their positions had become "surplus," advising them to put their names on lists of those requesting transfers, and telling them that refusal to accept transfers might be considered as the equivalent to the tendering of their resignations. At one point, we refused to continue to meet with Mr. Doucet unless the employer stopped these mandatory transfers. The employer agreed to stop them, and we resumed the conciliation hearings. Also, a federal election had taken place on September 4, and the Progressive Conservatives under new Prime Minister Brian Mulroney had won a clear majority in Parliament.

Negotiations continued until early October, when Mr. Doucet finally submitted his report. On October 11, 1984 we met with new Labour Minister William McKnight, who informed us that he had received Mr. Doucet's report. The next step was for the Labour Minister to choose among three options: he could choose to appoint a three-person Conciliation Board, choose a single person as a Conciliation Commissioner, or choose not to move forward with further conciliation efforts. If the Minister chose one of the first two options, we would acquire the legal right to strike seven days after the release of the final report of the Conciliation Commissioner or Board. If he chose the third option, we would be in a legal strike position seven days after the Minister's decision. While waiting for the Minister to make his decision, we continued meetings with the employer and reached agreement in some minor areas, mostly the renewal of clauses from the previous collective agreement that were not in dispute.

In late October, Labour Minister McKnight named Stanley Hartt, a Montréal lawyer, as Conciliation Commissioner, and Mr. Hartt informed us that his conciliation efforts would start on November 5, 1984. At Mr. Hartt's request, Canada Post agreed to stop all compulsory and other redeployment of our members, and to stop sending threatening letters to workers during Mr. Hartt's conciliation efforts.

During the first two days of Mr. Hartt's conciliation meetings, we presented our brief, while Canada Post used the following two days for one of its Vice-Presidents, Stewart Cooke, to present the employer's arguments. Our brief contained 175 pages of text, providing Mr. Hartt with a short introduction, a historical perspective from 1965 through 1984, and an explanation of the reasons behind each of our demands.

In late November, we made significant progress on three issues. First, we reached an agreement that the maximum weight of any package to be handled by a single employee would be reduced from thirty to twenty-five kilograms. We managed to have management agree to reverse Judge Tremblay's 1978 arbitration decision that put the onus of proving innocence on the worker in cases where management accused that worker of carelessness because of a shortage of cash or stamps at a postal wicket: the onus for proof of guilt would now fall upon the employer. And, we received guarantees that all closed-circuit television systems would be dismantled within sixty days of the signing of a collective agreement and that no new ones would be installed in future.

These developments encouraged us into believing that perhaps Canada Post negotiators really had been given a mandate to do their best to reach an agreement without a strike. Certainly, the new Mulroney government didn't need one at that time.

In December, we began to see high-level Canada Post representatives across the bargaining table. In mid-December, we won another important gain: management agreed that part-time workers would be treated the same as full-timers when it came to the accumulation of annual leave, vacation leave, and sick-leave credits during maternity leave.

On January 25, 1985, Canada Post presented us with a global offer. The next day, we presented a global counter-proposal and explained to Mr. Hartt that Canada Post's offer was unacceptable because several very important issues were not addressed in it, because it still proposed rollbacks, and for other reasons. We now felt that it was time to show some determination and that same day the National Executive Board decided we would conduct a strike vote before the end of February. The next day, Canada Post presented us with a second global offer, which, however, was little different from the previous one. Nevertheless, two days later, we presented another global counter-proposal in order to better position ourselves in light of the upcoming release of Mr. Hartt's Conciliation Report and our upcoming strike vote. That strike vote took place among our members between February 15 and February 25, and 80.3 percent of the membership voted in favour of a strike.

On February 27, 1985, Mr. Hartt discussed the draft of his Conciliation Report with us, and he probably did the same with Canada Post. (Mr. Hartt had an excellent reputation as a mediator, and, although I know that I will never be certain, I have a suspicion that what he showed the two sides in his "draft report" may not have been exactly the same thing. This is the sort of tactic a good mediator might use to convince the parties that their best interests would be served in accepting what was finally recommended.) We then agreed to resume negotiations with Canada Post in his presence, in a final effort to reach a settlement without a strike. On March 1, we presented another global counter-proposal for a settlement without a strike to the employer. Finally, on March 10, 1985, we reached a tentative agreement. In it, we won many important concessions, including some in areas such as job security that were even better than what we had been shown in Mr. Hartt's draft report.

When a union reaches a settlement with an employer without a strike settlement, it often raises the suspicions of some the most militant of the union's members over the motives of the union's leadership. I believe this is a good thing: it keeps the leadership careful about what it compromises before submitting an agreement to the membership. But, in this case, our National Executive Board was not worried about presenting the tentative agreement to the membership with its recommendation for acceptance. Other than those already mentioned, among the major gains we made in the tentative contract was agreement on the following points:

- total job security with no re-deployment to other postal locations except in cases beyond the control of the employer, in which cases the redeployment would be to postal locations no more than forty kilometres away;
- the creation of new jobs through the opening of fourteen "New Direction Outlets" (retail centres located in malls and other strategic locations where a wider range of goods and services were available than in standard postal outlets), in major centres across the country, the conversion of nine postal sub-post offices into full-fledged postal stations, a further reduction of fifty-three in the number of existing postal sub-post offices, and the phase-in of new products and services in the New Direction Outlets and subsequently, if successful, in other outlets;
- one week of pre-retirement leave per year to a maximum of five for employees having reached fifty-five years of age with at least twenty years of service, as well as for employees having reached sixty years of age with at least five years of service;
- three days of night-recovery leave per year to allow additional time off for workers to recover from the negative health effects of working night shifts;

- four weeks' vacation after seven years of service;
- a thirty-seven-cent wage increase retroactive to October 1, 1984, and a further thirty-eight-cent increase effective as of October 1, 1985;
- a cost-of-living allowance effective June 1, 1985, which would be triggered when inflation reached an annual rate of 5 percent;
- a two-year collective agreement retroactive to October 1, 1984, and due to expire on September 30, 1986;
- a cap of 4,500 in the number of part-time employees in the bargaining unit, with no more than 1,000 of these to be in small post offices;
- New dental, hearing, and visual-correction plans paid for by Canada Post;
- an increase in shift and weekend premiums;
- wage increases for temporary Christmas workers.

The tentative agreement was approved by a majority of 87.5 percent of CUPW's membership in the referendum. I'm sure that none of these gains would have been possible if we hadn't had a clear strike mandate from the membership. I also believe that, because the 6- and 5-percent wage increases provided for postal workers under the wage-control legislation turned out to be more than what most other workers had been able to negotiate during that period, fewer workers looked upon the wage package with quite the scrutiny that would normally have been the case.

I was pleased that our first round of negotiations with the new Crown Corporation was resolved without a strike and hoped that this would lead to improved labour-management relations. But I knew negotiations were going to be difficult in the years to come: I expected no miracles from the Progressive Conservative government of Brian Mulroney.

1986–87 Negotiations: Early Stages

We held our National Convention in April of 1986, a few months before we would begin the next round of negotiations with Canada Post. As part of our strategy, we adopted a program of action to mobilize the public to pressure politicians to defend, preserve, and expand postal services. Then, under the umbrella of the CLC, the five major postal unions met to develop a joint campaign to stop the cutbacks in postal services and to promote their expansion. CLC President Shirley Carr, who was accompanied by myself and representatives of the other four unions representing workers in the post office, announced this campaign at a press conference on August 25, 1986.

Local joint committees were established to organize activities in communities across the country. The program of action also included newspaper ads in major dailies coast to coast, the distribution of more than a million postcards to be mailed to politicians, the distribution among unions of a detailed backgrounder providing up-to-date information on

National Executive Board members elected at the 1986 CUPW Convention. From left to right, back row: Chief Steward John Fehr, Second Vice-President Mason Duffy, President Jean-Claude Parrot, First Vice-President Bill Chedore, and Secretary-Treasurer Caroline Lee (the first woman elected a CUPW national officer). Front row, from left: Richard Forget (Québec Region), Pat Miller (Western Region), Darrel Tingley (Atlantic Region), and Joe Alviano (Ontario Region).

the state of affairs in the post office and what they could do about it, and a brand-new video dealing with cutbacks in services and post office closures.

Meanwhile, on June 25, 1986, the President of Treasury Board reported to the House of Commons on changes proposed to eliminate legislative guarantees of full indexing of all pension benefits earned after the date of the change. This was shortly before we were due to begin the next round of negotiations, and it was an advance indication of the sort of hardball the employer and the government were going play.

That next round of negotiations with Canada Post was set to begin on July 2. It would prove to be a classic example of employer dishonesty, a two-year period of management's hard-line approach toward its workers. Its only goal was to win rollbacks and stop the evolution that had taken place in the previous round of negotiations towards job creation through improved and expanded services. It would also prove to be another example of direct involvement by a government determined to impose its terms, whether through negotiations or legislation. But these negotiations would also prove to be another example of the determination of postal workers and their union to negotiate while maintaining a thoroughly progressive vision of what the future should hold for workers.

Our national program of demands was ratified by a majority of 56.6 percent of the members in the spring of 1986. The reason for the lower-than-normal support of the membership for our program of demands was a major difference of opinion regarding our demand for a shorter workweek. The Montréal local argued that our demand would create part-time week-

Occupation of the cafeteria at Canada Post headquarters during the 1986 CUPW National Convention in Ottawa.

end workers and it campaigned against the program of demands. (I will deal further with these differences among our membership in Chapter Eleven.) In addition to a shorter workweek, the program called for progress in the resolution of longstanding issues between the union and the employer, for the maintenance of job security through job-creation measures, and for improvements to the important breakthroughs we had made in previous rounds of negotiations in the area of job creation.

We served our notice to bargain on July 2, 1986. When we arrived outside the Ottawa meeting place where we were to exchange our demands on July 21, we were met by a demonstration organized by the Montréal local and the Québec Regional Executive Committee. We returned to our office because we didn't want to provoke controversy by passing through the demonstrators. And, it was not our practice to cross a line of demonstrators, even if it was not technically a picket line. Another meeting was scheduled, and we met with the employer to exchange our demands for negotiations on July 24, 1986, which, coincidentally, was my fiftieth birthday and the thirty-second anniversary of my first day of work in the Montréal post office.

On July 22, I sent a bulletin to the membership explaining the internal differences within the union that had caused the delay in the presentation of demands, and added:

> Your National Executive Board is convinced that, despite these differences of opinion, on the national program of demands, we are united on the objectives we want to achieve in this round of

Picketing in July 1986 to protest the closure of Postal Station "C" in Winnipeg.

> negotiations. We all want the reduction of night work and the
> creation of day-shift positions, and we are convinced that the time
> has come to make this a reality.

When we met on July 24, the employer presented us with a sweeping
program of proposals, most of which were demands for rollbacks. In fact,
their proposals attacked almost every article in the collective agreement,
which were divided into three categories: monetary, organization of work,
and rights and protections.

In the monetary category, the employer proposed, among many other
rollbacks, to take away workers' wash-up time, as well as an end to both
retroactivity and our cost-of-living allowance. In the organization of work
category, it proposed, among many other demands, to amend the collective
agreement to give it total flexibility in the use of part-time and casual
workers, as well as in the scheduling of work. In the rights-and-protections
category, it demanded, among many other concessions, more restrictive
transfer rules, a system to measure individual workers' productivity, additional steps and time limits in the grievance procedure, and a new clause
stipulating that there would be no strike or lock-out during the life of the
collective agreement. (This was precisely the clause that "BS" MacKasey
had ripped up in 1975.)

After the exchange of demands, the first issue discussed at that meeting was a proposal from the employer to end the practice of simultaneous
translation at the bargaining table. To this, eleven years after we had won
this important demand, our first gain at the bargaining table after leaving
the Council of Postal Unions, I made the following response:

> Let me put it very simply for you. We are not going to have any

meeting without our negotiators having the right to speak and listen to the discussions in any one of the two official languages. So, if you maintain your position on this issue, we won't have any other choice than to apply immediately to move to the step of conciliation.

We immediately adjourned the meeting to see whether the other side would review its position on this important issue. Given the issues of simultaneous translation, the no-strike no-lock-out demand, and management's proposals for concessions on technological changes, on staffing, and on work measurement, it seemed that we were about to relive the difficulties of the 1975 negotiations. And, given its proposals for rollbacks in the area of job creation through service improvement and expansion, and on job security, it seemed we were also about to relive the 1985 negotiations.

The employer finally agreed to maintain the simultaneous translation, and negotiations resumed. We held fourteen meetings up to October 14, 1986, during which we discussed most of our demands. On August 19, we discussed the shorter workweek, and André Sauriol, who was the spokesperson for the employer said, "I know a group of your people who are against this demand, and I don't understand why you are still asking for it." I responded: "Mr. Sauriol, the union represents its members, who have ratified this demand, and I can assure you that none of our members are against the shorter workweek."

That was the end of the employer trying to use the opposition to the wording of this demand within the union against our negotiating team. I must say that Mr. Sauriol had a special sense of humour, and he often tried to be funny in his remarks on our demands. I remember, for example, at this same meeting, he argued against an increase in meal allowances by saying, "If I give you more, you'll eat too much and won't be able to work!"

During this series of meetings, we reviewed one another's demands but made no progress. On October 14, 1986, when management refused to initial the renewal of even clauses where neither party had a demand, we decided we'd had enough. Their argument for not initialing any of these clauses was that, until we agreed to rollbacks, they would not sign anything whatever with us.

On October 16, we filed an application for appointment of a Conciliation Officer, and on October 30 the Minister of Labour appointed André Drouin to assist the parties. The first meetings with Mr. Drouin took place November 24–26, at which time both parties provided an overview of their demands to the Conciliation Officer.

In mid-December and early January, Mr. Drouin met with the parties separately, and he also visited some postal facilities. By January 22, 1987, the employer had agreed to sign 126 clauses where neither party had a demand.

A press conference in March 1987 held by postal unions about a publicity campaign against privatization in the post office. From left to right: Jean-Claude Parrot, Nancy Riche from the CLC, and LCUC President Robert McGarry.

But, that was all that Mr. Drouin was able to get from the employer. Throughout these negotiations, Canada Post had continued to close post offices and boycott the arbitration process.

Given this lack of progress, we explained to Mr. Drouin in early February that we had no choice other than to move to the next step. At our request he withdrew and informed the Minister of Labour that CUPW had asked for the appointment of a three-person Conciliation Board, while Canada Post had requested the appointment of a sole Conciliation Commissioner.

The Minister of Labour appointed a Conciliation Commissioner in the person of Claude Foisy, and we knew by his reputation that he wasn't going to break any new ground in his report. The way the government appoints conciliators in disputes at the federal level is outrageous. One would think that, in looking for someone to appoint as a conciliator, the government would look for individuals who understood their role as bringing the parties to really negotiate and so avoid a strike. But, too often, those appointed understand very well that they had been chosen for very different reasons. And, those so chosen know very well that, if they want the government to give them similar appointments in future, then their reports should fit in nicely with government's agenda, whether hidden or not. In this case, it was clear that the government's agenda was to deny the aspirations and demands of the union and promote management's ability to run the business of the post office as they saw fit.

Unfortunately, this is also the best way to guarantee that a strike will occur, because it ignores the aspirations of workers for a better future. However, the Mulroney government wouldn't mind a strike, because it planned to introduce back-to-work legislation. And neither did Canada Post mind: it planned, for the first time, to use strikebreakers.

Conciliation hearings before Mr. Foisy began in early March of 1987, and they dragged on for months with very few signs of progress. All the while, we worked hard to assure that our members were kept well informed, through activists at the local level, about what was happening at the bargaining table. This was, of course, part of our strategy of negotiating on the strength of our membership, as well as on the strength of the solid arguments we developed in support of our demands. Good communications, especially while union negotiators are at the bargaining table, are as important as good arguments in keeping the membership confident in their union.

In March of 1987, we held a referendum to ratify our specific wage demands. When we had developed the program of demands prior to the beginning of negotiations the previous year, we had deliberately decided to not be specific in this area, identifying only some basic principles: a real wage increase above the inflation rate, full retroactivity, and a cost-of-living allowance to fully protect the negotiated wages. We believed that holding a referendum on separate, more specific wage demands at a time of our choosing during negotiations would strengthen both our position at the bargaining table and solidarity among our members.

By 1987, we had lost 5.9 percent of our wages due to inflation since our last increase, so we demanded an increase of 8 percent as of October 1986 and 6 percent as of October 1987. This wasn't unreasonable, since it also took into consideration management's position at the bargaining table. Among other rollbacks, it was proposing to eliminate our cost-of-living allowance. The referendum on our wage demands passed by a wide margin.

A month after the beginning of conciliation before Mr. Foisy, I had to recommend that the National Executive Board replace Brother Clément Morel on the Negotiating Committee. I took this step in view of his decision to indicate to the Conciliation Commissioner his dissenting position and that of the Montréal local regarding our demand for shortening the workweek. My recommendation was adopted, though the National Director for the Québec region registered his vote against it. Beginning on April 2, 1987, Brother Valère Tremblay from the Québec City local replaced Brother Morel on the Negotiating Committee.

One of the big issues for management was staffing. There had been a large increase in the number of part-time and casual hours worked in the

CUPW cleaners from Toronto demonstrate at the Prime Minister's residence on Sussex Drive in Ottawa.

post office when compared with full-time hours. Now, management wanted to tear up the clause they had signed in 1985 and take away every staffing restriction contained in the collective agreement. They argued that they needed the flexibility the use of part-timers would give them. They also wanted to eliminate the cap on the number of part-timers they could use relative to the number of full-time workers. We argued that, given management's own delivery standards, the changes were unnecessary.

When we discussed the protection of our jobs through job creation, we explained in detail the experiment we had gone through with the New Direction Outlets, the new postal outlets in major malls across the country that were providing more services than were provided in regular postal stations. The creation of these outlets had been part of the 1985 collective agreement. We argued that by offering these new services, Canada Post had increased its revenues. Management's reply to this was that revenues would rise a lot more in privately run sub-post offices where they would only have to pay workers $4.50 an hour.

This attitude upset me at the time, and it upsets me still today. I rose and explained how we had managed to protect our members' jobs through work in these new facilities and that they generated revenues for Canada Post and took nothing away from the employer. These new services were very much appreciated by the public, but now Canada Post wanted to move this work to sub-post offices where they could pay non-unionized workers minimum wage.

I pointed out that I had never argued that the union jobs in the new facilities were making huge profits for Canada Post, but I did argue that they were not in any way a drag on revenues. I argued that this was a positive role to play in our society, that the new facilities protected and created decently paid jobs while providing new services to the public. And, it had given Canada Post a positive image among the general public.

I went on, speaking of the obligation we all have in our society to improve the well being of people and to move away from exploitation through cheap labour. This could be accomplished by creating more full-time employment and providing the same benefits for part-time as for full-time workers. I explained that the contracting out of cleaners' work in the post office, which had taken place a few years before, had led to the exploitation of migrant workers, who were among the most vulnerable in our society. Now, I said, it is our wicket work, our truck maintenance, our data processing, and very much more that management wants to throw open to non-unionized workers getting minimum wage with no protections or benefits. I also underlined the fact that in 1986 casual and over-time hours had increased by 1,600,000 while full-time hours had fallen by 1,300,000.

I began a conciliation hearing on June 9, 1987 by proudly announcing that we were successful in winning a collective agreement for contracted-out cleaners at a plant in Toronto. It took a five-month strike to win the twenty-seven cleaners at Toronto's South Central plant a collective agreement. Their wages immediately increased from $4.65 an hour to $6.25 for light duties, and to $7.25 an hour for heavy duties. They also won seniority rights, a grievance procedure that included third-party arbitration, paid sick and vacation leave, job security with no more contracting out, protection against arbitrary discipline or dismissal, health and safety protections, and union rights in the workplace.

Organizing these workers was not an easy battle. I am sad to have to write here that postal workers did not respect the cleaners' picket lines because they felt that their work had nothing to do with that of the cleaners. The plant was a large, wide-open place, so postal workers didn't actually have to walk through picket lines because, with their small numbers, the cleaners were unable to cover all the entrances. However, our members cooperated inside the plant by not contributing to its cleaning, while some workers joined the cleaners' picket lines before or after their shifts.

I must say that mail-service couriers, members of LCUC were very helpful in this long struggle by lining up with their trucks before entering the plant and allowing us to speak with each of them individually for a few minutes before going in. Sometimes a truck would be lined up for hours before it got in the plant.

Canada Post pretended to ignore the cleaners' strike but it was clear to me that they were working to defeat them. On many occasions, Canada Post sent its security people to try to intimidate the mail-service couriers and CUPW members who were helping on the picket lines.

The executive of the Toronto local was very active in this strike, and it organized help on the picket lines, media coverage, and much more. It provided bus transportation for the cleaners and their supporters to go to Ottawa on a number of occasions to protest at the premises of the cleaning company's owner. These protests were very successful, and posters were plastered on telephone poles on the street all around the owner's premises. The poster included the owner's photograph and details about his minimum-wage exploitation of cleaners in postal plants. He finally gave up: he agreed to negotiations and we signed a collective agreement with him on June 7, 1987. It was a great victory for the cleaners. (We would eventually organize many other cleaners in postal facilities across the country.)

The LCUC Rotating Strikes of 1987

On June 16, 1987, while CUPW was still in the midst of conciliation hearings under the auspices of Mr. Foisy, LCUC began rotating strikes in the face of demands from the employer for major concessions at the bargaining table. The decision of the LCUC Executive to proceed with the rotating strikes was provoked when Canada Post insisted that new provisions in the collective agreement provide for letter carriers to drive their own cars to their walks and forbade them from returning to their stations for lunch. If agreed to, these concessions would have eliminated thousands of positions.

This was a direct attack on job security and on a walk-evaluation system that had been developed by letter carriers through several rounds of negotiations. During LCUC's rotating strikes, the employer used strike-breakers in an effort to intimidate and demoralize LCUC members. The New Democratic Party, the opposition Liberals, the CLC, and the entire labour movement condemned the use of strikebreakers.

Canada Post didn't limit itself to strikebreakers — let's not be too polite from here on in: let's use the term "scabs" — in its efforts to intimidate LCUC members. It called on police to escort scabs through picket lines, it used provocateurs to incite violence and the arrest of letter carriers, it used cameras and other security measures to monitor picket lines, it used disciplinary measures, including firings, to intimidate workers, it used management personnel to do LCUC work, and it threatened CUPW members with discipline for supporting LCUC picket lines.

Nevertheless, this attempt by Canada Post to conduct "business as usual" during the rotating strikes failed, because LCUC maintained strong picket lines, was consistent in its strike strategies, and signed an accord with other postal unions to provide mutual support both inside the workplace and outside on the picket lines.

After nineteen days of rotating strikes, LCUC won its battle against management rollbacks, and I sent a message of congratulations to its National Convention, which was held July 25–29, 1987, in Saskatoon. In my message, I congratulated LCUC members for their "magnificent struggle" and told them that their firm stand against concessions was a tribute to the entire trade-union movement. I added, "Your struggle has strengthened CUPW's determination to withstand the employer's demands for concessions and layoffs."

In August 1987, we reproduced in our national journal, CUPW *Perspective*, the following letter that I received from LCUC president Robert McGarry:

> This letter is to thank the brothers and sisters of the Canadian Union of Postal Workers for their cooperation and support in our recent strike.
>
> I am particularly grateful for the support of your members on the picket lines and for the information received from your union during this difficult period. When LCUC members were picketing all day in order to protect their jobs, groups of CUPW members came forward to join them in support. The feeling of such an action is most difficult to express in words. I wish to personally convey my thanks, through your national office, to you, Jean-Claude, and to all the members of your executive and staff who walked the picket lines with us.
>
> Our victory was gained through the assistance of your membership and I hope that the contract gained by our membership will make your struggle a little easier. In the event that strike action becomes necessary, however, you can be assured of the support of the Letter Carrier's Union of Canada and its membership.
>
> Once again — to the membership of the Canadian Union of Postal Workers — thank you for your cooperation and support.

I must say that LCUC's successful fightback and strike was not only a source of encouragement to our members in our ongoing negotiations; it

Police "line dancing" during the LCUC 1987 strike. The workers on strike and their supporters refused to join in the line dancing, preferring their picket lines.

also confirmed something that I had always believed, that LCUC members would not hesitate to fight when the employer attacked them. And what a fight they gave Canada Post! Nobody can suggest that the strikebreakers intimidated them. If anyone was intimidated, it was the strikebreakers and management.

Some felt that the pictures seen on television gave LCUC members a bad image. But I have never thought that the sight of workers fighting for their security and future was a bad image. Management made a big mistake when they thought they could use the public against LCUC, and they had to drop their demand for concessions.

1986–87 Negotiations: Going Nowhere

Following the LCUC settlement, the struggle against Canada Post's privatization and contracting out continued, and postal workers all across the country participated in national days of action to express both their support for better postal jobs and services and their opposition to Canada Post's plans.

By July 24, 1987 — yes it was my birthday again — a year had passed since that initial meeting where both parties had exchanged their demands. Mr. Foisy, whose conciliation efforts had been taking up much time with very little result to show for it, demanded that we zero in on what we felt were strike issues for our members. These were our demands for job security, an end to contracting out, contracting in of work that had formerly been done — or that might reasonably be done — in postal facilities, service expansion, the closing of sub-post offices, and no franchising of retail outlets.

Speaking of retail outlets, Mr. Foisy pointed out that it was the government that had prevented Canada Post from competing with the private sector in such areas as catalogue sales and franchising retail outlets. He compared CUPW wages of $24.90 an hour to the $5.00 minimum wage offered in the private sector. I responded:

> We are not going to stand for this government making money on the backs of the workers, because this would mean no future for us or our children. We will not be afraid to take on this issue publicly. Canadians are not in favour of cheap labour and we can prove that Canada Post can still make money without cheap labour. It is clear that the issue is how much profit and who will get it, the post office and government or the private sector.

Of course, we felt it should have been Canada Post, which could then afford to pay its workers a living wage, but it was clear that the government wanted the private sector to pocket these profits on the backs of poorly paid workers.

At a meeting on July 27, Canada Post made what it called a "global offer." However, this only led to more meetings, agreement on some uncontroversial clauses, and the tabling of new global proposals and counter-proposals. The final meeting with Mr. Foisy was on August 12, after which he retired to write his report.

While he was so engaged, we held a membership vote on the following recommendation of the National Executive Board:

> Whereas Canada Post and the Tory government have decided to destroy Canada Post through privatization and by reducing the deficit through the elimination of jobs and services;
>
> Whereas Canada Post and the Tory government have refused to address the deficit of Canada Post as is done in other countries, that is, through creating revenue-generating services;
>
> Whereas Canada Post and the Tory government have decided to attack the hard-won, acquired rights of post office workers to achieve their strategy of privatization, cutbacks in services, and cheap labour;
>
> Whereas Canada Post and the Tory government, despite the obvious failure of their strategy with letter carriers, appears determined to try the same strategy again with CUPW and the other unions;
>
> Whereas all postal unions under the umbrella of the Canadian Labour Congress have joined together to fight back for new and improved services instead of the deterioration of services;
>
> Whereas one year of negotiations has not produced any results at the negotiating table;

Whereas the National Executive Board has identified, for the Negotiating Committee, some flexibility on our demands in order to provoke progress in the last stage of the meetings with the Conciliation Commissioner;

Whereas like all the other post office workers, we in CUPW are fighting for our survival and that of the post office as a service to Canadian citizens;

Be it resolved that the Negotiating Committee be given the mandate by the National Executive Board to put the emphasis on the following issues in the last stage of negotiations.

- The protection of all hard-won, acquired rights — that is, no rollbacks;
- Full job security for every employee in the bargaining unit at the signing of the collective agreement;
- The protection of our jobs by opposing any privatization, contracting out, or franchising of our work;
- Job creation and job protection through expansion of services, contracting in of work, and reduced working time;
- The creation of full-time positions through the conversion of part-time positions, casuals, and overtime hours;
- The creation of day-shift positions wherever it is possible to do so;
- Ways to deal with health and safety issues, especially in regard to night work, excessive noise, and workplace injuries;
- A yearly wage increase of one per cent above inflation.

Be it further resolved that the National Executive Board be authorized to call strike activities to achieve the above issues.

The result of the vote was a clear majority in favour of the National Executive Board's recommendation.

In putting this vote forward we encountered one difficulty: the Montréal local wanted the last "be it resolved" to read "to call a general strike" of our members rather than "to call strike activities." The Montréal local completely opposed the idea of rotating strikes, arguing that members inside postal facilities would be at the total mercy of the employer once we acquired the right to strike, because there would be no collective agreement in effect.

The National Executive Board rejected the Montréal local's request on the basis that the type of strike to be called was a strategic issue best decided in light of the circumstances at the time our strike mandate is implemented.

Mr. Foisy's report was released on September 22, 1987, and, as expected, it offered nothing positive for postal workers. He recommended major rollbacks in the areas of job security and staffing. He had told us during the course of our meetings that his recommendations were going to hurt both parties. In his report, he made *statements* that did in fact hit both sides, but when it came to his *recommendations*, only postal workers got hurt. Given the demands of the two sides in this case, there was a major difference between Mr. Foisy not agreeing to a demand of the union and his agreeing to one of the employer: in the first case it meant the status quo would prevail, while in the second case it meant taking away existing benefits, protections, or rights from the workers.

On the issue of job creation, his approach was that it was up to the employer to determine what services and what level of services would be offered to customers. By doing this, and thus ignoring our demands for no contracting out of our work, he not only rejected our demand, but he also gave the employer leave to proceed with the franchising of private retail outlets, despite the existing provisions to the contrary in the last collective agreement.

He made no recommendations on monetary issues but suggested there should be some compensation for postal workers in return for their "concession" on the franchising of private retail outlets. It's up to the parties, he decided, to discuss the cost of such concessions. So, apparently it was up to him to recommend concessions from the union, but it was up to some undefined and indeterminate future discussions between the two parties to determine what might be proper compensation for the recommended "concessions." This showed in just what a cowardly way Mr. Foisy wrote a report that was supposed "assist the parties in reaching an agreement" and so avoid a strike.

On staffing, he recommended that Canada Post be allowed to put part-time workers on all shifts, thus eliminating full-time jobs, including many of limited number of preferred day-shift positions.

Finally, Mr. Foisy wrote: "If the parties maintain their extreme positions, all we can do is let them engage in the clash of Titans." This was an apt confession from Mr. Foisy that the task he agreed to undertake when he accepted the position of Conciliation Commissioner was one he couldn't do. He lacked the courage to make recommendations that would have forced both parties to sit down and negotiate in earnest.

Still, we did try to negotiate a settlement in the days following the release of what would become known as the Foisy Report and even after we began our strike action on September 30. But the employer was quite aware that the government had already announced that back-to-work legislation was going to be adopted in the House of Commons, imposing a government-appointed arbitrator (read "employer-appointed arbitrator"), to decide on the content of a new contract (I couldn't bring myself to write "collective agreement" here) for postal workers.

On Saturday, September 26, the employer tabled what it called its final offer — an offer of rollbacks and more rollbacks on the part of postal workers Just to give an idea of the scope of the proposed rollbacks, the following are examples included in a bulletin I sent to our members on September 28, 1987: the elimination of full job security for all employees; "surplus" employees to be laid off unless a vacant position exists and they are willing to move anywhere in Canada; a restrictive definition of technological changes; no restrictions in contracting out or franchising to the private sector; wicket employees who lost work for more than a year would receive $1,000; wicket employees who lost work for more than two years would receive an additional $2,000, subject, of course, to them accepting another position anywhere in Canada; no job creation through improved and expanded services; elimination of the peak period for part-time workers and an increase of part-time hours; in case of high mail volumes, overtime would be offered first to part-time employees; and the elimination of the cost-of-living allowance and of full retroactivity. And, this is but a partial list of the goodies contained in Canada's Post's final "offer." Attention to any of our major demands was nowhere in sight

Canada Post released its "final offer" to the media prior to presenting it to us at the bargaining table. This clearly showed us the contempt the employer had for postal workers. This "offer" had nothing to do with an effort to resolve the issues in dispute; rather it was a media event that had everything to do with Canada Post's expectation of back-to-work legislation whenever we chose to take strike action.

The union was left with practically no choice other than to take strike action, which we would be in a legal position to do on September 29, seven days after the release of the Foisy Report. On September 28, in a last-ditch attempt to reach a settlement, we presented a global counter-proposal in which we dropped seven of our demands and moved on wording in many other areas, but in which we maintained our major demands on job security, service expansion, job creation, priority staffing by full-time workers, and a wage increase of one percent above the inflation rate.

After a long discussion on individual demands and proposals, we agreed to meet again the next day, the last before strike activities would begin. Before adjourning, Harold Dunstan, Vice-President of Human Resources for Canada Post, told us, "The inevitability of it all becomes a pain in the ass. It doesn't look like we will have a settlement tomorrow night. We are so far apart on the key issues."

At the meeting the following day, all we were able to agree on was the identification of twenty more uncontroversial clauses in the existing agreement.

However, we learned through the media that the Minister of Labour had appointed his Deputy Minister, Bill Kelly, ostensibly to embark on a fact-finding mission on the state of negotiations. He held separate meetings with the parties to assess the situation in order to see how far apart the parties were and to determine whether either side was willing to compromise and, if so, in what areas. It was only in the following days that we ascertained that Mr. Kelly's fact-finding mission was not designed to gather information about the state of negotiations. Rather, the facts he gathered were to be used by the Mulroney government to justify its pending back-to-work legislation.

By this point it was crystal clear that the employer felt no pressure to resolve anything, knowing back-to-work legislation was waiting in the Parliamentary wings should we initiate any strike action. It knew that the legislation would, as usual, impose an arbitrator, who in turn would impose a contract between the parties.

That afternoon we continued meeting with the employer, dealing particularly with the whole issue of grievances and arbitration procedures. We had reached a situation where thousands upon thousands of grievances were pending arbitration, because the employer took no grievances seriously until a date was set for a hearing before an arbitrator. But there was an ominous sense from the other side of the bargaining table that they were simply watching the clock tick off the final hours and minutes of the negotiating process. With our right to strike about to come into effect as the second hand ticked past midnight, André Sauriol, Canada Post's Chief Negotiator, said, "There are three things certain in life: dying, going to the bathroom, and signing a collective agreement." Though I might have said more, my reply to him was brief: "We never signed a collective agreement in 1979," I said, referring to the collective agreement imposed on us after we defied the Trudeau government's back-to-work legislation. My implication was that we wouldn't sign this one either.

Days One to Fifteen of the Strike

Day One — Wednesday, September 30, 1987

As expected, the last-minute meetings of September 29 ended without any real progress. I reported this to the National Executive Board, which decided to move forward with our strike strategies. As mentioned earlier, there was serious disagreement between the Montréal local and the National Executive Board on how to proceed.

While there was some truth in the local's argument that a series of rotating strikes would leave workers in other locations at the total mercy of the employer, we felt there were great advantages in rotating strikes in view of the circumstances we were in. First, it was costly to the employer because it had to pay almost all workers while getting less revenue than normal. Second, it was politically more difficult for the Mulroney government to get back-to-work legislation through Parliament while mail was being stopped for only a day or two here and there. Third, we knew Canada Post was going to use scabs as they had in the LCUC strike, and with rotating strikes the employer wouldn't know where they were going to be needed, and so it would need to have them at the ready all across the country. Finally, it was better for our public image, because the public generally had no problem with mail delays so long as they were brief.

The Montréal local also took the position that using rotating strikes went against CUPW's orientation. I argued that we shouldn't confuse a strategy with an objective, a goal, or an orientation. (While I was still working in Montréal in 1970, CUPW had used rotating strikes, and my local had objected to them, not because we had been opposed to rotating strikes as such, but because they had become more the objective than a strategy to achieve our objective. Also, we had disagreed with the strategy at that time of not moving to a general strike when the time came for a show of strength. Nevertheless, our objection in 1970 had been of matters of strategy, and the Montréal local had not acted contrary to any decisions of the National Executive Board.)

In 1987, when we discussed our strike strategy, I made sure everyone understood that we might feel it necessary at some point to switch to a general strike of our membership as the situation changed. I explained that the employer might resort to a partial or total lock-out, but that if it did, Canada Post would be the side the public would blame for shutting down the post office. And, if the government chose to introduce back-to-work legislation in response to our rotating strikes, we would then have to decide on our course of action.

Because the Montréal local had told the National Executive Board it was going to strike that night and stay out until a settlement was reached, we decided that the first two locals asked to go out on the first day of our rotating strike would be the Montréal and Victoria locals. They walked out just after midnight on the morning of September 30.

The Montréal local had made no secret that they intended to go out and stay out, so Canada Post was ready to send busloads of scabs through the picket lines there. In Victoria, the employer wasn't able to organize scabs until the morning shift but, to their surprise, we asked Victoria to return to work for the day shift. So, all the scabs that had shown up at the plant at 6:45 am were sent home.

We wanted to show that CUPW was still interested in negotiating a settlement so, on the evening of September 30, we presented a global counter-proposal, approved by our National Executive Board, to Canada Post. We needed to show some real movement, while not losing sight of our overall objectives for this round of negotiations: progress and job security. My presentation of our counter-proposal was an oral one because, at this point, we were dealing with issues we hoped would lead to serious negotiations, rather than wording. I said that, while we still rejected the concept of franchising as unacceptable, we were no longer rejecting the concept of franchising itself, but we wanted a share of it for our members at union wages. I outlined various ways our job security might be maintained. I said that we had dropped our demand for a shorter workweek and that we were willing to compromise on vacation time, on the length of the collective agreement, and on our demands for child care. I outlined ways we were willing to move on grievance and arbitration procedures, as well as on health and safety issues. I concluded my presentation as follows:

> We feel that this package could get us into serious negotiations. We ask that you look at matters seriously and come back to us. If we don't get a negotiated settlement this way, it will create a lot of problems and hard feelings, and we will end up with an imposed agreement and still have to work together afterwards.
>
> Canada Post has a mandate to improve labour relations and we ask you to take this seriously. We do not intend to be governed by "religion" on any specific demands. We are prepared to be objective and to look into these areas, but this would involve serious negotiations.

Within an hour, the employer came back and outlined its position. It didn't want any references to franchising in the collective agreement, it needed to lay off workers, it wouldn't give us a straight answer on job creation, it didn't want a limit on the number of part-timers, and it would insist on the terms of the Foisy Report on all other issues. There were no more meetings with the employer for several days.

Day Two — Thursday, October 1

Naturally, Canada Post's use of scabs caused resentment on our picket lines. Over the more than twenty years since our 1965 strike, there had never been violence on our picket lines — other than a minor incident here and there — which was quite an achievement for a union of more than 23,000 members spread out in more than a thousand postal installations across Canada. Now though, as had been the case in the recent LCUC strike, our members were facing provocation, harassment, and violation of their rights.

On the second day of the strike, picket lines went up at 1:00 am in Hamilton, Ontario. All was very peaceful until a private mail service truck tried to drive through the lines. Police used excessive force and six of our members were hurt, two of them having to be hospitalized. At 5:45 am, about sixty scabs went into the plant by bus, accompanied by seventeen police cars. Two sisters were arrested for allegedly throwing eggs at the buses.

In St. John's, picket lines also went set up at 1:00 am, with about 150 members present. A busload of scabs arrived a few hours later and four people were arrested, one for assaulting a police officer posing as a journalist in "support" of the picketers. (At some point, the imposter pushed one

of our members, who pushed him back and was immediately arrested.). Of
course, *agents provocateurs* on picket lines are nothing new to the labour
movement, which is why striking unions often try to keep track of just who
is on a picket line. In our case, it also helped in determining who was
entitled to strike pay.

Picket lines also went up at postal stations in the Halifax-Dartmouth
area on Day Two, but it was very peaceful there: no scabs tried to go
through the lines and police did nothing more than observe some picketers.
Postal workers handed out leaflets to the public asking them not to use the
post office during the strike, and these were generally well received.

Day Three — Friday, October 2

On Day Three, Canada Post resorted to new tactics. When picket lines
went down in Hamilton, St. John's, and Ottawa, postal workers who were
scheduled to work were not allowed to do so until scabs inside had finished
their shifts. In Hamilton, management asked the local to inform it, facility
by facility, when picket lines would come down and told the local that it
would then determine the time and date of members' return to work.

In Grimsby, part of the Hamilton local, when postal workers returned
to work the employer refused to give them their paycheques. They then sat
down, chanting, "No cheque, no work." They got their cheques.

The Yellowhead Distribution Centre Facility in Edmonton and the
Dieppe Bulk Mail Facility near Moncton were also out on Day Three.

In Toronto, where workers had yet to set up picket lines, local officers
— who were following busloads of scabs waiting to be put into action on
word of local strike activities — were themselves followed by management
security and investigation personnel. Managers worked extra hours keeping groups of scabs ready in anticipation of a local strike.

All across the country, security and investigation personnel and other
management employees were assigned to monitor rallies and demonstrations.

During the day, Deputy Labour Minister Bill Kelly reported to his
Minister, Pierre Cadieux, who then told the House of Commons that the
government would prefer CUPW and Canada Post to reach a negotiated
settlement rather than introducing back-to-work legislation. However, he
said, he had the perception that neither party want to reach a settlement
and added that he had decided not to appoint a mediator at this stage. But
he declared that the government would not tolerate a disruptive, pro-
tracted work stoppage. (Earlier in the week, Harvie Andre, the Minister
responsible for Canada Post, had said that massive economic losses to
businesses dependent on postal services or undue violence on picket lines
might justify government interference.)

Day Four — Saturday, October 3

Our rotating strikes strategy was clearly making it impossible for the government to introduce back-to-work legislation at this stage. However, we knew it was just a question of time and we needed to put additional pressure on both the employer and the government.

So on Day Four locals across the country stepped up efforts to reach out to the public. Demonstrations took place in front of Canada Post's divisional offices, constituency offices of Tory Ministers and Members of Parliament, in front of halls where scabs were being hired, in front of scab bus company offices, and other places.

One of our strategies was for some locals to organize huge demonstrations in front of their places of work, forcing management to prepare for a strike, and then, a few minutes before the beginning of shifts, shutting down their picket lines and showing up on time for work.

Demonstrations were organized with the assistance and participation of provincial Federations of Labour and their affiliates in Saint John, Vancouver, and Toronto. In Saint John and Toronto, they called for anti-scab legislation, and in Toronto they protested privatization. I had the privilege to speak at the Saint John rally and received a good response from the assembled crowd of 300.

Messages of support from unions and other supporters from all across the country came into our national office every day. By this stage we had received a message of support from, among many others, Robert White, President of the Canadian Auto Workers. He also wrote this to Prime Minister Mulroney:

> Once again your government is encouraging the use of strike-breakers to try to steal the jobs of workers in the post office. Surely this insanity, which can only lead to violence, demands the condemnation of yourself and your government. With respect, Mr. Prime Minister, you cannot take credit for not crossing a picket line while on the other hand not stopping what Canada Post management is doing. Again, you of all people know what these actions do to labour relations. In the name of fair and free collective bargaining, I urge you to condemn the actions of Canada Post management immediately.

The 8,500-member United Steelworkers of America Local 1005 in Hamilton issued a press release in which they called on labour and all fair-minded citizens to stand firmly together in support of CUPW and to oppose the unprincipled actions of Canada Post. We also received encouraging words from Liberal Leader John Turner opposing postal franchises: "Apart from the worrisome implications for government patronage, we believe they could affect the quality of service and give undue competitive advantages to certain businesses. Be assured that we will be vigorous in our opposition."

Another message came from the Congress of South African Trade Unions, which we supported for many years in its struggle against apartheid. They ended their message by saying, "Your fight is our fight. Your victory is our victory. An injury to one is an injury to all."

While our rotating strikes were taking place, members of the Canadian Postmasters' and Assistants' Association (CPAA), were under tremendous pressure from Canada Post to sort mail normally processed by CUPW members. If they refused, Canada Post threatened to lay them off due to lack of work. But, protected by provisions in their collective agreement, they refused to handle our mail and sent it back to the offices from which it had come. On September 29, the Canadian Labour Relations Board rendered a unanimous decision declaring that CPAA officers had the right to speak out publicly in an effort to represent their membership, whether it be to the media, government, other influential bodies, or in any other forum, and to attempt to influence the employer on matters that directly affected CPAA's membership. The Board ordered Canada Post to remove disciplinary notes from the file of a sister who had spoken out against Canada Post's business plan and to "cease and desist from interfering with the rights of [CPAA members] acting in [their] capacity as a union representative." Canada Post had argued that criticism of it by any employee could not be tolerated, that only paid union officers could do so, and she was not one. The Board's response was that, just as Canada Post has the right to promote its business plan in its own way, "It is only fair that the union through its chosen representatives be allowed as well to express to the public its own view of the same Corporation plan." Our members and members of other postal unions faced similar situations, so this decision was very welcome because it would apply to all Canada Post employees.

Day Five — Sunday, October 4

We informed the membership that the employer had written to CUPW declaring that it had changed the collective agreement effective one minute after midnight on September 30, 1987. Among the changes management had unilaterally decided upon were: no more access for union officers to premises under the control of the employer; union dues would no longer be collected from workers' paycheques; no more right to grieve; articles on health and safety and on technological change were to be replaced by the provisions of the Canada Labour Code; and the denial of many other benefits, leaves, and other rights.

It was clear to me that this was just another effort to intimidate our members to either put pressure on the union leadership to settle or provoke us to declare a full-scale strike. The first of these hoped-for outcomes was a forlorn one, because by now our solidarity was stronger than ever. As for management's second hope, we were well aware that a full-scale strike at this point would make it easier for government to push back-to-work legislation through Parliament, thus imposing a collective agreement on us through arbitration and also that it would make the strike cheaper for Canada Post, which would then not have to pay salaries to CUPW workers. We weren't foolish enough to fall into such a transparent trap.

In response to this latest management tactic, we argued that the employer didn't have the right to unilaterally change the terms and conditions of employment. In fact, not long before, a unanimous decision in a similar case of the British Columbia Court of Appeal had rendered a decision to just this effect.

The employer came back to the table on Day Five, perhaps because of the show of determination and support we had received in the previous few days. At one point during that meeting, someone on the employer's side made a remark about the Montréal local not being in tune with the National Executive Board. I told him he was confused: we were organizing rotating strikes, with some locals being asked to go out for a few hours, others for a full day, and others for more than a day, which was the case for the Montréal local. (The local hadn't given us any choice in this, but the struggle they were carrying out locally was quite impressive. And, a few days later, we adopted a resolution that brought the Montréal local under the umbrella of our national strategy, which would entitle them to strike pay after being out for ten days, as provided in our national constitution.)

Harold Dunstan opened the meeting by explaining that management still felt it was possible to find the necessary compromises to reach a negotiated settlement, but that we were still very far apart and there would have to be compromises on both sides. They were prepared to seek a settlement on basic principles, he said, adding that Canada Post had to deal with seven different bargaining units and that there had to be a similar pattern in the negotiation and settlement processes with each union.

The first pattern, he explained, is compensation. Deviations from the pattern have to be explainable to other unions. The second pattern is job security. Canada Post needs to have similar benefits and employee protections in all its collective agreements, recognizing that different circumstances can lead to some variation.

Mr. Dunstan continued with this long explanation of Canada Post's position on different issues, but his bottom line was the offer of nothing more than the Foisy Report. His talk of patterns was simply his rationale for this position.

"There is a pattern you forgot to mention," I told him. "It's the pattern established in the last round of negotiations, the pattern reflected in the existing collective agreement we both signed without a strike." His answer to that argument was this: "The last time around it was a roll of the dice with the experiment of service expansion forced upon us." When I pointed out that Canada Post had reduced its deficit since the last round of negotiations, Mr. Dunstan responded that Canada Post was going to change and that we could either fight the change or go along with it. "We will not go along with change," I told him, "if it means layoffs and cheap labour."

The dialogue then deteriorated into simple repetition of the previous arguments used by each side to justify its position. I noted that, after the signing of the previous agreement, we had expected service expansion at postal wickets, but that this hadn't happened. Mr. Dunstan argued that Canada Post had been told by government not to compete with the private sector. After further discussion, we agreed we were at an impasse.

I had earlier provided the employer with a list of hundreds of articles sold at wickets in the Australian post office, something I'd brought back with me on the occasion of a trip I took to address a convention of the postal workers' union in Melbourne. I've always found it incredible that, other than some pre-stamped ones, we didn't even sell envelopes at our wickets. I worked at postal wickets for ten years, and I heard requests from customers for a wide range of products that we couldn't provide.

I see no merit in the argument that the post office shouldn't compete with the private sector. It was the private sector that began to compete with the post office when it saw there was money to be made. For example, when I began work, the post office was the only player in the parcel business. And, at one time we offered savings accounts because banks weren't willing to open branches in many smaller communities, but that service was stopped many years ago. Today, banks are closing in smaller communities across the country — many of which still have post offices — forcing people to drive to nearby towns to do their banking.

My vision is of a society where we all have a responsibility to our communities and that applies to employers as much as anyone else. But what we see today, with profit seemingly the only criterion, is companies closing in many communities, often after having exploited natural resources for years, leaving only unemployment in their wake. Other companies just pack up and move to other countries to exploit cheap labour there, abandoning the workers and communities that allowed them to thrive in the first place.

The fact is that private business doesn't want government to be an example of a good employer. But what would be wrong with that? What's wrong with sharing some of the wealth with people other than company shareholders? After all, aren't workers, as citizens, really the largest group of shareholders in Canadian society? As citizens, we should expect the benefits we get from our governments to come in the form of services and social programs, as well as in the form of decent employment. So, I can't accept the argument that it's somehow wrong to compete with the private sector, which only takes what is profitable, leaving the unprofitable to government. And then, the private sector has the nerve to speak out against government deficits.

I never had any doubts that the post office could be a profitable business, providing great service to the public at a reasonable cost and at the same time offering decent employment in every community across the country. I don't believe Canada Post should exist only to ensure that corporate shareholders see their profits forever rise, with complete disregard for the rest of the people. I firmly believe that there must be a social dimension to what we do with, and in, our lives. So, I tried throughout my working life to do the best I could to see that the working conditions of those I represented contributed to a better world for workers, their families, and their communities.

Day Six — Monday, October 5

On Day Six, more than a thousand CUPW members in twenty-seven locals in seven provinces went out on strike, in addition to the Montréal local, which, of course, was still out.

Day Seven — Tuesday, October 6

On the morning of Day Seven, 1,600 more members in six provinces were called out on strike. As well, the employer locked out the workers who had gone out the day before, threatening that they would remain locked out for up to three days.

At 3:00 pm, the union received a letter from Labour Minister Pierre Cadieux reminding us that the government was ready to proceed with back-to-work legislation. "Since no [negotiating] meeting is scheduled," he wrote, "I will give notice to the House of Commons today that the government intends to introduce a Bill to resolve this dispute... the decision to table the Bill or not depends on your willingness and ability to resolve your dispute through the collective bargaining process."

We asked for a meeting with Mr. Cadieux, but he refused.

Day Eight — Wednesday, October 7

Negotiations resumed between the parties, but positions on both sides being unchanged, it was another long and fruitless exchange between Mr. Dunstan and myself.

We then moved to discussions on grievance and arbitration procedures, which involved the participation of our National Chief Steward, Brother John Fehr. In total, the meeting lasted five hours and was unproductive. I indicated that, in view of the letter we had received from the Labour Minister the day before, we now wished to have a mediator appointed, and we asked the other side to join us in this request to the Canadian Labour Relations Board. Mr. Dunstan said that he felt strongly that, given how far apart the two sides remained, appointing a mediator at this point would be of no use.

Before the meeting ended, I confirmed to my office that we had failed to get agreement from the employer to jointly request a mediator. At about 4:00 pm, a letter with my signature was sent to the Labour Minister confirming that we had returned to the bargaining table and asking for the appointment of a mediator, independent of Labour Canada, to assist the parties in reaching an agreement.

It was clear at this point that neither party wanted to be seen as the one that broke off talks. At the end of the meeting, we asked the other side whether it was calling it quits. They answered that they wanted to continue meeting to discuss grievance and arbitration procedures.

Meanwhile, we were reaching out to more and more people in communities across the country, and there was increasing pressure on the Tory government to order Canada Post to begin to negotiate seriously.

Supervisors in many locations were taking small groups of workers aside to tell them the collective agreement was no longer in force and that they had no rights. Locals that took part in the rotating strikes were being locked out by management for different periods of time in hopes of dividing the membership and provoking extended walk-outs. Members were being suspended for petty reasons, with supervisors challenging other workers to "go on strike if you don't like it." The discipline of our members was incredible, in view of the many methods of provocation they suffered all across the country.

Day Nine — Thursday, October 8

During the entire period of these rotating strikes, the National Executive Board held meetings to deal with the issues requiring their attention. We discussed strategies and monitored movement — or more accurately, the lack of movement — at the bargaining table. We held regular press conferences and did interviews with reporters to keep the public informed of our position and actions and to counteract media statements from Canada Post representatives.

We also held meetings with the opposition parties in Parliament, the CLC, and many others to explain our position and try to win their support of our call against the introduction of back-to-work legislation. We organized demonstrations and rallies on a daily basis.

On Day Nine, the National Executive Board decided that we would move to an all-out strike of our 23,000 members across the country as soon as the government introduced back-to-work legislation.

Day Ten — Friday, October 9

The government introduced back-to-work legislation, Bill C-86, in the House of Commons, and from coast to coast to coast, our 23,000 members were out on strike. We called on locals to join those already out, and they all did so without any hesitation.

Postal workers in Toronto prevented scabs and vehicles from entering postal facilities by linking arms all around the plant. Canada Post then resorted to helicopters to move a very small amount of mail, and residents in the area complained about the noise. Canada Post told them to take their complaints to the federal Transport Department.

In Timmins, Ontario, a mail truck was delayed by a picket line, and letter carriers were given two-day suspensions because they didn't wait for the mail to arrive. Another local reported that windows and windshields of buses transporting scabs had been painted black, which must have made the bus drivers' jobs more than a bit challenging. Demonstrations and other actions in support of postal workers took place across the country, and they all underlined the message that, whatever might happen in the next few days, our struggle was far from over.

Bill C-86 had not received the consent of the New Democrats or the Liberals, which was necessary for its speedy passage in the House of Commons. The Bill would make our legal strike an illegal one and immediately order postal workers back to work. It called on CUPW and each of its officers and representatives to give notice to postal workers that they must return to work, take all reasonable steps to ensure they comply with that order, and refrain from any conduct that might encourage workers not to comply.

For any individual who contravened any provision of Bill C-86, the penalty would be no less than $500 and no more than $1,000, except for individuals acting in the capacity of an officer or representative of the union, in which case the penalty would be no less than $10,000 and no more than $50,000. In the case of the union itself, the penalty for contravention of any of the legislation's provisions would be no less than $20,000 and no more than $100,000 for each day or part of a day the offence continued. Furthermore, no individual convicted of an offence under Bill C-86 while acting on behalf of the union would have the right to serve as a CUPW officer or representative for a period of five years.

As expected, the legislation called for the appointment of a mediator-arbitrator to determine the provisions of a new collective agreement. The mediator-arbitrator was to first mediate the unresolved issues and then, on any matters still in dispute, arbitrate the matter and render a decision. In doing so, the legislation stipulated, the mediator-arbitrator had to give "due cognizance" to the Foisy Report.

With the assistance of the staff in our Ottawa office and our lawyer, I managed to arrange meetings with the opposition parties and even with the committee dealing with Bill C-86. I explained to them that, in fact, under Bill C-86 there would be no real arbitration. It would face us with the legal imposition of the Foisy Report, and this would leave the parties in a real mess, because the Foisy Report had failed to address many areas in dispute, and in others it failed to recommend any specific wording. Furthermore, I argued, it would put the mediator-arbitrator in a very difficult position, because he would have to decide on all the many issues still in dispute. All this would make a mockery of both the mediation and the arbitration processes provided for in the legislation

Fortunately, members of the committee dealing with Bill C-86 recognized the points I made and, with the help of the New Democrats, an amendment was added to the legislation before third reading. It was not all we wanted, but it changed the wording instructing the mediator-arbitrator from "give due cognizance to the Foisy Report" to "give cognizance to the Foisy Report."

I believe this change of a single word was what would eventually enable us to convince the mediator-arbitrator, Lucien Cossette, that Parliament's intent was not for him to impose the Foisy Report but simply to read it before rendering his decision.

Bill C-86 also stipulated that the term of the collective agreement would take effect from October 1, 1986, and would expire on a date to be fixed by the mediator-arbitrator, but not earlier than September 30, 1988, or later than September 30, 1989. This legislative provision meant that the collective agreement had continued to be in effect during the strike period, contrary to the numerous statements to the contrary made by the management.

Day Eleven — Saturday, October 10

Hundreds of messages of support streamed into our national, regional, and local offices across the country. They came from the labour movement — from the CLC and its affiliates, from small locals of many unions, from provincial Federations of Labour, and from national and international unions. They came from the political field — from representatives of federal and provincial parties. They came from the social movement — from church groups, women's organizations, the unemployed, and from those advocating for the poor, for rural Canada, for peace, for the environment. And they came from many more sources. The content of these messages, conveyed to picket lines, bolstered the resolve of postal workers.

In reaction to constant provocations, there were confrontations on picket lines, which the government used to denounce opposition parties for their refusal to fast-track Bill C-86. Both the New Democrats and the Liberals blamed the Tory government for introducing the legislation in the first place, thus increasing tempers on picket lines.

Police continued to escort scabs through picket lines across the country, and judges were quick to grant injunctions limiting the number of picketers at various locations.

Day Twelve — Sunday, October 11

We sent the following message to every one of our locals:

> At this time, it is not known when the strikebreaking legislation will
> be passed. However, it could happen as early as Tuesday afternoon.
> Based on this, demonstrations should be scheduled by all locals on
> Tuesday, October 13, 1987. Demonstrations should be held at
> constituency offices of Tory Members of Parliament, and at divi-
> sional offices of the Corporation or at post offices, whichever is
> appropriate. Picket signs should have slogans that oppose the
> removal of the right to free collective bargaining and the right to
> strike, repressive legislation, court injunctions, police brutality, etc.
>
> The National Executive Board will meet following the pas-
> sage of the legislation to determine our strategy. Until a decision is
> made, locals should maintain strong picket lines. Take advantage
> of the strike to maximize local activities.

Day Thirteen — Monday, October 12

This was a sad day. Sister Marie Taylor, from St. John's, Newfoundland, was
hospitalized after her pelvis was broken when a private mail service truck
struck her early in the morning. The truck was already half way through
the picket line when the driver suddenly accelerated, injuring Sister Taylor,
demolishing a gate, and hitting a guardhouse.

We denounced Canada Post's astronomical spending during the strike.
In one case, $300,000 was paid for sixty school buses to carry scabs
through picket lines in Toronto. These buses, bought from a company in
Drummondville, Québec, couldn't pass the required Ontario safety in-
spection, and most of them were ordered off the road on Sunday night.

Canada Post then tried to arrange for taxis to drive the scabs through
picket lines, but taxi companies would have no part of any such plans. It
then arranged for some local transit buses, but their unionized drivers
refused to cross picket lines. Eventually, the scabs walked through picket
lines under heavy police escort. When they came back out, they were
greeted with eggs and insults.

Arrangements had previously been made to sell the school buses, in
whatever condition they might be, for $1,000 each at the conclusion of the
strike. Canada Post had agreed in advance to absorb the $240,000 loss on
these buses.

The *Toronto Star* reported that drivers for these buses had been re-
cruited in Montréal and were paid $240 a day, plus expenses such as hotels
and meals. The twenty-two security guards hired from a Montréal firm
specializing in strikebreaking to accompany these buses were paid $1,000
a week in take-home pay, and each bus carried one or two "bus captains,"
who received $220 a day and whose responsibility it was to hand out time

cards to every scab. The scabs themselves were paid $13.25 an hour, with time-and-a-half after forty hours and a guarantee of twelve hours pay even if they worked far less. And, if they showed up when called during the first seven days of the strike and remained at work until sent home, they received a $200 bonus.

Day Fourteen — Tuesday, October 13

The back-to-work legislation reached second reading in the House of Commons. New Democrat Members of Parliament proposed three changes to the bill: the deletion of the reference to the Foisy Report (so as not to tie the hands of the mediator-arbitrator), the separation the mediation and arbitration processes, and deletion of that section of the legislation that stipulated five-year suspensions from office for union representatives who defied the back-to-work order. These attempts to amend the legislation were unsuccessful, and it was sent back to committee. Third reading, however, was imminent, and we knew that C-86 would soon become law.

Judges across the country granted several more injunctions limiting picketers. In Victoria, lines were limited to five picketers, in Bathurst, New Brunswick, to two. Previous injunctions had limited picketers in Vancouver and New Westminster to five at each truck entrance, and caps were put on the numbers that could picket at main entrances to post offices

The Vancouver local managed to keep the scabs from the post office, probably because the police already had their hands full providing security for a conference of Commonwealth leaders. Canada Post applied to the courts for a contempt charge against the local's president and grievance officer. A hearing was immediately granted, and another injunction was issued to further restrict the number of picketers.

It's amazing just how quickly judges manage to make themselves available to hear requests for injunctions by the employer during legal strikes. It's even more amazing how quickly they agree to grant injunctions against workers on legal strike.

Despite the strikebreakers, the courts, the employer's provocations, and the impending passage of Bill C-86, the morale of postal workers remained high. They devised creative ways to continue the struggle: for instance, on Thanksgiving Day they held turkey dinners in front of the homes of Tory Members of Parliament, and there were demonstrations in front of Tory constituency offices, police stations, and elsewhere. One local's members demonstrated in front of strikebreakers' homes, and the next day the number of scabs showing up for work dropped from forty-one to six. The same local also visited a car rental company, which had not been aware that their vans were being used to carry scabs across cross picket lines. The company then asked Canada Post to return them and, when it refused, the company towed the vans back to its premises.

In Winnipeg, there were seventy picketers on the line, but they were outnumbered by the seventy uniformed officers, the dozen plain-clothed officers, two paddy wagons, and other police vehicles parked near the post office. The picketers decided to reduce their numbers, leaving just three members on the line, and the media made much hay about the resulting imbalance.

The Postmaster in Rouyn-Noranda, Québec, drove a Canada Post car through a picket line and two women had to jump onto the hood of the car to avoid being hit. The local immediately laid charges and, thankfully, the police responded promptly. The Postmaster appeared in court the next day and was fined $600 and had demerit points put on his driver's licence.

At one point during the strike, I went to Toronto, where Canada Post's strikebreaking activities were at their peak, to take part in some of the local's actions. Local president Andre Kolompar told me that he knew where the employer was marshalling scabs before bringing them to the plants and having them cross picket lines under police escort. We drove there and slipped inside. There were about two hundred people waiting to be escorted to the plants. I jumped onto a table and spoke to them about what they were about to do. I told them that we were fighting for permanent, decently paid jobs for people just like them and indicated that if they took these very temporary jobs Canada Post was offering them they would have to carry the label "scab" for the rest of their lives. Knowing that security personnel might descend upon me at any moment, I told them quickly that we knew who they were and encouraged them to go home. We then left before any police or the employers' goons made an appearance.

In Ottawa, scabs were asked to gather in the parking lot of a shopping mall a couple kilometres from the Alta Vista plant. There, they boarded waiting buses that city police officers then escorted to the plant and across our picket lines. In a speech I made on an Ottawa picket line, I wondered why our municipalities were using our tax dollars to have local police do Canada Post's dirty work. They were doing much more than ensuring there was no violence on picket lines: they were taking part in the breaking of a legal strike. After the strike was over, I invited locals across the country to ask municipalities to send bills to Canada Post so they could recover the cost of all the extra police work done on the employer's behalf.

Throughout the strike, and especially as the passage of back-to-work legislation was working its way through Parliament, rumours were flying about whether we would defy the law. One day, in answer to a reporter, I said:

> I have never been a candidate for suicide. I was not in 1978 when we defied the law and I will not be in 1987. If you interpret this to mean that we will defy legislation, you're wrong, and if you interpret this to mean we will not defy legislation, you're wrong, because the National Executive Board has not determined its position yet.

Postal workers confront Halifax police during the 1987 CUPW strike. CUPW Sister Carol Woodall makes it clear to a policeman what she thinks of the police interfering in our rights to strike and to picket.

Day Fifteen — Wednesday, October 14

Bill C-86 became law, and it was now time to determine our course of action. After some discussion, the National Executive Board decided to comply with the legislation, because we clearly saw that, if we failed to do so, the Tory government was determined to break CUPW, regardless of public opinion on the matter. We immediately began to prepare for the mediation-arbitration process imposed by the legislation.

Some Reflections on the 1987 Disputes

In looking for a cause for the 1987 disputes at Canada Post, one must question whether the strikes were provoked by management in an effort to influence a decision the Canadian Labour Relations Board was soon to make that might have reduced the number of bargaining units the employer had to deal with. The strikes by LCUC, CUPW, and the cleaners all happened while the Board was reviewing the number of bargaining units in the post office. If Canada Post provoked both the CUPW and LCUC strikes to demonstrate to the Board the need for reducing the number of units, the cleaners' strike demonstrated to the employer that contracting out of work wasn't going to prevent strikes. It also showed that Canada Post's desire to contract out work contradicted its argument that units needed to be merged to limit the number of postal disputes. It was neither the first nor the last time Canada Post held contradictory positions at the same time.

Before negotiations had even begun, we had heard from reliable sources that, this time, the government planned to take CUPW head-on. It knew that neither LCUC nor CUPW was going to accept concessions and that both unions would opt for the process of conciliation with the right to strike. It was therefore important to ensure that CUPW would be the last of the two to reach the stage where the right to strike became a legal option. The employer would put on a good show that they were also after LCUC but would eventually reach a settlement with it. Then, tough back-to-work legislation would be passed — with provisions for severe penalties in the case of our defiance — to end the CUPW strike and allow an arbitrator to impose a collective agreement.

So, we had a situation where a review of the bargaining units by the Labour Relations Board was underway and the employer was taking a very hard line in negotiations with both LCUC and CUPW. Both unions were working together under the umbrella of the CLC in a broad public campaign to demand job security through improved and expanded services. We had collaborated with LCUC to apply for conciliation on the same date in the hope that we would win the right to strike at the same time. Our applications for conciliation were submitted on the same day, and, in both cases, a Conciliation Commissioner was appointed. However, the conciliation processes unfolded in a way that ensured that the two unions would win the right to strike at different times.

The government appointed Mr. Swan, a professor who had previous experience in dealing with cases involving the post office, to conciliate the LCUC dispute. He was not known as pro-union, but neither was he known as pro-employer or pro-government. Much to LCUC's satisfaction, he indicated that he was free during the two to three weeks following his appointment and that he would love to have the case settled in that time.

But in our case, the government appointed Mr. Foisy, who had never dealt with postal disputes before. As mentioned earlier, we knew him as someone very likely to be sympathetic to the employer. And, unlike Mr. Swan, he indicated that his schedule was very busy, with only a few days here and there available in the coming months. Still, the Tory government appointed him.

The government knew that CUPW and LCUC had a mutual policy to respect one another's picket lines. When LCUC went on strike first, it believed CUPW would ask its members to respect the picket lines. This would provide the employer with a legal excuse to fire CUPW shop stewards who encouraged members to respect LCUC picket lines. This, the government believed, would create heavy pressure on CUPW and possibly

CUPW Archives

Sister Maureen Cormack in the Ottawa post office speaks about her repetitive strain injury before Judge Cossette during his 1987–88 tour of postal facilities.

sow internal divisions that would make us an easier target when our turn came to strike.

The government strategy to get LCUC on strike first was successful, but from there its plans went awry. The two unions signed an agreement under which LCUC would open its lines to allow CUPW members to go to work and we would do the same for them when it came our turn to strike. The agreement also provided that members of the two unions would not do work normally performed by members of the other.

So, the government's plans to get rid of CUPW activists failed. However, the back-to-work legislation did force us to end the strike, and the government hoped that Judge Lucien Cossette, who was mediator-arbitrator, would interpret the legislation to mean that he had to impose the terms of the Foisy Report.

So, we were well aware of what the government and the employer were planning. It's one of the reasons we decided to return to work after Bill C-86 was passed. Another reason was that we had managed, when arguing before the Parliamentary committee responsible for Bill C-86, to get its wording slightly changed. This was the change in wording mentioned earlier from "to give due cognizance" to give cognizance" when instructing the mediator-arbitrator regarding the Foisy Report. As mentioned earlier, we were successful in convincing Judge Cossette that his obligation was simply to read the Foisy Report, not to impose its terms.

Rather than have a short period of arbitration followed by final arguments by our Ottawa-based national officers before Judge Cossette, we decided to take him into the field and involve our members in the process. And, we managed to do some real damage control: we marshaled solid arguments before Judge Cossette, presented him with a well developed, written presentation and a long list of exhibits, and accompanied him on visits to twelve different postal facilities. In all, seventy-nine CUPW members made presentations before Judge Cossette. This decision to bring the arbitration process into the field allowed locals the opportunity to speak directly to the person who would decide on the content of their collective agreement.

In the end, Judge Cossette didn't touch the job security protections that had been in the 1985 collective agreement. The gist of these protections was outlined in a section of that agreement known as "Appendix T." It's interesting to note that Mr. Foisy in his report said: "It seems to me that the employer's proposal — which would allow the Corporation to lay off an employee in a position declared surplus if he is unwilling to relocate — is reasonable." Judge Cossette, in his arbitration decision, said: "The mediator-arbitrator is of the opinion that it would be not only untimely but also unjust and unfair to modify 'Appendix T,' [which] has been in existence only since April 1985, and no change in circumstances has been demonstrated to me which might call for an amendment."

Another area where Judge Cossette ruled differently than had Mr. Foisy was in his decision to grant a five-minute rest period to coders every hour. Mr. Foisy had recommended that coders be assigned to other duties for five minutes every hour. Given the evidence provided by locals across the country, Judge Cossette also decided to include a clause in the collective agreement to protect workers against management harassment for absenteeism. On wages, he decided that we would receive the same percentage increase that LCUC had recently won, but he also agreed to some of the rollbacks proposed by the employer in the areas of casual staffing and overtime. Finally, while he did not feel in a position to order the employer to close or open particular postal facilities, to order specific service expansions to the public, or to supplant in any other way the responsibilities of Canada Post administrators, in referring to CUPW's job creation proposals, he wrote: "I consider the union's initiative excellent, commendable, and probably even viable." Nevertheless, Judge Cossette removed provisions we had negotiated in 1985 in regard to retail outlets.

Overall, while the collective agreement outlined by Judge Cossette didn't give us everything we wanted, it allowed us to make progress on many important health-and-safety issues, included improvements in health-care plans, and provided for a joint child-care study, increases in shift premiums, and improved vacation leave.

We surprised a lot of people when we decided to go back to work after the passage of Bill C-86 but, as I said before, I've never been a willing candidate for suicide. We had surprised the government with our strategy of rotating strikes and with our discipline and solidarity, despite the situation with the Montréal local. And, the right to negotiate and to strike is so fundamental to CUPW that we knew we couldn't leave the employer and the government under the impression that, if necessary, we wouldn't defy the law again. The history of the labour movement shows that workers have to fight, generation after generation, to insist that employers treat workers with respect and dignity.

CUPW's slogan, "The struggle continues," was used extensively during our national program of action after the 1978 strike, and it still had strong symbolic resonance during the 1986–88 negotiations. I'm convinced that this slogan reflects, not only the realities workers have faced in the past, but also what they face today and what they will face in the future.

10 My Final Years With My Union

The 1989–92 Negotiations

When we began negotiations in the summer of 1989, CUPW was in a unique position. We had just won a vote that certified us to represent all 46,000 postal workers in the operational bargaining unit. We had made a series of constitutional amendments to integrate members of LCUC, the Union of Postal and Communications Employees (UPCE, a component of the Public Service Alliance of Canada), and the International Brotherhood of Electrical Workers into CUPW. We faced a group of dissidents from within the former LCUC who were determined to see CUPW fail in our efforts to make all these workers feel at home and well represented. We faced the difficult task of integrating the provisions of six collective agreements into one. And, we had an employer that was introducing a whole series of changes affecting all our members. (For more on relations with other unions, see Chapter Eleven.)

Fortunately, CUPW's National Executive Board chose, on recommendations from our regional directors, a good negotiating team that reflected our newly expanded membership. They were Jeannie Campbell (Atlantic), Serge Drouin (Québec), Jeff Bennie (Ontario), and Peter Whitaker (West), all from the former CUPW; Raynald Robitaille (Québec), Don Lafleur (Ontario), and Lynn Bue (West), all from the former LCUC; and Bob Butcher (West), from the former UPCE. These eight representatives, with myself as Chief Negotiator, made up our Negotiating Committee.

The national program of demands presented to our 46,000 members for this round of negotiations underlined the importance of maintaining acquired rights. Our process of developing a program of demands wasn't well known to our new members. First, local delegates at area council meetings across the country identified and discussed issues they wanted dealt with in the next round of negotiations, and then they went back to their locals, where resolutions were adopted. These resolutions were then sent to regional conferences where delegates adopted resolutions reflecting what they believed our demands should be. These were then sent to the national office, where a sub-committee composed of the national directors of each region and the National Chief Steward developed a program of demands that was then submitted to the National Executive Board for its approval. Finally, the proposed program was voted upon in a referendum of our members across the country.

I think this process impressed most of our new members. Yes, there was a dissident group, led by most of the former leaders of LCUC, which encouraged members to boycott the voting process or to vote against the program of demands. (More on this in Chapter Eleven.) However, their strategy regarding the vote on our programs of demands was unsuccessful, partly because the workers they had convinced not to join CUPW had no right to vote. Of those who did vote, 89 percent approved of the programs. Negotiations began with three former LCUC members on our Negotiating Committee.

Our new members were also quite impressed by the high level of communication we used to keep members and their representatives informed during negotiations. One of the ways we did this was through background documents we provided to local officers and shop stewards. They were full of information on the different issues and they helped our representatives answer questions from the shop floor and from the media.

The first backgrounder we produced in January of 1990 was a twenty-page document entitled, *An Overview — Job Security — A Must for Post Office Workers*. Unlike during previous negotiations, we decided to distribute this backgrounder to all 46,000 CUPW members.

In an editorial message, I underlined the importance of the issue of job security in this round of negotiations, especially in view of the full-scale assault on our jobs by the employer. Every day, full-time positions were being eliminated as more and more positions were declared "surplus." In some cases, mail service couriers were being forced to perform letter carriers' functions, while wicket clerks with long years of service had to go back to the plants on night shifts. And, most vacant positions were not being filled.

I briefly explained how, with an expansion of services to the public and with the contracting in of work rather than contracting out, real job security was possible. I also pointed to the importance of members becoming familiar with both the employer's plan and the union's solutions outlined in the backgrounder.

I then underlined the importance CUPW has always attached to communications. "The strongest weapon of post office workers," I wrote, "is their union, and the strongest weapon of any union is an informed membership." I pointed out that we used bulletins, letters, pamphlets, backgrounders, newsletters, newspapers, shop stewards, and other local officers to communicate with our members.

Because there was a large number of dissidents among former LCUC members at this time, we knew that some local officers or shop stewards weren't transmitting information to members, so I concluded my editorial by suggesting members use a coupon in the backgrounder and send it to our national office if they wished to receive information from us directly.

CUPW members participate in a huge protest during a 1989 Tory convention in Toronto. Thousands of people visited "Mulroneyville," a site developed by the social justice movement for the occasion.

This didn't please some local leaders who felt we were going over their heads directly to the members but, in view of the situation, most approved of the move.

We had good reason for making job security a central issue in this round of negotiations In the years of 1989 and 1990 alone, the size of the internal bargaining unit (the inside workers) fell by more than 1,800 full-time positions, a reduction of 10 percent. Casual hours among those performing collection and delivery functions went up from 2,633,100 to 4,136,400, an increase of 57 percent. The number of wicket clerks (all full-time, day-shift positions), dropped by 325, a reduction of almost 10 percent. By December 1989, CUPW had received notices of more than 400 positions that had been declared "surplus," and, in some post offices, the employer simply notified us that when positions became vacant in future, they would simply be eliminated.

Management was also introducing an array of measures at this time, all of which were designed to eliminate jobs, and job opportunities, for postal workers. Massive technological changes were being introduced, including new optical character readers, letter sorting machines, and a new video encoding system. A ten- to eleven-digit postal code was being contemplated that would reduce sortation time for letter carriers. Mail service courier positions were being eliminated through contracting out and restructuring. The use of private vehicles for letter carriers was being expanded, as was the use of non-unionized admail "helpers" to deliver mail. "Supermailboxes," mail kiosks, and group mail boxes were being introduced, and some parcel sortation work was being contracted out. Postal counters were being privatized through franchising, and letter carriers' redirection time was being eliminated. And, all this was happening while Canada Post was making large profits, which could have been used to end service cutbacks and offer the public expanded services.

Instead, the federal budget handed down by Finance Minister Michael Wilson in April of 1989 decreed that by 1993–94 the post office would be expected to earn a return on equity similar to the private sector. Over the following five years, Canada Post was expected to pay the federal government $300 millions in dividends, and the government would consider privatizing Canada Post by selling shares.

This meant that, after eight years as a Crown Corporation, Canada Post would be required to earn a 14- or 15-percent rate of profit in order for it to be considered by government as having met its legislative mandate of breaking even. So, by an accounting sleight of hand, a $100-million profit became a $130-million deficit. A profit target of $278 million for 1993–94 was established for Canada Post.

Corporate Strategy

During the mid-1980s, Canada Post planned to get into the parcel delivery business, but government insisted that there wasn't any funding for such a move, especially in a time of government deficits and while Canada Post was already failing to meet its financial targets. And, the Mulroney government insisted, Canada Post was not to compete with the private sector.

Governments have continued with such arguments over the past several years in their re-shaping of the public service. It gives profitable parts of the public service to the private sector, and so the remaining public services cause higher deficits that are used as arguments for further cutbacks in services and staffing. The corporate media then enflame public dissatisfaction about reduced public services, blames "big government" for the problem, and calls for further privatization, leaving only the completely unprofitable services to the public sector.

The result of all this is that public assets and tax dollars flow increasingly to the private sector. As well, we ourselves now pay the private sector for services that used to be provided by the public sector. And, while the corporate sector pressures government for tax reductions that might mean something like two hundred dollars per year for workers, these reductions mean far more for already wealthy Canadians and many, many millions for corporations.

So, as they reduce taxes and facilitate the flow of millions of dollars in profits to the private sector, governments act to reduce deficits by cutting jobs and services and calling for rollbacks at public-sector bargaining

An unusually tie-less Jean-Claude Parrot at a June 1989 demonstration outside the Royal York hotel in Toronto, where the Fraser Institute was holding a conference on privatization and deregulation in Canada Post.

tables. And, as real wages fall in the public sector, corporations are under less pressure to improve the wages of their own workers.

Another consequence of the drop in wages is that governments take in less income tax and so are less able (and usually less willing) to improve and expand public services and provide proper social programs to Canadians.

Unfortunately, this corporate strategy isn't obvious to the public, largely because the media that millions of Canadians rely upon for news, and for news analysis, is itself an integral part of the corporate sector.

The Fraser Institute is a British Columbia-based, corporately funded "think tank" that for three decades has been putting forward arguments and publishing "research papers" — always well covered by the media — that seek to move a right-wing agenda forward and obscure the reality of this corporate strategy. In June of 1989, just as we were beginning another

Women postal workers were strong on CUPW picket lines. Here in Toronto, in 1989, they protest against the privatization plans of Don Lander, who had replaced Michael Warren as Canada Post's President. He was there to speak at the forum organized by the Fraser Institute.

CUPW Archives

round of negotiations, it organized a conference at the Royal York hotel in Toronto on privatization and deregulation at Canada Post. The CUPW local in Vancouver held a demonstration in front of the Institute's offices denouncing its promotion of the dismantling of Canada Post as a public service. On the eve of the conference, more than 200 people filled the Steelworkers Hall in Toronto to hear speakers who provided analysis of the Fraser Institute and the effects of postal privatization and deregulation. On the day of the conference, more than 200 postal workers and friends rallied in front of the Royal York, where Don Lander, President of Canada Post, and Harvie Andre, the Minister responsible for Canada Post, were to speak. I told the rally that "the ultra right-wing Fraser Institute cannot expect to advocate the destruction of the post office without a fight from CUPW."

Why did we pay so much attention to a conference organized by a group whose interests were so obviously opposed to those of our members? Because, while the Fraser Institute and a growing number of other organizations pose as academic forums or claim to be speaking in the public interest (the Business Council on National Issues comes to mind here as a body serving a similar purpose), such organizations receive their funding — and directly serve the interests of — the already wealthy corporate sector. And we believed — and we still believe — that the public should know who they serve so citizens can better understand the propaganda doled out by such right-wing organizations.

Negotiations

Between May and late September of 1989, we met with the employer at the bargaining table twenty-seven times. Very little was achieved, and so we applied for a Conciliation Officer. The government appointed André Courchesne, and we met with him seventy-eight times between September 25, 1989, and early September of 1990. Again, very little progress was made.

On August 31, 1990, in view of the scant progress over the course of many months of negotiation and conciliation, we asked the Minister of Labour not to appoint a Conciliation Board. This would allow us to acquire our right to strike immediately.

While waiting for his decision, we conducted a strike vote. The National Executive Board unanimously recommended the following to our members:

> Whereas following fourteen months of negotiations no agreement has been reached with Canada Post on a collective agreement covering the 46,000 members of the bargaining unit;
> Whereas while we are negotiating, the employer is introducing programs seriously affecting all post office workers such as the transfer of jobs and work outside of our communities, the cutting back of twenty percent of letter carrier and mail service courier jobs through changes to the work measurement systems and the contracting out of wicket services, mail delivery, maintenance, etc.;
> Whereas these programs also include serious cutbacks in service to the public such as the closing of post offices in both rural and urban areas, the introduction of supermailboxes, a reduction in the hours of service, a reduction of street mailboxes, etc.;
> Whereas the employer is proposing major rollbacks at the bargaining table, including the power to lay off employees, to move them from one office to another or from one class to another, and to change seniority provisions;

Bob White of the Canadian Auto Workers, Leo Gerrard of the United Steelworkers, Don Holder of the Communications, Energy, and Paperworkers' Union, and Jean-Claude Parrot of CUPW committing themselves to a pact of mutual assistance in collective bargaining struggles at the Canadian Auto Workers' Convention in the spring of 1990.

Whereas the union has ended the conciliation process with André Courchesne, the Conciliation Officer, on the basis that the employer refused to make any moves on important issues such as job protection, service protection, no privatization and no contracting out, job creation and no changes to walk/route measurement systems without agreement;

Whereas there has been no progress on other important priorities: wages and cost-of-living allowance, a stop to harassment, day-shift work, more full-time jobs, no introduction of changes until the employer meets all obligations under the collective agreement, reduced working time including the half-hour paid lunch for everyone, and many more demands affecting different groups of workers;

Therefore the members of the National Executive Board recommend that you vote "yes" —

To authorize the national Negotiating Committee to put the emphasis on the following demands: job, service, and wage protection, the right of an arbitrator to stop the employer from introducing a change when the collective agreement is not followed, an increase of full-time and day-shift jobs, and no rollbacks;

CUPW Negotiator Jeannie Campbell at a Post Office with Jean-Claude Parrot during the Conciliation Board's 1989 tour.

To mandate the national Negotiating Committee to take the necessary steps to obtain the many more demands of the membership, such as those affecting senior employees, part-time employees, night workers, wicket clerks, casual and term employees, electrical labourers, general labour and trades workers, general service workers, letter carriers, mail service couriers, postal clerks, mail handlers, and mail despatchers; and

To authorize the National Executive Board to call strike activities to achieve the above demands.

Our 46,000 members voted in favour of this recommendation by a clear majority. On October 31, 1990, the Minister of Labour turned down our request, deciding instead to appoint a Conciliation Board, naming Marc Lapointe as Chairperson. We nominated Jacques Desmarais, who had ably represented us in the past, while Canada Post named Arnold Masters, a consultant, to represent management.

Conciliation Board hearings began in mid-December, during which

During a tour of post offices with the 1989 Conciliation Board, from left to right: Jacques Desmarais, union nominee on the Board, speaking with CUPW Negotiator George McKenzie. CUPW Negotiators Jean-Claude Parrot and Peter Whitaker look on.

the Board visited mechanized postal facilities in Québec City, Montréal, Toronto, and Hamilton, as well as the post office in Aylmer, Québec. Locals from London, Hamilton, Toronto, and Québec City made presentations to the Board, as did our national union in Ottawa

In April of 1991, the Board began serious conciliation and mediation sessions, and by late June and early July we were into intensive bargaining. We made real progress toward merging all the previous agreements into one, and the scope of the dispute was narrowed considerably. Still, we were unable to settle on a number of basic issues. On July 5, the Board withdrew to draft its report.

On August 12, 1991, Board Chairperson Mr. Lapointe sent his report, which was also signed by Mr. Masters, the employer's nominee, to the Minister of Labour. Our nominee, Mr. Desmarais, disagreed with much of the report, and he submitted a minority report. His decision to do this reflected a greater honesty than Mr. Masters could muster: He signed the report — which indicated he was largely in favour of its recommendations — but then indicated that he reserved the right to forward some additional comments to the Minister. In fact, these so-called "additional comments" turned out to be a clear disagreement with the Chairperson's report.

In his report, Mr. Lapointe, who had been with the Canadian Labour Relations Board for many years, described the context of the dispute between the two parties as follows:

When Saddam Hussein was powerless to counter the air assault in the Gulf War, he announced that the forthcoming ground war would be "The Mother of all Battles." He was wrong. But the author of these lines, an old hand at labour relations, can state that the renewal of this collective agreement at Canada Post constitutes "The Mother of all Battles" in this field.

Mr. Lapointe went on to explain that the central causes of the dispute were the size and attitudes of the two parties, the scope of their disagreement, and the shadow cast by politics on the dispute. In summary, he wrote:

> It can be said that the Corporation has moved to the offensive in the collective bargaining process and that the union has tried every possible means to preserve the status quo, resulting in a host of demands.
>
> Increasingly, Canada Post Corporation wants to act as a private business, while the Canadian Union of Postal Workers wants it to continue to act like an operation devoted to what it terms the public service of delivering the mail to Canadians. In a certain sense, the parties are headed in opposite directions.

The efforts of the Conciliation Board were successful in reducing the number of each party's demands. The two parties initialed 195 clauses, to add to the ninety agreed to during Mr. Courchesne's earlier conciliation efforts. But the Board's majority report identified nine "major" points still in dispute, along with twenty others it described as "minor clauses."

Mr. Desmarais raised what he called "a substantial deficiency" in the majority report. He wrote that there remained a major point of contention between the parties regarding job security and staff management, but that the majority report had failed to adequately address this issue. In my opinion, this statement from Mr. Desmarais' minority report pointed to a fundamental flaw in the majority report:

> In view of the significant effort (in time, documentation, explanations, and discussions) devoted by the parties to explaining their positions on this issue, to send them away without direction and without guidance seems to me ill advised. The dispute resolution system initiated nearly twenty years ago by the Canada Labour Code includes ultimate recourse to methods of economic pressure (strike or lock-out) to force the parties to reach a collective agreement. By giving the Minister of Labour the power to require the intervention of a Conciliation Board before the start of any strike or lock-out, the Code explicitly provides for the

involvement of a third party in the system and makes the submission of its report the crucial factor for exercising methods of economic pressure. A report that is silent on a major element and one, moreover, likely to be the source of a major conflict, seems to me not only to violate the economy of the system but also to be ill considered. The period of seven days between the time when the report is submitted to the parties and when the strike or lock-out may begin must be used to make a decision as to whether or not the report is acceptable. It is too short to attempt to resolve an issue of such magnitude without guidance from the Board's report.

Mr. Desmarais' criticism turned out to be correct: No agreement was reached between the two parties in the seven days following the release of the Conciliation Board's report, and between August 24 and September 5, 1991, we conducted rotating strikes across the country.

Rotating Strikes and Solidarity Pacts

On the eve of the strikes, Tony Clarke, Chairperson of the Action Canada Network — a coalition of major Canadian labour and social organizations — called a meeting of representatives of groups representing seniors, students, people with disabilities, unemployed workers, farmers, and anti-poverty activists to discuss ways CUPW and these civil organizations might support one another. These groups and the union agreed to sign a series of "solidarity pacts."

The first groups to sign such a document with us were the National Anti-Poverty Organization, Disabled People for Employment Equity, and the Canadian Council of Retirees (Ontario Sector). It outlined CUPW's commitment to "develop a contingency plan to sort and deliver social assistance cheques in the event of strike action." The three groups expressed their appreciation for this commitment and pledged to inform their members of CUPW's "extraordinary initiative."

The second solidarity pact with CUPW was signed by the Canadian Federation of Students and the Ontario Coalition Against Poverty. It denounced the use of scab labour and supported our position calling for the creation of decent full-time jobs. The two groups agreed to communicate with their members, urging them not to accept work as scabs during any postal strike.

A third pact was signed by Rural Dignity of Canada, the National Farmers' Union, and the union. It expressed our mutual commitment to fighting closures of rural post offices and for the expansion of rural services.

Finally, the Action Canada Network endorsed all three pacts, and Tony Clarke concluded: "Our member groups are concerned with protecting those Canadians who are the most vulnerable during a labour-management dispute like this one. And they are concerned about decent jobs, at decent wages, for all Canadians. That's what the solidarity pacts are about."

All these signings took place at a press conference well attended by the media, but I have never seen one media report about it or about the solidarity pacts. Perhaps it was because this was just two days before we began our rotating strikes and these immediately became "the news." But surely these agreements should have merited at least some coverage by unbiased media sources. It certainly didn't take business and right-wing media sources long to condemn our rotating strikes and point out how much they were "hurting the public." Well, the solidarity pacts showed that, without doubt, large sections of the public understood and supported our position. But, I guess the media didn't feel this qualified as "news."

As follow-up to the first of the solidarity pacts we had signed, on August 22, CUPW made an offer to the President of Canada Post Donald Lander to set up a contingency plan to deliver government cheques in the event of a strike. But we received no response from Mr. Lander and, on the following day, Canada Post announced it would deliver the mail during the strike using its own contingency plan. A Canadian Press story reported that the Supply and Services Department, which issues such cheques, had said that the August cheques were already in the mail stream.

We began our rotating strikes the following day, and Canada Post withheld cheques from the mail system, and even from the bags of letter carriers about to leave to deliver mail. On August 27, a Canada Post spokesperson announced that, despite the rotating strikes, people would get their cheques. We again contacted Don Lander, warning him that Canada Post's contingency plan for delivering the cheques would lead to disaster and urging him to allow letter carriers to deliver them.

On August 28, Canada Post placed ads in newspapers across the country advertising locations of distribution centres where people could pick up their government cheques. The next day, thousands of senior citizens and others due to receive government cheques lined up for hours in the summer heat. A large number of them went home without receiving their cheques.

Across the country, postal workers went to these lines to provide those waiting with assistance, offering them water, chairs, donuts, and coffee. We told them not to be surprised if they didn't get their cheques, explaining that it was one of Canada Post's strategies to make them suffer so that postal workers would take the blame.

Mr. Dunstan's Error

With our members helping out people at these waiting lines all across the country and reporters beginning to ask the right sort of questions, the public mood was clearly turning against Canada Post and the government.

Harold Dunstan, Canada Post's Vice-President and Negotiator, is confronted by a CUPW picket line during the 1991 rotating strikes.

CUPW Archives

On August 30, Harold Dunstan, Chief Negotiator for Canada Post, tried a devious ploy to gain public sympathy.

He arrived at a scheduled negotiating meeting in Ottawa accompanied by a lot of media. He appeared to be very angry, and he shouted at me that he was not going to meet with us that morning because our members in Toronto were holding back trucks containing cheques for needy citizens. He made a long speech denouncing the union's lack of civic responsibility toward seniors and others dependent on government assistance.

When he finished his speech, Mr. Dunstan walked out of the room, saying that he wouldn't be back as long as we continued to deprive these citizens of their cheques. Once he was gone, reporters turned to me for my reaction.

At that moment, an idea struck me: I knew Andre Kolompar, the president of the Toronto local, and I knew the character of CUPW members. I felt there was something fishy about Mr. Dunstan's theatrics. "Wait," I told the reporters. "Let's check out Mr. Dunstan's story right now." I took the phone and dialed Andre's cellular number. I expected I'd reach him on the picket line. I did, and without giving him any explanation of what had just taken place at the Ottawa meeting, I asked him if it was true that his members were stopping government cheques from getting into the post office.

"Jean-Claude," he said, "all we've done is to ask that they open the doors of the trucks so we can see if there are scabs inside. If there aren't, we'll let the trucks go in, but they refuse to open the truck doors. We've told the police and the reporters here now that we only want to see if these trucks are being used to get scabs into the plant." I asked him to repeat what he had just told me, and I held the phone out so the Ottawa reporters could hear his explanation.

When they had listened to Andre's account, I told them to immediately get in touch with their media counterparts in Toronto, who were probably at that picket line, and ask them to determine what was inside the trucks. The Toronto reporters then asked management to let them see what was in the trucks. Backed into a corner, management had little choice but to grant their request.

When the truck doors slid open, the reporters saw they were full of strikebreakers and that there was almost no mail on the trucks. It turned out that my hunch that Mr. Dunstan's antics amounted to a media stunt was correct.

The issue of the delivery of government cheques to the needy had so far been a big part of media coverage of our rotating strikes. Reports the next day about what happened at the Ottawa meeting and on the Toronto picket line now made Canada Post's earlier position seem weak, if not downright deceptive. I spoke to Canada Post President Don Lander that day, and he agreed that letter carriers could deliver the cheques on their own volunteered time during the Labour Day weekend.

The letter carriers were well received as they made their weekend rounds delivering cheques, and people thanked them for their kindness on their days off. Seeing the public relations disaster they had created, Canada Post now insisted on giving each of the volunteer letter carriers a $100 cheque. All across the country, letter carriers gave their honoraria to seniors' organizations and to other groups helping people in need. I was really proud of them and of other CUPW members who had helped them in making their rounds.

I never again saw Mr. Dunstan at the bargaining table, and he was eventually transferred to another position in the Atlantic region. I still wonder what might have happened had I not been able to immediately reach someone on the Toronto picket line and the media had taken Mr. Dunstan's act at face value.

We had managed to get cheques to needy people and to win a public relations victory over Canada Post, but, unfortunately, this didn't lead to any agreement in negotiations. In early September, the Labour Minister appointed Judge Allan Gold as mediator to assist the parties. These mediation talks went on for seven weeks and, to the surprise of everyone, we decided to stop our rotating strikes during those talks. This was an unusual step on our part, but it's also one of the reasons CUPW has been a success story over the years.

We are unpredictable, imaginative, principled, and determined, all at the same time. Our goal is always to make progress and to position ourselves for future situations. In this case, we were aware of the quality of the mediator and that the government was once again ready to impose a collective agreement on us through an arbitrator, and we carefully considered both of these factors in making our decision.

Such a move showed everyone who was looking that postal workers across the country were fully able to act together to strategically pursue their interests. Some have suggested that we went back to work at this juncture because we didn't want to complicate matters during an upcoming national strike of most of the workers in the federal civil service, those represented by PSAC. Though this wasn't our reason for our strategic move to suspend our rotating strikes, I believe our decision to end them during Judge Gold's mediation efforts may have worked to PSAC's advantage.

PSAC had much to prove to the government and to others, including many in the labour movement. Some members of the CLC Executive Committee considered PSAC a relatively weak union, but I thought their strike was an important opportunity for its leaders and members to show that they could take on a tough struggle on their own.

And they did. After the PSAC strike was called in September, Ottawa was like a war zone. I'm sure that many residents had never known that PSAC members worked in so many places around the city. Their picket lines were everywhere.

By early October, despite our best efforts to reach a negotiated agreement, there were still 185 issues outstanding between the parties, and the government had back-to-work legislation ready to introduce before Parliament if we struck. Judge Gold suggested that the outstanding issues be referred to binding arbitration. We replied that we would not voluntarily see these issues sent to arbitration and that we still believed a negotiated settlement could be achieved. On October 10, 1991, our National Executive Board decided we would resume strike activities on October 16.

Negotiations were at a crucial juncture. Canada Post knew that the government was ready to introduce back-to-work legislation if we went on an all-out strike. But management also knew that Judge Gold was a very experienced mediator who was respected by the union, and they couldn't be sure of the terms they would get if Gold was unsuccessful in getting the parties to reach agreement and an arbitrator was appointed to write an agreement that would then be imposed on both parties.

After Judge Gold held further meetings with both parties, our Negotiating Committee put before our National Executive Board a proposal that we make a verbal presentation to Judge Gold of a global offer we would make to the other side. The National Executive had intense debates about many of the positions suggested by the Negotiating Committee. October 16 came and went, and the National Executive Board decided to assess the situation on a day-by-day basis. Postal workers remained on the job.

On the evening of October 21, 1991, I reported to the National Executive Board after another meeting between our Negotiating Committee and Judge Gold. I told them that, after these latest discussions with Judge Gold, he felt the best we could achieve was the following: full-time employees on staff as of September 25, 1988, would have job security; 80 percent of retail outlets staffed by CUPW members would be retained until July 31, 1993; there would be some notice prior to the contracting out of the work of mail service couriers; management would have the right to contract out visual encoding work; management would agree, in general terms only, to some job creation initiatives; there would be improvements in clauses dealing with the issue of harassment; there would be an increase as of August 1 of each year of 57 cents in 1989, 50 cents in 1990, 46 cents in 1991 and 50 cents in 1992, raising salaries from $14.24 to $16.27 an hour, an increase of $2.03 over four years with full retroactivity; a union education fund would be established; and there would be a half-hour paid lunch for those in our bargaining unit who hadn't yet won this right.

But, despite all the efforts we made, we were unable to reach an agreement and, on October 27, the National Executive Board decided unanimously to give twenty-four hours' notice of a full-scale strike as soon as back-to-work legislation was introduced. This legislation, Bill C-40, was brought before Parliament on October 28, 1991.

In view of the fact that the two parties had made quite a bit of progress through Judge Gold's efforts, we convinced the Labour Minister to agree to an amendment to the legislation that would require the arbitrator who was to be appointed to respect agreements that had been made between the two sides during Judge' Gold's mediation efforts. This amendment was important to us, because it meant that the employer would not force us to go back to square one before an arbitrator.

In view of this amendment to Bill C-40, our National Executive Board then adopted a resolution accepting the swift passage of the legislation. Canada Post had indicated it would speedily pay a wage increase. On the morning of October 29, the National Executive Board called a national strike of our members to last until the adoption of the legislation, largely as a symbolic act to protest the government again taking away our right to strike. The strike ended a few hours later, when Bill C-40 was passed by Parliament.

The National Union Education Fund

The question of including a Union Education Fund in the collective agreement created a very interesting debate among members of our Negotiating Committee. Most union activists knew that the Canadian Auto Workers' Union had for some years included in their collective agreements a clause entitled "Paid Education Leave," which required the employer to deposit into a special account three cents for every hour paid to workers in the plants. The union was then permitted to use these funds to pay workers attending education seminars it organized.

From the beginning of the preparation of our program of demands for this round of negotiations, I had promoted the inclusion in the program of a provision for a Union Education Fund paid by the employer. In developing the program, we agreed to ask for five cents for each hour worked by CUPW members. This proposal was duly submitted to the employer as part of our program of demands. Being a monetary demand, it was not discussed until we reached the issue of wages and benefits, and so no problems surrounding it arose until late in negotiations, when the employer was refusing to move on any benefits other than wages and retroactivity. We were at a point where we had to make compromises on our demands, but I insisted that we maintain our demand for a Union Education Fund. We had already reduced our demand to three cents per hour, and I made it clear that, as far as I was concerned, we shouldn't make any further concessions on this demand. Choices are never easy during the final stages of negotiations, and we had lively discussions among the members of our Negotiating Committee on this matter. Some suggested that if it were simply a three-cent matter it should be added to general wages or benefits, but I felt strongly about the issue, and decided to bring it to the National Executive Board, which, under our constitution, had final authority over our negotiating position.

At first, Canada Post argued that CUPW would use a Union Education Fund simply to campaign against the employer, and it wanted a provision in the collective agreement that this would not be the case. I responded that, three cents or no three cents, we would, when we thought it necessary, denounce the employer's policies when we believed it affected our members negatively and that we would carry out our campaigns to that effect. Did Canada Post, I asked, want us to allocate other funds for such campaigns and leave this three-cent-per-hour fund in a separate account? I suggested that we avoid useless wording in this provision of the collective agreement.

In the few previous years leading up to our mergers with other postal unions, CUPW had cut its internal education budget to less than $100,000 per year, which was clearly inadequate for a union of 23,000 members that wanted to both develop future leaders and to keep its members informed and educated about important issues such as the interpretation and application of collective agreements, grievance and arbitration procedures, the roles of shop stewards and other union officers, the collective bargaining process, and health and safety issues. Now, after mergers with other postal unions, the amount available for education for union members was doubly inadequate.

I confess I was stubborn on this issue, and I admitted as much to our negotiators and national officers. I told them what we all knew, that our purpose was to negotiate benefits and protections for the membership. But, I said, in order to be able to continue to do this in future years, we'll need activists who will have a good understanding of the issues facing the members, who will understand the underpinning democratic principles of our union, and who will be able to well represent our members and so become good and effective leaders at all our various organizational levels.

I went on to argue that, without this Union Education Fund, we would eventually fail in our responsibility to negotiate the best possible benefits and protections for our members. I strongly believed that without the educational tools to adequately and democratically represent our members, future leaders would inevitably fail in their efforts to best represent the interests of our members, no matter how noble their initial intentions may be.

Some members of our team felt that this was just a minor three-cent issue, but I continued to argue that, without an adequate education system to help new members rise through union ranks to future positions of principled leadership, our future would be clouded at best. And, with a Union Education Fund, we would have at hand more than $2,000,000 that we could use to keep our union strong through good education programs for our members.

One member of our Negotiating Committee, Peter Whitaker, who had already been frustrated by the fact that we were not getting any monetary benefits beyond a wage increase and retroactivity, decided to resign over this issue. I told him that I hoped he would reassess his position and, after a couple of days of reflection, Peter came back. His return was well appreciated by all of us because, facing the probability of an upcoming arbitration process, we knew that our unity would be our strongest asset.

After the adoption of Bill C-40, we began preparing for the arbitration process. The Labour Minister appointed Jean Bergeron as mediator-arbitrator, who began his work early in 1992. By this time, I had already announced that I was going to run for the position of Executive Vice-President of the CLC at its convention in Vancouver in June of 1992.

The arbitration process was a long one, and much of our efforts were spent trying to convince Mr. Bergeron that the employer had agreed to things before Judge Gold that it was now denying. I explained to him that the amendment made to the legislation was precisely to ensure that he would not have to start the whole process over and that he should respect what had been agreed to, even if these agreements had not yet been signed. Canada Post argued that the points agreed to in the various global proposals and counter-proposals put before Judge Gold were meaningless outside the context of a final agreement between the parties.

I countered that there were many areas of agreement in these exchanges — including the establishment of a Union Education Fund — which the employer now wanted to withdraw from the table. Knowing that this would underline our point, I indicated that the employer had not implemented the wage increase that was on the bargaining table when talks broke down, but a lower one that Gold had outlined as "achievable."

During these hearings before Mr. Bergeron, I was elected to my new position and Brother Darrell Tingley became CUPW's new National President. I had worked with Darrell for many years and there was no doubt in my mind that he would be a good National President. He agreed with me about the importance of the National Education Fund, and he was also aware that the employer had indicated quite clearly in its last offer that it would be willing to agree to it, but only as part of an overall package.

After I began my new job with the CLC on July 2, 1992, the employer and the union decided to meet independently of Mr. Bergeron to see if there was any possibility of arriving at an agreement before he had rendered a decision. Each party was worried that Mr. Bergeron might decide some issues that it felt were fundamental in favour of the other party.

These talks were successful, the wage issue was resolved, and an agreement was reached on all other points in dispute. When I read the new contract and saw that the provision outlining the Union Education Fund was still there, I was pleased I had stood firm and was also grateful to Brother Tingley for ensuring that it wasn't sacrificed in last-minute bargaining.

When I look at CUPW's national education program today, I'm proud of my union. I don't understand why, even today, other unions don't make similar provisions. A union education fund can be an incredible tool to ensure that new leaders continuously come out of union ranks to pursue the work of their predecessors and address the new issues that will inevitably face their memberships. It prepares new leaders for the challenges they will face, fosters pride in the history of the trade union movement, and attracts new, young activists.

Reflections on Leaving My Union

It's hard to explain the feelings I had in July of 1992, when I left CUPW to serve as Executive Vice-President of the CLC. I was leaving a life I had enjoyed very much.

I remember my first days at the CLC, when I had some free time alone in my office without much work to do. All the years I had spent in both the post office and CUPW raced through my mind. What had been my life had become my past, and I was left with thirty-five years of memories. During that first week at the CLC I relived the good times of those years, along with the not-so-good times. I also thought of my personal life, my marriage to Louisette, the birth of our two daughters, our move to Ottawa, and the blessings of two granddaughters. Despite the fact that I spent a lot of evenings and weekends at the office and that I was often away from Ottawa, I was still able to reflect on the wonderful times I'd spent with my family.

After being elected to the CLC post, many people asked me whether I was going to miss CUPW. If the person asking was a CUPW activist, I would say: "I'm quite excited that someone else will be chairing these long hours of conventions trying to maintain some unity among these activists from the different regions of the country. What I'll miss most is the people I've met and worked with through the years, all these sisters and brothers that have made CUPW the union it is today."

CUPW's evolution through the years has been incredible but so too has been the evolution of postal workers themselves. Most, like me, came to the post office with little knowledge of what it meant to be a union member. But I saw many of them became strong activists who realized that representing their sisters and brothers was important and who believed that we could really change things for the better if we worked hard and maintained our unity and solidarity. I thought in particular of members intervening at conventions. Some had never spoken in public before, but there they were delivering passionate speeches on issues they cared about. I could often see from the expressions on their faces that they believed in the importance of their participation.

I thought of the personal development of activists in key union positions whose involvement, when I first met them, had been limited to voting at referendum meetings. I saw them at union education seminars, speaking at conferences and conventions, participating in demonstrations, and, in time, leading their locals or moving up to regional or national positions. I thought of all the officers, union representatives, specialists, and other staff I worked with at the national office and of those in our regional offices, all working hard for the members. They all shared one thing in common: they were proud of CUPW.

Together, we worked to create a union that was attractive and open to postal workers who wanted to become active in the struggle for their rights, justice, and dignity. We made CUPW one of the most democratic organizations in our society. We made it a union that believes that its strength is its members, one where leaders understand they are responsible to members. And we also made our members responsible for their union, understanding that without their solidarity no progress was possible and that, without them, there would be no union.

I thought of how we had brought the employer, and governments, to change the way employees are treated, of how we forced them to replace unilateral decisions with negotiations. I also thought of the impact we had on the labour movement, especially the CLC: a broadened democracy, quality policy papers, the singing of *Solidarity Forever* to open conventions, the quality of debates, the adoption of progressive policies, and much more.

Another question people asked me after my election to the CLC was this: what were the greatest memories, achievements, or events of my life in CUPW? This was hard for me to answer, because there were so many, but I mentioned several. There's no doubt that the solidarity of postal workers when we defied the law in 1978 was one of the greatest moments of my union life. It was a tremendous feeling to see these 23,000 postal workers tell the world that the Trudeau government was both wrong and dishonest in imposing a collective agreement on us through back-to-work legislation. Winning the vote for a new, much larger bargaining unit in 1989 was another great moment in my union life, especially as I believed that "one union for all" was the road to greater solidarity among postal workers. (More on this vote in Chapter Eleven.) I will never forget my first election to a full-time union position, in 1968, when I became vice-president of the Montréal local. The same goes for 1971 when I was elected National Chief Steward, and for 1977, when I was elected National President, a position I never dreamt of holding. Nor did I ever dream of becoming one of four full-time CLC officers.

I'll never forget my first arbitration hearing in English, or the great progress we made in negotiations, or the spirit of postal workers at demonstrations and on picket lines. I remember all the special moments that occurred day after day in my union life: the smile of a worker I helped to resolve a problem; the smile of a secretary proud of a bulletin I asked her to prepare for the membership; and the smile of a union representative arriving back from an arbitration hearing knowing he or she did a good job.

I remember the great friendships that developed among members of the National Executive Board, despite the thorough and sometimes exhausting discussions that took place from time to time. I remember the great spirit of workers deciding to fight for their rights. I remember the faces of our negotiating team when we got the people on the other side of the bargaining table to agree to something they had said they would never agree to. And I remember the faces of countless others as we worked together, day by day and year after year, to make a better union. This was my everyday life in CUPW, and I will always remember it.

Finally, there was one other thing that filled my thoughts during those first days at the CLC: what *I* got out of my involvement in CUPW. I've always been a shy person, but I learned through CUPW how to control that shyness when it was important to do so. It is because of my work in our union that I learned how to express myself at meetings, to write bulletins and articles in union publications, to act as a legal advisor representing members at arbitration, to teach union education courses, to negotiate working conditions and benefits for our members, to deal with the media, to deliver speeches on important issues and causes, and to chair conventions. These were all things that, as a younger man, I had never dreamt of doing.

I thought about how my life in CUPW made me discover who I really was, someone who believed in social justice, in the rights of people to a decent job, to a better sharing of wealth among people. But I also learned things — though not all at once — I hadn't known in my youth: the importance of tolerance and the rejection of all forms of discrimination; the rights of women, gays and lesbians; and the rights of people with disabilities and other groups of people to be free of any harassment and to participate fully in the union.

I also learned about issues of peace, the environment, human rights, aboriginal peoples, and the situations of workers around the world. I learned about the exploitation of people, especially of women and children, and the role of governments and the corporate sector in maintaining that exploitation.

Throughout my life, I've always thought I was a lucky man. During those first days in my CLC office, I realized again how lucky I was. I always enjoyed my work, I have a wonderful family, I enjoy good health, and I've known people who were worth fighting for and who it was a pleasure to work with. I guess I was feeling nostalgic that week, but it was nice to relive some of these wonderful moments of my life in CUPW. I was privileged to have been there, and I'm proud of my union.

11 Union Unity

The previous ten chapters have essentially dealt with the chronology of my years in the post office and as an officer of the Canadian Union of Postal Workers. In these final two chapters, I will try to deal with three overarching areas that have influenced my own, and to varying degrees my union's, history and contribution to the betterment of Canadian society: inter- and intra-union relations, the role of the media in its relations with CUPW, and CUPW's role in the wider world over the years.

Struggles With the CLC

When I left CUPW in 1992 and went to work at the CLC, I hoped to continue my efforts to strengthen the Canadian labour movement, this time in a different role. I saw the CLC as a progressive central labour body that could build solidarity among Canadian workers. But it hadn't always been so: in earlier years there had been sharp differences between our union and the CLC leadership.

Back in 1978, after our strike and our subsequent defiance of back-to-work legislation, we had to react to a letter that Dennis McDermott, then the CLC's President, sent to all ranking CLC officers. (For details of this period, see Chapter Six.) In this letter, dated November 3, 1978, he tried to explain the actions or inactions of some CLC leaders during our recently concluded strike. The letter created much confusion about the CLC's actions — and its lack of actions — both before and during the strike. So, one of the first things we did after the strike was over, and all our officers had been released pending their trials or sentences, was to provide a "statement of fact" in response to Dennis McDermott's letter. This was sent out to all ranking CLC officers under the signature of CUPW Secretary-Treasurer Leroy C. Hiltz on December 7, 1978.

McDermott's letter had given the impression that CUPW had not kept the CLC informed of its struggle prior to the strike. Brother Hiltz pointed out that, through both letters and meetings, the CLC President had been kept better informed of our struggle than he was about the struggles of most other CLC-affiliated workers. Three letters, dated from June of 1977 to September of 1978, had been sent to McDermott from our national office. The first of these was sent by Joe Davidson before he stepped down as National President at our National Convention in the summer of 1977. It informed McDermott that at a recent press conference, CUPW had called for a Royal Commission of Inquiry into the administration of the post office in light of its poor service to the public, its financial irresponsibility, its poor labour relations, and its refusal to implement institutional changes recommended by numerous independent reports. Joe wrote, in part: "CUPW is also concerned that the government will try to direct public frustration with poor postal service and the large deficit of the department against members of our union and the labour movement in general. Already, Postmaster General Jean-Jacques Blais is publicly advocating a strike for next fall." The letter concluded: "Events since October 1975 have demonstrated that the strength of the labour movement lies in its ability to overcome past differences and forge new bonds of solidarity. I trust you will support us in our present action which we believe to be in the interest of postal workers, the labour movement, and the Canadian public."

The second letter was sent a year later, on June 23, 1978, about a month after a meeting between McDermott and myself, during which we discussed CUPW's negotiations with the employer and the implications of legislation denying CUPW its right to strike during the upcoming election campaign. At that meeting, McDermott expressed his support of CUPW and promised to fight restrictive legislation against public-sector unions.

My letter brought to McDermott's attention the fact that the Postmaster General, the Deputy Postmaster General, and the Progressive Conservative critic for the post office were all using his name to attack CUPW and our policies. I informed McDermott of developments in our negotiations and included documentation, including a newspaper clipping outlining his opposition to our demand for a reduced workweek. (This same article had been submitted to the Conciliation Board by the employer to support its bargaining position.) I also stressed in my letter that the Liberal government was obviously trying to divide the labour movement, and I concluded by asking for a meeting with him to discuss the situation more thoroughly.

We met in July of 1978, and I stressed that if the government's use of his name to attack postal workers remained unchallenged, it would be interpreted as a sign that the CLC didn't support CUPW. McDermott then told me, "I object to this misuse of my name and I am committed to support postal workers."

As the summer went on, the government escalated its attacks on CUPW through a vast public relations campaign. It lied about our demands at the table, constantly violated the terms of the existing collective agreement, and continued to use Dennis McDermott's name, asserting he was opposed to postal workers. Still, the CLC remained silent.

On September 8, 1978, I sent McDermott another letter raising my concerns over his silence and asking that he publicly demonstrate his solidarity with postal workers. A Conciliation Board report was due to be handed down on September 21, leaving us without a contract but with the legal right to strike as of September 28, 1978. I suggested that, as CLC President, McDermott should take a stand. I urged him to make a public statement supportive of postal workers, in order to increase pressure on the government to seriously negotiate.

Still, McDermott remained silent. It wasn't until October 18, a few hours before our decision to maintain the strike despite back-to-work legislation, that he issued a press release accusing the government of using postal negotiations to help it politically in an expected upcoming federal election, instead of trying to bring about a fair settlement. His statement denounced the government and called on it to resolve outstanding issues through negotiations.

I met again with McDermott on October 19, and he tried to apply pressure on us to go back to work, as now required by federal legislation, and to use the arbitrator-mediator process to pursue negotiations. At this point, we asked McDermott that, if the CLC wasn't going to support us, the CLC at least refrain from making public statements against us.

Meanwhile the CLC prepared a three-page press release strongly opposing our actions. Though it was dated October 25, 1978, the same day we decided to return to work, it was never officially released, but its contents leaked out. It ended as follows:

> CUPW embarked on this course of action without consultation with the CLC. They have rebuked all efforts on the part of the CLC to change their suicidal direction. They therefore cannot reasonably expect the CLC to lend their support, or that of their affiliates, to a course of action which takes us down the road of anarchy, and which will, at best, leave the labour movement in total disrepute and, at worst, create nation-wide havoc and the possible destruction of the movement we have all struggled for so long to build.
>
> We have an obligation to our affiliates. We and our affiliates have an obligation to our members. As painful as it may be, that obligation compels us to state:
>
> The CLC will not support CUPW in their current course of action. We will endeavour to make every effort to assist in resolving the situation wherever and whenever possible, but we will not place our resources at the disposal of CUPW, neither will we counsel our affiliates to provide substantive support.

This document was widely quoted in the media, even though it was never officially released. Even the judge in my trial used a quote from this CLC statement in passing sentence on me.

In the statement of fact released over the signature of Brother Hiltz on December 7, 1978, we indicated that, contrary to Dennis McDermott's assertions, we had kept the CLC informed of our situation consistently over the previous months. Never, at any time, had we asked, or even implied, that the CLC should call a general strike in support of our struggle. Yet, for months, Dennis McDermott had chosen to remain silent.

He even convinced NDP Leader Ed Broadbent to stay away from us. For Dennis McDermott, the real issue was that a federal election was expected, and CUPW's actions would give a bad image to both the labour movement and the NDP. For my part, I never believed that CUPW ever gave a bad image to the labour movement. While some didn't agree with our goals and objectives, this didn't mean they had no respect for us. Both the NDP and the labour movement have had a problem with this idea of "image" for many years. In order to win public support, we are encouraged to take a low-profile approach, so that we aren't seen as "too militant."

Without a militant approach, postal workers wouldn't have succeeded in winning the working conditions and collective agreement they enjoy today. Our major breakthroughs, our gains for minority groups, our job security provisions — these were only made possible by our militant determination to fight and so change things for the better.

I felt so strongly about this that in March of 1981 I wrote an article entitled "The Low-Profile Approach — A Disaster," which appeared in our monthly publication. This was just after 12,000 Ontario hospital workers had defied provincial legislation and walked off the job in what I called "a bitterly fought struggle with an employer whose view of industrial relations belongs to the Stone Age." My article went on:

> The response of the labour movement to this most important labour struggle launched by CUPE was very eloquent in its silence. The absence of visible support for these workers by either the leadership of the labour movement or the NDP in the face of one of the most significant labour struggles in Ontario since the Inco workers' strike in Sudbury opens to question what I call "the low-profile approach."... In the final analysis, this low-profile approach is, in my opinion, perceived as a sign of weakness and, therefore, does not prevent the government from introducing bad legislation and does not help NDP candidates at election time. If leaders in the labour movement expect support from the membership, and if NDP candidates expect support from the public, they must be perceived as being strong, committed, dedicated, and prepared to take a stand on controversial issues. Respect must be earned.

Looking back now on the crucial time CUPW went through in the fall of 1978 and the lack of support we received then from the CLC, perhaps I might have expected as much, based on how CUPW delegates were treated at the CLC's Convention in May of 1978.

In view of the vicious attacks against labour at the time — wage controls, rollbacks, and other repressive measures — and the CLC's apparent lack of response to such measures, we in CUPW decided to present a "Program of Action for the Labour Movement" at that convention. We felt that this was timely. Workers were facing the highest unemployment levels in forty years, major layoffs were being announced all across the country, and inflation was reaching new heights.

At the convention, the CLC leadership's approach was to avoid discussions of the specific directions and actions contained in our resolutions. Both the outgoing CLC President Joe Morris and incoming President Dennis McDermott used their positions as chairpersons of the convention to try to duck any serious discussions. They used tactics such as making remarks from the chair dismissing a delegate at a microphone as being "frivolous" and ignoring a delegate at one microphone to focus instead on a delegate at another who could be counted on to better serve the leadership's agenda.

This was my first CLC convention since becoming CUPW's National President the year before. Leading our delegation and the debates on many of our resolutions, I often found myself at the microphones and was subjected to the evasive tactics of both Morris and McDermott. On one occasion, I had to stand on a chair at a microphone in an effort to get the chairperson to grant me the floor. He had already jumped over my microphone several times, which made delegates in my area of the hall start to object.

On the first day of the convention, Brother Darrell Tingley, CUPW's National Director for the Atlantic region, rose on a point of order and argued that the chairperson couldn't arbitrarily call the question on an issue before the delegates. He quoted CLC rules of procedure to support his point. President Morris responded by telling Brother Tingley that he was out of order.

Brother Tingley was so angry with this that he gave Joe Morris the "one-fingered salute." Morris declared that Brother Tingley was being "obscene" and that a repetition would lead to his immediate eviction. This repetition took place immediately, and Morris then ordered the sergeant-at-arms to escort Brother Tingley from the hall.

This angered many delegates, and it was impossible to conduct any business for about an hour. Twice, Morris declared that delegates had voted to support him in his expulsion of Brother Tingley, but this raised loud objections from the floor. At one point, I succeeded in getting recognized, and I said that it must have been a long time since the chairperson had attended a local union meeting and that, if such a hand signal offended him so much, he should in future avoid union meetings.

Finally, Morris invited Brother Tingley to return to the hall, but we had not yet seen all the techniques used during that convention. A major issue at the convention was the policy of tripartism, which the CLC leadership had pursued since 1976. The idea behind tripartism was that labour would sit together with business and government representatives on different boards and agencies that were given the task of developing or administrating public policies. The idea was that, though business and labour could usually be counted on to take different positions, the third party — government — could be assumed to take a neutral position, and so tripartite bodies would be likely to come to decisions leading to the public good. CUPW and many others in the labour movement took the position that tripartite bodies, in almost all cases, served business interests, because government representatives, especially under Conservative and Liberal administrations, would almost always side with business. We argued that, when labour representatives took part in tripartite bodies, workers would be the inevitable losers, yet the decisions taken would enjoy the veneer of "impartiality."

After having brought over a million workers to the streets on October 14, 1976, for a National Day of Protest against "wage and price controls," it was sad to see the country's central labour body giving credence to a tripartite body such as the National Labour Market Board. Given the strong opposition of progressive trade unionists, with the support of many other activists from a broad range of unions, it was clear that it would be difficult for the CLC leadership to have resolutions sympathetic to tripartism accepted on the convention floor.

The solution Joe Morris hit upon was to move from the chair that all policy documents referring to the Labour Market Board be tabled for the consideration of the incoming CLC Executive Committee. Thus, Morris managed to avoid any debate on tripartism. Of twelve CLC policy documents due for discussion at this convention, in this way four of the most important never reached the convention floor.

I couldn't resist going to the microphone and suggesting that, since it was seen fit to refer all major policy issues to the incoming Executive Committee, it might seem logical to refer all resolutions to the wisdom of that body, thereby saving both time and money on such insignificant matters as the CLC's convention. Of course, Joe Morris labelled my comments "frivolous."

In addition to tripartism, other CLC policy documents called for "a unity of purpose... through a revitalized, strengthened, and more relevant Congress," "electoral support for the NDP," "increased lobbying in the legislative arena," and "increased support for the system of collective bargaining."

In contrast, the CUPW's Program of Action presented a far more concrete labour strategy. Perhaps it was best described by Brother Evert Hoogers in an article in *Canadian Dimension* magazine about the 1978 CLC Convention. Brother Evert Hoogers later became a national officer in

CUPW, but was a member of the Vancouver local at the time:

> In retrospect, the document itself (CUPW's "Program of Action
> for the Labour Movement") was not as important as the incisive-
> ness of criticism it inspired. It did not direct its attention to a
> criticism of tripartism: it did provide the forum for that debate to
> develop. It did not explicitly raise the question of unequivocal
> support for Québec's right to self-determination: its presence did
> bring that debate into focus. It did not constitute a full-blown
> program for the trade unions based on class struggle: yet its hard-
> nosed, clear delineation from the non-policies put forward by the
> CLC leadership pointed irresistibly in that direction.
>
> The program calls for a strong national centre for labour. It
> points out that labour's power will be based "on the economic and
> political strength of our membership. Our national centre will be
> respected to the extent that it can coordinate and lead the mem-
> bership in their struggles — for we have learned that business and
> governments respect only power.'
>
> The document sees the defeat of wage controls in any form as
> a number-one priority for the labour movement. It rejects any
> attempt by government to "institute any brand of formula bar-
> gaining" on either the private or public sector. Noting that the
> government must understand that, "should it re-impose wage
> controls it will be faced with opposition of unprecedented scale."
> It calls upon the CLC to build towards "an unlimited general
> strike."
>
> Among its proposals for a labour fight-back campaign:
>
> • distribution of existing work to deal with unemployment: it
>   calls for a thirty-hour workweek at forty hours pay, early volun-
>   tary retirement, triple time for all overtime, with CLC-mobi-
>   lized support "for all workers engaged in industrial action to
>   achieve these priorities";
> • short-term policies to reduce unemployment: proposals here
>   include public campaigns to secure housing projects at afford-
>   able costs, increased entitlement to unemployment insurance,
>   fully indexed pension plans for all Canadians, rollbacks in en-
>   ergy prices, etc.
> • increased protection for employed workers through six-month
>   notice of all layoffs, employer justification of any proposed
>   plant shutdown, and government expropriation of enterprises
>   that "can still be operated for the benefit of society";
> • a workers' publication for all members of all unions to be pub-
>   lished twice weekly, covering current struggles being under-

taken by workers, promoting all campaigns and boycotts being undertaken by the CLC and its affiliates… and providing general education on the economy and labour history.
• a program to endorse and develop secondary industry in Canada.

The last part of Hoogers' article shows what Dennis McDermott thought of CUPW:

President McDermott is a self-described "intelligent militant," but is at pains to explain that this doesn't mean "butting your head against a brick wall." Upon his election he pronounced, in reference to the activities of CUPW delegates and their supporters at the convention, that "militancy isn't just screaming your head off either."

He described CUPW's "Program of Action" as "indefensible and reactionary" and (most telling) as "negative rhetoric… about as popular as the advance man for Asian flu." Trade union leadership, then, is nothing if not "popular." The weatherman must first be consulted to determine the direction of the wind. Workers' struggles, or fighting for workers' interests in the face of (often popular) attacks on the union movement, are not for the likes of President McDermott.

During the convention, he outdid his distinguished precursor in evoking the good ole' commie bogie. He informed the citizenry of Canada, through *Globe and Mail* columnist Wilfred List, that opposition to the CLC Executive Council's policies was the work of "communists, a small assortment of Maoists and Trotskyists," and threw in CUPW, the "new bible-thumpers of labour," just to round things off.

Further, he speculated on the motivations of this motley crew. Such delegates, he opined, amounted to "a small but vocal group of people who are dedicated to opposing anything that any other mortal attempts to do. You can't do anything with people like that unless you lay them down on a psychiatrist's couch for fifteen or twenty years."

The appearance of this diagnosis touched off some vocal concern among certain oppositional delegates who apparently felt more mentally fit than Brother McDermott was wont to admit. But in the face of protest over these disgraceful remarks, the new President was not to be swayed. Pointing his finger directly at Marcel Perreault, Montreal local president of CUPW, he made a statement that may well serve to characterize what can be expected from his administration. "CUPW officers," he lectured, "can't stand at these microphones day after day pouring buckets of shit over the platform and not expect retaliation."

A clearer warning to worker militants can hardly be imagined. Despite the flamboyance of McDermott's stewardship, the struggle to end class collaboration in the labour movement will not find succour from the CLC executive.

A few years after our strike in the autumn of 1978, Mr. McDermott's friend, Pierre Trudeau, named him Ambassador to Ireland.

Dennis McDermott was asked by the media for his reaction to the "Program of Action for the Labour Movement," which we put before this convention. He said we "were marching to a different drummer," and that "we were skunks urinating on the labour movement."

Such statements were an attack against the democratic rights of delegates to participate in convention debates and against their right to hold opinions on various issues that differed from those of the CLC leadership. But, we understood that his approach wouldn't, in the long run, succeed in devaluing our contributions to debates in the labour movement.

CUPW delegates may have been frustrated by what happened at this CLC convention, but when we look back today at the progress the CLC has made in adopting more progressive directions, we can only be proud of the contributions we made in that regard. While it's certain that the CLC leadership has become far more progressive since the days of Joe Morris and Dennis McDermott, I'm proud of the interventions CUPW made at the 1978 convention and am certain that they helped steer the CLC toward a more positive course.

When the 1978 convention adjourned, our delegation stood and sang *Solidarity Forever,* while other delegates left the floor. Two conventions later, all CLC delegates were singing that noble refrain, accompanied by artists invited by the CLC for just that purpose.

After the 1978 CLC Convention, CUPW remained very active in the CLC. We associated ourselves with the left in the labour movement and got involved in its Action Caucus, which brought together many of the more progressive delegates to work together at conventions. CUPW was one of the few unions officially involved in the Action Caucus, but many other delegates also took part, with or without the official approval of their own unions. We helped move the CLC toward more progressive positions, first on international issues and then on national ones. Over the years, the work of the Action Caucus helped the CLC become a much more democratic organization.

By the time I was elected to the CLC Executive in 1992, its policies had changed considerably, and for the better. Today, the CLC is seen internationally as one of the most progressive central labour bodies in the world. Its unique composition of leadership provides a forum for the voices of working women, people of colour, aboriginal workers, the disabled, youth, and those with varying sexual orientations. International delegates to CLC conventions are always surprised by the number and variety of delegates and by the quality of their interventions in debates.

Negotiations for One Union

The idea of having one union to represent all postal workers was something that made so much sense that it was hard for me to understand why anyone would oppose it. CUPW and LCUC members understood this when they voted early in 1969 in favour of a merger of the two organizations, as recommended by the respective leaderships. This was after the two unions had formed the Council of Postal Unions in order to be certified without delay to begin negotiations after the adoption of the Public Service Staff Relations Act in 1967.

However, following a decision at the LCUC convention in 1969 that the leadership didn't have the right to conduct such a referendum, delegates rejected the merger, preferring instead to maintain the Council of Postal Unions. This soon proved to be a disaster. As we said at the time, "We're in a car with two drivers going in different directions."

The Council of Postal Unions was the subject of debate at both the 1971 and 1974 CUPW Conventions, and after the 1974 gathering CUPW decided to leave the Council and apply to be sole representative for our members. The Public Service Staff Relations Board determined there would be separate bargaining units for members of the two unions.

Between 1975 and 1985, we demonstrated that leaving the Council had been a good decision, given the major progress we had made in negotiations. In 1981, we even succeeded in getting the government to turn the post office into a Crown Corporation, with its labour relations falling under the Canada Labour Code. This eliminated previous restrictions on what could be negotiated.

This forced the postal unions to work together to protect the rights of both their members and their unions. We won a guarantee from the government that, at least until all unions had negotiated one collective agreement under the Canada Labour Code, the existing bargaining units would remain, as would the existing collective agreements.

I was sure that the time had come for the unions in the post office to sit down for serious discussions on their futures. There was no doubt in my mind that the employer would demand a review of the bargaining units and that there was a serious possibility that all postal workers — excepting administrative and supervisory personnel — would be put in the same bargaining unit.

I was right. On May 6, 1985, Canada Post filed an application with the Canadian Labour Relations Board for a review of its twenty-six bargaining units. In November, the Board rejected objections to the review raised by some unions representing Canada Post workers. This was shortly after the

Joe Davidson and Bob McGarry, leaders, respectively, of the CUPW and LCUC locals in Toronto, during the days of the Council of Postal Unions.

Tory government had established a private-sector Review Committee to examine the mandate and productivity of Canada Post. It was composed of four business representatives and a former CLC Vice-President who had retired. Neither the CLC nor any of the unions in the post office had been consulted regarding that nomination.

The five postal unions under the CLC's umbrella — CUPW, LCUC, the Union of Postal and Communications Employees, the Canadian Postmasters' and Assistants' Association, and the International Brotherhood of Electrical Workers — presented a joint brief to the Review Committee recommending that improved and expanded services replace financial self-sufficiency as Canada Post's number-one priority, that Canada Post maintain its exclusive privilege of delivering mail to Canadians, that the date for Canada Post to achieve financial self-sufficiency be set back, that its deficit be reduced by the introduction of new revenue-generating services, that services that had been cut be reinstated, that Canada Post make a long-term investment in parcel distribution and electronic mail, that it end an absentee harassment program it had introduced, that it reduce workplace injuries, and that it increase staffing to an adequate level.

The private-sector Review Committee, chaired by Alan Marchment, president and chief executive officer of Guaranty Trust, rejected our proposals and made forty-three recommendations of its own, including greater use of part-time and casual labour, a reduction in service standards, and a scaled-down post office that would only deliver mail the private sector didn't think was profitable.

An interesting part of the Review Committee's report was the release of a survey on the opinions and attitudes of the public towards Canada Post. The survey showed that 60 percent of Canadians used the post office at least once a week, that 22 percent received mail daily, that 11 percent sent personal letters daily, that 70 percent felt postal workers were knowledgeable, that 64 percent believed postal workers were efficient, and that 52 percent believed the post office should be a public service under a Crown Corporation or a government department. Only 31 percent favoured privatization, while 63 percent favoured daily home delivery, even if it increased postal rates or taxes.

In late 1985 and early 1986, postal unions held discussions under the umbrella of the CLC on the issue of a merger of bargaining units. The CLC officials participating in these discussions strongly urged the parties to reach a merger agreement, but both LCUC and the Canadian Postmasters' and Assistants' Association rejected the idea.

In April of 1986, leaders of the Union of Postal and Communications Employees and CUPW approved the formation of a joint committee to negotiate a merger agreement between the two parties. UPCE members worked in the post office, and their union was a component of the Public Service Alliance of Canada. That same month, Brother Denis Gagnon, UPCE's National President, along with Brother Stephen White, director of UPCE's Pacific division, were guests at our National Convention, where they were warmly welcomed. After a few meetings, on May 21, 1986, CUPW presented UPCE with a full merger proposal. On May 28, PSAC's National Executive adopted a resolution "authorizing a referendum vote of the members employed in Canada Post on a bargaining unit basis if an acceptable merger agreement is reached and approved by the UPCE National Executive and the Executive Management Committee of PSAC." On September 25, leaders of both unions approved a tentative merger agreement and adopted resolutions recommending their members vote "yes" in the referendum on the tentative agreement. There was one dissident vote on CUPW's National Executive Board, that of Brother Richard Forget, National Director for the Québec region.

The UPCE National Executive adopted a resolution to hold a special convention on November 8 and 9, 1986, to assure that all the legal requirements for finalizing the merger were met. However, PSAC's national leadership didn't think this special convention was necessary and it refused to cover its cost, so CUPW's National Executive Board adopted a resolution to allocate up to $100,000 to underwrite the cost of the special UPCE convention.

Signing of the CUPW-UPCE tentative merger agreement in 1986. From left to right: David Migicovsky, lawyer, Denis Gagnon from UPCE, and Jean-Claude Parrot and Bill Chedore from CUPW.

Up to this point, our merger negotiations with UPCE had gone relatively smoothly, but here's where difficulties arose. While PSAC's Executive Management Committee approved the tentative merger agreement and the referendum among UPCE members, on October 8 it informed UPCE that it would be sending the voting kits to the membership around October 11, 1986 — before UPCE's special convention and before it had held any meetings with members in the field. To add to the difficulties, LCUC representatives had just tried to raid UPCE by offering to sign up its members. UPCE President Denis Gagnon then issued a bulletin asking members to delay voting until UPCE had been given the opportunity to address their concerns and questions. Meetings across the country for this purpose were planned between mid-November and mid-December, which were to be attended by Brother Gagnon, myself as CUPW President, and an elected PSAC officer.

CUPW's National Executive Board decided to hold our referendum meetings and local votes between November 8 and November 30, with completed ballots to be returned by locals to the national office by December 2. (There was one dissenting vote on this Executive Board decision, that of the National Director for the Québec region.)

On November 5, PSAC's National President, Daryl Bean, on behalf of its Executive Management Committee, informed Denis Gagnon that an elected officer would attend meetings in the field only if no representatives from other unions were permitted to participate in the meetings. Nevertheless, at UPCE's special convention on November 8–9, delegates voted 68–2 in favour of merging with CUPW and urged its members across the country to support the merger in the upcoming referendum. Meetings of UPCE locals then took place across the country up to mid-December.

On December 5, 1986, I announced the result of CUPW's referendum on the merger: 70.2 percent voted in favour, 29.3 percent were opposed, and 0.5 percent spoiled their ballots. Considering the strong opposition of the Montréal local and the dissent of the National Director of the Québec region on the Executive Board, this represented a clear mandate for us to proceed with the merger.

Now we had only to wait for the result of the UPCE vote, and ballots were to be sent into its national office by January 9, 1987. But, on January 8, Daryl Bean wrote a letter to Denis Gagnon informing him that he had become aware on January 5 that a resolution had been adopted at PSAC's 1982 National Convention "opposing vigorously a merger of all postal unions in Canada Post [and to] to take all steps deemed necessary to protect our jurisdiction; and that PSAC gives its full support to achieve the above objectives and to protect the interest of all our members." In his letter, Bean asked for UPCE's view on how to deal with this problem. Meanwhile, completed ballots were flowing into UPCE's national office, but had yet to be counted.

On January 28, at a meeting of PSAC's National Board of Directors, Brother Burke, PSAC's National Vice President, seconded by Brother Denis Gagnon, moved, on behalf of PSAC's Executive Management Committee, that the 1982 resolution be rescinded. A vote was held and the motion was defeated, for lack of the required two-thirds majority. Despite the earlier support of PSAC's Executive Management Committee for the proposed merger, a majority of directors of PSAC's other components were now telling UPCE members that they strongly opposed any merger with other postal unions.

On February 2, 1987, Daryl Bean sent a letter to all UPCE members informing them that, in view of this, the referendum on the merger has been cancelled and ballots would not be counted. However, all indications were that UPCE members across the country would have approved the tentative merger agreement if the ballots had been counted. As Denis Gagnon said at that time, "Without any explanation or rationale, PSAC's National Board of Directors denied UPCE members the democratic right it had previously granted."

The UPCE Executive then decided to propose to its members that they individually sign applications to join CUPW. Given Canadian Labour Relations Board regulations, UPCE members applying to join CUPW had to pay a fee of five dollars in order for their applications to be considered valid.

During this period, a dirty campaign was carried out through PSAC's regional offices. At one point, PSAC reported, falsely, that the UPCE's Executive had resigned. On March 19, PSAC placed UPCE under trusteeship. On March 30, following the signing of CUPW applications by a good number of UPCE members, PSAC filed a complaint before the CLC charging CUPW with raiding.

On April 16, 1987, I wrote Daryl Bean asking that he withdraw his complaint. I told him that CUPW had acted in good faith in all our discussions with PSAC and that UPCE had spent a lot of energy and money to try to effect a merger with CUPW. Furthermore, I wrote, CUPW shouldn't be penalized because UPCE's Executive had decided it was left with no other choice than to have its members apply to join CUPW.

On May 7, 1987, I wrote to CLC President Shirley Carr to explain our view of the situation. I informed her that I had written to Brother Bean and told her that we were prepared to take advantage of any mediation that might be offered. By this time, we had begun to file applications to be certified as bargaining agent for some UPCE units where we knew a majority of members had signed CUPW cards.

Brother Bean, however, did not withdraw his complaint, and the CLC appointed Carl Goldenberg to rule as an impartial umpire on the matter. On December 10, 1987, he issued this ruling:

> I find that in applying for certification for units of employees of Canada Post Corporation with respect to whom PSAC is the certified bargaining agency [that] without claiming justification before taking action, CUPW was in violation of sections of the constitution of the Canadian Labour Congress. However, I find extenuating circumstances in the conduct of PSAC in authorizing merger negotiations with CUPW by the employees for whom it was certified, approving a tentative agreement, authorizing a referendum vote thereon, and, in a surprise move, annulling the referendum in the midst of the vote.

Unfortunately, some in UPCE decided to suddenly switch sides, convinced that by this means they could keep their members in separate bargaining units. Stephen White, the director for UPCE's Pacific division, was one of them. I'm sure he knew, as I did, that we would end up representing blue-collar UPCE members, while administrative UPCE members would most likely stay in a separate unit. After Denis Gagnon was suspended by PSAC, Stephen White became President of what was left of UPCE. CUPW then hired Denis Gagnon to prepare for a referendum among LCUC and CUPW members on who would represent workers in the post office in the future. He was eventually elected a national officer of CUPW and he became a great brother on our National Executive Board.

The Giant Step Toward One Union

Meanwhile, the Canadian Labour Relations Board continued its review of the number of bargaining units at Canada Post. We in CUPW argued that there should be one bargaining unit for all postal workers other than supervisory personnel. This was in keeping with policies we had adopted over the years at conventions and in referenda of our membership. With one bargaining unit, we said, it would be much more difficult for the employer to play one group of workers off against another. Other unions, however, argued for multiple bargaining units. As the hearings were drawing to a close, we indicated our willingness to have a separate unit for workers in LCUC classifications.

To the surprise of many, the Canadian Labour Relations Board rendered a decision to reduce the number of bargaining units to only four. These were: a unit to include all the administrative workers still represented by the UPCE component of PSAC; one unit for all workers then in CUPW, LCUC, the International Brotherhood of Electrical Workers (IBEW), and the blue-collar workers who had recently changed their affiliation from UPCE to CUPW; one unit for supervisory workers, members of the Association of Postal Officers of Canada; and a fourth unit for the Canadian Postmasters' and Assistants' Association, which would continue to represent workers at small, rural post offices.

In view of this decision, we entered into negotiations with LCUC on the formation of one union to represent all workers in what was referred to as the "urban operational bargaining unit." (In fact, IBEW also took part in these meetings, but they represented only a relatively small number of workers in the post office, and it was clear to all that they would end up in whatever union organization emerged from the discussions between CUPW and LCUC.) Our talks made some progress, but only very slowly. Eventually, on November 3, I sat down with Brother Bob McGarry, National President of the LCUC, to see whether we could finalize points still in dispute.

While we were trying to reach a merger agreement with LCUC, our National Executive Board adopted a contingency plan we would use if the merger talks failed: in that case, it would come down to a single certification vote among the members of both unions. Pamphlets were produced geared towards groups such as smaller locals, mail service couriers, and general labour and trades workers. They outlined CUPW's bargaining history and our job security provisions and made other comparisons between the collective agreements and the constitutions of CUPW and LCUC.

We set up phone banks to be used by all CUPW representatives and those responsible for the campaign in Ottawa. Kits were sent to all locals to help them in their communications work, and different committees were struck. We scheduled a meeting of representatives of larger CUPW locals on Sunday, November 6, 1988, in Toronto and another the following weekend for representatives of locals with fewer than seventy-five members. On November 4, we held a meeting at an Ottawa hotel of national and regional full-time CUPW representatives to review where we were in our discussions with LCUC toward reaching a merger agreement. We also discussed preparations for a certification vote should the merger talks break down. I gave my opinion at that meeting that, if the vote were to take place the next day, we would lose it. I pointed out that, in order to win, we first had to ensure that our own members would support CUPW and we had to demonstrate that CUPW had always been a union that supported the unity of all postal workers. Everyone at this meeting knew the negative consequences that would result if merger talks broke down and LCUC won certification for the new bargaining unit, so I knew they would all do their best to win a vote, if that's what it came to.

Still, both Brother McGarry and I knew that an agreement between us was preferable to an all-out war. We met together later on the same day of the CUPW meeting at an Ottawa hotel, and we finally reached an agreement, on the following terms:

- members would retain democratic control of the union;
- there would be representation from each region of the country on the National Executive Board;
- negotiations would remain under membership control and members would receive continuous updates on the progress of negotiations;
- all locals would be integrated at least one year before our 1993 convention;
- all locals would be entitled to representation at all national conventions;
- the national union would continue to provide the same standard of service as before;
- all members would be covered by a group life insurance policy paid by the union;
- salaries and benefits for CUPW officers would be adjusted, while salaries for LCUC officers would be frozen. (Salaries for LCUC officers were significantly higher than were those of equivalent CUPW officers, often by many thousands of dollars.);
- there would be co-presidents until a referendum vote in three months to determine the new union's President and Executive Vice-President;
- starting in 1993, amendments to the constitution to change union structure, salaries, dues structure, and sick-leave benefits would require a simple majority;
- there would be nine divisional offices, each with four elected union representatives;
- the National Executive Board would be made up of eleven resident officers and nine divisional officers;
- dues would be set at $35.60 per month, to be distributed as follows: 15

percent to a defence fund, 30 percent to locals (a 5-percent increase in the case of CUPW locals), and 55 percent to the national union;

- during an interim period until 1990, the National Executive Board would have nine members from LCUC, the nine existing CUPW members and one UPCE representative;
- CUPW and LCUC would be guaranteed equal delegate representation at the 1990 convention.

Brother McGarry and I also came to a personal understanding that we would both run for National President of the new union, but whoever lost would not seek any other position in the union. At first we had talked about one becoming President and the other Vice-President, but we both agreed that this might look more like we were protecting one another's jobs than a democratic way to determine a new leader.

CUPW's National Executive Board immediately endorsed the agreement and we prepared to present it to a vote of our members. We also had time to inform, before they returned to their locals across the country, our representatives who had attended our Ottawa meeting that a merger agreement had been reached. We had prepared materials ready to go out for the vote when Brother McGarry phoned me and told me that his Executive had rejected the agreement. When he told me this, I initially thought that we would have to resume negotiations to try to reach an agreement both sides might live with, but he then told me his Executive had rejected the agreement because they thought they would win a certification vote.

I couldn't believe they were willing to gamble their union's future on the simple feeling that they would win a vote. To me, this meant that power, not unity, was their goal. It meant that by winning the vote they wouldn't have to share leadership of the new union. By winning a vote, they could get rid of CUPW's leadership and have all CUPW members suddenly fall under their existing constitution, with no regard to our own history of union democracy.

It wasn't long before I learned that Bill Findlay, LCUC's National Vice-President, had spearheaded the argument against any agreement with CUPW. They were going to win the vote, he said, so why negotiate with CUPW?

He argued that workers in small post offices would vote for LCUC, because, under their constitution, all locals sent delegates to LCUC conventions. He claimed that people working at the wickets would vote for LCUC because they were in close daily contact with LCUC members. Finally, he argued, members of CUPW's Montréal local would vote for LCUC because they had been at odds with their national leadership for some time. Findlay concluded that LCUC would win the vote by a majority of more than 70 percent.

I thought these arguments displayed an incredible lack of understanding. As for the small locals, it was true that our constitutional formula was such that the members of these locals had to go through a regional conference to be elected as delegates to our national convention. But these were held only every three years, and our structure gave them the opportunity to participate in regional conferences prior to each round of negotiations and prior to each national convention. They were well represented in negotiations, had much input into union affairs, and many of them went through regional conferences and became delegates at our national conventions. I didn't think they were going to throw this away for a chance for one of them to attend a national convention every third year.

I had worked at postal wickets for many years and I knew that these workers had faced difficulties in their working relationships with LCUC members and would be unlikely to abandon their union.

But surely, I thought, Bill Findlay's greatest lack of judgment was in his assessment of our Montréal local. It had opposed CUPW's national leadership because it thought we were not militant enough, but they were hardly likely to abandon us to vote for LCUC, which was widely perceived to be a far more conservative union than CUPW. In fact, I thought, Montréal would be the last local in the country to vote for LCUC.

We had no choice other than to prepare for the vote. We immediately informed our representatives across the country that there was no deal. We sent out material that outlined the agreement LCUC had rejected, and we encouraged our members to show it to local LCUC leaders and members. In the days that followed, we also sent out the material we had, fortunately, prepared in case the merger talks broke down.

While we were fairly confident we would win the vote, we were worried about the lists of eligible voters the employer sent to the Canadian Labour Relations Board, which was to conduct the vote. We knew that Canada Post hoped LCUC would win the vote, but we were able to have our locals go through the lists. We opened campaign headquarters at different locations across the country, and they did a great job of getting the lists supplied by Canada Post adjusted by the Labour Relations Board.

This was a time of personal strain for me, and on one occasion it showed. The particular issue at hand was the list of eligible voters for a large local, and it seemed to me that the employer had stacked the list against us. A colleague, Geoff Bickerton, came to me and said, "Jean-Claude, everyone here is doing the best they can trying to make sure we cover all the bases we need to." I think he was distressed by the panic he might have seen on my face, and when he said this to me I was disappointed in myself, but it seems that others working closely with me either didn't notice my distress or overlooked it. I was thankful to them.

The next day, I made certain to exude confidence that we were going to win the vote, and I recognized the great work everyone was doing to

Denis Gagnon, left, and Darrel Tingley holding Jean-Claude Parrot on their shoulders after the announcement of the result of the certification vote between LCUC and CUPW on January 17, 1989.

assure our victory. A pool was organized on what the result would be, not with any money involved, but simply to allow us all to make our predictions. Mine was that we would win by a very small majority of 51.7 percent. My guess represented very closely the relative strength in numbers of the two unions. The logic behind my prediction was that there were no major reasons for members of the respective unions to vote to be represented by the other. This is why a merger agreement would have been a good solution to avoid an all out battle, which could prolong our division, no matter who won the vote. As of November 6, 1988, the Canadian Labour Relations Board had mailed 45,871 ballots for the vote.

On January 17, 1989, the Labour Relations Board announced the results of the vote at an Ottawa hotel. I won the pool: we won the vote by a 52.2 percent majority, a half-percent more than I had predicted. This was quite a shock to LCUC supporters, because most had believed their Executive, which had told them LCUC would win the vote by a good majority. This shock was also visible in the faces of both employer and LCUC representatives present at the announcement.

It was a great moment for CUPW and myself, as we realized we had out-organized LCUC in the campaign. In the spirit of the moment, I was taken up on the shoulders of both First National Vice-President Darrell

CUPW staff welcoming LCUC staff following the integration of LCUC members into CUPW. To the left, Jean-Claude Parrot shakes hands with Louise Vaillancourt, shop steward for LCUC staff. Standing beside them is Yvonne Demalpas of the Office and Professional Employees International Union.

Tingley and CUPW technical advisor Denis Gagnon, who were as exuberant as I was in the joy of victory. The owners of both these sets of shoulders had done great work to assure our victory, as they did later in building unity inside the new CUPW. The same can be said of countless other CUPW members, from workers on the shop floor to regional and national officers.

I recall this now as one of the greatest moments of my career in the labour movement. I had always strongly believed that unity would be a great thing for all postal workers. I was also pleased that I never engaged in attacks against LCUC members, despite a clear lack of respect I'd felt from some in that organization. For example, I had differences with Brother Bob McGarry, but I always respected him as a leader. I'm afraid I can't say the same for Bill Findlay.

We owe many thanks to all those at the national and regional levels, and especially those in the field, who did their homework. They made this victory possible. I am sure that in their hearts, as in mine, their thanks were to their fellow CUPW members who all across the country stuck with their union. I was also thankful for the support we received from both UPCE and LCUC members, whose contributions surely made a difference in the vote.

On February 1, 1989, CUPW was certified by the Canadian Labour Relations Board to represent more than 45,000 workers in all the urban operations of Canada Post.

Unfortunately, those in LCUC at the national and local levels who had always opposed a merger of the two unions and who had rejected the agreement in principle that had been finalized between Brother McGarry and myself didn't accept the result of the vote they had imposed on all of us. This made the integration of LCUC members into their new union much more difficult and left some bad feelings among them. While Brother McGarry urged them to get involved in their new union so they could influence its development, others encouraged locals to spend their assets so they wouldn't have to transfer them to CUPW.

However, other LCUC locals, such as those in Québec City and Edmonton, immediately merged with our locals and new structures were quickly put in place. After a few months in their new union, many former LCUC members demanded we go to court on their behalf to have their money either returned to them or transferred to CUPW. (We did initiate court action, but it has dragged on for several years. At the time of the writing of this book, a fund totalling about $3,000,000 is in the care of a court-appointed trustee. It seems likely that the disbursement of these funds will be decided by a vote of former LCUC members. They will probably be given a choice of splitting it among themselves, giving it to a charitable organization, or turning it over to CUPW's defence fund.)

One of the first things we did after the vote was to meet a commitment we had made to LCUC's support staff. Prior to the vote, we had given them a clear commitment that we would take them all into CUPW should we win the vote, and we did. CUPW's staff had been unable to obtain a similar commitment from LCUC.

Winning the vote should have made things easier for CUPW because there was no need to implement a merger agreement. All members previously in LCUC and IBEW, as well as some from UPCE, were now represented by CUPW and therefore fell under our national constitution. So technically, we didn't have to make any amendments to our constitution, but we decided to make changes to our structure and constitution that reflected the agreement that the LCUC leadership had turned down at the last minute. We decided to do this despite the fact that we knew that, had LCUC won, Bill Findlay and his supporters would have made no changes to their organization to accommodate former CUPW members. CUPW's National Executive Board felt that, if we were to well represent our new members and make them feel welcome, we needed to get them involved in the day-to-day life of the union.

I always believed that if members of the different unions came together in the same meetings, they would all gain a better understanding of each other's needs and that this could only increase their sense of solidarity. Soon after we won the vote, we encouraged all our locals to review their by-laws to integrate members of the other unions in their structure at all levels. Nationally, we led by example, adopting a series of amendments to our constitution that were put to a vote of the membership through a national referendum. These changes reflected principles and created positions at national, regional, and local levels that had been called for in the agreement that was ultimately rejected by the LCUC leadership.

On March 1, 1989, CUPW members voted in favour of these constitutional changes, and on May 13 we proceeded with an election to fill the seventeen new positions that had been created at the national and regional levels.

In June, LCUC held a special convention in Sudbury and created a twelve-person "power base" to whom it gave control of LCUC's assets. Each "power base" member received an annual salary $37,000, plus benefits. LCUC was transformed into an entirely new sort of organization, no longer accountable in any way to its members. All decisions were made by four executive officers, who would remain in office indefinitely.

Resolutions passed at the Sudbury gathering also gave the "power base," a mandate to file a request with the Canadian Labour Relations Board to rescind its original decision. They were to ask the Board to divide CUPW into two units, one for inside workers and one for outside workers.

But the "power base" never did approach the Board, knowing full well they would be turned down. In fact, they knew this even when they recommended that delegates adopt this resolution, giving them the false impression that it might be possible to bring back their old union.

Instead of carrying out its mandate, the "power base" did everything possible to interfere in the affairs of the new CUPW. They actively worked against the referendum on amendments to the CUPW constitution to integrate the new members. They eventually participated in three unsuccessful raids against CUPW, and we had no choice but to suspend, on clear evidence, all those who actively participated in these raids.

Some local leaders didn't want to identify those who participated in these failed raids, but I was determined that any member who participated in a raid would be suspended. I wasn't ready to tolerate members who organized against their own union from the inside.

I stuck firmly to this position. I made it clear at meetings that the new CUPW would work for its members, but not for those who would try to break the union. I said that the new CUPW would work to represent letter carriers, mail service couriers, and maintenance workers just as we had always represented inside postal workers. I said we would integrate the different collective agreements into one and protect the acquired rights of everyone in doing so. I concluded:

> Those who want to work with us will find that they have their place in this union, but those who wish to continue to break this union will find that we are not going to sit back and let them do whatever they want in this union. When you signed a card, you

agreed to give your allegiance to that organization. In exchange, the Executive of this union will make sure you will be able to identify with it as really being your union.

We didn't budge from this position, and I believe it encouraged many whose loyalties were wavering to really join our ranks, rather than stay in the "empty field" suggested to them by the well-paid leaders of the "power base." They understood that the actions of the "power base" were strictly based on the desire for vengeance.

In numerous interventions I made at meetings across the country at this time, I directed the following comments to Bill Findlay:

> You are the one who imposed a vote on the members to decide which union was to represent all workers. We offered you a merger that would have united all these workers, but you decided you were not going to work with the CUPW leadership, and you forced a vote because you were sure you would win it and, therefore, be able to run the union without the CUPW leaders. You lost, my friend, and we now see what your true colours really are. Despite knowing that you would not have offered us a position on the Executive, we were still willing to offer you one after the vote, but you chose instead to raise hatred among former LCUC members against their new union.
>
> Stop lying to your members and spending their money on your own crusade. They need to prepare for the next round of negotiations with the employer to solidify and improve what they built when in LCUC. Like it or not, Bill Findlay, this is what I will fight for with them.

I was pleased with the attitude of Brother Bob McGarry, who encouraged his members to get involved in their new union and then gracefully retired from the scene. In fact, he deserved our thanks for his cooperation in numerous cases where LCUC members filed grievances before an arbitrator for violations by the employer of provisions in the last collective agreement LCUC negotiated. He often appeared as a witness in such cases, helping former LCUC members win arbitration decisions.

Many LCUC activists across the country followed Brother McGarry's advice and immediately got involved in their new union. Today, Lynn Bue is CUPW's First National Vice-President and Chief Negotiator. These were her reflections after becoming the first former LCUC member on our Negotiating Committee in 1989:

> Emotions were pretty raw at the beginning, and there was an obvious mistrust on both sides about the integration of the mem-

bers from LCUC, but I soon believed it was a good thing CUPW had won the vote.

I was impressed with their quality of research, by their vision for a changing post office, by their education program, and I believed CUPW could better adjust to the addition of our members than vice versa.

Perhaps internal workers had dealt with so much technologi-cal change they had been forced to acknowledge that the world of postal work would not stay the same. The approach by CUPW, though, was inspiring. It was not to "hold the line," even though we were seeing rollbacks in many other workplaces, but to fight to improve our work, expand our work, and build a solid public institution that delivered good service. No apologies. As Jean-Claude said, "If we don't look after the future of our children and grandchildren, who will?" And, they knew the value of building allies in the community for this vision.

The resistance of the "power base" lasted a long time in some former LCUC locals, but eventually, even those most opposed to what they called a "forced merger" decided to follow Brother McGarry's advice as they came to see it as the sensible course of action.

It is hard to believe that more than fifteen years have passed since the Canadian Labour Relations Board's decision to bring almost all postal workers under the same bargaining umbrella and the subsequent decisive vote. By now, the collective agreements have long been integrated, as has the new and larger membership. Now, the union negotiates with strength on behalf of all postal workers. Today, there are former members of other unions in positions at all levels of CUPW. In fact, there are many today who were hired by Canada Post after January 1989 and who therefore have only ever known one union for all postal workers.

Postal workers now discuss together changes they want to see in their collective agreement, and this gives all of them a better understanding of one another's issues. Every good trade union leader understands how important such understanding among the membership is when facing the employer at the bargaining table.

I am proud of having contributed to the making of one union for all workers in the "urban operational bargaining unit" and of having been their leader during the time of their integration. Union leaders may have influence on policies adopted at conventions, but it is always the delegates who have the last word. A strong, democratic union often has to deal with issues that demand serious debate, mutual respect, a passion for justice, and a desire to ensure a better world for our children and grandchildren. And, this is precisely what CUPW has been all about through the years of our struggle.

The Worst Period of My Life in the Union

I had many great moments during my life in CUPW, but not all my experiences were happy ones. From time to time, situations arose that were difficult to handle on a personal level. The worst of these were serious internal problems that, unfortunately, led to personal attacks against the National Executive Board, against regional activists, and against myself.

I never took exception to healthy debates within the union, but I did object when these reached the level of personal attack. Differences of opinion on issues, on strategies, or on leadership are all fair ball, and there are forums in the organization to address these, but personal attacks have no place in an organization like CUPW.

I've always accepted that people are different. Not all people have the same education, knowledge, or aptitudes. One has to respect every individual who makes an effort to be active in the organization and to never discourage them. I also accepted that there were often rivalries for elected positions within the union, but that's what democratic elections are all about.

What I never accepted was rejection of the democratic process and the turning of issues into personality conflicts. Sure, from time to time I had honest disagreements with others on various issues. Sometimes, members in different locals or regions didn't think we got all we could have in a round of negotiations or that some of the things we agreed to were unacceptable. These members were always able to strongly express their points of view in the field or at Executive meetings.

I had a particular habit of language when I wasn't pleased with someone at meetings of the National Executive Board or other union functions: I would begin my comments addressed to him or her with the expression, "Listen, my friend." Everyone then knew that I was angry, whether rightly or not. But they also knew that by the time we reached the next issue or the end of the meeting, my anger would have been forgotten.

But none of the internal disagreements in the union ever reached the proportions of the struggle between the national leadership and the Montréal local in the period between 1985 and 1988, when this problem reached its peak. Our differences were so serious that we felt the need to call a Special National Convention in Toronto in February of 1988. (Another reason for calling this Special Convention was the need to implement a National Program of Action to counter a five-year business plan developed by Canada Post that would have very negative effects on postal workers.)

At a meeting in Ottawa on November 18, 1987, the National Executive Board, as provided for under the terms of our national constitution, adopted the following resolution calling for this Special Convention:

Whereas the union must deal with serious internal problems of democracy;

Whereas the CUPW membership is entitled to expect these problems to be resolved without delay;

Whereas the CUPW membership is also entitled to be assured that we will enter the next round of negotiations in the knowledge that the National Executive Board will be in a position to deal with any problems that may occur;

Whereas, following the repressive back-to-work legislation, it is essential that we ensure full human and financial resources to implement the national program of action;

Whereas the Québec Superior Court decided that investing money from the defence fund into a building for the national headquarters of the union was not, in its opinion, the kind of investment provided for under our national constitution;

Whereas the settlement of these three issues may necessitate amendments to the national constitution;

Be it resolved that the National Executive Board call a Special Convention as there is an urgent requirement for such action;

Be it further resolved that the National Executive Board authorize the National Executive Committee to finalize the urgent question(s) that require the calling of the Special Convention subject to the approval of the National Executive Board at its meeting in December 1987;

Be it finally resolved that the National Executive Committee be authorized to announce to the locals the decision of the National Executive Board in a notice which will indicate that the official call will be sent following the December meeting and will indicate the urgent question(s) that require the calling of the Special Convention, this in order to provide locals with the necessary time to choose their delegates for the regional conferences that will precede such Special Convention.

The National Director of the Québec region, Brother Richard Forget, recorded his dissenting vote against this resolution.

It was obvious that the situation was serious, or the National Executive Board would not have taken such a decision. When the official notice of the Special Convention went out, five issues were put on the agenda. The National Executive Board adopted resolutions to address each of these issues, and these were presented and debated at the Special National Convention. The five issues were:

- the financing of the National Program of Action;
- the decision of the Québec Superior Court in regard to the National Executive Board's decision to buy the national headquarters building;

- the appeal procedure for disciplinary charges laid under the terms of the national constitution;
- the absence of adequate powers in the hands of the National Executive Board to enable it to resolve the serious problems of democracy and operational problems within the union; and
- members subjected to disciplinary measures by the employer.

By the time we got to this Special Convention, I was quite upset by a number of ongoing personal attacks by the Montréal local against myself and members of the National Executive Board. These attacks were prompted by the local's objections to the national leadership's actions in three areas: the decision of the National Executive Board to buy a head-quarters building in Ottawa, the merger agreement with UPCE, and the local's rejection of some of the demands included in the national program of demands that had been put before, and approved by, the membership prior to the beginning of negotiations in 1986.

I was especially displeased that the Montréal local had chosen to bring its national union before the courts on a number issues that had no place there, but I'm getting ahead of myself. Some background is in order here.

When we began negotiations in July 1986, there was strong opposition from the Montréal local over some of the points included in our national program of demands. Its strongest objection was to our demand for a shorter workweek of four eight-hour days. The local objected on the grounds that this would create too many part-time weekend workers. Most locals in Québec also supported the position of their regional executive committee against these demands being included in our national program of demands. This is why, nationally, we received only a 56.6 percent major-ity in favour of the program. Nevertheless, the program was ratified, and we were set to present it to the employer at a meeting scheduled for July 21, 1986.

Prior to that meeting, the National Executive Committee met with the members of the Québec regional executive committee and the Mon-treal local's executive about their concerns regarding our national program of demands. On the eve of our meeting with the employer, the National Executive Board discussed a resolution from the Québec regional execu-tive committee and nine other Québec locals demanding that we change the program of demands that had been ratified by the membership.

At that meeting, the National Director for the Québec region, Brother Forget, moved that the National Executive Board should change the program of demands to bring them in line with objections raised by the Québec regional executive committee. No other member of the National Executive Board seconded the motion, and it was then decided to proceed with the presentation to the employer the next day.

The National Executive Board had already given serious consideration to the arguments used to try to convince us to change the program of demands. We spent quite some time in debating the issue, and I asked, despite personal attacks, that the Board members focus on the issue itself. After considerable debate and analysis, we came to the conclusion that the opposition to the few demands raised in the Québec resolution in fact reflected their disapproval of our approach, rather than of the objective itself — the reduction of the workweek without a drop in pay. Therefore, we didn't feel justified in changing the national program of demands.

As mentioned in Chapter Nine, when we arrived for the meeting with the employer on July 21, several members from the Montréal local were picketing the location, and the meeting had to be rescheduled. (There may also have been some members from other Québec locals on that picket line.)

In a bulletin sent out on July 22 informing members of the delay in presenting our demands because of the picket line, I tried to indicate to the Montréal local and others who had concerns about the program of demands that our objective was the reduction of working time, and on that we were all in agreement. We all knew that compromises are inevitable in negotiations. And, even if the employer were to accept our demand, we would then have insisted on measures to mitigate the impact it could have regarding the possible use of part-time weekend workers by the employer.

But this wasn't enough for representatives of the Montréal local. For them, nothing short of deleting this demand for a shorter workweek from the national program would do. Without holding another referendum, we felt we had no right to do so, and we had no intention of doing so, especially in light of the fact that we had already looked closely at the issue and had thoroughly discussed the concerns of those in opposition to us.

A meeting was organized in Drummondville by several Québec locals to discuss this situation and they invited me and First National Vice-President, Brother Bill Chedore, to attend it. Soon after this meeting began, a delegation from the Montréal local and the Québec regional executive committee, led by Brother Richard Forget, National Director for the Québec region, arrived. Brother Forget then told other members present to leave, saying Brother Chedore and I had no right to be there. He then accused me of trying to create a division among the Québec locals.

I replied that, as National President, I don't refuse invitations from CUPW locals to discuss important issues unless I'm unavailable due to other important commitments. The presidents of these locals had invited me, I said, because they want to hear our side of the story and to express their dissatisfaction over this public division within the union.

I think the tone used by Brother Forget, ordering members to leave the meeting, was the wrong one. These local leaders were seriously concerned about the internal differences that had arisen in the union, and they all remained.

Brother Forget and his delegation left the meeting. Members then told me that, despite their reservations about some our demands, they didn't want to be associated with the ongoing crusade of the Montréal local against the national union and myself.

They accepted my explanation about the difference between negotiating strategies and objectives, and my explanation of other issues, such as buying the national headquarters building. The attitude of the Montréal local and the Québec regional executive committee was such that most other locals in the Québec region eventually demanded that all locals outside Montréal be put in a different region with a new regional executive that would represent their interests inside the union.

This wasn't my idea of to how to resolve the conflict, but I must admit that the Montréal local and the Québec regional executive committee didn't offer any help in finding an alternative solution. Many other Québec members soon came to see them as an arrogant group that took members outside the Montréal local for granted. For the Montréal local, there seemed no room for compromise, and they were determined to continue their fight against the national leadership, as represented by the members of the National Executive Board.

The attacks from representatives of the Montréal local continued. As mentioned in Chapter Nine, when we reached the conciliation process, the Negotiating Committee member from the Québec region, Clément Morel, told us that he would raise his opposition before the Conciliation Commissioner should our demand for a shorter workweek be discussed. In light of complaints that had already been received from locals across the country, Brother Morel had already been warned by the National Executive Board in writing in October of 1986 that, if he persisted in his attacks on our program of demands, his appointment to our Negotiating Committee would be terminated. Because this would have shown us to be weakened by internal divisions before both the employer and the Conciliation Commissioner — and, most importantly, because Brother Morel had continued his public attacks on our program of demands — I had no choice but to recommend that Brother Morel be replaced at a meeting of the National Executive Board in March 1987. In the discussion that followed the resolution to remove him, I was asked whether we had the right to remove Bother Morel. The atmosphere in the room was tense, and in an effort to defuse the situation, I replied, "If we have the right to appoint, we have the right to disappoint." This helped to ease the tension in the room, and the National Executive Board passed the resolution. Brother Morel's place on the Negotiating Committee was eventually taken by Brother Valère Tremblay from the Québec City local.

Obviously, this didn't please the Montréal local's executive, but despite their challenges I maintained my position and that of the National Executive Board. The numerous criticisms by the local against the national union and the fact that the local brought us before the courts on our dismissal of Brother Morel, as well as on our purchase of the building for our national office, led many Québec locals to raise concerns over the dispute.

At a meeting of the National Executive Board in August 1986, Brother Forget reported that he had undertaken a campaign to try to modify the program of demands because of the 87.5 percent vote against the program in the Québec region. He also said that, while Brother Chedore and I had attended the meeting in Drummondville with representatives from several locals in the Québec region, nobody from the Québec regional office had been invited to this meeting. He denounced Brother Chedore and myself for what he described as an abuse of our duties.

At the same meeting, the National Executive Board reviewed a letter sent by eighteen locals from the Québec region in which they dissociated themselves completely from an August 4, 1986, bulletin issued from the Québec regional office. That bulletin accused Brother Chedore and myself of "improper conduct" because we had attended the Drummondville meeting.

In February 1987, Brother Forget brought four resolutions from the Québec regional executive committee to the National Executive Board. The first asked for a review of their concerns over our program of demands. The Board asked me to respond, and I explained that thorough discussions had already taken place on this issue and that the program could not be changed.

The second resolution asked that we declare the CUPW vote on the merger with UPCE null and void. Again, the Board asked me to respond, and I explained that UPCE was still interested in working towards a merger and that we therefore could not declare the vote null and void.

The third resolution called for my resignation as National President for allegedly "deceiving" the membership about the merger with UPCE. The National Executive Board asked me to respond, and I explained that incurring the costs of the merger had been a decision taken by the National Executive Board and that the membership had not been "deceived by the National President," and the Board did not ask me to resign.

The fourth resolution called for the National Executive Board to change its position and not purchase a building for our national headquarters. Again I was asked to respond, and I explained that considerable previous discussion had taken place on this issue and that our position would remain unchanged.

At the beginning of the Board's afternoon session, Brother Forget arrived with the two other members of the Québec regional executive committee and read a statement indicating that, because we had no intention of settling the issue of our program of demands to their satisfaction, they would take whatever further steps they felt were required. They then left the meeting.

For reasons noted in Chapter Nine, at the March meeting of the National Executive Board I had no other choice than to recommend that we expel Clément Morel from our Negotiating Committee, and this was agreed to. Later on at that meeting, we were interrupted by a delegation from the Québec regional executive and the Montréal local executive.

Brother Marcel Perreault, president of the Montréal local, then read six resolutions that had been adopted at a meeting of his local. The delegation then left the meeting, as did Brother Forget, National Director for the Québec region, who parted saying he would not return to the National Executive Board until Clément Morel was reinstated on the Negotiating Committee.

The six resolutions from the Montréal local were:

- to call an emergency National Executive Board meeting to delete the demands objected to by the Montréal local from the national program of demands;
- the National Executive Board should not purchase a building for our national headquarters;
- the National Executive Board should give priority to negotiations and not to other trade union activities;
- the National Executive Board should declare the results of CUPW's merger vote with UPCE null and void;
- the National Executive Board should call for the resignation of the National President due to the declaration by PSAC that the UPCE ballots would not be counted;
- an emergency meeting of the National Executive Board should be held in order to obtain the resignation of the National President for meeting with various locals from the Québec region.

Suddenly, out of nowhere, the president of the Montréal local was objecting to my involvement in the trade union movement. This same issue had been the subject of a number of resolutions from his local at the 1983 CUPW Convention (see Chapter Eight), where I had been prepared to resign my position if a narrow vision of the proper role of CUPW had been adopted.

I later discovered that what Brother Perreault had actually been saying to the members of his local was that I was travelling too much instead of representing the members. This was an issue on which the two of us were in total disagreement. According to him, I should always stay at the national office. As explained in Chapter Eight, whenever I travelled outside Ottawa, I touched base with locals and appeared at other gatherings to further CUPW's cause. But, for Brother Perreault, this was simply a question of orientation. For me, it was also a question of vision. I was not only CUPW's Chief Negotiator, which demands long periods in Ottawa, but I was also National President, which required that I also represent the membership away from the bargaining table. The 1983 Convention had long ago decided on this issue.

During this period, I often had to appear in court in Montréal to deal with charges made by the Montréal local against the National Executive Board over decisions it took that the local considered unconstitutional. The first legal challenge was to our decision to buy a building for our national headquarters. A second legal challenge was against our decision to remove Clément Morel from our Negotiating Committee. A third legal challenge was against our decision to reach a merger agreement with UPCE. All of these challenges were defeated, but they took up valuable time and union resources.

I didn't find it distasteful that I had to appear in court to represent the national union. But I did find it distasteful that the other side treated us as if we were an enemy of workers that took actions contrary to their interests. Although I was successful in defending the positions of the National Executive Board in the courts, I was personally attacked with a hatred that has no place in a democratic organization such as ours.

Even after I moved to Ottawa in 1971 I always maintained my membership in the Montréal local, and the issue of union democracy became something that I had no choice to take on if I was going to continue to have any credibility within CUPW and with others I had to deal with in representing our membership. So I stood up against the president of my local, Brother Marcel Perreault, when I saw him clearly crossing the line of democratic organization. I had accepted my full share of attacks in my years with CUPW, but, until now, I had never taken these as personal.

It is not that I never myself criticized the national union or its leaders. I certainly did, but never with hatred in my voice. I would argue my point on an issue without taking the tone that those who disagreed with me did so for personal reasons. I also don't believe union leaders are elected to their positions to run their organizations through referenda. There are policies, a constitution, and mandates that are sufficient to provide leaders with guidance in their decisions.

That being said, the membership remains the highest authority of the union, and there were specific situations where the constitution clearly called for a referendum: amending the constitution between conventions, the adoption of our national program of demands, ratification of a collective agreement, strike activities, changes in seniority rules, increases in union dues, agreements with other unions or a central labour body, merger with other unions, and affiliation or disaffiliation with a central labour body.

I strongly believe that the Montréal local played a very important role in making CUPW a strong union of principles and determination. Marcel Perreault, Clément Morel, and I worked hard to make the Montréal local a strong and democratic local long before the national union became a strong one. I sincerely believe that, at crucial points in CUPW's history, the Montréal local had a tremendously positive influence in the development of the national union. Even after I moved to Ottawa and Clément Morel moved to the Québec regional office in Montréal, all three of us continued to work hard to make our union, and our local, strong. By the time CUPW emerged from under the shadow of the Council of Postal Unions in 1975, I believe we had become the union of principles and determination I am proud of.

The working demands on our national union grew through the years, and it got to the point at our national office where we needed more space than we had. At the same time, rental costs were reaching levels that were having quite a financial impact on our organization. The idea of buying our own building was floated and my first reaction was the same as the Montréal local's: I didn't think we should become managers, maintainers, and administrators of a building at the cost of our regular duties and responsibilities.

The National Executive Board had a study made of the situation, and it clearly demonstrated that we could save a substantial amount of money if we owned our own building. Furthermore, the study showed that we wouldn't have to manage, maintain, and administrate the building, yet we could still save a substantial amount of money.

I was still sceptical of the idea, but I eventually ran out of rationales for my opposition, so I supported the resolution to accept the report going into the 1983 Convention. It was adopted there, with the understanding that it was to be reported back at the 1986 National Convention. Unfortunately, there was so much other business to attend to that we were unable to deal with the matter during the 1986 Convention. But the problem didn't go away and, seeing how the situation at the national office was deteriorating, the National Executive Board decided to proceed with the purchase of larger premises.

But, we still had to find a way to finance this project, and we decided that the union's defence fund would invest in a building. At the time of purchase in 1987, we had $19,000,000 in the defence fund: we invested $3,200,000 in the purchase of the building in which we were already a tenant. This saved us the considerable cost of moving, and, as other tenants moved out, more space became available for our use.

The Montréal local took us to court, arguing that the purchase was unconstitutional. The judge granted an injunction in the local's favour but, on being informed that we were planning a Special Convention to deal with this issue, he asked the local whether, if we were to have the purchase ratified by a referendum, this would resolve the issue. The local's answer was in the negative. It argued that we didn't have the right to call a referendum on this issue.

In any event, the Special Convention was held in February 1988 to deal with this and four other issues that needed to be resolved if the union was to be able to move on with its work in representing the membership. After a three-hour debate, the Convention supported the National Executive Board's recommendation to hold a referendum on the matter. The referendum was held, and the membership supported the purchase of the building. The court then rejected the charges of the Montréal local on this matter.

I was also a witness in other cases brought before the courts by the Montréal local. At first, quite a few members of the Montréal local attended the court sessions, but their numbers soon fell to the few on the local's executive.

I particularly remember one point during the Montréal local's legal efforts to overturn the National Executive Board's decision to remove Clément Morel from our Negotiating Committee. During cross-examination, the lawyer representing the local mentioned that I had nominated someone to run for election against the local's incumbent secretary-treasurer in the local elections, held in the autumn of 1986. Surely, the local's lawyer said, this was not something the Ottawa-based National President should be doing at the local level.

Under questioning from my own lawyer, I had the opportunity to clarify the reasons for my behaviour. First, I said, I was a member of the Montréal local and, as such, had the right to participate in its meetings and activities. However, I agreed that, as National President, I didn't normally see such actions as my proper role, but in this instance, I didn't feel I had any other choice. I explained that Brother Normand Marin had asked me to nominate him as a candidate for the position. I told him that I didn't see this as my role, in view of the position I occupied. I added that I didn't want to be involved in the local's election.

Still, as a member of the Montréal local, I attended the meeting. Brother Marin had already found someone else to nominate him. At the start of the meeting, local president Marcel Perreault gave an outline of the work done by the outgoing executive committee. In concluding his remarks, he said that, despite the fantastic work done by the local executive, there were some individuals who had organized to run against some incumbents, forcing them to close the office for two weeks in order to campaign to get re-elected.

He spoke in this vein for several minutes, offering up scathing criticism for those who would dare to stand for nomination against incumbent executive members. I remember feeling that it was outrageous for a local president with such experience and knowledge of the importance of democracy in the labour movement to be talking in such a manner. I couldn't believe it: the same individual who was accusing us of not being democratic was objecting hatefully to individuals who might dare to run against members of the local executive. This was contrary to the most fundamental principles of democracy — the right to run for office and the right to vote.

When nominations were called for the position of secretary-treasurer, I immediately went to the mike. "It had not been my intention to make any nomination," I said, "but in view of the remarks by the president that it is a crime for anyone to run against the existing local executive, I nominate Brother Marin, who has the right to run for election, for the position of secretary-treasurer." I had nothing against the incumbent secretary-treasurer, but the right to participate in the most fundamental act of democracy in our society, and in the labour movement, was very important to me.

I think the explanation I gave in testimony to the court on that occasion, and on others, allowed members of the Montréal local attending the hearings to hear for the first time another side of the story Marcel Perreault had been telling them. It didn't turn them against him, but that was not my goal. Still, I'm sure it made them think that not everything was quite as portrayed by the local's leadership.

I was hesitant to write about all these events, but the activists involved in the union at the time know how difficult that period was for the union, and for myself. To avoid writing about this would have taken away any credibility this book may have. One thing is certain in my mind about this period of my life in the union: I honestly felt I had no choice in taking the actions I took. I never did anything out of vengeance or to simply show I had power within the union. I felt at the time that there should have been less confrontational ways to deal with these issues, but for the other side it was their way or nothing. Still, even today I feel sad about the conflicts we faced during that period.

But not every aspect of that time was sad. One day during this period of conflict with the Montréal local, a florist phoned our Ottawa home, and Louisette answered. "Madam," he said, "I have a funereal wreath of flowers to deliver to your address, but I find it strange that this is to a private home and want to verify with you that all is in order."

"Do you know who is sending this?" Louisette asked. He replied that he didn't know, that it was an order placed and paid for at the counter. "Well," Louisette told the florist, "this is obviously a joke someone is playing, but I wonder if, as it is already paid for, whether you could send me a nice arrangement for my dining-room table instead of the wreath." The florist agreed to her request, and said he was glad he had called.

A couple hours later Louisette received a nice flower arrangement, and when I got home, she had a great time telling me what had happened. We had a good laugh at this, and the next day when I went back to union meetings, I couldn't resist telling this story, knowing it would get back to the Montréal local. I didn't think Marcel Perreault was necessarily behind this, but I could think of a couple other members of the Montréal local who might have done something like it. Mind you, I could also think of some people who were not members of the Montréal local who might have done this. I hope that whoever it was heard the story or that they read of it here. Louisette and I thank you for the nice floral arrangement.

Eventually, relations between the Montréal local and the national leadership improved. Once the 1988 Special Convention and the membership referenda on the issues that had prompted it were over, things got back to normal. We worked closely on the integration of the UPCE and LCUC members into CUPW. When I decided to run for the position of CLC Executive Vice-President in 1992, both the Montréal local and the Québec regional executive actively supported my candidacy.

So, despite strong differences of opinion on approaches and strategies toward certain issues and a disagreement on the orientation or vision of the union, we came through this period as a strong, united union, because in the end, CUPW was more important to all of us than were our differences.

Despite everything, one of my greatest memories in CUPW is of the time Marcel Perreault, Clément Morel, and I worked together as full-time officers of the Montréal local from our small office on St. Denis Street. We were three hard workers who shared the same vision in building our union and defending and extending the rights of our members.

I had the good fortune to meet Marcel just a few years ago, when the Montréal local, under the presidency of André Frappier, asked us to participate in a film entitled *Gains For Everyone*, about the history of the Montréal local. We both enjoyed doing this. Unfortunately, Clément Morel passed away before that film was made.

I believe the three of us made major contributions to CUPW in different ways and, despite some differences along the way, we had one thing in common: we knew which side we were on.

12 The Media and the Wider World

The Media and the Trade Union Movement

During my life in the trade union movement I dealt with the media quite regularly, especially when I was CUPW's President and Chief Negotiator. I was impressed by the knowledge and talent of almost all the reporters I met.

I had very little experience in dealing with the media before I moved to Ottawa in 1971. During our fourteen-day strike in 1974, I helped President Joe Davidson in our dealings with the media, but I was quite nervous. I dealt with the French media while Brother Davidson handled the English reporters. The hour-long debate I had with the Postmaster General at a Montréal television station during that strike was a first for me. After my election as National President in 1977 I had to deal with the media in both languages. I was helped immensely through the years in my media dealings by the staff at our national office in Ottawa. Our staff kept in close contact with reporters, keeping them up to date on negotiations, and on union affairs in general. I eventually became more comfortable in my role as a media spokesperson.

I made myself available for interviews and was impressed with how generally well-informed labour reporters were. This was a good indication that our staff was doing a good job. Articles by these labour reporters were, generally speaking, quite fair and accurate. I adopted a policy of never complaining about what these reporters wrote, but when I felt a reporter had got things wrong, I'd usually ask someone else from our national office to speak to the reporter and provide him or her with additional information This would show our interest in their work, while keeping them informed at the same time.

I was never dishonest with reporters and I always showed respect for their work. As well, I always refused to provide "scoops" to any favoured reporters: major announcements and press releases were issued to all the media at the same time.

For their part, media workers knew that any press release from us could lead to real news in the days and weeks to come. I have a collection of many articles by reporters that I considered fair and informative. Even

One of the numerous media scrums Jean-Claude Parrot held through the years as CUPW's Chief Negotiator.

during a strike, there were often many articles that essentially dealt fairly with issues in dispute or with statements we issued.

Whenever I was engaged in a press conference or an interview, I took the view that I was both talking to our members and reaching out to the broader public. Therefore, I made it a habit to speak in the same language whether talking to the media or to our own members. I never accepted that it was necessary to say one thing to the media and another thing at membership meetings. I know that not everyone in the labour movement agreed with me on this, but I suspect that their reasons were probably related to an obsession of "not giving a bad image" to the labour movement, as I mentioned earlier.

Despite what the media may have reported or opined, postal strikes were never directed against the public. Rather, they were the use of a right that was part of a legal process to encourage the employer to negotiate with us seriously. In fact, I have great respect for the public and I always made an effort when we struck to explain publicly why we felt we had no other choice.

In fact, I wonder why some labour leaders are defensive about being forthright in such situations. What's wrong with fighting to protect decent jobs? What's wrong with fighting for secure full-time and part-time jobs instead of lower paid, insecure jobs? What's wrong with fighting for good health and safety protections in the workplace? Obviously, nothing is wrong with fighting for these things. One thing the media rarely reminds people is that workers with decent jobs — and therefore decent pay —

spend their money in their communities for locally available goods and services. (In contrast, the corporate sector almost always takes its profits and goes home.) Decently paid workers also pay more taxes, so governments can maintain and improve public services and social programs.

I don't pretend that coverage in the media was always perfect. While reporters' articles were generally fair, media owners use their editorial powers to influence public thinking on many issues.

Sadly, media coverage of labour issues has changed drastically in our country over the past twenty years. Labour issues are almost always now a very low media priority, as owners have restructured their operations with much more attention paid to making profits than to providing information to the public. Media owners are far from neutral, and while they may not directly tell reporters what to write, they have ways of manipulating information to make the trade union movement look bad.

First of all, media owners eliminated labour reporters from their staffs. Today, the same reporters who cover other matters, such as the House of Commons or provincial legislatures, also cover labour issues. When the House of Commons or a legislature is in session there is no way any reporter will miss something in such forums to cover a labour issue. No reporter today is willing to risk missing an unexpected statement by a Member of Parliament that would be reported in all the other media. And, whether or not the statement contributes anything positive to civil society, the employer would reprimand any reporter who missed such "big news."

Not only are there no longer any labour reporters in the mainstream media: many new reporters are hired today because of their pro-business orientation. Many of these reporters don't see covering social issues as a priority, let alone labour issues.

When there is labour coverage in the media today, it is usually because of a strike that affects the public or because of some union activity designed to attract the attention of the public or of the employer. But coverage is rarely about what workers are fighting for: it is almost always about the public impact of the strike or other activity. The media focus tends to be on the sensational, such as on an isolated act of violence or vandalism, rather than on the positive social impact a union might achieve by winning certain rights for its members.

Media owners and senior management staff have any number of ways of slanting articles on labour issues. Often, I would see a very good newspaper article written by a knowledgeable reporter who was trying to be fair. However, the article was often skewed by a headline added by an editor. An article about a difference we had with the employer, even one that would never be the subject of a possible strike, would often appear under a headline such as, "Will postal workers strike again?"

Editors know that, unless readers are really interested in a particular issue, most are apt to simply scan the first paragraph of an article and then decide whether to continue. So, editors often add an opening paragraph to what the reporter has written. This paragraph often skews the story in a manner similar to the headline mentioned above. (In our society, newspapers are not judged to be successful based upon the quality of information they give to their readers. Rather, it is the profits they deliver to their shareholders that determines their "success.")

On other occasions, a photo might be used to skew an article. Many times, I saw a photo of myself accompanying a reporter's well-written story, but often the photo was several years old and captured me at an angry moment, thus leaving a generally negative impression with readers. Other old photos might also be used to accompany a perfectly acceptable article, but they would be of workers or confrontations on a picket line during a long-since-ended strike. Inevitably the captions under the photos would deal with the image itself rather than the meat of the story.

The worst case of this sort of editorial manipulation I ever saw in a newspaper was occasioned by a very good article that outlined CUPW's issues. But the title and the added first paragraph were negative, there was another bad photo, and the caption under the photo was terrible. In addition to all this, there was a cartoon detrimental to our struggle, an editorial denouncing us, and two pages of letters to the editor that were far from supportive of postal workers. No such letters had appeared the day before and there were none the day after. Were readers supposed to believe that the newspaper had received all these letters to the editor on the same day? The biggest problem with such attitudes among media owners and senior management is that they increase the likelihood of a strike taking place, because, through such media coverage, the employer will come to believe that the public is against us and so will wait for government to introduce back-to-work legislation, leaving the real issues unresolved.

If a union calls a strike, there is sure to be lots of media coverage. But if it signs a collective agreement without a strike, there might be a small paragraph about that fact somewhere hidden deep in the newspaper. And there would probably be nothing about it on the radio and certainly not a word on television.

But whether media attention comes during a strike or when a contract is signed without a strike, the coverage rarely addresses the issues. It is the strike that becomes the news, not the issues that forced the strike. And sometimes it's even worse: there is very often a clear bias against the union, against its leaders, or against the workers themselves.

I must say that I didn't at all like it when the media referred to me as a "union boss" in a very derogatory way. However, I liked the fact that by using such a term they recognized that a "boss" is something disgusting, reflecting my view that employers (the bosses) are ever ready to exploit workers.

In order to look neutral despite their obvious anti-labour biases, the media will often hide behind studies done by so-called think tanks such as the Fraser Institute or the Business Council on National Issues (now called the Canadian Council of Chief Executives), both of which are funded by large employer groups, such as non-unionized banks, insurance companies, and other financial institutions.

But if it is a study that comes from the Canadian Labour Congress, from a particular union, or from populist movements, there is little if any coverage, on the grounds that these are biased studies. But, in fact, these groups are particularly careful to make sure their facts are correct before including them in their studies.

Sometimes, people in positions of communicating news to the public can be downright dishonest. One day, around the time of our 1978 strike, Gord Lomer, a columnist with the *Ottawa Journal,* used his column to write an article about the strike. One would have thought it would be an appropriate place to analyze the issues in dispute and the positions of the parties. Instead, the title of the column was "746-7053." This was my home phone number and the entire column urged people to phone me and "give him hell for holding people at ransom with his strikes and his greedy demands." I would have bet anything that Mr. Lomer didn't even know what our demands were. He certainly never took the time to phone my office to hear our side of the story. He never even dialed 746-7053 himself.

As it turned out, not too many people phoned my home, but the few who did reached my father-in-law who was alone at home during this period. He had heart problems and he was very affected about these few abusive calls. In fact, a few months later, he died of a heart attack. I am not asserting that the phone calls were the reason for his death, but I never forgot that coward of a columnist. If he had contacted my office, he would have learned that I worked long hours and that it was much easier to reach me at my office than at home. He would have also have found out why we were on strike and what the issues were that led us to use this last means we had of pressuring the employer to negotiate seriously.

Fortunately, there are not many media workers who would stoop to the depths Mr. Lomer did. As I have already written, most reporters are very professional, competent, and diligent at doing their homework. Unfortunately, especially on private radio, those being hired today far too often bring an openly anti-labour bias to their work.

My experience in dealing with the media taught me that it is almost constantly in conflict between its duty to provide information to the public and its position as a profit maker. Always — though, I must admit, to varying degrees — the desire for profit will trump the duty to provide real information to the public. Nowhere was this more clearly evidenced — especially in the print media — than when it came to coverage of the issue of ad-mail workers in the post office.

Businesses in that period had three ways to get advertising flyers into the hands of potential customers. They could use a firm that hired low-wage workers, they could have their materials inserted in local newspapers and magazines, or they could use the post office, which was able to provide them with information on residential and business addresses, francophone and anglophone speakers, and other pertinent information to help the firm determine where best to distribute their flyers. The post office employed ad-mail workers to deliver these promotional materials.

Following an agreement between Canada Post and CUPW worked out in 1991 as part of negotiations on a first collective agreement for the new merged union, ad-mail workers in the post office became protected by important sections of our collective agreement and their salaries increased substantially. I must say that the print media's battle against the use of ad-mail workers in the post office was disgusting and obviously self-serving. How could the print media support, on one hand, international tripartite agreements on the creation of decent work in our society and then, on the other hand, vigorously oppose the use of decently paid ad-mail workers in the post office? The answer, of course, is that they wanted the flyer business for themselves.

When we negotiated working conditions for ad-mail workers, we gave them decent salaries, benefits, and protections. We tried to make their jobs decent ones, but this was not important to newspaper owners. In their greed for profits, they argued that the post office should not compete with the private sector. Never mind that, out of the other side of their mouths, these same newspaper owners were saying that Canada Post should break even. Logical consistency never stood in the way of making a profit.

The real issue here was that it was not the post office competing with the private sector to make profits, because, after our agreement with Canada Post on ad-mail workers, the profits went to the ad-mail workers themselves in the form of better wages and working conditions.

Sadly, in 1996, the ad-mail workers were all fired. They lost their jobs because of the pressures brought to bear by newspaper owners and their supporters. Flyers are now commonly distributed as newspaper inserts. Some are delivered by children. Isn't the private sector wonderful?

The International Labour Organization (ILO) is made up of four representatives from each of its 175 member countries: two from government, one representing employers, and one representing workers. At the beginning of this century it unanimously adopted the concept of decent jobs for all workers. In 1998 it also unanimously adopted a declaration renewing its commitment to the fundamental rights included in its constitution: freedom of association, free collective bargaining, no child labour, no forced labour, and no discrimination in employment or occupations.

How often do we see an editorial defending the rights of freedom of association and free collective bargaining? Maybe sometimes, if the country is far enough away and the case is too obvious to be ignored, but when it comes to here in Canada or the United States, media owners always turn a blind eye to such violations.

Newspaper owners and managers know that workers in Canada have the right to strike, but when we use it, they accuse us of "taking the public hostage," or they tell us we are denying other people their rights, or — as we've seen in some columns — they simply accuse us of being ignorant and stupid. They never defend our right to strike. Worse, they don't take any interest in the issues that caused us to strike in the first place.

On many occasions in recent years, federal and provincial governments have been denounced unanimously by the ILO for being in violation of international conventions they had agreed to. But not a line, not a word, in our media.

I once wrote to every newspaper in Ontario about an important ruling the ILO issued condemning Ontario's Harris government for its repressive labour policies. I was Executive Vice-President of the Canadian Labour Congress at the time and had been elected as the Canadian workers' representative to the ILO. The fact that I was representing in that capacity a large segment of the population in Canada was irrelevant to all of these newspapers, and they ignored my letter. Nor was there any mention of this condemnation of the Harris government by an international body in the pages of these newspapers. I can imagine how much coverage there would have been if it had been the unions struggling against Mike Harris that the ILO had condemned. It would have made the front pages of almost every newspaper in Ontario and probably would have been covered nationwide.

There were several unanimous decisions taken against the Harris government by the ILO. One was against legislation that took away existing rights to organize and negotiate from farm workers and declared their collective agreements null and void. Another condemned legislation denying other workers the right to organize.

Over the fifteen years I served as CUPW's President and Chief Negotiator, the number of invitations I received to take part in public-affairs programs and hot-line shows diminished. I'm not too bashful to say that this might have been because my appearances in such venues led to increased public support for our struggle, and this was not something that media owners were anxious to encourage. Today, you don't often see labour leaders on these programs, and when you do, there are often a whole handful of other guests on the same program arguing from the employer's point of view. Although, as I have already said, I think most reporters had respect for CUPW and its leaders, a few seemed to live for the thrill of getting a sensational statement. One of the worst of these was the reporter who in 1975 pestered Joe Davidson incessantly about the effect of a possible strike on the public until he finally responded with his "to hell with them" quip, which I outlined in Chapter Five.

I remember once appearing on a hot-line show on a private Ottawa radio station hosted by an anti-labour media host named Lowell Green. We were on strike at the time and, as usual, he was ranting against postal workers and inviting the public to phone in to speak against us. He obviously thought I was going to be destroyed by the callers, and he led the anti-union charge from the beginning of the program. His questions were long and the way they were framed made his point of view very clear. When I tried to answer one question, he would interrupt me with another long question, or with an extensive statement.

I can sometimes be very patient, and I let him go on like this for the first fifteen minutes of the program. Then he asked me another long question, and I remained silent. He asked me again, but I wouldn't answer, and I could see that he was wondering about my sudden silence. So he asked me yet again, and implied that my silence showed that I had no respect for his listeners. I again remained silent for a moment, but then answered — I don't have a transcript of that program, so I can't be exactly sure of the precise wording — to the following effect:

> Mr. Green, you invited me to this program. I accepted your invitation because I thought you wanted to know what CUPW had to say about the present situation. If you didn't want me to answer your questions, then why have you invited me? For the last fifteen minutes you have stopped me every time I've tried to answer any of your long questions. If you wanted to speak for the whole hour, you should have told me. I would have stayed on the picket line with the other workers, and we both would have been better off.

For the rest of the program, Mr. Green asked only short questions, and he allowed callers to ask me questions directly. As the program went on, more and more callers said they understood our position and that, even if they didn't like our strike, they had gained newfound respect for our position. When I left the studio, there were about a hundred postal workers and friends cheering me outside.

In CUPW, we always respected the right of the public to agree or disagree with us. But we always made a sincere effort to explain the issues that had forced us to strike or led us to hold a national day of protest or simply a local demonstration.

What I experienced on the Lowell Green show was repeated many times over the years. After twenty minutes or a half hour on a hot-line program, callers began to sympathize with our position or at least indicated that they understood the common sense of our positions. By the end of these programs, most callers were usually in support of what we were trying to achieve because by now they understood our underlying motives.

That is why media owners and managers prefer to talk about the effects of strikes rather than the issues that lead to them. People are capable of forming their own opinions when they are properly informed about the issues at stake.

I have already written in Chapter Ten of how the Action Canada Network organized seven national organizations to sign, before the media, three different solidarity pacts with CUPW prior to the beginning of our rotating strikes in 1991, and I have detailed the complete lack of media coverage these signings generated. Media executives didn't have to meet among themselves to decide on this: their rejection of such was a natural extension of structural aspects of for-profit media organizations that instinctively deny coverage to pro-labour groups and events. So there was not a word about the fact that national organizations representing women, students, retirees, seniors, poor people, the unemployed, farmers, churches, people with disabilities, and rural Canadians were behind our demands.

The Canadian labour movement is one of the most democratic organizations in our country. Our locals meet every month to allow workers to bring their issues to their elected union representatives. In CUPW, we hold referenda by secret ballot on our program of demands prior to entering negotiations, on the ratification of collective agreements, and on calls for strike action. We hold conventions where our policies are established through representatives of locals across the country, and delegates elect our national leaders through secret ballot.

In earlier years, labour reporters would attend our conventions, but now media organizations have decided that these are of no interest to the public, the same public they say we "take for ransom" when we exercise our legal right to strike. This is true today of both CUPW and CLC conventions, which represent the interests of more than 2,000,000 Canadians.

Now that I have managed to vent my spleen about many of the most negative aspects of our national media, I would be remiss in not recognizing some of its best aspects. We have the good fortune in this country to have both the Canadian Broadcasting Corporation and Radio-Canada. They do what they can to create public awareness of important social issues, because, as publicly owned institutions, they feel less pressure to generate profits, and so they are under less pressure to skew their coverage of labour issues than are privately owned media. Their contributions are valuable to Canadians.

I encourage them to continue in their positive work and hope that the federal government will grant public broadcasters the funding they need to do their job effectively, although government funding for public broadcasting has been shrinking alarmingly in recent years. Although less common in the for-profit sector of the broadcast media, there are also a few good programs on private television and radio stations, and I encourage them to see that more public debate takes place on important issues.

I'll end my musings on the media with one short story. During the 1991 rotating strikes that followed soon after the non-coverage by the media of solidarity pacts signed with CUPW by several organizations representing the most vulnerable people in our society, Canada Post decided to use scab workers. One of these pacts was signed by both the Canadian Federation of Students and the Ontario Coalition Against Poverty in support of our demands that would create decent full-time jobs.

During the strike, I saw on the television news, as did millions of others, an interview with one of the people who had been hired as a temporary scab in Toronto. She was a black woman, the single mother of two young children, and had been unemployed before finding this most recent work. Here she was, exploited by both that television station and Canada Post, in order to show the public what a heartless organization CUPW was in keeping this woman from work with our picket lines.

This is what I said to postal workers at meetings across the country about that television piece at the time:

> Like me, one night recently on the news you saw a woman, who is among the most vulnerable people in our society, who chose to work as a scab in the Toronto postal plant. She is a young black woman, single with two small children, and she was unemployed. She said she couldn't afford to turn down the job she was offered. Don't be angry with her, because she's right. She might have been told she would lose her unemployment insurance or right to welfare benefits if she turned down this job opportunity. We know just that has happened to some others.
>
> However, do get angry at both Canada Post and that television station for not saying that if we are successful in our strike, that woman might have an opportunity to work in the Toronto post office as a permanent, full-time employee, rather than as a temporary scab, needed only until the end of the strike, when Canada Post will throw her again onto the unemployment lines. By then, both Canada Post and the televisions station will have forgotten all about her.

We in CUPW are not ashamed of our history or of the vision of a better future for working people we have always fought for. Through the years, we will continue to fight for that better common future. Private profit will never be our cause: our cause will always remain justice, dignity, and respect through decent and honest work.

CUPW and the Wider World

Should unions be involved in activities other than directly representing their members in the workplace? I believe that people are entitled to respect, dignity, and justice in all aspects of their lives. That's why I support a good public education system, good adult literacy programs both at the workplace and outside, good job training programs, and good education programs for workers in the labour movement. People need to know how social and economic factors affect their lives at home, at work, and in their communities. This is essential if we are to have a real democracy that can help all citizens achieve respect, dignity, and justice.

In CUPW, we believe that, in order to well represent postal workers and their families, we have to closely follow developments in the labour, social, and political worlds that can affect our members. Decisions and policies of international bodies, and of federal, provincial, and even municipal governments affect the lives of all Canadians, including trade union members, and so I believe it is the proper role of trade unions to do their utmost to do what they can to influence the development of those decisions and policies and to battle against the policies that have negative impacts on their members, while supporting those policies and decisions that have positive impacts. Unfortunately, given the stranglehold corporate interests have on almost all aspects of government policy, trade unions are far more often than not put in the position of condemning bad policies, rather than of supporting good ones.

The move of the Canadian and other governments to "liberalize" trade over the past several years is a good example of the sort of policies made outside the workplace that affected Canadian workers in all aspects of their lives. The World Trade Organization, which determines the rules of international commerce, believes that there shouldn't be any barriers to business investment anywhere in the world. In fact, it argues that business rights are more important than social rights. On such matters, trade unions and other progressive organizations have a moral — and a political — obligation to stand on the side of social justice.

The Canada-United States Free Trade Agreement, the North America Free Trade Agreement, and the proposed Free Trade Area of the Americas Agreement all diminish the ability of governments to make decisions for reasons of the common good if they have the slightest impact on the power of the corporate sector. In effect, they take away our national sovereignty. Ottawa can't adopt policies to assist Canadian industries because this might interfere with the power of international capital. Even providing decent social benefits to Canadian workers can be challenged under the terms of such international agreements.

Trade liberalization allows employers to use the threat of moving their operations, and the jobs associated with them, to other countries as a way of exacting concessions in labour negotiations. They force workers around the world to see themselves as in competition with one another to be the "lowest bidder" in order to land or maintain jobs. Under the regime of trade liberalization, to be "competitive" means having to cut labour costs. That's what I call achieving prosperity through poverty.

As I mentioned previously, the ILO is a tripartite, United Nations

Some CUPW members pose for a photo after a Toronto rally opposing "free trade" on May 26, 1986.

organization whose mandate is to adopt standards and policies on workers' rights and protections. Its constitution guarantees workers around the world the right to organize, the right to negotiate, freedom from child and forced labour, and freedom from discrimination in employment and occupations. When the World Trade Organization says that there will be no social impediments to trade, this is what they are talking about — the right of employers and investors to increase profits by ensuring that these international labour standards don't stand in the way of such private profit.

The labour movement can't remain indifferent or evasive in the face of such an inhuman approach that values profit and ignores the costs in human misery such profit exacts. The international trade liberalizers don't believe there should be regulations to protect the health of our planet: profit reigns supreme. They don't believe in health and safety protections: profit reigns supreme. They don't believe that government regulations on universal access to clean water and clean air should stand in the way of profit: profit reigns supreme.

These trade liberalizers are the same people who demand the privatization of public services whenever a profit can be made, who call for smaller governments, who demand an end to rules and regulations that protect the public interest, who support cuts in social programs, and who push for an end to all the other fundamental rights and protections trade unionists and other Canadians have fought so hard for over many, many years.

Over the years, we in CUPW have made efforts to build a better world for our members and their families, and for all the other people in our communities, through our involvement in the world outside the workplace.

We got involved in coalition work with other social groups, such as organizations of students, the unemployed, women, the impoverished or homeless, aboriginals, seniors and retirees, farmers, the disabled, gays and lesbians, peace and disarmament activists, environmentalists, rural and church activists, and many others.

We became involved in campaigns against "free trade" agreements, privatization, high interest rates, wage controls, rollbacks to unemployment insurance, and other issues that affected our members as much as they did the rest of Canadian society. We worked with other groups to develop alternatives to government budgets and to improve education, health care, and other public services. We did what we could to help bring about the fall of apartheid in South Africa, to end sweatshop and child labour the world over, to counter the American trade embargo on Cuba, and to fight racism and violence against women.

Our participation in supporting the struggles of other workers, in working in coalition with others on different issues, and in playing our role in the outside world was as beneficial to our members as it was to those we supported outside CUPW's ranks. In Chapter Nine, I mentioned Bishop Remi De Roo and his statement on New Year's Day in 1983 entitled "Ethical Refection on the Economic Crisis." I'll never forget an address he made at our National Convention on April 7, 1986, in which he drew the connections between our support for broader issues and our work on behalf of our members. It was one of the best summaries I ever heard about the dangers of the neo-liberal agenda. He said, in part:

> The postal system, as you well know, constitutes another major example of a public service being subjected to privatization. In recent years, you have seen firsthand a series of steps aimed at changing Canada Post into a profit-making enterprise. You have experienced job losses that result from the contracting out of services. You have encountered the social impact of new technologies on your working conditions. You have witnessed the deteriorating quality of service in the postal system that has resulted largely from this privatization process. And you know what impact this has all had on your fellow workers and on public confidence in the postal system as a public service.
>
> Today, we all need to recognize that the public service sector, as we have known it in this country, is under concerted attack. Increasing emphasis is being put on remaking public services into profitable enterprises. The priority is not on serving people's needs but on generating maximum profits for capital. To be certain, there are problems of waste and inefficiency in many of our public services in this country. Much more could be done to improve their quality and effectiveness, but should it not be done

Pat Miller, CUPW National Director for the Western region, and Jean-Claude Parrot lead postal workers into a Vancouver stadium for an "Operation Solidarity" rally in 1983. Operation Solidarity was a huge social-justice coalition that opposed the right-wing policies of British Columbia Premier Bill Bennett and his Social Credit government.

by revitalizing our public sector in this country rather than by turning these vital services over to the private sector, leaving them at the mercy of the market system?

I, for one, firmly believe that the labour movement has an essential role to play in revitalizing the public sector in this country.

I want to commend CUPW for the efforts you have made as a union to give leadership on some of these fronts. I know that the public does not generally appreciate this dimension of CUPW. There is a tendency still to see only a militant union, just striking postal workers.

What the public does not see or understand is the struggle you have had to wage inside the postal system to humanize technological changes, to maintain job security, to improve the quality of service. What they may not see is the positive role that you have played in supporting the struggles of the unemployed and the working poor, many of whom are women. What they may not see are the initiatives CUPW has taken in solidarity with other people suffering from oppression in Africa, Chile, and other repressive regimes. What they may not see are the efforts you have made to generate greater commitment on the part of the labour movement to peace and disarmament in this country.

For the common good and the progress of mankind, I encourage you not only to pursue, but to intensify the activities I have just mentioned. The more we are heading towards a market-based society, a culture dominated by high technology, the more we must consolidate and reaffirm our fundamental human values and human spiritual priorities. I invite the entire Christian community to intensify its efforts and to support you in a common essential effort. A people that lives in hope knows that the depths of night will soon yield to the dawn of a new day. Tomorrow will belong to those who really care. May your solidarity inspire your debates. May your unity happily crown your victories.

This was a great encouragement to me to pursue our struggle and to reject the low-profile approach too often suggested by some labour leaders who should have been the first to encourage workers to stand up and be visible in their opposition to the neo-liberal agenda.

I remember, in my first years at the national level of my union, how proud I was of its involvement in the struggle of South African workers against apartheid. I also proudly remember our support for thirteen striking workers of an insurance company in Ottawa — twelve of them women — who were otherwise alone and vulnerable on the picket line. CUPW members and others from the Ottawa District Labour Council added to their numbers and strength to their cause. And CUPW members have supported picket lines of international, national, and local workers who were defending their rights. We've walked the picket lines of workers fighting for rights denied them by international financial institutions and the picket lines of workers in front of small restaurants whose owners would likewise deny their workers rights and decent working conditions.

CUPW participated actively and financially to national coalition work among progressive organizations to collectively fight back against the impacts on Canadians of neo-liberal policies, regulations, and legislation.

What should trade unions do in the area of partisan politics? I believe that they should look at the interests of their members on the one hand and the platforms of the political parties on the other, and then judge whether the implementation of the policies contained in those platforms would help or hinder the union's members. If one party has policies that would help workers more than other parties would, then they should support that party.

However, support for a political party should never be automatic: it should be a decision taken a few months before each election. That way, no party can be assured of labour's unconditional support without regard to its actions and policies.

Through the years, labour has supported the New Democratic Party, except in Québec, where in the past few decades labour has usually backed the Parti Québécois provincially and the Bloc Québécois federally. However labour in Québec doesn't give its support to these parties automatically, as the CLC does to the NDP.

Looking back, I see clearly that the best legislative advances for Canadians outside Québec were introduced by NDP governments or were prompted by strong NDP pressures. On paper, it is the one major national party that advocates progressive policies that would benefit the vast majority of working Canadians. In Québec, the Parti Québécois has played this role, and Québec has the most progressive provincial legislation in the country. Its anti-scab legislation and regulations in the fields of parental rights and childcare are among the best examples of progressive leadership. Still, at the provincial level we have seen both NDP and Parti Québécois governments take some stands that workers have no reason to be proud of.

I recognize that the pressures brought to bear by the corporate sector and international economic institutions such as the World Bank and the International Monetary Fund can make it difficult for our governments to implement progressive policies. But, to me, it is a question of courage and conviction.

For the labour movement, support for a political party is given in the interests of trade union members. However, as many NDP leaders have told us through the years, once elected, they have to represent all the people. Unfortunately, this argument has been used by provincial NDP governments to justify implementing policies contrary to the positions of their own party.

In 1989, for the first time ever, the NDP was elected to govern Ontario. The party had a new leader, Bob Rae, who raised the right issues during the election. Being a very good speaker and communicator, he was able to clearly express the need to take on the previous government during the election campaign. Activists across the province were attracted by the quality of debate, and they got involved in the election.

This was the first time that almost the entire left in the province united to support the NDP, and more activists than ever before worked for an NDP victory. On election night, people felt inspired by what they saw as their collective victory. Sadly, we were soon to be disappointed: it seemed that Bob Rae saw it as his personal victory, and from then on, he acted as if he alone knew the way forward

After his victory, I wrote to Bob Rae to remind him of the importance of consolidating the support of those who, for the first time in their lives, had worked for and voted NDP. I suggested that he should, very early in his mandate, take steps to implement some of the progressive policies he had articulated during the election campaign.

One of the most discouraging trends in Canada over the past thirty years has been the increasing disillusionment people feel for politicians. People hear promises during a campaign and then see victorious governments take actions that have no regard whatever for those promises. So I felt it was essential, given the lukewarm support a large number of voters had given the NDP, that the new Rae government show it was different, that it wouldn't deceive the people who had elected it.

Unfortunately, Bob Rae chose another road. His first announcement after his election was that his government would not go ahead with the public auto insurance he had promised during his campaign. He then tried to convince business leaders that his government would be a good thing for them. Then he took on Ontario's public-sector workers. All these policy reversals were made on the basis that the Rae government had discovered that the deficit was much higher than what the previous government had said it was.

This was the beginning of disaster for the Rae government. The abandonment of private auto insurance was seen as caving in to the insurance companies. This NDP government was just another one that would not live up to its promises. This immediately turned away many of those who had worked for Rae's election, including trade unionists. They would have become strong supporters of the new government if they had immediately seen Rae implementing one of his promises, rather than abandoning one. It gave ammunition to those who had never had any faith in the NDP.

The Rae government introduced some progressive labour legislation, but it took over a year to enact it because Bob Rae launched a campaign to convince the business community that it would be a good thing for them, as well as for workers. I didn't understand this. To try to convince employers that progressive labour legislation is in their interests will always be a lost cause. He might just as well have tried to convince them that better-paid workers were in their interests.

The business sector spent hundreds of thousands of dollars to fight this new labour law, and it forced the labour movement, through the Ontario Federation of Labour, to spend $100,000 on an ad campaign in support of the new law.

I found it totally unacceptable that we had to spend this amount of money to force a "friendly" government to implement a major promise of its election platform. It was ironic that Bob Rae didn't give us a chance to have the same kind of public debate on his decision to drop the auto insurance promise that he offered the business community over the new labour law.

To me, it was clear that, even before he began his attack on public-sector workers, the soft supporters of the Rae government had already disappeared. That was certainly true among trade union activists. Then, when the Rae government attacked public-sector workers in the name of the deficit, I began to feel that with "friends" like Bob Rae, workers had no need of enemies.

Naturally, workers were angry at this attack on public-sector workers. Even those who agreed with Rae's decision to take on the public sector thought his government's approach was political suicide. His arguments for this attack were the same ones we had heard from the Mulroney government for years for its attacks on working people.

This is what most discouraged activists: to hear Bob Rae using the same language they fought against during the Mulroney era. He even tried to divide the labour movement. Very few activists, in either the public or private sectors, tried to defend the Rae government on the shop floor.

Perhaps the most negative impact of the Rae government was that it persuaded many Canadians, by its attitudes and actions, that the policies of the left were irrelevant and that the right-wing parties were correct in making the deficit their priority. A year before the federal election of October 1993, the CLC met in Toronto to discuss the impact the Rae government's policies was having on the labour movement, both provincially and nationally. This meeting was attended by federal NDP Leader Audrey McLaughlin, as well as the three NDP provincial premiers, from Ontario, Saskatchewan, and British Columbia: Bob Rae, Roy Romanow, and Mike Hartcourt.

Before entering the meeting, Bob Rae told the media he was there to tell the labour movement about the importance of eliminating the deficit. In the meeting, all the provincial premiers agreed that our priority had to be the elimination of the deficit, but none argued this more loudly than Bob Rae. At one point, he said that there were still some in the labour movement who didn't believe this should be a priority. I was not planning to intervene, because CLC President Bob White was representing us very well. But, when I heard this statement, I immediately raised my hand, indicating that I wanted to say something. I was given the floor almost immediately, and I said the following:

> I just want to say to Bob Rae that I am one of those who do not believe that the deficit is the issue here. First of all, how can any one of you at the provincial level pretend you will eliminate the deficit when you don't have control over it? None of you has control over monetary policies such as inflation, interest rates, the value of our dollar, transfer payments to the provinces, trade agreements, and the like.
>
> Even if you were successful in eliminating or reducing the deficit, what if the federal government adopts policies leading to new high interest rates, further cuts in transfer payments to the provinces, and new trade agreements? Are you going to cut more social services to the people of your provinces and attack more public-sector workers to get out of your mess?
>
> Instead, here's what I suggest we do here. We should join together to make sure that we elect a federal NDP government under Audrey McLaughlin so that we can then address the issue of balancing between efforts to reduce the deficit and policies for full employment, while at the same time protecting hard-won social programs. We can then have the three NDP provincial

governments take on the task of showing the public that, without a federal government that will work with them, they will never be able to really put their provinces and the country back on track.

I suggested that the three premiers and Audrey meet to develop a strategy to this effect. I believed at the time, and I still think today, that there would have been a strong possibility of her being elected Prime Minister in 1993, if policies had been articulated that would have spurred progressives to get out and support the party.

But, Bob Rae wasn't a team player: he didn't care about the federal party. The first thing Bob Rae told the media when the meeting was over was, "I hope they understood that the deficit is the major problem we need to resolve." By the time the federal election was called, there were few people willing to work for the party, perhaps least of all the three provincial leaders. In fact, by the time the election was called, the federal party could not even afford to be seen with them. And so, it came as little surprise that the NDP did not fare well in the 1993 federal election.

The fact was, we had lost our activists. Who wanted to knock on doors only to see them slammed shut by angry people? Bob Rae, of course, was defeated in the next provincial election, and a few leaders, even then, accused labour and other long-time NDP activists of abandoning him. But they were wrong: Bob Rae had abandoned the party long before anyone else did. Those labour leaders who argued that we had abandoned the NDP need look no further than to their own membership to see that NDP support had disappeared.

Perhaps the saddest legacy of the Rae government was that, by moving to the right, it made it far easier for the federal Liberals to move farther to the right themselves. Canadians all across the country have been living with that legacy through four federal elections.

I still don't understand how three provincial NDP premiers, who continuously blamed federal policies for a large part of the financial mess they faced, didn't see it as appropriate to go back to those who elected them and campaign for the election of a federal NDP government that would allow them to pursue their provincial objectives. People would have seen that this made a lot of sense. But Rae, Romanow, and Hartcourt didn't see this. Perhaps this was because their provincial NDP parties chose as leaders people who did not believe in the policies of their own parties.

Once, after I left CUPW, someone questioned my support for the NDP. I was able to show that in every election while I was CUPW President, the leadership had supported the NDP and asked our membership to do the same. We also produced material used during election campaigns by many other unions. I know that I had more credibility with CUPW members than Bob Rae had with NDP activists.

When the federal NDP asked the CLC Executive Council to support the use of an NDP credit card, I supported the idea and encouraged members to do the same. Rather than support the NDP, some labour leaders decided to imitate it by developing their own union credit cards. I still have my NDP credit card, and I use it regularly. I still believe in the party's platform, but will never automatically support a different platform that might be implemented by future NDP governments.

One day, Bob Rae told me that, as social democrats, we can't accept living with a deficit. My answer was, "As a social democrat, I can't live without a social democrat government, and your approach guarantees your defeat in the next election and another decade or two without an NDP government." To me it was better to live with a deficit while implementing a strong full-employment strategy that would eventually have reduced the deficit.

After Bob Rae's defeat, we in Ontario had to suffer the ravages of the Mike Harris government for two terms. Perhaps he was re-elected because people believed that he did what he said he was going to do. I know this wasn't really the case, but it seemed so to many people, and this allowed him to consolidate his voter base.

Bob Rae may have kept the province of Ontario's credit rating high with the World Bank and other financial institutions, but he lost Ontario to a right-wing government. Despite eventually introducing some good labour laws, the Rae government was defeated in the next election because it failed utterly in building on the support base that had elected him in the first place.

I believe that Bob Rae is one of those who feels that I brought a bad image to the labour movement during the time I served as CUPW President. I can only say this to him:

> I have not only won an election, Bob Rae, but I was re-elected several times, by both CUPW and the CLC. I, along with my Executive, created solidarity among postal workers, built relations of trust between them and the leadership, and made very important gains and breakthroughs for all postal workers, including minority groups. We set negotiating precedents that were later achieved by the entire federal public sector. As far as image is concerned, I can only say that I kept my reputation among those who elected me. It isn't enough to win one election: you also have to win the respect of the people you represent.

Obviously, not all postal workers support the NDP. This is why in CUPW we don't automatically support any party. When an election is announced or about to be announced, we analyze the positions taken by the various parties on issues of interest to postal workers and workers in general, and then we make a recommendation to the members to support the party that best represents their interests. It is up to the members whether to follow our recommendation or not. This process helps politicize members about the importance of considering the parties' positions on the issues before voting. I strongly believe that workers have as much right as anyone else in our society to get involved in politics and I will continue to defend that right.

Some CUPW members, and many other Canadians, hold more radical views than the NDP's. Through my years in CUPW, it was common to go to meetings and see activists who were members of political parties or groupings far to the left of the NDP. I have always admired the tenacity of such people in distributing their materials at meetings, seminars, and conventions of progressive organizations, their ability to intervene in debates, and their continuous questioning of positions taken by different organizations.

They belonged to many different political or ideological organizations, such as Marxist-Leninists, Trotskyites, Maoists, Communists, and the like. They distributed their publications, pamphlets, and other materials that supported their cause, denounced the capitalist system in general, and criticized labour leaders for accommodating oppression.

Most of these people were politically knowledgeable, and they never hesitated to intervene at the microphones during meetings. They often became targets of those presiding at meetings and were sometimes ejected and banned from meetings.

One day near the end of the 1970s, I spoke at a CUPW referendum meeting in Toronto. When I went in, there were the usual sorts of people outside distributing leftist pamphlets and magazines. After I spoke, many of the members belonging to these leftist groups began to ask questions and make other interventions. This was during a question period allowed by the local before proceeding to a vote. Unfortunately, the questions, and especially the comments, were long and, as time wore on, many members were becoming discouraged.

One member came to the microphone and asked me to end the question period and proceed with the vote. I said that it wasn't my decision to make, that it was that of the local member who was chairing the meeting, but I then added this:

> I don't hire the people who work in the post office. Our union has nothing to do with that. So for me, as long as the person who asks questions is an employee of the post office and a member of this union, I will not deny them the same rights other members of this union have to ask questions or make comments on an issue as important as the one we are discussing today. However, I will appreciate if, when you come to the microphone, that you do not ask the same questions or make the same comments time and

time again so that all members can exercise their democratic right to vote.

To my surprise, I was applauded, and the question period soon came to a natural end. I think that some of these members were not used to being told that they had a right to participate in a manner they felt was important to them. I felt that this was a very important message to give to the membership: the enemy is not those who come to the microphones to speak, but post office management, which tried to turn members against members under the pretext that these people were "just a bunch of" Trotskyites, Maoists, Leninists, Communists, or whatever. But management never reminded the workers that it was the post office that hired these people.

I remember one other time in a public forum, I said, "You know, I have been called a Communist, a Maoist, a Trotskyite, a Leninist, a Marxist, a Péquiste, and many other names, but I've never been called a Liberal or a Progressive Conservative, and I'm very proud of that."

One day a reporter mentioned to me that it seemed we had a lot of leftists in our union. I replied:

> You know, we do have a lot of postal workers hired by the post office who believe that the system under which we are working is wrong and who are quite happy to belong to a union that does not exclude them and, in fact, recognizes them like any other union member. But one thing I can tell you, these postal workers who were hired by the post office are very good members, and we know we can count on them when we need to fight the boss or defend a good cause.

I was always bothered by the attitude of some in the labour movement regarding the left. Many leaders rejected the participation of leftist members in their unions. I have seen them ridiculed, kicked out of meetings, attacked by their leaders, and denounced continuously for their constant opposition to the positions of the leadership on many issues. In fact, sometimes members who were not part of any left party or ideology were treated as if they were, simply because they opposed resolutions or policies put forward at meetings or conventions. I also saw people denounced and attacked by their leaders as leftists, not because of their positions on the issues, but simply because they opposed the leadership.

This happened all across the country at meetings of provincial labour federations, as well as at CLC conventions. It was weak positions taken by the labour movement on international issues and the way opposition to these positions was attacked by union leaders that made my union become involved in the Action Caucus at CLC conventions.

The Action Caucus denounced apartheid in South Africa long before the CLC did. The CLC didn't want to be seen to be supporting the Congress of South African Trade Unions because it was Communist-led, but we eventually got the CLC to actively support the struggle against apartheid. In fact, the CLC was later very proud of its contribution to that struggle, and while I was with the CLC, we sent a delegation to South Africa to help celebrate the end of apartheid.

While most of our early activities at CLC conventions focussed on international affairs, the Action Caucus became increasingly influential on the convention floor. We managed to get some bad policy papers presented to delegates by the leadership returned to committees where improvements were made to them.

CLC leaders opposed the participation of what they called "the radical left" among their ranks, claiming that their ideology was "undemocratic." Talk about contradictions! Workers who were members of our unions wouldn't be allowed the right to speak enjoyed by other members of the same union.

What sort of democracy is this? It's the sort of "democracy" exercised by chairpersons of conventions where you could stand at the microphone for a long time and not be recognized. This happened to me at CLC conventions many times, especially, as I noted earlier, in 1978, when both Joe Morris and Dennis McDermott seemed to have vision problems. Once, McDermott even had arithmetic problems: he recognized the microphones in numeric order, but kept jumping over the one where I stood.

I wanted to change the attitude of the labour movement towards the left. After all, are we in the labour movement not ourselves supposed to be on the left? If some think I may be exaggerating about the role of labour leaders in attacking the left, let's look at the case of my "good friend" Dennis McDermott. In the fall of 1979, he was invited to speak at the National Convention of the Canadian Union of Public Employees. During the debate that took place before he spoke, delegates dealt with a resolution demanding his resignation as CLC President because of the lack of support it gave postal workers in our 1978 strike. Here was McDermott's contribution to that debate: "The Marxist-Leninists are accommodated in CUPE and CUPW and they will take the CUPE convention's decision as a green light to continue their campaign. I have declared war on them. Otherwise, they will destroy the labour movement and the country if they have their way."

McDermott criticized CUPE President Grace Hartman, saying, "She has demonstrated time and time again that she's a lightweight." He accused her of not having properly explained to delegates the CLC's reasons behind its decision not to support CUPW. Wilfred List of the *Globe and Mail* summarized this disagreement on November 5, 1979:

> While Mrs. Hartman defends the right of delegates to their views, Mr. McDermott says he does not accept her "weak-kneed excuses and rationale of how the lunatics took over." To Mr. McDermott, it's a matter of leadership. As he sees it, there is none in CUPE when it comes to making decisions that may offend some within the union. He says the unions are back to the early 1940s when they had to fight the traditional Communist Party, a political force regarded as conservative and bourgeois by the Marxist-Leninists organizations in Canada. "If these people are on the march, we are going to have to put them to death," Mr. McDermott says.

Dennis McDermott never had much respect for public-sector unions, on the basis that they were weak. But once they became strong, he didn't support them on the pretext they were led by Marxist-Leninists. To him, when public sector unions became strong, not only in negotiations but also at conventions within the labour movement, it could only be because they were led by Marxist-Leninists.

I am proud of my union, its leaders, and its activists for having taken on this struggle for democracy within the labour movement. It was because of this struggle that we changed the CLC policies on international issues. It was because of this struggle that we changed the CLC's structure to make elections more democratic. And it was because of our participation in this struggle that CUPW became a union very much respected by the entire labour movement.

When I moved to Ottawa after my election in 1971, I had already long been a strong supporter of Québec independence. While still working in Montréal, I supported the formation of the Rassemblement pour l'Indépendance Nationale and later became a member of the Mouvement Souveraineté Association, and then of the Parti Québécois (PQ). I was a great admirer of Pierre Bourgault and André Dallemagne, who both wrote and spoke in the 1960s on Québec independence.

I first became involved in the early 1960s when Marcel Chaput, a federal government employee in Ottawa, began a fast to protest the lack of recognition of the French language in federal government departments. I collected money to support his cause at the postal station on St. Laurent Street in Montréal where I worked. I worked early, preparing registered mail for letter carriers. I had a good relationship with them, and I had no problem getting them to put something into my collection box. In fact, I think some who may not have been at all interested in Chaput's fast probably contributed simply because of the good relations I had with them.

When I first moved to Ottawa, I attended PQ meetings in Hull but, because I lived on the Ontario side of the Ottawa River, I was soon told that I could no longer be a member. This made sense, and I stopped going to PQ meetings, but I never stopped supporting the cause.

After the PQ came to power in 1976, the issue of Québec's relationship to the rest of Canada was the subject of sharp discussion across the country. This was certainly true of the labour movement, and at CUPW's 1977 National Convention in Halifax, delegates adopted a policy that called for the right to self-determination for the people of Québec. It took no particular side on the issue of Québec's place in Canada, saying only that this was a matter for the people of Québec to decide on.

The first to speak on this resolution was Brother A. Galley from the Burlington local. He raised concerns that this could divide our union in two. He ended his comments by saying, "First and foremost, I am a Canadian, and I wish and hope that there will be no such thing as the withdrawal of the Québec region from this union and that we stay as one united national union."

The next speaker, Brother Marcel Perreault from Montréal, indicated that there was no question of making a regional union with this resolution, only that Québec was one of two nations within Canada.

One speaker, Brother T. Penney, said that twenty-eight years earlier Newfoundland, which had the right to self-determination, had used that right to join Canada and that nobody was going to tell him that today the people of Newfoundland didn't have the right to leave Canada if they wanted to. "This is a right that Québec must also have," he said.

Brother Hoogers from Vancouver also spoke, saying that he stood irrevocably for the principle that the people of Québec had the absolute right to determine their destiny:

> I stand here as a Canadian worker, and I say that the only way I can have unity with my brothers and sisters in Québec, with Québécois workers, is to underline and actively work for their right to decide on their own destiny themselves. When people, workers especially, in English Canada respond to the phony issue of national unity, I just want to bring to their attention that what they are responding to is the call of a man — and the call of a government — who has hardly been the friend of CUPW. If we look over the history of the regime of Pierre Elliott Trudeau, we see a Prime Minister who has consistently worked in the interests of big business and large corporations. Never once has he worked in the interests of workers in this country. Why do we think, because he is calling for us to unite with him around the issue of national unity, that somehow he is working in our interests now? To the call of Prime Minister Trudeau for unity with him, I say never.

All other speakers spoke in favour of the resolution, and it was adopted unanimously.

Brother Hoogers was certainly correct in his comments on Prime Minister Trudeau. Although Trudeau oversaw the implementation of the Official Languages Act in 1969, which recognized the French language in Canada, he never had the courage to meet the aspirations of the people of Québec.

Trudeau pretended to never recognize that people in Québec were looking for sovereignty-association with the rest of Canada, not outright independence. To him, they were just a bunch of "separatists" who wanted to destroy "our country." Trudeau used the term "separatist" in a very derogatory way, and because of this many Canadians turned against the people in Québec.

Trudeau was admired in English Canada because of his intelligence and charisma. He came from Québec, was fluently bilingual, and he made it look to many in English Canada as if the country was under attack by Québec. Many in English Canada had been asking, "What does Québec want?" Trudeau managed to get many of these people to change that question into a statement: "If Québec gets it, we want it too."

Trudeau successfully put Québec in the position of being just one among ten provinces. He never tried to find a solution to the aspirations of the people of Québec. On the contrary, he encouraged many in English Canada to oppose any accommodation with Québec.

Whenever I hear people say that Trudeau saved Canada, or that he united it, I get a knot in my stomach. This guy never united Canada: he divided it. Many people in the rest of the country don't want to hear about the aspirations of the people of Québec. In some parts of the country, there is even hatred against people from Québec. Bilingualism in federal government services is seen by some as a way to give jobs to French-speaking people ahead of English speakers. In 1980, some even suggested that the army be used if the people of Québec voted "yes" in the referendum on sovereignty-association that was held that year. The appointment of a francophone as director of an Ottawa hospital was denounced fanatically, despite his recognized competence, because at one point he had shown sympathy to the PQ.

It was never properly explained to the rest of Canada what the PQ was really asking for in the 1980 referendum. There was a clear difference between sovereignty-association and full independence. René Lévesque's position was quite clear, and he never deserved to have the term "separatist" used against him in the derogatory manner Trudeau did.

Today the provinces are demanding that the federal government give them more power, yet, strangely, nobody calls them "separatists." This is all that Québec under René Lévesque had demanded, that more power be delegated to Québec without affecting the existing status of the other provinces. Québec wanted much more responsibility in such areas as immigration, social programs, and a larger voice in the international field.

I wasn't at all surprised when the Bloc Québécois was formed as a strategic move to let the Liberals and others in English Canada understand that, whether they liked it or not, Québec *is* a distinct society. Indirectly, that "great Canadian," Pierre Elliott Trudeau, was largely responsible for the formation of the Bloc.

The fact remains that people in Québec believe in a strong Canada, and whatever happened in the past or will happen in the future, Québec will never be a province like the others. Québec, whatever form its relationship to the rest of Canada may take in the future, will always be a good thing for Canada, especially once Canadians accept Québecois as friends, not enemies.

The policy CUPW adopted in 1977 in support of Québec's right to self-determination has been renewed at every convention since, and it remains the policy of CUPW today. Not long after we adopted this position, it was also adopted by the CLC.

I was happy to see, in 1994, the CLC, on behalf of all the provincial Federations of Labour, sign an agreement with the Fédération des Travailleurs et des Travailleuses du Québec (FTQ). We in the labour movement love to call it our sovereignty-association agreement. It allocated more funds to the FTQ to allow it more autonomy on issues that had before been strictly the responsibility of the CLC. It also recognized a role for the FTQ in the international activities of the CLC. It was agreed that one of Canada's two seats on the International Confederation of Free Trade Unions be given to the President of the FTQ. The role of the CLC in the francophone countries around the world was also transferred to the FTQ.

I hope that someday our politicians will have the courage to act in a similar manner regarding the relationship between Canada and Québec. The CLC-FTQ agreement shows that Canadians and Québécois can find solutions that work for both parties.

A few months after my re-election as CUPW National President in 1990, I indicated to some of my national officers that I was not going to run again at the 1993 Convention. It had long been my goal to unite all postal workers in one bargaining unit, and we had achieved this during my previous term as CUPW President. I felt that I had reached my long-term goals, and the time for my departure had come. And, I believed, new leadership and new debates within CUPW were needed to continue making progress for postal workers.

When I learned that two CLC officers were leaving, one of them being the representative from Québec, I felt that I should run for that position. I had always been interested in the CLC, and it was at a very important turning point in 1992, with Bob White of the Canadian Auto Workers incoming as President to replace Shirley Carr. I saw an opportunity to

Bob White congratulating Jean-Claude Parrot on his election as Executive Vice-President of the CLC in June 1992.

make the CLC a better force to represent Canadian workers. At the same time, I knew that the FTQ would need a strong voice and I felt I could be that voice.

I agreed with the FTQ's policies and positions. I had spoken in English Canada to explain why the FTQ was right to support the PQ in Québec. I was a member of the CUPW's Montréal local and that meant I was an FTQ member. I also felt it was very important for the FTQ to have a strong CLC in view of what was on the political horizon, such as the North American Free Trade Agreement.

Unfortunately, by the time I approached the FTQ on this matter, I learned that it had already agreed to support another candidate. Also, at that time, CLC elections were run under a "slate system" that was less than fully democratic, and this would complicate my election. (The conduct of elections in the CLC has since become far more democratic.) However, I decided to run anyway.

In the months preceding the Convention, I gained the commitment of many labour leaders to support my candidacy. During the Convention, I spoke to many union caucuses where candidates were invited to make a few comments. I was surprised at what seemed to me the FTQ's weak efforts to promote its candidate. I will never forget the support I received from CUPW delegates, including those from the FTQ. All CUPW members from across the country did a fantastic work for my candidacy, none more so than Jim Crowel from Edmonton, who spearheaded my campaign during the Convention itself.

When the result of the election was announced, I was nervous and wasn't sure I'd heard it correctly. I turned around to Daryl Bean from PSAC, and asked him if I had won. He told me I had, as cheers went up around me. It was quite an emotional moment for me. From what I gathered from what people told me, I apparently had a constant grin on my face for the next two weeks!

My election created some hard feeling among many in the FTQ. Indeed, after the FTQ President Fernand Daoust, denounced my election, FTQ delegates walked out in protest. But, guided by good advice from CLC President Bob White, relations improved, and I was invited to speak at the following FTQ Convention. In this way, the FTQ showed there was no grudge held against me. The new FTQ President, Clément Godbout, and the General Secretary, Henri Massé, both made it clear to delegates that they were very satisfied with our relationship. From then until I retired from the CLC in 2002, I presided over elections at every FTQ Convention.

Conclusion

Every postal worker and trade unionist in Canada should be proud of the history of how CUPW became the union it is today. It's the history of workers whose determination became their badge and of a union whose principles became its trademark.

It's the history of a union that has faced brutal attacks by government against our right to strike, attacks by management on our right to negotiate, attacks from the media, and even attacks from other segments of the trade union movement. It's a history that has seen the police, the courts, and the entire judicial system all arrayed against us as we sought to protect and extend our rights. Against all odds, we built a strong, militant, and united union that won the respect of all.

If we in this country are to maintain our rights to freedom of association and free collective bargaining with the right to strike, we will have to continue to struggle against challenges to these rights from employers and governments. And, so will our children and our grandchildren. These rights are the only tools we have to fight for a more equitable share of our nation's wealth and for protections in our places of work.

In my life in the labour movement, I've always said, "An employer is an employer, and will always be an employer." What I mean by this is that employers will always try to buy their labour at the lowest possible cost. This is an instinct fundamental to being an employer. Once, when speaking before a group of employers, I expressed it this way: "In order for you to understand where I come from, I want you to realize that I am one of those who believe that if, as workers, we were to depend strictly on employers, we would all be slaves."

The bottom line is that the employers and governments have never accepted the right to free collective bargaining with the right to strike. Only through the solidarity of the labour movement have we been able to maintain these rights up to now. Even today, these rights remain under constant attack.

There are many, many "export processing zones" around the world (in Mexico, they are known as *maquiladoras*) where governments attract businesses by ensuring that there is a complete lack of collective rights, no protection against child labour, no health and safety regulations, no environmental protections, and no minimum wage. There are 250 million children working around the world, most of them in these zones, which I call "exploitation zones." This is where many of the goods being sold in Canada today are being processed.

Even in North America, we have the United States, supposedly the most "democratic" country in the world, where many states don't recognize workers' rights. Under the guise of ironically named "right to work" legislation, many states in effect nullify the right to strike, or even the right to belong to a union. I call these states America's "export processing zones."

Should we be surprised that the world of business continues to search out these places where workers face the same sort of working conditions that were the everyday life of Canadian workers more than a century ago? I am not: employers always have and always will resist any interference in the way they do business, and profits will always be more important to them than the lives of their workers. Every year in Canada, a thousand workers are killed on the job, and many more thousands suffer debilitating injuries.

For the last ten years of my working life, I served as the Canadian workers' representative at the ILO, and I also served as a member of its governing body. Over the past seventy-five years, it has instituted rights and protections for workers around the world. Some of these deal with health and safety, others with the right to form an association or the right to free collective bargaining. Yet others deal with protection against discrimination, the impact of technological change, or prohibitions against child labour. Such rights and protections are adopted at the ILO's annual meetings, and are then submitted by representatives of governments around the world for ratification by the competent authority in each country.

Only very rarely does Canada ratify any of these ILO rights and protections: Ottawa often uses the excuse that it can't get the unanimous approval of the provinces and territories, even in cases where representatives of provincial and federal governments had supported them at the ILO. Canadian government officials, like representatives from other governments around the world, make soothing noises at the ILO, pretending they care about workers. But the way officials from these same governments talk at gatherings of such other international bodies as the World Trade Organization is quite different. There, the influence of the corporate sector is obvious: no social considerations are allowed to impede the liberalization of trade. No regulations are permitted that would negatively affect investments of the corporate sector. Collective rights are not allowed to stand in the way of the pursuit of private profit.

In 1998, the ILO unanimously adopted a declaration committing all member governments to respect its five basic principles: freedom of association, free collective bargaining, no child labour, no forced labour, and no discrimination in employment or occupation. But declarations like this must never be allowed to stand in the way of maximizing profits.

Why is this so? Because "an employer is an employer, and will always be an employer." If we were to depend on them we would all be slaves.

On September 14, 2000, I gave a speech in Ottawa at a rally organized by the Ontario Coalition Against Poverty. My talk was entitled, "Defending the right to dissent." I think this extract well expresses my views on the subject:

> We live in a country where the right to protest is recognized, which is part of living in a democratic country. This right, however, is respected only as long as it is carried out peacefully. The problem is the definition given to our right to protest "peacefully."
>
> Protest has to be such that nobody will know we have protested. The media will not cover it, it will not raise the attention or the interest of politicians, it will not raise any awareness among the population, and it will not disrupt anything. In fact, it will be such that only the protesters will know they were there. If your protest is such that it will have a real impact, then the police will be there to stop you.
>
> We live in a country where freedom of the press is a right. This is nice, but it is the owners of the media, the employers, who implement this right. By ignoring the peaceful protests of the most vulnerable in our society, they encourage protesters to make their protests more visible, more exciting.
>
> In our society, police forces are often used to protect the interests of those in power. They do it during strikes, protests, and rallies. The police forces are not often called to protect people, but as we have seen in a recent protest in Toronto by the homeless, they can be called to protect an empty, abandoned building.
>
> The public has the right to know that, since a resolution was passed by Parliament in 1989 to eliminate poverty by the year 2000, poverty has increased by 50 percent, food banks have become a necessity all across the country, homeless people of all ages are dying in our parks, and many children go to school without the benefit of breakfast. Cuts in our social programs have contributed to all this, leaving to charitable organizations the task of dealing with these situations.
>
> More important than knowing, the public should have the right to participate in debates on what needs to be done, debates over whether we should reduce taxes or provide homes for our people, food and clothing for our children.
>
> I live in a country where there are no debates anymore, and where our rights are respected as long as we don't use them. So, I will continue to participate in protests that attract the media and if this means that the laws of the land will be used against us, so be it.
>
> We don't have the rights we have today because they were given to us. We have them because our fathers and grandfathers

fought for them. Our ancestors were also jailed, and some even died to win these rights. By our actions, we simply continue the same struggle and, unfortunately, continue also to face attacks.

More and more people are being marginalized today, as the gap between the rich and the poor widens, leading to the growth of poverty. We must continue in the tradition of our ancestors.

I'm all for peaceful protest, but not under their definition of "peaceful." To be effective, peaceful protests need to disrupt. An occupation, the blockade of a road, a march on the streets, a picket line, and a strike are all peaceful protests.

Imagine for a moment the use of police force, including riot squads using their long sticks, police on horses running into crowds, the pushing of people onto the ground to handcuff them. All these actions were taken against homeless people and their friends at a small demonstration in support of the right of the homeless to occupy an empty, abandoned building instead of having to sleep in a park where several have already died in recent years.

This happened in Toronto at a demonstration I attended. Some in our movement think we create a bad image when we protest in a disruptive way. I say to them that we are not the ones who run cars and trucks through picket lines, killing and handicapping our people. We are not the ones who use tear gas or pepper spray on people. We are not the ones who beat people in demonstrations or on picket lines. We are not the ones who reject any solutions to the problem of poverty in our country.

When I was the President of CUPW, I was once told by the President of the CLC that we were creating a bad image for the labour movement. He was dead wrong: we never got more support from the public than when we stayed on strike in spite of legislation ordering us back to work.

Yes, we were disruptive, but we were also sending a clear message that the government was wrong. We won that debate. We created an image of people fighting for justice, fighting a government trying to gain politically by using violence against us.

We must continue to protest peacefully under our own definition, meaning that we need to disrupt to be effective. Protests that do not disrupt are like the right to negotiate without the right to strike, the right to strike without the right to have a picket line, the right to attend meetings without the right to speak, the right to vote without the right to participate in the electoral process.

We are here tonight to reaffirm our right to effective protest, our right to disrupt so we can be heard. We are here to defend our right to dissent.

CUPW National President, Deborah Bourque, holding CUPW's "The Struggle Continues" flag at a demonstration during CUPW's 2002 National Convention.

Behind the denial of our rights to strike and to dissent, something else is being attacked — our right to negotiate. In the summer of 1979 I gave a speech to the national convention of the Confederation of Canadian Unions (CCU) in Vancouver. It dealt with the fundamental issue of "negotiations versus consultations." I also spoke of the type of trade unionism we should practice, of the difference between business unionism and class-struggle unionism. Although it was twenty-five years ago, I still believe today what I said then:

> I know the CCU is no stranger to the type of attacks that postal workers have faced over the last year. Police harassment, injunctions, unjust firings and dismissals, union-busting campaigns, the government's manipulation of and straight-out violation of the law, red-baiting, hysterical stories in the media, jail sentences — these are all as familiar to you as they are to us.
>
> Why, with ongoing attacks on our jobs and rights, do we continue to struggle? Why do some unions have a more difficult time than others? Are the employers' allegations true — are we just a bunch of wild-eyed anarchists, hell-bent on destroying everything around us? What's at stake?
>
> The law can recognize or not recognize our right to strike, and the law can impose penalties on us for striking. But the law

never gave us the right to strike, and it cannot take it away. The right to strike is simply part of being a worker, not a slave.

But the right to strike is not the reason for our struggles. It is only a small part of what's at stake. What's at stake is our right, as workers, to some control over our lives, to decent living standards and working conditions, and to the minimal protections, on and off the job, that workers have won over hundreds of years of struggle. What's at stake is our right to form democratic, militant unions, unions responsive to workers' needs, not to the employers' wish for higher productivity and higher profits at workers' expense...

The government's message to postal workers was, and still is, "consultations, not negotiations." Is it not the same message employers are sending to other workers?

Whatever name it goes under — "industrial democracy," "worker participation schemes," "worker self-management," "quality of work life experiments," and so on — both private and public sector employers are pushing the concept of replacing collective bargaining with consultation schemes. And let's make no mistake: they are pushing this concept very hard.

But why? Is it because employers like ours, who have refused to offer anything at the bargaining table unless they are confronted by the strength of our membership, have suddenly realized the injustice of their ways and are now interested in the welfare of their employees? Or is it because, through these "industrial democracy" schemes, all these employers know they can remove issues away from the collective bargaining process, away from democratic control of the membership, away from the strength of the membership, away from any possibility of collective worker action or reprisals — and into the cozy atmosphere of back-room deals and bartered privileges that they call consultation?

Why do companies push "industrial democracy"? Because it will increase profits and productivity, and, most of all, because unions officials can then be used to impose employers' orders and exercise a "restraining influence" on members.

But even where the employers' efforts to impose "industrial democracy," "quality of work life," and all their other attempts to co-opt us fail, legalized union-bashing to coerce workers into consultations schemes remain the order of the day. The tactics may be a little different, but the object is exactly the same: to destroy the power of workers and reassert the unchecked arbitrary power of corporate bosses, not just at the workplace, but throughout our society.

Chief steward Dan Tippins (standing), with other brothers from the Ottawa local, staying warm on the picket line in 1997.

And this, brothers and sisters, is something we in the organized labour movement have a duty to fight. If we care about workers' rights on the job, if we care about the social programs we have won in the past — like unemployment insurance, pensions, welfare, medical care, workers' compensation, and so on — if we care about the ownership, direction, and control of our country, we must move away from "industrial democracy" and toward the strengthening of collective bargaining. And this means we must create new mechanisms that will enable us to more effectively wield our collective strength.

The challenge before us is to create a situation where every employer who considers forcing his employees to strike will do so in the knowledge that those workers will receive financial help from all organized workers. Where every employer who considers using scabs will know in advance that such action will provoke a mass picket organized by local labour organizations. And where every employer realizes that when the labour movement calls a boycott of anti-medicare doctors or of products of a single company, that boycott will be actively promoted and supported by millions of workers.

It will not be easy to transform the trade union movement into a unified fighting force. There will be differences of opinion concerning priorities and strategy. But these differences can and

CUPW Archives

Postal workers, still fighting for their rights, march on Parliament in 1998 to protest back-to-work legislation.

should be handled in a fraternal way, in the knowledge that the enemy is not those who desire change within the labour movement. The real enemy is to be found in corporate boardrooms across the country. The enemy is not workers who wish to protect their rights — the real enemy is those who wish to repress and eliminate our rights.

When I delivered that speech in 1979, I didn't know that twenty-five years later, we would still be looking to transform the trade union movement. We need to transform it so we can effectively fight the international pressures on workers to accept the corporate sector's "free-trade schemes," which have no regard for our rights or social conditions. We need to transform it so we can successfully provide financial assistance, mass picket lines, and active, effective boycotts.

Freedom of association and free collective bargaining with the right to strike are not negotiable rights. They should be supported through legislation and they should be respected by the judicial system. They are fundamental rights, and they have been recognized as such by governments, employers, and workers' representing more than 170 countries.

Workers around the world have been arrested, jailed, and killed while fighting for these rights. For all those workers and for all those we represent today, we should never let anyone take these rights away from us. It was worthwhile to fight for them in the past and it is still worthwhile to fight for them today, as it will be tomorrow.

The entire labour movement, and its leaders, must accept that we

Members of the National Executive Board at CUPW's 2002 National Convention, during a tribute to former National President Jean-Claude Parrot who was retiring from the CLC. From left to right, Denis Lemelin, Jean-Claude Parrot, Deborah Bourque, Lynn Bue, John Fehr (at the mike), Donald Lafleur, and George Kuehnbaum.

must work together to support workers' struggles. Otherwise, we will be left to fight individually, and we will regress rather than progress.

I have tried to spend my life working for the cause of postal workers in particular and for the cause of workers in general, and I have no regrets about any of it. The only sadness I felt was in knowing I was stealing precious hours from my family. Without the understanding and support of Louisette and my two daughters, Manon and Johanne, I don't know what would have happened.

I gained much from what I have experienced in my life. I discovered who I really was, and which side I was on. As a youngster, I was a quiet, shy boy raised in a Catholic environment who left school early and whose main interest was watching sports. My reading was limited to the sports pages of newspapers, comics, and detective and spy novels. I grew up going to the movies to see cowboys win battles against Indians, Americans win battles against communists, and watching war movies in which the Americans were always the "good guys." The only sign of revolt in my teen years was my support for the arrival of rock and roll.

I had no real sense of what life was all about when I entered the post office on my eighteenth birthday in July of 1954. I think that in those first years I was a good worker, though shy and quiet. During breaks and at lunch hours, I learned to play ping-pong. Two days a week, I played in bowling leagues with other postal workers. Then, after seven years in the post office, I attended a union meeting. I never thought it would change my life, but the rest, as they say, is history.

I learned to have more confidence in myself. I found out who I was and what I stood for. I started to like what I was discovering about myself.

I cared about others. I was upset about injustices. I could have ideas of my own. I could be an activist. The more I got involved in my union, the more I got out of it. I met new friends. I became a shop steward and then a member of the executive committee of my local. Seven years after my first union meeting, I was a full-time officer.

I never thought I would one day be able to write bulletins and articles that appeared in union publications and elsewhere. I never thought I would one day be able to speak before a large crowd. I never thought I would one day know how to represent a worker and act as a lawyer in front of an arbitrator. I never thought I would one day be able to handle negotiations for all postal workers. I never thought I would one day give press conferences. I never thought I would one day give education seminars. I never thought I would one day represent Canadian workers in an international forum. I never thought I would one day chair national conventions and an international tripartite conference of delegates from more than 170 countries. I never thought I would one day do all that work in two languages.

For all this I thank postal workers and CUPW for having given me the chance to learn to do all these things and much more. I thank them also for the support they gave me over the years. I'm sure that they, like me, are proud of what we accomplished together, often against all odds.

I cannot end this book without giving special thanks to all the officers and union representatives I've work with through the years. I have appreciated their support and their efforts to help make CUPW a great union. My thanks go also to all CUPW communications, research, and translation workers whose advice helped guide me through the years. As well my thanks are due to all the support staff who worked so hard to make the union what it is today. Without them all, we would never have succeeded in our work.

There are three people who need to be recognized that worked closely with me during the whole period I was Chief Negotiator and President of the union: Geoff Bickerton, the first research and communications person we hired, helped me gain confidence in myself as a labour leader; my secretary, Jacqueline Hélie, for her patience; and Gaston Nadeau, our lawyer and a great friend of postal workers, for his good advice on legal matters and on the wording of collective agreements.

All these people are part of this story, a story of which we can be very proud. Our history is now part of the history of the Canadian labour movement. I hope it will never be forgotten, and I hope it will serve as an encouragement to those facing future struggles.

BENEFITS OBTAINED BY THE COUNCIL OF POSTAL UNIONS AND CUPW			1968 – 1992 COLLECTIVE AGREEMENTS	
COUNCIL OF POSTAL UNIONS FULL-TIME	COUNCIL OF POSTAL UNIONS FULL-TIME	COUNCIL OF POSTAL UNIONS FULL-TIME	CUPW FULL-TIME AND PART-TIME	CUPW ARBITRATION AWARD
OCTOBER 1968	OCTOBER 1970	MARCH 1973	DECEMBER 1975	MARCH 31, 1979
• EMPLOYER TO DEDUCT MEMBERSHIP DUES AS CONDITION OF EMPLOYMENT • 8 HOURS PER DAY / 40 HOURS PER WEEK • 2 x 10 MINUTE REST PERIODS • 2 x 5 MINUTE WASH-UPS • $1.50 MEAL ALLOWANCE / IF OVERTIME MORE THAN 3 HRS. • 15¢ PER HOUR NIGHT & EVENING SHIFT PREMIUM • 11 STATUTORY HOLIDAYS • 3 WEEKS VACATION LESS THAN 20 YEARS • 5 WEEKS FURLOUGH AFTER 20 YEARS • 4 WEEKS VACATION AFTER 25 YEARS • 15 DAYS SICK LEAVE PER YEAR-CUMULATIVE • 25 DAYS SPECIAL LEAVE-MAXIMUM • 4 DAYS BEREAVEMENT LEAVE - IMMEDIATE FAMILY • 1 DAY BEREAVEMENT LEAVE GRANDPARENT AND IN-LAWS (SON, DAUGHTER, SISTER OR BROTHER) • 1 DAY LEAVE FOR BIRTH OF CHILD • 8 MONTHS LEAVE WITHOUT PAY (LWOP) MATERNITY LEAVE (2 MONTHS BEFORE AND 6 MONTHS AFTER TERMINATION OF PREGNANCY) • INJURY ON DUTY (IOD) WITH PAY FOR REASONABLE PERIOD, DETERMINED BY EMPLOYER • UP TO 3 DAYS TRAVEL LEAVE – ISOLATED POST • ISOLATED POST ALLOWANCE (IPA) TO CONTINUE TO BE PAID • UP TO 28 WEEKS SEVERANCE PAY FOR LAY OFF • UP TO 13 WEEKS PAY ON RESIGNATION • UP TO 28 WEEKS PAY ON RETIREMENT • EMPLOYER CONTRIBUTE TO GSMIP • EMPLOYER TO PROVIDE UNIFORMS AND PROTECTIVE CLOTHING • 4 _ ¢ TO 15¢ PER MILE FOR MILEAGE ALLOWANCE • $70 PER YEAR BOOT ALLOWANCE • $5 PER YEAR GLOVE ALLOWANCE • 3¢ PER HOUR BOOT ALLOWANCE PART-TIME • $3 PER YEAR GLOVE ALLOWANCE PART-TIME	• 18¢ PER HOUR EVENING AND NIGHT SHIFT PREMIUM • 10 MINUTE REST PERIOD FOR 2 HOURS OR MORE OVERTIME BEFORE OR AFTER SHIFT • OVERTIME OF 3 HOURS OR MORE _ HOUR PAID MEAL PERIOD PROVIDED • 3 WEEKS VACATION LESS THAN 18 YEARS • 4 WEEKS VACATION AFTER 18 YEARS • LEAVE WITH PAY (LWP) JURY DUTY • LEAVE WITH PAY SUBPOENA AS WITNESS • COUNCIL OF POSTAL UNIONS JOINT COMMITTEE ON TECHNOLOGICAL CHANGE • EMPLOYER TO PAY 50% OF PREMIUM IN THOSE PROVINCES THAT HAVE A MEDICAL CARE INSURANCE PLAN • 5 MINUTE VEHICLE SAFETY INSPECTION • SAME SCALE OF PAY SHALL APPLY TO MALE AND FEMALE EMPLOYEES IN SAME CLASSIFICATION COUNCIL OF POSTAL UNIONS PART-TIME EMPLOYEES NOVEMBER 1970 • HOURS OF WORK NOT MORE THAN 30 HOURS AVERAGED OVER 12 WEEKS • 10 MINUTES REST PERIOD IF SCHEDULED FOR MORE THAN 2 HOURS • 5 MINUTES WASH-UP FOR SHIFT OF 3 HOURS OR MORE • 5 MINUTES WASH-UP ADDITIONAL IF REQUIRED TO WORK MORE THAN 6 HOURS • 11 STATUTORY HOLIDAYS • VACATION PAY OF 4% OF PAY AND OVERTIME DURING PREVIOUS YEAR IF LESS THAN 8 YEARS • VACATION PAY OF 6% AFTER 8 YEARS • SICK LEAVE 5 HOURS PER MONTH FOR EACH MONTH ENTITLED TO PAY FOR 40 HOURS • SICK LEAVE WITH PAY GRANTED FROM THE 6TH WORKING DAY FROM START OF ILLNESS OR NON COMPENSABLE INJURY • UP TO 8 MONTHS LWOP FOR MATERNITY LEAVE • LWP FOR JURY DUTY AND WITNESS UNDER SUBPOENA • COUNCIL OF POSTAL UNIONS JOINT COMMITTEE ON TECHNOLOGICAL CHANGE • 5 MINUTE VEHICLE SAFETY INSPECTION • EMPLOYER TO PROVIDE UNIFORMS AND PROTECTIVE CLOTHING • SAME SCALE OF PAY SHALL APPLY TO MALE AND FEMALE EMPLOYEES IN SAME CLASSIFICATION • 4 _ ¢ TO 15¢ PER MILE FOR MILEAGE ALLOWANCE • IPA ALLOWANCE TO CONTINUE TO BE PAID	• OT MEAL ALLOWANCE RAISED TO $2 • 3 WEEKS VACATION LESS THAN 16 YEARS • 4 WEEKS VACATION AFTER 16 YEARS • 5 WEEKS VACATION AFTER 30 YEARS • 1 DAY BEREAVEMENT LEAVE – ADDED GRANDCHILD • 1 DAY WITH PAY FOR ADOPTION OF CHILD • MATERNITY LWOP – 11 WEEKS BEFORE AND 6 WEEKS AFTER TERMINATION OF PREGNANCY • LEAVE WITH PAY TO ATTEND ADJUDICATION HEARING IF PARTY TO, REPRESENTATIVE OF, OR A WITNESS • UP TO 28 WEEKS PAY PAID TO ESTATE OF FT EMPLOYEE IN THE EVENT OF DEATH • MANPOWER COMMITTEE TO DEAL WITH THE INTRODUCTION OF A CHANGE OR TECHNOLOGICAL CHANGE • BOOT ALLOWANCE $84 PER YEAR • GLOVE ALLOWANCE $8 PER YEAR • EMPLOYEES RECLASSIFIED TO A LOWER LEVEL CONTINUES TO BE PAID AT FORMER RATE • TREASURY BOARD TRAVEL DIRECTIVE TO BE USED TO REIMBURSE MILEAGE • LETTER OF UNDERSTANDING OF ERIC KIERANS PMG OF SEPTEMBER 1ST, 1970 – "…THE PLANNED MODERNIZATION PROGRAM WILL NOT RESULT IN LAYOFFS…" COUNCIL OF POSTAL UNIONS PART-TIME EMPLOYEES MARCH 1973 • VACATION PAY FOR LESS THAN 4 YEARS - 4 % OF PAY AND OVERTIME • VACATION PAY FOR MORE THAN 4 YEARS, LESS THAN 16 YEARS – 6% • VACATION PAY FOR MORE THAN 16 YEARS – 8% • EMPLOYEE ENTITLED TO VACATION LEAVE OF 3 WEEKS OR 4 WEEKS IF ENTITLED TO PAY • SICK LWOP FOR 3 WORKING DAYS OR LESS • SICK LWP FROM 4TH WORKING DAY • MATERNITY LWOP – 11 WEEKS BEFORE AND 6 WEEKS AFTER TERMINATION OF PREGNANCY • LEAVE WITH PAY FOR ADJUDICATION LEAVE • 4 DAY BEREAVEMENT LEAVE - IMMEDIATE FAMILY • 1 DAY BEREAVEMENT LEAVE GRANDCHILD, GRANDPARENT AND IN-LAWS (SON, DAUGHTER, SISTER OR BROTHER) • 1 DAY LWP FOR ADOPTION OF CHILD • MANPOWER COMMITTEE TO APPLY • IN LIEU OF BOOT ALLOWANCE, 4¢ PER HOUR • GLOVE ALLOWANCE, $4 PER YEAR • TREASURY BOARD GUIDELINE FOR TRAVEL USED FOR MILEAGE	• FULL-TIME AND OVERTIME MEAL ALLOWANCE RAISED TO $2.50 • 40¢ PER HOUR EVENING AND NIGHT SHIFT PREMIUM • 60¢ PER HOUR ON SATURDAY REGULAR HOUR PREMIUM • 75¢ PER HOUR ON SUNDAY REGULAR HOUR PREMIUM • FT – 3 WEEKS VACATION LESS THAN 14 YEARS • FT – 4 WEEKS VACATION AFTER 14 YEARS • FT – 5 WEEKS VACATION AFTER 27 YEARS • PT – LESS THAN 4 YEARS – 4% OF PAY AND OVERTIME • PT – MORE THAN 4 YEARS, LESS THAN 14 YEARS – 6% • PT – MORE THAN 14 YEARS – 8% • 4 DAY BEREAVEMENT LEAVE ADDED GRANDPARENTS • PT COVERED BY IOD LEAVE WITH PAY • DEFINITION OF TECHNOLOGICAL CHANGE WITH RIGHT TO ADJUDICATION ON DISAGREEMENTS • GUARANTEED EMPLOYMENT, CLASSIFICATION, PAY, RETRAINING AND PAID RELOCATION • EMPLOYER TO CONTRIBUTE TO COST PROVIDED UNDER PLAN OF "PUBLIC SERVICE HEALTH INSURANCE REGULATIONS" • FT – BOOT ALLOWANCE $125 PER YEAR AND $8.25 FOR GLOVE ALLOWANCE • PT – 6¢ PER HOUR IN LIEU OF BOOT ALLOWANCE AND $4.15 FOR GLOVE ALLOWANCE PER YEAR • COST-OF-LIVING-ALLOWANCE (COLA) CAPPED AT 10¢ MAXIMUM QUARTERLY • NO INDIVIDUAL WORK MEASUREMENT	• REST PERIOD INCREASED TO 15 MINUTES • FULL-TIME AND OVERTIME MEAL ALLOWANCE INCREASED TO $4 • FT – 3 WEEKS VACATION LESS THAN 10 YEARS • FT – 4 WEEKS VACATION AFTER 10 YEARS • FT – 5 WEEKS VACATION AFTER 25 YEARS • PT LESS THAN 4 YEARS – 4% OF TOTAL PAY, OT SHIFT AND WEEKEND PREMIUMS, COLA AND VACATION LEAVE PAID • PT MORE THAN 4 YEARS AND LESS THAN 10 YEARS – 6% • PT MORE THAN 10 YEARS AND LESS THAN 25 YEARS – 8% • PT MORE THAN 25 YEARS – 10% • PT ENTITLED TO TAKE 5 WEEKS VACATION LEAVE FOR MORE THAN 25 YEARS SERVICE • PT CAN ACCUMULATE UP TO 10 HOURS SICK LEAVE PER MONTH • PT ALLOWED TO USE SICK LEAVE CREDITS FROM 1ST DAY ILLNESS • PT RIGHT TO 5 DAYS LWP FOR MARRIAGE LEAVE • COMMON-LAW SPOUSE ADDED TO DEFINITION OF IMMEDIATE FAMILY, 4 DAYS BEREAVEMENT LEAVE • PT UP TO 28 WEEKS SEVERANCE PAY FOR LAY OFF • PT UP TO 13 WEEKS PAY ON RESIGNATION • PT UP TO 28 WEEKS ON RETIREMENT • PT UP TO 28 WEEKS PAID TO ESTATE OF EMPLOYEE IN THE EVENT OF DEATH • FT AND PT SERVICE CALCULATION USED TO DETERMINE AMOUNT OF SEVERANCE PAY • DISPLACEMENT ALLOWANCE LUMP SUM $100 OR $300 ACCORDING TO DISTANCE DISPLACED DUE TO TECHNOLOGICAL CHANGE, 2 OR 4 MILES • FT BOOT ALLOWANCE $140 PER YEAR • FT GLOVE ALLOWANCE $10 PER YEAR • PT 7¢ PER HOUR IN LIEU OF BOOT ALLOWANCE • PT $5 PER YEAR GLOVE ALLOWANCE • COLA ROLLED INTO WAGE RATE

BENEFITS OBTAINED BY THE COUNCIL OF POSTAL UNIONS AND CUPW			1968 – 1992 COLLECTIVE AGREEMENTS	
CUPW	**CUPW**	**CUPW**	**CUPW** POSTAL SERVICE CON- TINUATION ACT	**CUPW** INTERNAL, EXTERNAL, GLT, GS AND EL'S
JUNE 1980	**AUGUST 1981**	**APRIL 1985**	**1987**	**JULY 1992**

• FT _ HOUR PAID MEAL PERIOD AND WORK WEEK REDUCED TO 37 _ HOURS
• PT HOURS NOT TO EXCEED 25 HOURS PER WEEK AVERAGED OVER 12 WEEKS
• 72¢ PER HOUR EVENING AND NIGHT SHIFT PREMIUM
• 90¢ PER REGULAR HOUR WORKED SATURDAY AND SUNDAY
• FT 6 WEEKS VACATION FOR MORE THAN 30 YEARS
• FT 7 WEEKS VACATION FOR MORE THAN 35 YEARS
 	
• PT FOR MORE THAN 30 YEARS – 12% OF TOTAL PAY AND COMPENSATION
• PT FOR MORE THAN 35 YEARS – 14% OF TOTAL PAY AND COMPENSATION
 	
• PT ENTITLED TO TAKE 6 WEEKS VACATION LEAVE FOR MORE THAN 30 YEARS SERVICE
• PT ENTITLED TO TAKE 7 WEEKS VACATION LEAVE FOR MORE THAN 35 YEARS SERVICE
• UP TO 26 WEEKS PAY MAXIMUM FOR EMPLOYEE RELEASED FOR INCAPACITY
• FT $155 PER YEAR BOOT ALLOWANCE
• FT $11 PER YEAR GLOVE ALLOWANCE
• PT 8¢ PER HOUR IN LIEU OF BOOT AND GLOVE AL-LOWANCE
• COLA ROLLED INTO WAGE RATE – 6% ADJUSTMENT FACTOR TRIGGER
• PT FOR PART-TIME OP-ERATIONAL REQUIREMENTS PEAK PERIOD
• A LETTER INDICATING THAT SURPLUSES DUE TO CHANGES OUTSIDE CANADA POST CONTROL WOULD BE OFFERED ALTERNATIVE EMPLOYMENT
	• PT ENTITLED TO PAID MEAL PERIOD AND ADDITIONAL 15 MINUTE PAID REST PERIOD FOR 8 HOUR SHIFT
	• FULL-TIME AND OVERTIME MEAL ALLOWANCE TO $5.50
	• 81¢ PER HOUR EVENING AND NIGHT SHIFT PREMIUM
	• $1.01 PER REGULAR HOUR WORKED SATURDAY AND SUNDAY PREMIUM
	• 3 WEEKS VACATION FOR LESS THAN 8 YEARS
	• 4 WEEKS VACATION AFTER 8 YEARS
	• 5 WEEKS VACATION AFTER 20 YEARS
	• PT FOR LESS THAN 8 YEARS SERVICE – 6% TOTAL PAY AND COMPENSATION
	• PT FOR MORE THAN 8 YEARS SERVICE – 8% TOTAL PAY AND COMPENSATION
	• PT FOR MORE THAN 20 YEARS SERVICE – 10 % TOTAL PAY AND COM-PENSATION
	• 1 DAY BEREAVEMENT LEAVE ADDED GRAND-PARENTS OF SPOUSE
	• PAID MATERNITY LEAVE – FIRST 2 WEEKS 93% OF WEEKLY WAGE
	  • UP TO 15 ADDITIONAL WEEKS UI BENEFITS TOPPED UP TO 93% OF WEEKLY WAGE
	• RIGHT TO REFUSE WORK UNSAFE "IF HAS REASONABLE GROUNDS TO BELIEVE"
	• FT $195 PER YEAR BOOT ALLOWANCE
	• FT $17 PER YEAR GLOVE ALLOWANCE
	• PT 11¢ PER HOUR IN LIEU OF BOOT AND GLOVE AL-LOWANCE
	• NO FURTHER INSTALLATION OF INVESTIGATIVE (CCTV) AND RESTRICTIONS ON EXISTING CCTV
	• PEAK PERIOD FOR PT NOT TO EXCEED 5 HOURS
	• CONTRACTED OUT WORK EMPLOYEES OFFERED ALTERNATE POSITIONS
	• COLA ROLLED INTO WAGE RATE
	• APPENDIX N – RIGHT TO OPEN AGREEMENT FOL-LOWING PROCLAMATION OF CPC ACT
	
	CUPW C-124 LEGISLATION 1982
	• AUGUST 1981 AGREEMENT THAT EXPIRED ON DECEMBER 31, 1982 EXTENDED BY BILL C-124 TO SEPT 30, 1984
	• APPENDIX M AND N CHANGES NEGOTIATED ADDED
	• CONCILIATION BOARD REPORT ADDED THE PARTICULAR WORKING CONDITIONS OF CASUAL EMPLOYEES
	• CASUALS PAY RAISED TO MINIMUM HOURLY WAGE RATE OF REGULAR EM-PLOYEES
	• HOURLY WAGE RATES CHANGED ONLY TO REFLECT C-124 (6 AND 5) LEGIS-LATION
		• COMPULSORY MEMBERSHIP IN UNION
		• NIGHT SHIFT WORKERS RIGHT TO 2 CONSECUTIVE DAYS OFF 2 OUT OF EVERY 3 WEEKS
		• FULL-TIME AND OVERTIME MEAL ALLOWANCE TO $6
		• 85¢ PER HOUR EVENING SHIFT PREMIUM
		• $1.05 PER HOUR NIGHT SHIFT PREMIUM
		• $1.05 PER REGULAR HOUR WORKED SATURDAY AND SUNDAY PREMIUM
		• 3 WEEKS VACATION FOR LESS THAN 7 YEARS
		• 4 WEEKS VACATION AFTER 7 YEARS
		• PT FOR LESS THAN 7 YEARS – 6% TOTAL PAY AND COMPENSATION
		• PT FOR MORE THAN 7 YEARS – 8%
		• PRE-RETIREMENT LEAVE – 5 WEEKS PAID LEAVE FOR WORKERS 55 YEARS OF AGE AND 20 YEARS OF SERVICE OR 60 YEARS OF AGE AND 5 YEAR OF SERVICE – 1 WEEK PER YEAR
		• MATERNITY LEAVE CAN BE EXTENDED AN ADDITIONAL 24 WEEKS LWOP
		• PATERNITY LEAVE – LWOP UP TO 24 WEEKS FOR CARE AND CUSTODY OF NEWBORN
		• ADOPTION LEAVE – LWOP UP TO 24 WEEKS
		• DENTAL PLAN COST ASSUMED BY CPC
		• HEARING AND VISION PLAN COST ASSUMED BY CPC
		• DISABILITY INSURANCE PLAN AVAILABLE TO ALL EMPLOYEES
		• EMPLOYEE NOT REQUIRED TO LIFT OBJECTS OVER 25 KGS
		• NIGHT RECOVERY LEAVE – 3 DAYS LWP PER YEAR TO EMPLOYEE WHO WORKED 200 OCCASIONS ON NIGHT SHIFT
		• 26¢ PER KILOMETRE MILEAGE ALLOWANCE
		• COLA TRIGGERED AT 5%
		• CCTV TO BE DISMANTLED WITHIN 60 DAYS
		• JOB CREATION – 19 NEW DIRECTION OUTLETS
		  • PHASE IN ELECTRONIC BULK MAIL
		  • PRESENT NUMBER OF SUB PO TO BE REDUCED BY 53
		  • LEAD HAND WICKET CLERK
		  • DISPATCHERS TO BE MOBILE MOTORIZED EQUIPMENT INSTRUCTORS
		• JOB SECURITY APPENDIX – NO LAY OFF OF REGULAR EMPLOYEE RENDERED SURPLUS
		  • BUY OUTS BY SENIORITY
		  • SURPLUS IDENTIFIED BY REVERSE SENIORITY
		  • ONLY SURPLUS "BEYOND THE CONTROL OF CPC" CAN BE FORCED TO REDEPLOY TO VACANCY WITHIN 40 KILOMETRES
		• PT POSITIONS TOTAL IN BARGAINING UNIT (BU) NOT TO EXCEED 4,500
		• PT IN GRADE 7 AND 8 PO NOT TO EXCEED 1,000
			• PT HOURS AT LEAST 20 HOURS PER WEEK AND NOT TO EXCEED 30 HOURS PER WEEK AVERAGE OVER 26 WEEKS
			• FT MEAL ALLOWANCE ON OT RAISED TO $6.25
			• 95¢ PER HOUR EVENING SHIFT PREMIUM
			• $1.15 PER HOUR NIGHT SHIFT PREMIUM
			• $1.15 PER REGULAR HOUR WORKED SATURDAY AND SUNDAY PREMIUM
			• 5 WEEKS VACATION LEAVE AFTER 14 YEARS
			• PT FOR MORE THAN 14 YEARS – 10% OF TOTAL PAY AND COMPENSATION
			• ADOPTION LEAVE AL-LOWANCE AND SUB PLAN THE SAME AS MATERNITY LEAVE
			• CHILD CARE STUDY – TO INVESTIGATE NEEDS AND AVAILABILITY OF CHILD CARE COST SHARED BY PARTIES NOT TO EXCEED $50,000
			• TECHNOLOGICAL CHANGE DISPLACEMENT ALLOWANCE RAISED TO $200 AND $400
			• CPC TO PAY 70% OF PROVINCIAL MEDICAL INSURANCE PLAN PREMIUM (PREMIUM PAYING PROVINCES)
			• 20% REIMBURSEMENT IN NON PREMIUM PAYING PROVINCES
			• DENTAL FEE GUIDE OF 1986 APPLIES FOR 1988, AND 1987 FEE GUIDE APPLIES FOR 1989
			• VISION BENEFITS - $130 FOR EACH 2 YEAR PERIOD
			• 1 DAY PAID RECOVERY LEAVE IF COMPLETED MORE THAN 3 YEARS AND WORKED ON NIGHT SHIFT IN PRE-CEDING 4 MONTH PERIOD
			• 5 MINUTE REST PERIOD EVERY HOUR GIVEN TO EMPLOYEES ASSIGNED TO CODING FUNCTIONS
			• PREGNANT EMPLOYEES WORKING ON VIDEO DISPLAY TERMINALS GIVEN OP-PORTUNITY TO BE RE-ASSIGNED
			• CPC TO REDUCE NOISE LEVELS IN MECHANIZED FACILITIES 85 DECIBELS
			• PREGNANT EMPLOYEES ENTITLED TO UNIFORMS REIMBURSED UP TO $130 FOR PURCHASE OF MA-TERNITY WEAR
			• FT BOOT ALLOWANCE $240 PER YEAR, GLOVE AL-LOWANCE $20 PER YEAR
			• PT 13¢ PER HOUR IN LIEU OF GLOVE ALLOWANCE
			• COLA TRIGGER 7%
			• CHRISTMAS CASUAL SAME PAY AS REGULAR CASUAL
			• POLYGRAPH TESTING PROHIBITED
			• IPA ALLOWANCE INCREASED TO CURRENT TREASURY BOARD GUIDELINES
			• PT POSITIONS IN BU NOT TO EXCEED 4,200
			NOTE:
			• ARBITRATOR COSSETTE DELETED JOB CREATION APPENDIX
				• RIGHT TO USE SENIORITY TO FILL VACANT POSITIONS IN OTHER GROUPS BEFORE HIRING FROM STREET
				• EXTERNAL WORKERS TO HAVE _ HOUR PAID LUNCH STRUCTURED INTO THEIR ROUTES WITHIN 30 MONTH PERIOD
				• GLT AND GS WORKERS TO HAVE _ HOUR PAID LUNCH INCLUDED IN HOURS OF WORK WITHIN 30 DAYS
				• 5 WEEKS VACATION AFTER 14 YEARS, ALL GROUPS
				• 6 WEEKS VACATION LEAVE AFTER 28 YEARS, ALL GROUPS
				• 7 WEEKS VACATION LEAVE AFTER 33 YEARS, ALL GROUPS
				• PT FOR MORE THAN 14 YEARS - 10% OF GROSS EARNINGS AS PER T-4
				• PT FOR MORE THAN 28 YEARS - 12%
				• PT FOR MORE THAN 33 YEARS - 14%
				• ALL REGULAR EMPLOYEES COVERED BY CPC PAID DENTAL PLAN
				• TECHNOLOGICAL CHANGE CLAUSE PROTECTIONS AND DISPUTE MECHANISMS TO COVER ALL GROUPS
				• JOB SECURITY PROVISION – NO LAY OFF REGULAR EMPLOYEE IN BU AS OF OCTOBER 27, 1991 IF SURPLUS PROVIDED AGREES TO BE DISPLACED TO ANOTHER POSITION UP TO 40 KILOMETRES – OTHERS, BU WIDE DISPLACEMENT
				  • SURPLUS JUNIOR IN THE GROUP
				• MAINTENANCE WORK ON NEW GENERATION EQUIPMENT NOT TO BE CONTRACTED OUT
				• CHILD CARE FUND ES-TABLISHED NOT TO EXCEED 1.2 MILLION IN ANY FISCAL YEAR AND FUND BALANCE NOT TO EXCEED 2 MILLION DOLLAR
				• JOINT COMMITTEE ES-TABLISHED TO DEAL WITH CHILD CARE FOR EMPLOYEES
				• PT EMPLOYEES RETIREMENT SAVINGS PROGRAM ES-TABLISHED
				• ADMAIL WORKERS WAGE AND WORKING CONDITIONS NEGOTIATED INTO AN APPENDIX IN COLLECTIVE AGREEMENT
				• SERVICE EXPANSION AND WORK PLACE DEVELOPMENT COMMITTEE ESTABLISHED APPENDIX "T" WITH A 5 MILLION DOLLAR CAP
				• UNION EDUCATION FUND – CPC TO PAY CUPW EDUCATION FUND 3¢ PER HOUR ACTUALLY WORKED BY ALL REGULAR FT AND PT EMPLOYEES
				• NO CONTRACTING OUT CLAUSE OF WORK PER-FORMED BY MAIL SERVICE COURIERS
				• THE CITY MAIL VOLUME INDEX, CPC TO PAY FOR STUDY UP TO $500,000.

Index